STANDING UP, SPEAKING OUT

In recent decades, some of the most celebrated and culturally influential American oratorical performances have come not from political leaders or religious visionaries, but from stand-up comics. Even though comedy and satire have been addressed by rhetorical scholarship in recent decades, little attention has been paid to stand-up. This collection is an attempt to further cultivate the growing conversation about stand-up comedy from the perspective of the rhetorical tradition. It brings together literatures from rhetorical, cultural, and humor studies to provide a unique exploration of stand-up comedy that both argues on behalf of the form's capacity for social change and attempts to draw attention to a series of otherwise unrecognized rhetors who have made significant contributions to public culture through comedy.

Matthew R. Meier is an Assistant Professor of Communication Studies at West Chester University in West Chester, PA.

Casey R. Schmitt is an Assistant Professor of Communication at Lakeland University in Plymouth, WI.

STANDING UP, SPEAKING OUT

Stand-Up Comedy and the Rhetoric of Social Change

Edited by Matthew R. Meier
and Casey R. Schmitt

NEW YORK AND LONDON

First published 2017
by Routledge
711 Third Avenue, New York, NY 10017

and by Routledge
2 Park Square, Milton Park, Abingdon, Oxon, OX14 4RN

Routledge is an imprint of the Taylor & Francis Group, an informa business

© 2017 Taylor & Francis

The right of the editors to be identified as the author of the editorial material, and of the authors for their individual chapters, has been asserted in accordance with sections 77 and 78 of the Copyright, Designs and Patents Act 1988.

All rights reserved. No part of this book may be reprinted or reproduced or utilised in any form or by any electronic, mechanical, or other means, now known or hereafter invented, including photocopying and recording, or in any information storage or retrieval system, without permission in writing from the publishers.

Trademark notice: Product or corporate names may be trademarks or registered trademarks, and are used only for identification and explanation without intent to infringe.

Library of Congress Cataloging-in-Publication Data
Names: Meier, Matthew R., editor. | Schmitt, Casey R., editor.
Title: Standing up, speaking out : stand-up comedy and the rhetoric of social change / edited by Matthew R. Meier and Casey R. Schmitt.
Description: New York : Routledge, 2017. | Includes bibliographical references and index.
Identifiers: LCCN 2016008424 (print) | LCCN 2016014846 (ebook) | ISBN 9781138100282 (hardback) | ISBN 9781138100299 (pbk.) | ISBN 9781315657738 (ebook)
Subjects: LCSH: Stand-up comedy–United States. | Comedy–History and criticism. | English language–United States–Rhetoric.
Classification: LCC PN1969.C65 S73 2017 (print) | LCC PN1969.C65 (ebook) | DDC 792.76–dc23

ISBN: 9781138100282 (hbk)
ISBN: 9781138100299 (pbk)
ISBN: 9781315657738 (ebk)

Typeset in Bembo
by Apex CoVantage, LLC

CONTENTS

Contributors ... ix
Preface ... xiii
Foreword: Stand-Up Comedy, Social Change, and (American) Culture ... xv
Judith Yaross Lee

Introduction: Standing Up, Speaking Out ... xxi
Matthew R. Meier and Casey R. Schmitt

PART I
Stand-Up and Identity ... 1

1 "You Gotta Get Chinky with It!": Margaret Cho's Rhetorical Use of Humor to Communicate Cultural Identity ... 3
Lacy Lowrey and Valerie R. Renegar

2 If Laughs Could Kill: Eddie Izzard and the Queer Art of Comedy ... 20
Christopher J. Gilbert

3 "No Damn Mammy, Moms!": Rhetorical Re-invention in the Stand-up Comedy of Jackie "Moms" Mabley ... 40
Abbey Morgan

Response
Laughing at Others: The Rhetoric of Marginalized
Comic Identity 57
Joanne Gilbert

PART II
Stand-Up, Race, and Culture 69

4 Rhetoric of Racial Ridicule in an Era of Racial Protest:
Don Rickles, the "Equal Opportunity Offender"
Strategy, and the Civil Rights Movement 71
Raúl Pérez

5 "Would You Want Your Sister to Marry One of Them?":
Whiteness, Stand-Up, and Lenny Bruce 92
Matthew R. Meier and Chad M. Nelson

6 Teasing the Funny: Native American Stand-Up
Comedy in the 21st Century 111
Amanda Morris

Response
From Insult to Reflection: Stand-Up
Comedy and Cultural Pedagogy 125
Alberto González

PART III
Stand-Up and Politics 133

7 The Comedic Prince: The Organic Intellectualism
of Bill Hicks 135
Aaron Duncan and Jonathan Carter

8 What's the Deal with Liberals?: The Discursive
Construction of Partisan Political Identities in
Conservative Stand-Up Comedy 152
Ron Von Burg and Kai Heidemann

9 Live from DC, It's "Nerd Prom": Political Humor at
the White House Correspondents' Association Dinner 168
Jonathan P. Rossing

Response
Wise Fools: The Politics of Comedic Audiences   185
Mary Stuckey

PART IV
Standing Up, Breaking Rules   **193**

10 How Can Rape Be Funny?: Comic Persona,
Irony, and the Limits of Rape Jokes   195
Christopher A. Medjesky

11 Louie C.K.'s "Weird Ethic": *Kairos* and Rhetoric
in the Network   213
James J. Brown, Jr.

12 Late Night Apologia: A Critical Analysis of David
Letterman's On-Air Revelation   223
Casey R. Schmitt

Response
Returning the Favor: Ludic Space, Comedians, and the
Rhetorical Constitution of Society   237
Stephen Olbrys Gencarella

Index   *249*

Comedy doesn't just make people laugh and think, but makes them laugh and change.

(Sam Kinison)

CONTRIBUTORS

Judith Yaross Lee, Ph.D., is the Charles E. Zumkehr Professor of Communication Studies at Ohio University and 2016 Fulbright Senior Professor of American Culture at Leiden University in The Netherlands. She is the Editor of *Studies in American Humor* and Director of the Central Region Humanities Center in the School of Communication Studies at Ohio University. Her most recent book is *Twain's Brand: Humor in Contemporary American Culture*.

Matthew R. Meier, Ph.D., is Assistant Professor of Communication Studies at West Chester University of Pennsylvania. His research concerns the intersection/s of rhetoric, comedy, and democracy. He has written essays on comedians such as Jon Stewart, Stephen Colbert, and John Oliver as well as popular culture texts including the Blue Collar Comedy Tour, *Shaun of the Dead*, and *The Office*. His published work can be found in the *Western Journal of Communication* and the *Journal of Public Deliberation*.

Casey R. Schmitt, Ph.D., is Assistant Professor of Communication at Lakeland University. His primary research examines environmental narrative, rhetoric, and the social import of American folk narrative and popular culture. He is the author of 15 peer-reviewed articles and chapters and has served on the editorial staff of several academic journals, including *New Directions in Folklore*, the *Oral History Review*, and *Western Folklore*. He is Vice President-Elect of the National Communication Association's Environmental Communication Division.

Lacy Lowrey, M.A., is an Instructor of Communication Studies at Metropolitan State University of Denver and the University of Colorado, Denver. **Valerie R. Renegar, Ph.D.**, University of Kansas) is Associate Professor in Communication

Studies at Southwestern University in Georgetown, Texas. Lowrey and Renegar have published work on other women in comedy (Sarah Silverman in the *Western Journal of Communication*; Amy Schumer in a forthcoming book) and believe that working together is far more fun than working alone.

Chris J. Gilbert, Ph.D., is Assistant Professor of English at Assumption College. His work is published across a number of leading journals like the *Quarterly Journal of Speech*, *Rhetoric & Public Affairs*, *Philosophy & Rhetoric*, *Rhetoric Society Quarterly*, *Text & Performance Quarterly*, *Critical Studies in Media Communication*, and more. His work traverses topics in rhetoric and cultural studies, but he has a particular interest in the politics of comic artworks and performances. Currently, Chris is looking at returning soldiers who have turned to stand-up comedy to ease their transition home, the role of pleasure and pain in portrayals of war trauma, and multiple case studies dealing with caricature and controversy.

Abbey Morgan, is a Ph.D. candidate in English at the University of Maryland, with interests in 20th century African American humor. Her dissertation examines racial formation along the color line in African American comedy and humor.

Joanne Gilbert, Ph.D., is the Charles A. Dana Professor of Communication at Alma College and author of *Performing Marginality: Humor, Gender, and Cultural Critique*. Her work has most recently appeared in *Fan Girls and the Media: Creating Characters, Consuming Culture* and *Women and Comedy: History, Theory, Practice*.

Raúl Pérez, Ph.D., is Assistant Professor in the Department of Sociology and Criminology at the University of Denver. His research and teaching interests span several areas, including race/ethnicity and racisms, social inequality, law and society, culture, theory, and humor/comedy studies. His current research examines how racial discourse shifted in the US from the pre-civil rights era to the present, with an eye on how racist humor evolved in the world of comedy as a result of the civil rights movement. His works appear in *Discourse & Society*, *Ethnicities*, and *Social Semiotics*. He received the 2015 Oliver C. Cox Article Award from the American Sociological Association's Section on Racial and Ethnic Minorities and the 2015 Cristina Maria Riegos Graduate Student Paper Award from the Latina/o Sociology Section. His research has also been featured in *Time* magazine, *The Grio,* and *Latina Rebels*.

Chad M. Nelson, Ph.D., is an Assistant Professor at Florida Gulf Coast University where he primarily researches and teaches in the areas of intercultural communication and rhetoric, with particular interests in race, culture, and the rhetoric of educational politics and economics.

Amanda Morris, Ph.D., is Associate Professor of Multiethnic Rhetorics at Kutztown University. Her research interests include contemporary indigenous rhetorics, specifically Native American Rhetorics, creativity in the classroom, and the power of stories.

Alberto González, Ph.D., is Professor and Chair of the Department of Communication at Bowling Green State University. His published research includes examinations of the political discourse of Mexican American activists and explorations of popular music as a mode of communication. His work has appeared in various journals, including *The Quarterly Journal Of Speech, Youth Theatre Journal, Western Journal of Communication, Southern Communication Journal,* and *Communication Quarterly*. He has co-edited several books, including *Our Voices: Essays in Culture, Ethnicity and Communication* (with Marsha Houston and Victoria Chen, now in its 5th edition) and *Mediating Cultures: Parenting in Intercultural Contexts* (with Tina M. Harris). González has served as the Chair of the International and Intercultural Division of the National Communication Association and, from 2007–2012, he served as chair of NCA's Affirmative Action & Intercaucus Committee.

Aaron Duncan, Ph.D., is Lecturer and Director of the Speech & Debate Program at the University of Nebraska-Lincoln. His research focuses on sporting culture, public mythology, and political communication. During his time as Director of Speech & Debate, UNL students have won 25 individual state championships, broken over 100 events at national tournaments, and competed in over 30 final rounds at national tournaments. **Jonathan Carter**, is a Ph.D. candidate in Communication Studies at the University of Nebraska-Lincoln.

Ron Von Burg, Ph.D., is Assistant Professor of Communication and Core Faculty in the Interdisciplinary Humanities Program at Wake Forest University. His research interests include rhetoric of science, public argument, public discourses on religion and science, and science fiction film studies. **Kai Heidemann, Ph.D.**, is Assistant Professor of Sociology at University College Maastricht within Maastricht University in The Netherlands. His research mainly focuses on social movements and the politics of education reform, but he has a serious affinity for the study of humor in politics. He completed his PhD in Sociology at the University of Pittsburgh.

Jonathan P. Rossing, Ph.D., is Associate Professor and Department Chair of Communication Studies at Gonzaga University. Jonathan's primary research focuses on humor as a critical, public pedagogy, particularly in relation to social and racial justice issues. He also studies intersections between improvisation, play, and rhetorical theory and practice.

Mary Stuckey, Ph.D., is Professor of Communication and Political Science at Georgia State University. She specializes in political and presidential rhetoric, political communication, and American Indian politics. She is the author, editor, or co-editor of twelve books and author or coauthor of roughly 80 essays and book chapters. She has received the Michael M. Osborn Teacher/Scholar Award, the Rose B. Johnson Award (with Zoe Hess-Carney), the Roderick P. Hart Outstanding Book Award, the Marie Hochmuth Nichols Award, and the Bruce E. Gronbeck Political Communication Award. She has served as editor of the *Southern Communication Journal* and is Editor-Elect of the *Quarterly Journal of Speech*.

Christopher A. Medjesky, Ph.D., is Assistant Professor of Communication at the University of Findlay. His research focuses on the relationship between rhetoric and media. This scholarship often focuses on the significance of humor, intertextuality, and interactivity in rhetoric.

James J. Brown, Jr., Ph.D., is Assistant Professor of English and Director the Digital Studies Center at Rutgers University-Camden. He conducts research in the areas of digital rhetoric, electronic literature, and software studies. His book *Ethical Programs: Hospitality and the Rhetorics of Software* examines the ethical and rhetorical possibilities of a number of networked software platforms.

Stephen Olbrys Gencarella, Ph.D., is Associate Professor of Communication at the University of Massachusetts Amherst. His research concerns the intersection of rhetorical studies, folklore studies, and performance studies. His work has appeared in the *Quarterly Journal of Speech, Rhetoric Society Quarterly, Communication and Critical Cultural Studies, Critical Studies in Media Communication*, and other scholarly journals. He is especially interested in the ways contemporary humor performances address, uphold, and critique social and political anxieties.

PREFACE

Origins of the Collection

This collection began, like so many before it, as an idea for a conference panel. The panel never happened. What did happen, though, was a handful of rhetoricians started a serious conversation about stand-up comedy. This collection is a reflection of the major ideas driving that conversation. What is more, it is an invitation to you, the reader, to join us and the authors included here as we continue to consider the relationship between comedy – stand-up or otherwise – and the rhetoric of social change.

Given its origin, the collection has been constructed as a series of conversations. As we, the editors, sought to fill out the content, we posted an open call for papers, received a few dozen submissions, and culled from them the very best chapters for inclusion here. Our decisions regarding chapter selection were based on scholarly rigor, quality, and fit for the collection's central themes. Simply, we chose what we believed to be the best chapters that were submitted. We declined several chapters that we were particularly fond of, some even after a revision or two. In every case, the final decision came down to rigor, quality, and fit.

The collection is organized into a series of conversations around four unifying themes that emerged as the chapters were revised and refined. Each part ends with a response from a senior scholar that synthesizes those chapters and extends their conversations into other areas of the literature that provide, we hope, new points of entry for future scholarly consideration. Each part, in this way, is constructed like a panel session. They are topical and thematic conversations contained within a broader conversation about stand-up comedy and social change. This organizational structure means that each part functions as both a discrete discussion that should be of interest to scholars and students concerned with the themes and topics even when they may not otherwise concern themselves with stand-up comedy and as a well-rounded engagement of the potentials and pitfalls of stand-up comedy as a rhetoric of social change.

These organizational and structural decisions have other ramifications, not the least of which regards those comics discussed and those omitted from these pages. In our limited space and structure, we have almost certainly excluded one of your favorite comedians from this book. In fact, we have left out some of our favorites, too. This is, at least in part, by design. There are simply too many comics that are important to the tradition of stand-up comedy and the culture it stands to change to address them all, and any attempt to rank them in order of significance is highly subjective at best. Nevertheless, we believe that all of the comics treated by the authors of this collection are worthy of scholarly consideration.

In the same way, there are topics and themes not covered by the authors of this collection. Because the subjects of stand-up comedy run the gamut between issues of grave importance and the utterly mundane, it would be just as difficult to catalog and adequately consider every theme used to wrest laughs from and change the minds of audiences. Because it originated as a conversation about specific comedians and specific issues, our collection was never intended to be comprehensive. We've left important comedians out, we've left commonplace themes unexplored, and we invite our reader to fill in those gaps as we continue the conversation together.

The editors would like to thank our friends, colleagues, and families for their guidance and assistance in bringing this collection to fruition.

FOREWORD

Stand-Up Comedy, Social Change, and (American) Culture

Judith Yaross Lee

Emily Dickinson did not have stand-up comedy in mind in 1868 when she advised, "Tell all the Truth but tell it slant," but her punning explanation that "Success in Circuit lies" (Dickinson 1961, p. 248) recognizes how indirection animates truth-telling in all comic forms. The observational monologue that has become stand-up's hallmark represents comic art at its purest – the humorous anecdote delivered in apparently ordinary conversation – and thus highlights humor as a rhetoric of, and for, social change.[1] Comedy went silent just after the 9/11 attacks, but soon Margaret Cho managed to tweak the hyperpatriotism of the times, reporting that she had gone to Ground Zero "day after day, giving blow jobs to rescue workers … because we all have to do our part" (Cho 2002). Whatever form it takes, narrative humor always presents a specific attitude or viewpoint aimed at eliciting a specific effect – laughter – from a specific audience whose social knowledge, in turn, specifies topics and values ripe for ridicule. The slanted truths of comic rhetoric exploit the zone of play, a zone that (like the sacred zone for ritual) takes place in "a playground," as Johan Huizinga (1955) put it in *Homo Ludens*, a location "marked off beforehand either materially or ideally, deliberately or as a matter of course" (p. 10). The punchline may surprise, but successful humor addresses an audience already within the humor zone; stipulating "That's a joke" does not neutralize offense after the fact. Within the humor zone, however, the humorist invokes social rules in order to transgress them, if only symbolically through language, visual art, or other mode. Humor thus serves as the advance guard of social change, mocking values in flux.

The stand-up comedy examined in this volume mainly reflects the social challenges of post-World War II American culture. But, as Abbey Morgan and Christopher Gilbert indicate in their chapters on Jackie "Moms" Mabley and Eddie Izzard, stand-up comedy challenged social norms long before the breakthrough performances of Mort Sahl and Richard Pryor, and stand-up comedians thrive beyond U.S. borders. Born Loretta Mary Aiken in North Carolina barely one generation removed from the Civil War, and just after the Supreme Court legalized Jim Crow apartheid in Plessy v. Ferguson, Moms Mabley (1897?–1975) developed a solo career in New York theaters during the Harlem Renaissance of the late 1920s after a decade performing sketch comedy in vaudeville shows that toured through the African-American Theater Owners Booking Association. Her mature act forged an intimate relationship with her audience from the stage of such distinguished venues as the Apollo Theater. One biographer notes that she "presented herself as … someone who would be welcome in their living rooms, bringing around the latest gossip, jokes, and news of the community" or sharing imaginary conversations with national and world leaders, an ideal posture for skewering racism as African Americans fought for civil rights (Logan 2005). Thus Mabley not only took on the stand-up comedian's classic role, the cultural mediator who appears as "a naked self"; she also adopted the stand-up's classic persona: the *eiron*, a figure whose unassuming manner or appearance is deceptive.[2] For his part, Izzard (1962–), born of British parents in Yemen and influenced by the Monty Python troupe, has performed in 28 countries around the world (and in four languages) from his base in London while undertaking theatrical and film roles to supplement his signature solo performances grounded in the impersonation and cross-dressing traditions of the British music hall (Plagens 2000; Beekeepers 2015). As Izzard's career tracks growing acceptance of gender performances beyond old binary norms, his outreach in recent years to celebrate "the 70th anniversary of peace in Europe" under the banner of "Comedy *Sans Frontieres*" suggests how he builds, and builds on, common political ground.

Overlap between the minstrel and music hall origins of Mabley and Izzard highlights the Anglo-American stage traditions underlying stand-up comedy as a medium of social change. English theatricals not only valorized the stage monologue, as Shakespeare's plays remind us, but also interwove comic and serious plots as far back as the medieval *Second Shepherds' Play*. At any rate, lowly characters who spoke truths in jest had a long history by the time British colonies in North America claimed their independence in 1776, when the carnivalesque impulse theorized by Bakhtin (1984) lost its chief political restraint. A free democratic society has less need than a monarchy for a social safety valve that restricts lower classes' comic license to critique their social superiors to a few ritual occasions. As part of that political shift, a major strand of American humor rejected the English tradition of learned wit (the sort of humor that befuddles students forced to read Alexander Pope's "Rape of the Lock," a long, mock-epic poem about a flirtation over a card game) and instead celebrated the uncouth but charming average Joe – or Robin or Jonathan, as the quintessential Yankee was then known. On stage and in print, this character represented the ordinary American citizen through three main traits: youth (symbolizing the new government in the New World), common speech (often marked by a regional, even rural dialect signaling rejection of aristocratic hierarchies), and common sense (usually in invidious contrasts demonstrating that book learning or social status did not confer wisdom). This so-called vernacular figure had his theatrical debut in Royall Tyler's stage comedy *The Contrast* (1787), a landmark in the divergence between British and American rhetoric.

When the play opened in New York City on April 16, 1787, the Articles of Confederation organizing the first postcolonial American government had failed, the nation was bankrupt, and the new constitutional convention that had been convened for the next month in Philadelphia was by no means certain to devise a better plan. In Tyler's comedy, Revolutionary War hero Colonel Manly gets the girl by proving his moral superiority to his foppish Anglophile competitor, Billy Dimple. But lowly young Jonathan, Manly's servant, gets the glory: he brought down the house in every performance with a rousing rendition of "Yankee Doodle," a song originating in British insults that American troops appropriated as a patriotic badge of honor. The so-called fourth wall of the stage keeps Manly and Jonathan from the direct, apparently authentic, and purportedly spontaneous communication that characterizes stand-up comedy, but the characters and their situations rely on the zones of play and laughter to give meaning to the dramatic social changes of their day. *The Contrast* symbolically resolved problems of contemporary economics, politics, and identity by upending the British status quo: the play literally and metaphorically laughs the Old World sophisticate off the stage in favor of American middle-class virtue and homespun verve. These old postcolonial stage traditions live on in media and genres across the spectrum of contemporary American humor, as I have detailed elsewhere (Lee 2006; Lee 2012), but they remain most visible in stand-up comedy's performance of marginality, as defined by Joanne Gilbert (2004), who has contributed to this volume a response to three chapters on the theme of stand-up and identity.

I cite the hoary 18th-century example to make three points. First, plot-based humor – as distinct from puns, parodies, and other plotless types – always feeds, and feeds off of, social change. Even the shortest anecdote imitates human action in society, in the sense that Aristotle defined imitation as a representational mode in *The Poetics* (c.335 B.C.E./1970). Consequently, insofar as any comic anecdote starts with a narrative instability that plot (and perhaps punchline) must resolve, it always plays with social values and norms, the more unstable the better for purposes of play, and in the end plot must either affirm or challenge the status quo. Second, comic rhetorics range across genre and place. Stand-up comedy not only has its own history, traditions, and tropes in each culture that produces and sustains it, but also borrows from and informs *other* comic forms and performance traditions wherever they circulate. No comedian is an island. On the other hand, and this is my third point, as a rhetoric tied to social reality, plot-based humor always speaks to a specific time, place, audience, and context. It is a paradigm of *kairos*.

For that reason, however, I must note that the comic monologue as a vehicle of social critique dates back even before *The Contrast*, and thrived off as well as on stage. In April of 1722, for instance, 16-year-old Benjamin Franklin channeled chatty criticisms of the ironically named Silence Dogood (get it?) in letters to the *New-England Courant*, and he published 14 monologues before admitting authorship and conceding that his "small Fund of Sense for such Performances was pretty well exhausted" (Franklin 1771-1789/2006). That Franklin saw these letters as performances testifies to the line between dramatic monologues in print and the deadpan tradition in stand-up comedy. So does the history by which newspaper humorists like Mark Twain became public personalities whose biographies disappeared behind their textual masks. In fact, between Franklin and Twain so many comic correspondents appeared in the vernacular mode (including that despicable Confederate sympathizer of the 1860s, Petroleum Vesuvius Nasby, created by David Ross Locke of the *Toledo Blade* and reputedly a favorite of Abraham Lincoln) that the distinguished British cultural critic and poet Matthew Arnold (1888) lambasted the very notion that the U.S. had a civilization, sneering at American "glorification of 'the average man'" and declaring that "addiction to 'the funny man' … is a national misfortune there" (p. 489). The development of radio meant that deadpan comic critique no longer needed print to reach a wide national audience, but the monologue tradition has continued to adapt to new media – nightclubs, television, podcasts, and the Internet – without forsaking the stage.[3] Consider, for instance, the "cowboy humorist" Will Rogers (born William Penn Adair; 1879–1935). In 1922, exactly 200 years after Franklin, he began a newspaper column, "Will Rogers Says," that eventually brought his homespun political commentary to 40 million readers atop great celebrity in vaudeville and silent films (Rogers 2003, p. 180). At a time of rising income inequality and new roles for women, this new success led fans to draft him as a candidate in the 1928 presidential campaign, a precedent for the mock-candidacies of the comic-strip possum Pogo in 1952 (and 1956) and of Stephen Colbert in 2012. Then, in 1929, Rogers moved to radio, where he feigned unawareness of his humor with his famously modest tagline, "Well, all I know is what I read in the papers," as he guided listeners through the Great Depression and New Deal. And although Walter Blair labeled the American tradition of the comic monologue "A man's voice, speaking," in fact women supplied many of the voices, and women's creations often had a life on stage as well as in print, as in the case of the influential antebellum Widow Bedott created by Frances Miriam Whitcher (1811–52), though Bedott was famously performed in drag. All these dramatic monologues offered a slanted truth, deflating received opinions and proffering unexpected wisdom. Like today's stand-up comedy, monologues in print translated the moralistic orientation of Anglo-America, with its puritan penchant for self-improvement, into a popular expression of individualism for society's sake.

Indeed, in this way stand-up comedy offers nearly infinite variety on what Louis D. Rubin Jr. (1973) called "the Great American Joke": "the incongruity between the ideal and the real" that symbolizes "the nature and problem of democracy" (p. 5). Rubin conceived this formulation for a 1971–72 radio series broadcast over the U.S. Department of State's Voice of America network for international audiences, and his conception reflects a nationalism perhaps more relevant to its time and its original context than to ours. But his vision retains resonance because the American project, which resides in ideals, reflects an impulse for equity and right action that fuels stand-up comedians around the globe. Not that they need even to stand. With a metaphor borrowed from physics, Rebecca Krefting (2014) shows in *All Joking Aside* that a comic rhetoric of social change can yield "charged humor": a type of stand-up comedy that exploits "principles of attraction and repulsion that mimic audience response" as its practitioners, including comedians with disabilities, "bring new worldviews that eschew inequality into public consciousness and discourse" (p. 25). Charged or otherwise, modern stand-up comedy deserves close critical attention as a rhetoric that tells the truth, but tells it slant.

Notes

1 Solo or duo comedy routines on other topics may also qualify as stand-up comedy if they break the fourth wall of the stage to communicate directly with the audience, whereas sketch comedy and solo monologues that maintain that barrier do not. For a good contrast in performances by a single comedian, consider Lily Tomlin. As the overgrown pre-schooler Edith Ann, Tomlin spoke directly to her audience ("Hello, my name is Edith Ann, and I'm 5½ years old"), but instead of social commentary she offered a character study that could include replies to questions from the audience (see, for example, Tomlin 1975). In her performances as Ernestine, the telephone operator, on the other hand, Tomlin addressed widespread mistrust in the 1970s of AT&T's powers as the nation's sole telephone company (a 1982 antitrust settlement with the Justice Department broke up their monopoly): Ernestine apparently had access to customers' tax records and threatened bodily harm for nonpayment of small balances, claiming, "We are not subject to city, state, or federal regulations; we are omni-petent." But the audience was eavesdropping on Ernestine, as well, and she did not acknowledge their presence, exemplifying the difference between sketch comedy and observational stand-up (see, for example Tomlin, n.d. [1970s]).
2 Lawrence Mintz (1985) wrote the classic statement on stand-up comedy; David Marc (1989/1992) described the stand-up as "a naked self, eschewing the luxury of a clear-cut distinction between art and life" (p. 13). John Limon (2000) offered a theory of stand-up comedy "as abjection" that no longer has much traction. The canonical description of the *eiron* (and his opposite, the *alazon*) in American humor is Walter Blair and Hamlin Hill (1978), *America's Humor*.
3 See, for example, Meserko (2015) on how stand-up comedy has adapted to the podcast medium.

References

Aristotle (c.335 B.C.E./1970). *Poetics*. Trans. & ed. by G.F. Else. Ann Arbor: University of Michigan Press.
Arnold, M. (1888). Civilisation in the United States. *The Nineteenth Century, 134*, 481–496.
Bakhtin, M. (1984). *Rabelais and his world*. Trans. by Helene Iswolsky. Bloomington: Indiana University Press.
Beekeepers. (2015). Force majeure reloaded. *EddieIzzard.com*. Retrieved from www.eddieizzard.com/news/201510/07/force-majeure-reloaded (accessed October 7, 2015).
Blair, W., & Hill, H. (1978). *America's humor: From Poor Richard to Doonesbury*. New York: Oxford University Press.

Cho, M. (2002). *Notorious C.H.O.: Margaret Cho filmed live in concert*. Wellspring Media.
Dickinson, E. (1961). *Final harvest: Emily Dickinson's poems*. Boston: Little, Brown & Company.
Franklin, B. (1771–1789/2006). Autobiography, Part 2. In S.V.F. Waite, W. Poe, P. Doherty, & D.W. Packard (Eds.), *Franklin papers online*. The Papers of Benjamin Franklin. Packard Humanities Institute, Yale University. Retrieved from http://franklinpapers.org/franklin/framedVolumes.jsp?vol=50&page=002a (accessed October 1, 2015).
Gilbert, J.R. (2004). *Performing marginality: Humor, gender, and cultural critique*. Detroit: Wayne State University Press.
Huizinga, J. (1955). *Homo ludens*. Boston: Beacon Press.
Krefting, R. (2014). *All joking aside: American humor and its discontents*. Baltimore: Johns Hopkins University Press.
Lee, J.Y. (2006). Mark Twain as a stand-up comedian. *Mark Twain Annual, 4*, 3–23.
Lee, J.Y. (2012). *Twain's brand: Humor in contemporary American culture*. Jackson: University Press of Mississippi.
Limon, J. (2000). *Stand-up comedy in theory, or abjection in America*. Durham: Duke University Press.
Logan, R.W. (2005). Mabley, Jackie "Moms." In D.C. Hine (Ed.), *Black women in America*, 2nd ed. New York: Oxford University Press. Retrieved from www.oxfordaasc.com
Marc, D. (1992). *Comic visions: Television comedy and American culture*. New York: Routledge.
Meserko, V.M. (2015). Standing upright: Podcasting, performance, and alternative comedy. *Studies in American Humor, Series 4, 1*(1), 20–40.
Mintz, L.E. (1985). Standup comedy as social and cultural mediation. *American Quarterly, 37*(1), 71–80.
Plagens, P. (2000). It's Izzard, isn't it? *Newsweek, 135*(12), 66.
Rogers, W. (2003). In A. McNeill, R.C. Hanes, & S.M. Hanes (Eds.), *Great Depression and the New Deal reference library*, Vol. 2 (pp. 176–184). Detroit: UXL.
Rubin, Jr., L.D. (1973). Introduction: "The great American joke." In L.D. Rubin, Jr. (Ed.), *The comic imagination in American literature* (pp. 3–15). New Brunswick, NJ: Rutgers University Press.
Tomlin, L. (1975). Lily Tomlin as Edith Ann: Edith Ann talks with the audience (Q & A). *YouTube*. Retrieved from www.youtube.com/watch?v=OufQ4vacywo (accessed October 1, 2015).
Tomlin, L. (n.d. [1970s]). Lily Tomlin as telephone operator Ernestine. *YouTube*. Retrieved from www.youtube.com/watch?v=SvesMBkduQo (accessed October 1, 2015).

INTRODUCTION

Standing Up, Speaking Out

Matthew R. Meier and Casey R. Schmitt

On March 31, 1964 Lenny Bruce was arrested. Again. His arrest in New York City for uttering obscenities from the stage before a mixed audience marked the genesis of a landmark trial regarding the freedom of expression in the United States. The conviction rendered at the trial's conclusion ended the career of one of the brightest comedy talents in American history. Admittedly, Bruce may not have been the funniest of his contemporaries – both Shelley Berman and Bob Newhart, not Bruce, won Grammy awards for their LPs – but his legacy, both in terms of the form of stand-up comedy and American culture more generally, casts an impressive shadow. Bruce's comedy was impactful, in part, because he delighted in pressing where it hurt for his audience. He prodded taboo subjects such as sexuality and racism. He questioned the motivation of the country's most well-respected religious figures. He toyed with language and revealed, at almost every turn, the hypocrisy of cultural institutions. His stand-up became the standard by which subversive comedy – comedy for social change – would be judged.

In his celebrated essay on social movement, Michael Calvin McGee argues that social movement occurs whenever a new term comes into fashion or an old term becomes associated with a new meaning (1980, p. 243). The result of Bruce's trial, conviction, and death (in 1966) was precisely this kind of social movement. The word "obscenity," a word whose definition was central to the trial proceedings, changed and for the generation of stand-up comedians who followed in Bruce's footsteps – notably Richard Pryor and George Carlin – so too did the culture. So much so, in fact, that when Carlin found himself in a courtroom in Milwaukee, Wisconsin, facing obscenity charges for performing his "Seven Words You Can Never Say on Television" routine at an outdoor festival, even the judge presiding over the hearing laughed out loud when the LP version of the bit was played in the courtroom.

Whether or not Bruce intended to do so, his comedy changed the meaning of obscenity. From Bruce's conviction to Carlin's courtroom comedy, what could be said and what could not be said in public changed. In the liner notes of Carlin's *Class Clown* (1972) – the record on which Carlin's "Seven Words" routine first appears – the comic thanks Lenny, to whom the album is dedicated, for "taking all the chances." His posthumous recognition of Bruce's significance to both the form and to freedom of speech speaks to the legacy of social change permeating Bruce's comedy for future generations.

Of course, we would be short-sighted to suggest that Lenny Bruce was *solely* responsible for changing society's understanding of obscenity. Social change is simply not that simple. Social change is the result of complex interactions between rhetors, discourses, audiences, and events. No singular oration, comedy routine or otherwise, can result in social change. Nevertheless, scholars of rhetoric persist in their efforts to characterize the process by which social change occurs and the rhetorical forms and strategies that encourage such change.

This collection joins that conversation by addressing stand-up comedy as a unique rhetorical form in terms of its ability to facilitate social change. Admittedly, this is not the standard approach to studying rhetorics of social change. Traditionally, scholars have addressed subjects such as protest movements or political rhetoric in their attempts to understand the rhetorical aspects of social movement and change. Such rhetorics operate under the guise of seriousness and therefore carry an assumed legitimacy not granted to other modes of discourse. Our argument over the course of this volume is that even though stand-up comedy is a decidedly non-serious form of rhetoric, it nonetheless participates in the discourse of social change. For this reason, stand-up carries unique potential to affect discourses for change by providing an alternative mode of expression while operating outside of the rules of serious discourse.

Rhetorical Scholarship and Stand-Up

In historical terms, stand-up comedy is a relatively new concept. The term itself didn't come into fashion in America until the middle of the 20th century. In the late 1950s, the rise of "new comedians" – people like Mort Sahl, Shelley Berman, Dick Gregory, and Lenny Bruce – introduced American audiences to a uniquely oratorical form of entertainment that was both captivating and provocative. Comedy had long since been a part of the American experience, but the joke tellers, vaudevillians, and radio performers of the past preferred rote gags and canned jokes. The rise of stand-up as a form also meant the rise of a new kind of popular rhetor. Stand-up comedians were not merely comic actors as were their predecessors – they were comic rhetors. Whereas the comedians of the past were primarily concerned with delivery, stand-ups turned their attention to invention. They wrote, improvised, and thought comedy. They became, as *Time* suggested, a new class of public intellectuals (1960, p. 44). Theirs was rhetoric more than a performance, and as such, their comedy was not only entertaining, it was also persuasive.

Molded in the Ciceronian notion of a speech for entertainment, stand-up comedy is an especially rhetorical form of popular culture. Stand-up comedy typically involves a lone rhetor offering a punchline-peppered monologue to an audience packed tightly into a nightclub for the express purpose of laughing for an hour or so. A decidedly oratorical spectacle, the stand-up comedy performance remains one of the last remnants of the rhetorical tradition in contemporary culture. As Andrea Greenbaum (1999) contends, stand-up comedy is a form of rhetorical argument whereby comics construct *ethos* (credibility) by creating comic *personae* (character or voice) while negotiating *kairos* (timing) to ensure the maximum impact of their punchlines. What is more, as Stephanie Koziski argues, stand-up comedians function as cultural critics who "jar their [audience's] sensibilities by making [them] experience the shock of recognition" and by revealing "the hidden underpinnings of their culture" (1997, p. 87). In this way, Koziski suggests that stand-up performers are not unlike anthropologists or other intellectuals preoccupied with the characteristics of public culture. Given the rhetorical features of stand-up performance and its tendency toward cultural critique, it is no surprise that rhetorical scholars have occasionally focused their attention on the form and its rhetorical potential.

Among the most significant contributions to the scholarly conversation about stand-up comedy and rhetoric is the work of Joanne Gilbert (1997). Writing from the perspective of a rhetorical critic and former stand-up comedian, Gilbert provides an important analysis of the style and function of female stand-up performers. She argues that female comics use their marginalized status as women to challenge authority by offering "potentially subversive critique of the hegemonic culture while simultaneously eliciting laughter and earning a living" in contexts where "the marginal are not only accepted but valorized" (p. 3; 2004, p. xii). That is, comics are unique because their criticism, though it may be harsh, is rewarded. Further, Gilbert suggests that comic rhetorical strategies such as self-deprecation can act as double-coded social critiques that are sanctioned by the audience because the stand-up performer simultaneously performs "self and culture" (1997, p. 317). In this way, the comic may make himself or herself the butt of a joke, but in so doing simultaneously externalizes some cultural incongruity or imperfection as the target of the audience's laughter's corrective capacity. Gilbert's analysis of female performers such as Roseanne Barr and Phyllis Diller challenges the conventional wisdom that comedy, even at its most acerbic, merely reifies existing hierarchical relations of power.

Other critics have addressed specific performers in terms of their rhetorical functions. Richard Pryor, for example, has received a good deal of scholarly treatment. In one essay on his stand-up, Evan Cooper (2007) contends that Pryor's hyper focus on foibles and idiosyncrasies of black culture as a well from which to draw punchlines fostered what he calls a "culturally intimate" humor (p. 224). Much as Gilbert suggests of comediennes, Cooper argues that Pryor's intense focus on his own culture and identity became the source of power for his comedy. In this way, Pryor's ability to use his stand-up to critique dominant culture relied heavily on his ability to make those critiques by working through his own cultural subjectivity and marginality.

In another essay, Jonathan Rossing (2014), whose work is featured in this collection, suggests that Pryor's humor became a resource for challenging dominant cultural assumptions and managing the risk of speaking truth to power. What is more, because Pryor's stand-up performances took the form of *parrhesia* or frank criticism, Rossing argues that his comic rhetoric teaches his audience "how meaning, experience, and systematic forces in a particular historical moment establish specific modes of authority and power relationships, sanction particular subject positions, and legitimate certain experiences" (p. 30). Pryor's comedy, in this way, functions as social criticism that speaks to oppression from the perspective of the oppressed. His jokes move beyond the guffaws and challenge his audience to think critically about power and culture. Thus, for both Cooper and Rossing, the form of stand-up comedy provides a means by which dominant discourses may be challenged and alternative truths can be spoken by people who may not otherwise be permitted to speak.

Korean American comedienne Margaret Cho, who is also featured in this collection, has been among the more fruitful examples of the rhetorical potential of stand-up comedy. Kyra Pearson (2009), for instance, suggests that Cho's comedy operates from a speaking position she calls the "symbolic assassin," which functions to "expand the space for dissent against disparate power relations (p. 37). From Pearson's perspective, Cho's stand-up uses language to challenge the discourse of dominant culture and create new associations between symbols and meanings. In another essay, Susan Pelle (2010) suggests that Cho's sexualized performances "make 'real' a form of national abjection that continues to violently and repetitively exclude, deny, and shape her" through her bodily expositions of "the performing vagina" (pp. 34–35). In this way, Pelle argues that Cho's comedy permits her to play with traditional notions of sex and gender in order to challenge how she is perceived by dominant culture. Both claims rest upon the capacity of Cho's performative venue – that is, stand-up comedy – to function as a safe haven for what Lawrence Mintz (1985) calls "staged antagonism." In this way, these analyses of Cho's stand-up suggest that the form itself carries unique potential to provide an alternative space for the symbolic contests of social change.

Together, these treatments of stand-up comedy all indicate that the form is at once uniquely rhetorical and capable of engaging discourses of social change by calling into question dominant cultural practices and assumptions. Although we are not suggesting that stand-up should be regarded as a panacea, its ability to speak truth to power, speak the unspeakable, and consider the world not as it is but as it should be cannot be ignored as a potentially powerful rhetorical resource for social change.[1]

"Standing Up"

In reflecting on the rhetorical potential of stand-up comedy, we consider the phrase "stand-up," itself, as a rhetorical concept. The act of "stand-up" has, in it, at least four significant meanings for our perspective.

First, of course, stand-up is comedy. It is the act of one speaker delivering humorous, monologic quips, observations, and anecdotes to an audience, who may then signal their approval or disapproval of the performance and concepts presented. It is *meant* to be funny. But it is also meant to be socially and rhetorically significant. The speaker delivering stand-up is presenting ideas to the crowd for review, seeking assent and affirmation. So "stand-up" is telling jokes, but jokes that carry judgments.

Stand-up is also a physical act. Sure, some stand-up comics sit or pace or change position through their acts, but most stand-up is still performed while standing. It is an embodied act of gaining attention and social prominence. Audiences for stand-up are generally seated and at leisure. The stand-up comic, standing up, is both uniquely powerful and uniquely vulnerable in the standing position. She or he is a central focus of attention. By standing up, the speaker physically takes on a role of social prominence and attention.

Third, as an extension, standing up – or "stand-up" – is a distinctly *active* process. Standing up is the verbal opposite of standing down or lying down, choosing to be inactive, passive, or silent. Stand-up, as a practice, is an act of selection and of interaction with the world. The stand-up comic is selecting to engage with her or his environment rather than stepping aside, standing or lying down in the face of surrounding actors and events.

And lastly, stand-up has the metaphorical or implicit meaning in English of confronting or challenging authority and/or oppression. In English, we speak of "standing up" for our principles or for the "little guy." We also tell tales of individuals or communities who "stand up" to bullies, corruption, or other antagonistic forces. In this sense, "standing up" is a direct assertion of resistance and justice in the face of adversity. Stand-up comedy can, at times, take on this resistive, progressive, activist sense as well.

The chapters in this collection consider stand-up comedy in each of these senses, contributing to a complex rhetorical act that is both grounded in traditional, monologic, speaker-to-audience oratory and potentially disruptive, resistive, and conducive to social change.

"Speaking Out"

In developing this collection, the contributing authors also reflect on oratorical performance as uniquely conducive to social engagement and disruption of widely shared social opinions. In addressing a crowd, large or small, the stand-up comic is a public speaker, using words and delivery to spread ideas and sentiments among those others that surround her or him. The traditional stand-up comic, on a stage and talking directly to an audience, face-to-face, is literally "speaking out," and this phrase, too, has multiple potential meanings.

On one level, "speaking out" can be quite literal. The live orator uses her or his voice to take what was internal – ideas, arguments, mental images, jokes – and make it external. The live stand-up comic, through performance, speaks her or his mind outwardly.

In this way, oratorical performance is inherently social, inherently outward looking. It is a practice of engagement with one's surroundings, one's society, one's immediate social environment. "Speaking out" is an acknowledgment of and engagement with a world and a social sphere outside of the individual (or physical) self.

In vernacular meaning, this acknowledgment and engagement with social surroundings is extended. To "speak out" is also, popularly, to speak against or in opposition. Individuals and groups "speak out" against injustice, against controversial policies, against powerful persons and interests. To talk of "speaking out" implies, at times, resistance or constraint that holds the speech, words, or ideas in, and a breaking of this constraint as the censored or unspoken concepts escape through oral performance.

And, in this sense, "speaking out" is frequently paired or associated with "breaking silence." The practice of speaking literally breaks a silence, but when we talk or write about individual activists, witnesses, political figures, or other citizens "speaking out" we recognize that a relative silence is broken as well, as underrepresented perspectives are given voice and attention, as topics that went unspoken due to taboo or hegemonic agenda-setting are loosed for public and social discussion.

The stand-up comic performing live before an audience is literally "speaking out" to the crowd, and inherent to this practice is a social engagement, with the potential to encourage social reflection and social change. Certainly not all stand-up comedy is performed with social commentary in mind, but the mere act of standing up and speaking out always holds this potential. As the chapters in this collection demonstrate, stand-up is a powerful tool for shaking the status quo, destabilizing assumptions of all things, including norms of propriety, political arguments, personal or social identity, and race.

Stand-up comics like Chris Rock, Roseanne Barr, Dick Gregory, and Amy Schumer, among others, have often explicitly used their stand-up microphone as a medium for channeling their social commentary, speaking out on injustice and imbalance, but in a jovial atmosphere; breaking taboo, sometimes with mere wordplay or bathroom humor, but also encouraging audiences to reflect as they laugh. Other comics may not leap to mind as social crusaders, but their action of standing up and speaking out makes their performances rhetorical and socially significant all the same.

For this reason, the chapters of this collection focus on traditional stand-up before an audience from a primarily rhetorical perspective. The uniquely jocular, taboo-courting form of the stand-up set is a significant genre in the study of oratory and social engagement. At the same time, though, this focus on the oratorical and rhetorical aspects of comedy invites wider conversation, and the response chapters following each main part of the book open the conversation to other fields and perspectives where humor is increasingly embraced as a vehicle for reflection, revision, and upheaval.

Chapter Summary

This collection is divided into four primary parts, each focused on one ways in which stand-up comics and their routines have functioned as a rhetoric of social change, encouraging audiences to question popular practices and assumptions, ludicly reorganizing categories and allowing audiences to collectively reflect upon and recombine ideals and ideas.

Stand-up as a genre displays special affordances, tropes, and strategies. The unique rhetorical situation in the comedy club or talk show environment, the comic persona, the comedy-laden strategies and techniques available to the speaker, and the special role of (often explicitly vocalized) audience reception allow stand-up to "push-the-envelope," and to comment on controversy, politics, and other social issues through jest and in other taboo ways. The individual chapters collected here explore these affordances through case analysis while engaging in rhetorical theory, and highlight particular comics and routines as notable cultural interventions, as sites of social challenge and change.

The first part considers "Stand-Up and Identity." This part's authors examine how stand-up comedy can deconstruct speaker and audience identities, ridiculing assumptions as it asserts more fluid, non-conformist identity through performance and providing audiences with alternative models for being.

In the part's first chapter, Lacy Lowrey and Valerie Renegar consider the power of stand-up to question and re-frame racial stereotypes and categories. Their chapter examines the stand-up of Margaret Cho as it negotiates and communicates Korean American bicultural identity. Humor, they argue, offers a rhetorically significant method for performing cultural identity membership, and the chapter traces themes of bicultural otherness, ironic essentialism of Asian culture, and stereotypical self-deprecating humor as a means of cultural separation in Cho's work. Through ironic essentializing of a cultural group, they explain, Cho is able to subversively highlight the absurdity of the stereotypes she has encountered and speak to both Asian and non-Asian audiences.

Following this, Christopher Gilbert's chapter moves beyond race to other social identity categories, using Eddie Izzard's celebrated *Dressed to Kill* stand-up special to highlight how absurdity in humor can disrupt all sorts of cultural categories and preconceptions, including gender, sexuality, and religious belief. Gilbert demonstrates how Izzard seamlessly melds his transvestitism with his comedy, as both transvestitism and comedy queer (or reorganize) social categories and expectations to reveal the inherent absurdity of those categories and expectations in the first place. As Gilbert writes, Izzard exploits "the comic stage as a relatively 'safe' space to embellish just how bizarre the familiar seems when compared to the strange" and provides counter-narratives to dominant cultural orders of masculinity, militarism, and faith. Taped during the late 1990s, the routine presents a direct challenge to several dominant American cultural narratives of the time.

In the final chapter of this part, Abbey Morgan considers the comedy career of Jackie "Moms" Mabley, whose vaudevillian adaptation of the African American "mammy" redeployed stereotype in the stand-up frame as a means of resisting limitations on race and gender in the 1950s, 60s, and 70s. Mabley's seemingly simple schtick, Morgan argues, was actually deeply invested in issues of representation, self-imaging, and re-imaging, and she traces these themes in several of Mabley's jokes and routines over the years. After giving a history of black humor and minstrelry, Morgan suggests that Mabley's comedy deconstructed and reconstructed black female identity in a public-private realm.

The established authority on rhetoric and comedy, Joanne Gilbert, provides a response to these three chapters, looking outward to expand the discussion of stand-up and identity beyond the rhetorical lens. Gilbert traces how stand-up comics like Cho, Izzard, and Mabley speak especially from and deconstruct positions of *marginal* identity, then further illustrates this concept through the case of contemporary comic, Wanda Sykes.

The second part of the collection considers the frequent intersection of "Stand-Up, Race, and Culture." The authors here consider the ways that stand-up confronts and addresses racial and intercultural tensions. Stand-up comics use their unique platform to confront these tensions head-on, often defusing conflict through an embrace of intercultural difference, though just as often skirting uncomfortably close to the very close-minded arguments they parody.

In Chapter 4, for instance, Raúl Pérez complicates the discussion by examining stand-up comedy that explicitly tackles social controversy through the unapologetic use of racial, sexist, and other potentially offensive language. Analyzing a 1968 routine by "equal opportunity offender" Don Rickles during the height of the American Civil Rights Movement, Pérez argues that the comic, with free rein to not only engage but also even embrace the taboo, can encourage communal catharsis, using acknowledgment of social difference to foster social understanding. He traces in Rickles' comic strategies of negative self-presentation, negative other-presentation, audience homogenization via insult, and appeals to humor to argue that these four strategies in combination allow the comic rhetor to promote community in ways inaccessible to other speakers and forms of speaking.

Matthew R. Meier and Chad Nelson address racialized stand-up performance from the perspective of the rhetoric of whiteness. In this fifth chapter, they draw upon examples from some of Lenny Bruce's most notable routines about race and racism such as "How to Relax Your Colored Friends at Parties" and "Are There Any Niggers Here Tonight?" Specifically, the chapter argues that stand-up comics like Bruce are able to move between performing whiteness and critiquing whiteness in such a way as to render their own privilege invisible while throwing the audience's privilege into relief. Through these examples, the chapter illustrates how the strategic use of whiteness provides the ground upon which a comedian may establish and maintain the rhetorical authority necessary to challenge discourses of racism, but at the same time draws attention to whiteness' capacity to maintain its centrality against critique.

In Chapter 6, Amanda Morris examines contemporary Native American stand-up as a vehicle for social commentary, cultural activism, and intercultural engagement. In a close analysis (coupled with interviews) of Jim Ruel and the Powwow Comedy Jam, Morris demonstrates how Native American stand-up comics deploy "trickster" strategies to "simultaneously reassure and unsettle the audience." Blunt reference to the strain and ignorance undergirding white-indigenous relations in his routines allows Ruel (like his Powwow Comedy Jam compatriots) to prompt reflection, education, and healing. By teasing American and Native American audiences alike, Morris argues, Native comics promote cross-cultural understanding.

Intercultural communication scholar Alberto González provides a response to these chapters and expands the conversation to humor, race, and intolerance at large, further examining cases in which race and cultural tensions are fueled by comic performance rather than eased.

The third part of this collection considers "Stand-Up and Politics." Beyond merely analyzing politically-toned stand-up routines as simple critique in part of a larger landscape of political oratory, the authors in this part draw heavily on rhetorical and social theory to demonstrate how stand-up may itself promote hegemony and stagnation or, conversely, stimulate change.

In Chapter 7, Aaron Duncan and Jonathan Carter examine the late Bill Hicks – considered by many to be the exemplar of the stand-up comic as social critic – as an organic intellectual in a Gramscian sense. With routines that deployed biting social commentary, political viewpoints, and, often, righteous anger, Hicks, they argue, worked to shock his audiences into awareness. His position as organic intellectual allowed him to articulate subaltern attitudes already existing yet not yet illuminated for his audiences and, they add, his comedy functioned as what Gramsci called a "Modern Prince," deconstructing political spectacle and rallying masses toward resistance. The chapter culminates in a discussion of how stand-up comedy – dismissed, by some, as "mere jokes" – can always, in fact, inspire audience sentiment and action, challenge complacency, and upend status quo beliefs.

In Chapter 8, Ron Von Burg and Kai Heidemann apply Burkean concepts to stand-up comedy and politics, examining the potential dangers of using humor in political spheres by analyzing Brad Stine, a uniquely conservative-leaning comedian and self-proclaimed "God's comic" at the 2012 Conservative Political Action Conference. Von Burg and Heidemann contend that while some taboo-courting comedy can forward social dialogue, in the political realm it can function as burlesque instead of as satire and foster division, stigmatizing, and scapegoating. Their analysis shows how stand-up laced with explicitly partisan appeals can drive populations away from one another, entrenching in-group/out-group sentiments of conflict and division, and they end with an appeal to comics mixing humor and politics to work more toward collaboration and deliberation.

In Chapter 9, Jonathan Rossing examines the use of stand-up oratory at the White House Correspondents' Association (WHCA) annual dinner. The century-old tradition of the dinner has in recent years become a star-studded fête where politicians, members of the press, and celebrities du jour mix and mingle, where a comedian frequently serves as headliner, and where, in recent years, political figures like George W. Bush and Barack Obama have taken the opportunity to try their hands at comedy. Rossing analyzes the WHCA dinner speeches during the Bush and Obama administrations. Contributing to an ongoing conversation regarding the role of political humor in democracy and the blurred lines of entertainment and politics, Rossing argues that with rare exception these speeches constitute a tripartite "demockery" of the critical potential and responsibilities of humor, the role of the press in democracy, and democracy itself.

Communication scholar and expert on American politics, Mary Stuckey contributes a response that both reflects on this part's arguments and challenges the authors by questioning them and presenting alternative perspectives of its own.

The collection's final part returns to the initial premise that the stand-up rhetor enjoys a uniquely disruptive social position and opens more broadly to the social repercussions of "Standing Up, Breaking Rules." On stage, on recording, or online, stand-up comics, by profession, push boundaries and thrive on the disruption of propriety and expectations. By making the otherwise unusual usual and the otherwise inappropriate appropriate, stand-up continues to be a powerful vehicle of social change in an age of TV, Internet, and other mass media. This power can be wielded to both socially beneficial and to more socially harmful, personally beneficial ends.

In Chapter 10, Christopher Medjesky tackles, for instance, the question of obscenity and offensiveness, and the responsibility of the comic not to promote insensitivity or hate. Considering stand-up jokes and routines about rape, Medjesky examines where and how comics and their audiences draw the line between outrageous hyperbole and outrageous harm. Using a single joke delivered by comedian Daniel Tosh as a starting point, the chapter analyzes common tropes of rape humor in contemporary popular culture. The chapter examines Tosh's use of "dark humor" to joke about rape, compares performances by Tosh with routines by David Cross, and examines Tosh's response to the ensuing controversy, demonstrating how Tosh used his position of power as a comedian to refocus the discussion in a way that benefited his comedic persona.

In Chapter 11, James Brown examines a more socially beneficial phenomenon in the case of comedian Louis C.K.'s self-produced and self-distributed comedy special, *Live at the Beacon Theatre*. Brown explores how C.K.'s unusual, even nonsensical distribution model set a new pattern for commentary and comedy in the current age. C.K., Brown argues, capitalized on a contemporary media environment in which authors and artists can distribute their work with fewer intermediaries. Brown argues that while this model is relevant to digital rhetoricians, C.K.'s potential contribution to a networked rhetoric resides in his method of invention, and C.K.'s approach to *kairos* – the timing and crafting of invention in response to rhetorical situation – offers an alternative to the dominant mode of contemporary networked rhetoric. In adapting to and with new media formats, comics like C.K. set a public model for social engagement and development online.

Finally, in Chapter 12, Casey R. Schmitt analyzes stand-up comic and talk show host David Letterman's 2009 on-air revelation that, as a result of sexual misconduct in the workplace, he had become the target of an extortion scheme. Schmitt argues that while other public figures in the early 2000s – including politicians and athletes – had developed a rhetorical genre of sexual misconduct apologia, Letterman's position as comedian allowed an unprecedented variation on the theme. Instead of gravity and remorse, Letterman's confession drew on stock comic structure and phrasing and prompted an audience to respond to him as comic rather than as penitent. His revelation was met, in the moment, by laughter and applause rather than shock or reprimand. This chapter highlights how a comic speaker can cue audience response in ways otherwise inaccessible to rhetors speaking on serious topics, and also then use this response to her or his own rhetorical advantage.

In the response to this final part, rhetorical and cultural critic Stephen Olbrys Gencarella speaks to the repercussions of this special power of the comic rhetor with any degree of social influence, and reminds readers that while stand-up comics enjoy a special degree of freedom and power by virtue of their ludic roles and performances, they often also benefit from systemic privileges of race and gender. Comics like Tosh, C.K., and Letterman, he notes, for all of their playful and/or subversive qualities, also demonstrate the dominance of straight white men in the American comedy landscape. His chapter reminds us that while the rhetoric of comedy can and does disrupt social norms and assumptions, the historic dominance and special privilege of straight white male comedians is also a major (if not the major) component of many comics' successes and he urges future rhetorical studies of stand-up to extend the conversation by looking more closely at those comics speaking from more marginalized social positions.

In presenting these chapter examples with critical responses, it is our contention that stand-up routines are never merely "laughing matters," but, rather, that sometimes the laughing is what makes a social topic matter in the first place. Stand-up comedy can rally an audience to attention and articulate concerns in engaging, memorable, and highly quotable ways. Through its invitation of the audience to reflect upon and engage critical perspectives in a favorable, lighthearted, and enjoyable manner, it encourages audiences to embrace their own questions, concerns, and doubts in times when they might otherwise suppress them. The stand-up comedy exchange and atmosphere allows a group, through laughter, to affirm mutual sympathies and commitments. The laughing promotes matters. The laughing, itself, matters. With this collection, we invite other rhetorical critics and students of public deliberation, social movement, and address to consider the rhetorical power of stand-up more closely and join the conversation only just now beginning over the coming years.

Note

1 Of course, this brief foray into the literature is not comprehensive. Our intention is not to catalogue and summarize every piece of scholarship on stand-up comedy in the existing literature; rather, it is to illustrate the rhetorical nature of stand-up comedy and to demonstrate its capacity to participate in the discourse of social change. Readers interested in further exploring stand-up comedy and other forms of comic rhetoric

may see Krefting (2014), Gray, Jones, and Thompson (2009), Gournelos and Green (2011), Tafoya (2009), Limon (2000), Haggins (2007), Boskin (1997a), and Boskin (1997b).

References

Boskin, J. (1997a). *The humor prism in 20th century America.* Detroit: Wayne State University Press.
Boskin, J. (1997b). *Rebellious laughter.* Syracuse: Syracuse University Press.
Cooper, E. (2007). Is it something he said: Mass consumption of Richard Pryor's culturally intimate humor. *The Communication Review, 10*(3), 223–247.
Gilbert, J. (1997). Performing marginality: Comedy, identity, and cultural critique. *Text & Performance Quarterly, 17,* 317–330.
Gilbert, J. (2004). *Performing marginality: Humor, gender, and cultural critique.* Detroit: Wayne State University Press.
Gournelos, T., & Green, V. (Eds.) (2011). *A decade of dark humor.* Jackson: University Press of Mississippi.
Gray, J., Jones, J.P., & Thompson, E. (Eds.). (2009). *Satire TV.* New York: NYU Press.
Greenbaum, Andrea. (1999). Stand-up comedy as rhetorical argument: An investigation of comic culture. *Humor, 12,* 33–46.
Haggins, B. (2007). *Laughing mad: The black comic persona in post-soul America.* New Brunswick, NJ: Rutgers University Press.
Koziski, Stephanie (1997). The standup comedian as anthropologist: Intentional culture critic. In J. Boskin (Ed.), *The humor prism in 20th century America* (pp. 86–114). Detroit: Wayne State University Press.
Krefting, R. (2014). *All joking aside: American humor and its discontents.* Baltimore: Johns Hopkins University Press.
Limon, J. (2000). *Stand-up comedy in theory, or, abjection in America.* Durham, NC: Duke University Press.
McGee, M.C. (1980). "Social movement": Phenomenon or meaning? *Central States Speech Journal, 31,* 233–244.
Mintz, L.E. (1985). Standup comedy as social and cultural mediation. *American Quarterly, 37*(1), 71–80.
Pearson, Kyra. (2009). "Words should do the work of bombs": Margaret Cho as symbolic assassin. *Women & Language, 32*(1), 36–43.
Pelle, Susan. (2010). The "grotesque" pussy: "Transformational shame" in Margaret Cho's stand-up performances. *Text and Performance Quarterly 30*(1), 21–37.
Rossing, Jonathan. (2014). Critical race humor in a postracial moment: Richard Pryor's contemporary parrhesia. *Howard Journal of Communication, 25*(1), 16–33.
Tafoya, E. (2009). *The legacy of the wisecrack: Stand-up comedy as the great American literary form.* Boca Raton: BrownWalker Press.
Time Editorial Staff. (1960, August 15). The third campaign. *Time,* 44.

PART I
Stand-Up and Identity

> People come up to me and say, "God, Roseanne, you're not very feminine." They say that, can you believe that they would say that to me? Can you even believe that? "You're not very feminine." So I say, "Well, suck my dick!"
>
> (Roseanne Barr)

1

"YOU GOTTA GET CHINKY WITH IT!"

Margaret Cho's Rhetorical Use of Humor to Communicate Cultural Identity

Lacy Lowrey and Valerie R. Renegar

When comedian Margaret Cho introduced herself to the American public in the early 1990s, it was the first time most, if not all, Americans had seen a popular Asian American – specifically Korean American – comedian (Rotella 2001). Though outspoken women comedians such as Roseanne Barr, Joan Rivers, and Brett Butler had already entered the typically male-dominated world of stand-up comedy before Cho, not yet had an Asian American man or woman offered a humorous voice to audiences on such a large scale. Unwilling to shy away from a predominantly white male profession, over the past 20 years, Cho has forged an unlikely path within the world of stand-up comedy, commonly discussing specific aspects of her Korean heritage. Whether it is because of or in spite of her minority status, Cho has developed a substantial and loyal following since her first appearances on the stand-up comedy stage and television shows, and was recently named the "Number One Asian American Comedian of All Time" (Fung 2010). She has become best known for her social commentaries about gender, sexuality, and, perhaps most notable, race. Additionally, to discuss such heavy issues, Cho routinely uses aggressive, confident, and unapologetic humor while voicing her opinions (Holden 2000). Though she has parlayed her talents into successful television, movie, and music careers, she began (and continues to be most known for) her work as a stand-up comedian.

In 1994, Cho's stand-up comedy routine was transformed into the sitcom, *All American Girl*, the first show in America to feature an Asian American family in primetime (Marin & Lee 1994). At that point, Asians had been underrepresented and misrepresented in the media and the production of this show seemed to signal a turning point for society's perceptions of minorities, particularly Asian Americans (Park, Gabbadon, & Chernin 2006). However, the show was cancelled after only 13 episodes, in part because critics accused Cho of not being "Asian enough" (Boone 2002; Strauss 2008). It was clear that Cho's race played a significant role in who she was as a comedian whether she wanted that aspect of her identity to take center stage or not. As her career developed, Cho, never one to flee from conflict, directly addressed her race, as well as the subsequent discriminatory encounters that have developed because of it (Fowler 2000; Holden 2000; Kelly 2000). The fact that Cho has been so humorous while addressing serious racial issues has elicited some backlash from the Asian American community (Fung 2010). In fact, some of her most predominant critics come from within the Korean and Korean American communities. While some may view her comedy as racially stereotypical, others laud Cho for her willingness to discuss topics otherwise avoided by the general population (Esther 1999; Holden 2000). To many, Cho is the voice of various minority groups due to her bravery and honest humor.

In an effort to better understand the importance of Margaret Cho's moniker as the first notable Korean American comedian, we argue that humor offers a rhetorically significant method for performing cultural identity membership. In order to do this, we examine Cho's stand-up comedy, specifically the ways in which she discusses her racial identity and cultural background. We offer an analysis of Cho's stand-up comedy followed by conclusions and implications that arise based on her use of humor to create a culturally-based identity.

Margaret Cho's Stand-Up Comedy

Margaret Cho is not afraid to directly address social issues that affect not only her, but the world at large. While her stand-up comedy has certainly provided a voice for women as well as for the gay, lesbian, and bisexual communities, Cho's use of racial humor provides a unique Korean American perspective through stand-up comedy (Holden 2000). Before Cho reached her current level of fame, she focused much of her performances on her Korean heritage, particularly her traditional Asian family. Through several short televised stand-up comedy performances in the early 1990s, Cho developed and perfected her most well-known character: an impression of her traditional, conservative Korean mother. With this impression as her vehicle, Cho routinely addressed Asian stereotypes, social and racial discrimination, and even the fact that few Asian American role models were available in the media (Esther 1999). Cho was a pioneer among stand-up comedians considering the fact that she was the first to offer a widely seen humorous voice for the Korean American minority population (Esther 1999; Kelly 2000).

With the release of her 2000 one-woman comedy special, *I'm the One That I Want*, Cho performed her first full-length stand-up comedy special solely devoted to her thoughts, opinions, and jokes (Boone 2002). Though various aspects of her life and personal identity are represented during the 96-minute performance, Cho pays close attention to her family, the discrimination she has experienced, and her personal struggles with her cultural identity (Esther 1999). Additionally, in light of the failure of Cho's sitcom *All-American Girl*, much of the content of this performance addresses the struggles and discrimination she faced during the show's production (Lee 2004). Cho utilizes various styles of humor from imitation to irony as a means of offering a completely unique perspective. Bolstering the popularity of her impression of her mother, much of the humor in *I'm the One That I Want* centers around the traditional perspectives of Cho's mother and the ways in which they routinely juxtapose with Cho's liberal behaviors and opinions. Further, Cho directly discusses more serious issues such as racism, cultural ignorance, and Asian stereotypes, all topics that Cho had discussed in her previous work, but never to this extent. Perhaps because of her willingness to be blatantly honest, combined with her unique sense of humor, Cho was awarded *New York Magazine*'s Performance of Year award for her performance in *I'm the One That I Want* (Kelly 2000). The social effects of this performance continue to impact the entertainment world and the public's perception of Asian American identity. Therefore, jokes from *I'm the One That I Want*, along with several jokes from various comedy specials filmed in 1992, early in Cho's career, provide the basis of this examination. Each of these jokes directly and humorously addresses aspects of Cho's cultural background, perspectives, or struggles, and they provide an adequate representation of Cho's body of humorous performances. While Cho has written and performed multiple stand-up comedy and television specials since the production of these particular performances, it is through her earlier stand-up comedy performance that she allows audiences into her life and Korean American identity in the most significant way.

Rhetorical Forces in Cho's Stand-Up Comedy Performances

Within Cho's distinctive humor – and, specifically, its focus on her Korean American background – three theoretical lenses emerge that offer a better understanding of humor as a tool for communicating culture. First, Cho highlights the problematic aspects of bicultural otherness. Individuals who identify with two distinct sets of cultural norms, practices, and values are categorized as bicultural (Mok, Cheng, & Morris 2010; LaFromboise, Coleman, & Gerton 1993). For instance, Asian Americans often identify and implement Asian cultural tradition while simultaneously incorporating Americanized values or behaviors in their identities. Attempting to combine aspects of both cultural affiliations can be problematic for the individual or the people around them (Mok & Morris 2010). Often, bicultural individuals suffer from cultural "othering" based on aspects of their identity that do not align with the majority group (Gianettoni & Roux 2010). When expectations stemming from one aspect of an individual's bicultural identity are challenged, it can create social dissonance and lead to cultural othering (Gianettoni & Roux 2010; Iwamoto & Liu 2010). This social separation delineates clear outgroups based solely on cultural group membership, and the formulation of these boundaries highlights the unique set of social issues that arise for bicultural individuals (Brewer 1999; Lwin, Stanaland, & Williams 2010; Mok & Morris 2010).

Second, in light of the impressions she constructs of Asian woman in general, and her mother in particular, Cho appears to ironically essentialize Asian identity. Essentialism is the mental tendency to apply a "fixed, underlying nature to members of a category, which is understood to determine their identity," and "render them fundamentally alike" (Haslam et al. 2006, p. 64). In other words, essentialist attitudes allow entire cultural groups to be reduced to a finite set of behaviors, characteristics, or attributes. Essentialized groups tend to be perceived as social outsiders, and, thus, are more likely to be discriminated against or ostracized (Bernstein et al. 2010). When essentialized ironically, however, the portrayal of specific social groups is not meant to be taken literally (Booth 1974). Irony allows a speaker to develop dual narratives: one within the literal words and one within the underlying meaning of the message (Partington 2007). Cho seems to implement a postmodern, rhetorical version of irony in that her messages are "multiple, complex, and inconsistent" (Shugart 1999, p. 436) and require a specific level of understanding from her audience (Booth 1974). By ironically essentializing a cultural group, a comedian is able to subversively highlight the absurdity embedded within this extreme form of cultural categorization (Shugart 1999) while simultaneously appearing to adhere to it.

Finally, through stereotypical self-deprecating humor, Cho not only implicates herself, but also her entire cultural group. In most jokes, there is an object and a subject, and self-deprecation places the joker in the role of the object. An individual who uses self-deprecating humor is ostensibly able to remain aligned with social hierarchies while placing themselves as the object of the joke (Gilbert 2004). Because this type of humor puts listeners at ease due to its lack of aggression, it often creates a sense of community among the joker and the audience (Meyer 2000). Additionally, self-deprecating humor routinely makes use of social or cultural stereotypes, which can serve to further separate the cultural out-group from the majority (Lin et al. 2005). In particular, Asian Americans are commonly stereotyped as being socially awkward based on American social standards, and humor that reinforces this perception justifies prejudicial attitudes from the racial majority and cultural discrimination toward this minority group (Lin et al. 2005).

Therefore, in light of these theoretical perspectives, we examine Margaret Cho's stand-up comedy with a specific focus on bicultural otherness of Asian Americans, ironic essentialism of the Asian culture, and stereotypical self-deprecating humor as a means of cultural separation. Through these specific units of analysis, we argue that Cho implements humor as a method of creating and communicating cultural identity to a large audience.

The stand-up comedy performances of Margaret Cho offer much more than just laughs. Her humorous implementation of bicultural "otherness," ironic essentialism, and self-deprecating humor highlight the rhetorical implications within her humor with regard to cultural identity development. Through an examination of Cho's culture-based jokes within her early stand-up comedy performances as well as from *I'm the One That I Want*, it is clear that the use of humor as a means of communicating cultural identity is rhetorically significant.

Bicultural "Otherness"

Bicultural individuals face a unique set of benefits and drawbacks when developing and maintaining their cultural identity (Mok & Morris 2010). Because they are able to draw upon two distinct sets of cultural values, norms, and practices, bicultural individuals can experience pressure from one or both sides of their heritage to fully adopt only one aspect of their identity, which can lead to uncertainty (Gong 2007; Mok, Cheng, & Morris 2010). It can be increasingly difficult for a bicultural individual to negotiate his or her personal identity as cultural boundaries become unclear or confusing at times (Palmer 2006). According to biculturalism theory, achieving a high level of bicultural competence requires an individual to "live effectively" among two cultural groups without displaying preference to one particular group (LaFromboise, Coleman, & Gerton 1993, p. 404). Because achieving a balanced identity is difficult among two separate cultural backgrounds, bicultural individuals are often perceived as rebellious against social norms if they choose to implement aspects from both of their cultural identities (Mok, Cheng, & Morris 2010). People who identify with two or more cultural backgrounds are often "othered," or forced into a position of an outsider by members of one aspect of their cultural background, because they are unable or unwilling to conform to only one set of cultural practices (Gianettoni & Roux 2010). Therefore, individuals who assume a bicultural identity often deal with the negative effects of cultural "othering" from members of one or both of their cultural backgrounds.

Cho discusses her bicultural identity numerous times throughout her stand-up comedy special *I'm the One That I Want*, paying particular attention to the ways in which she was the victim of cultural "othering." During the filming of her 1994 sitcom *All-American Girl*, Cho was criticized for not portraying enough "Asian-ness":

> This really scared the network. "She's not Asian enough. She's not Asian enough. She's not testing Asian." So, for my benefit, they hired an Asian consultant. Oh yes, because I was fucking it up so bad, they had to hire someone to help me be more Asian. She would follow me around, "Margaret, use chopsticks. Use chopsticks, and when you're done eating, you can put them in your hair. So, you're wearing shoes, which is something we don't do in the house. We don't wear shoes in the house. Now, I'm going to leave this abacus right here."
>
> *(Coleman 2000)*

Despite the fact that Cho was raised by Korean parents, and the sitcom was based on her stand-up comedy routine, it was clear that the American television studio had a clear idea of what it meant to be "Asian." Culturally appropriate behaviors are a significant factor within the development of a bicultural identity (LaFromboise,

Coleman, & Gerton 1993; Wei et al. 2010). When an individual does not adhere to socially accepted culture standards that are based on mainstream expectations, "othering" can be a result. Regardless of Cho's status as an American citizen, she was forced to comply with clear cultural stereotypes and expectations (Brewer 1999; Gianettoni & Roux 2010). Though stereotypical behaviors may not always be negative, applying them to a member of a particular cultural group emphasizes an individual's status as the social "other" (Maddux et al. 2008).

Also, Asian Americans often display a distinct physical difference compared to the dominant cultural group in America, and due to this clear physical difference, they are the victims of othering more often than many other cultural groups (No et al. 2008; Tafarodi, Kang, & Milne 2002). To illuminate a practical application of othering based on physical appearance, in one of her early stand-up comedy performances, Cho describes an experience she had during a promotional tour for *All-American Girl*. Though she was born in the United States and English was her first language, she highlights the fact that her Asian heritage was her primary social identifier:

> Then there were people who didn't understand the concept of Asian American. I went on a promotional tour for the TV show. And I went all over the country, and I went to one morning show, and the announcer said, "Hey Margaret, we're changing over to an ABC affiliate. So why don't you tell our viewers, in your native language, we're making that transition." So I looked at the camera, and I said, [pause] "They're changing to an ABC affiliate."
>
> *(Coleman 2000)*

Because her "Asian-ness" was perceived as a commodity, Cho was viewed as the "other" despite the fact that she was born in America and identified with the majority of the social norms and qualities of life within American culture.

Reinforcing the idea that her Korean cultural membership was often the most identifiable aspect of her social identity, in an early stand-up comedy special, Cho discusses the benefits and drawbacks of her biculturalism:

> Definitely one of the disadvantages of being Asian in America is that sometimes you can't communicate with your family. I think the biggest advantage of being Asian in America is that if you're in an airport or in a bar or something, and someone talks to you and you don't want to talk to them, you can just pretend you don't speak English. [adopts an exaggerated mousey, shy posture and voice] "Oh, no, I don't know [laughs into her hand]."
>
> *(Cho 1992a)*

Maintaining a balanced bicultural identity can be a difficult process, primarily because the individual has the choice to conform to or rebel against cultural expectations, and this choice is ongoing (Mok & Morris 2010; Mok, Cheng, & Morris 2010). The first aspect of this joke highlights one of the difficulties associated with a bicultural identity: the inability to easily communicate with certain family members (Wei et al. 2010). However, the second part of the joke includes Cho's humorous identification of a more advantageous aspect of her bicultural identity – though in this humorous explanation of the benefits of her bicultural identity she, in effect, is culturally "othering" herself, performing an Asian stereotype common in the majority of the American population (Gianettoni & Roux 2010).

Another aspect of cultural othering is the tendency for the dominant culture to disregard the validity of specific cultural groups (Brewer 1999). Cho recalls an experience in which one aspect of her bicultural identity was minimized during a fight with her manager:

> I fired my manager after that. He said some amazing shit to me. He said one time, "You know what Margaret, I think the Asian thing puts people off." What the fuck is the Asian thing? Like it's some gimmick that I pull out of my ass every couple of years. To jazz up my career, it's like [gestures, imitating karate moves] doing the Asian thing. Hey! Alright, is that ice? [mimics chopping a block of ice] Hi-ya! You know, you gotta chink it up sometimes. You gotta get chinky with it.
>
> *(Coleman 2000)*

In this instance, Cho's Asian cultural background is trivialized to no more than a simple choice, similar to choosing an article of clothing or changing moods. The categorization of Cho's Korean background as an "Asian thing" creates a distinction between what is deemed worthy of cultural classification (Brewer 1999).

As an Asian American, it seemed that Cho's Asian heritage often emerged as the most identified aspect of her identity. Cho often mentions the paradoxical nature of her identity as she looks Korean but sounds like a quintessential "white girl." Her bicultural identity, based on the nature of her stand-up comedy performances, has routinely led to being "othered" by the American public, which forced her into the role of a commoditized Asian, despite her bicultural identity.

Ironic Essentialism

Essentialism is the belief that all members of a social or cultural group possess an innate set of characteristics and behaviors (Haslam et al. 2006; Kashima et al. 2005). Cultural essentialism commonly leads to prejudicial attitudes as it ascribes a "normalized" identity to all members of a cultural group. When implemented literally, essentialist attitudes serve to unfairly and stereotypically categorize an entire race, ethnic group, or culture based on limited and often unrealistic social expectations (Bernstein et al. 2010). However, ironic essentialism is not meant to be understood in as straightforward a manner. Because irony requires the audience to understand both the literal and indirect meaning of a message, humorous irony has the potential to offer subtle critiques within seemingly direct communication (Booth 1974). Particularly, among comedians like Cho, ironic messages are often interwoven with other forms of humor (Pexman & Olineck 2002). The use of stereotypical, exaggerated, and hyperbolic cultural characteristics can indicate the inclusion of irony as a means of identifying and critiquing absurd expectations (Booth 1974; Colston & O'Brien 2000; Shugart 1999). Ironic depictions of essentialized cultural groups can be a subversive method for highlighting the ridiculousness of predetermined behaviors and attitudes (Shugart 1999). In other words, when essentialized ironically, the significance of a cultural group appears to be minimized; however, this form of communication serves to emphasize the unfair struggles and categorizations the members of the group face.

Cho utilizes ironic essentialism several times throughout *I'm the One That I Want*. For instance, as she discusses in her performance, when she began to lose weight for her sitcom, her Asian heritage was highlighted as a primary factor in her weight loss:

> I would still open up a tabloid and see the "Chow like Cho Diet," which was this fake diet that I never went on with all these fake quotes from me like "when I was young, I was raised on rice and fish so when I get heavy I go back to that natural Asian way of eating." That is so Mulan. You could almost hear the mandolin in the background. [in a sweet Asian accent] "When I was a little girl, I grow up on the rice patty [doing Asian dance very slowly and gracefully], and we have no food but even though we have no food I have a tendency to put on weight. Which is why I really hope I catch malaria. The pound fall away so kikly when you have malaria or dysentery" [shyly giggles and doubles over].
>
> *(Coleman 2000)*

In the development of this joke, Cho appears to appropriate stereotypical Asian characteristics in direct response to the appropriation of this culture within American tabloid magazines. Through her fictitious alter-ego, Cho highlights a "traditional" Asian speaking pattern, diet, and dance. Mirroring the magazine's use of essentialist attitudes, Cho mocks the assumption of her traditional Asian diet by reducing the Korean culture to the most well-known stereotypes and expectations (Chun 2004). Though her construction of this stereotypical image literally reinforces expected Asian characteristics, through her exaggeration and humor, Cho subtly creates a second message that challenges unfair cultural classifications and assumptions (Partington 2007).

Arguably, Cho's most famous stand-up comedy "bit" focused on an impression of her traditional, conservative Korean mother. Though the audience may or may not have had the opportunity to observe her actual mother, the impression served to encapsulate her identity, according to Cho. In one joke, Cho embodies her mother during an answering machine message:

> I have to tell you some-sing. Grama and grampa, gonna die. I don't know when they gonna die. But some time, so den mommy just tell you now. So when they die, you no surprised. Don' be surprised when dey die. But you don't have to tell dem. Don't say, "Oooh, mommy say you gonna die." Don't say. Dat not nice. And dey know already. But mommy know you gonna come home to pray the comedy club in two weeks, so mommy wants hope, mayyybee they die before you come home, just so you don' have to make two trip.
>
> *(Coleman 2000)*

While this impression may be completely accurate, it still serves to address prominent American ideologies regarding Asian identity (Chun 2004). Through the way in which she elongates certain words and shortens others, along with her clearly exaggerated body and facial movements, Cho reinforces the dominant culture's expectation of the Asian style of speaking.

Often, among Americans, various Asian ethnicities are condensed, and people from a Chinese background are mistaken for Korean or Japanese. This tendency to incorporate multiple ethnicities within one category serves to essentialize Asians not only based on a specific nationality but on appearance and assumed sameness as well (Haslam et al. 2006; No et al. 2008). In *I'm the One That I Want*, Cho humorously recalls an instance in which her Korean cultural background was essentialized in such a way that it was equated to the Chinese culture:

> I recently did this showcase of international talent, and they chose me because I'm so very "international." And they had a real problem with me because I look [one way], but I talk this way. There's like a problem, and they're trying to be sensitive about it. They were like, "Margaret, we don't want you to take this the wrong way, but could you be a little bit more, oh, I don't know, Chinese?" "Actually I'm Korean." "Whatever." And I was supposed to go on this show and tell jokes. What was I supposed do? [squints her eyes, puts her head back, and speaks in a stereotypical Asian style] "Oh, my husband is so fat, that when he sit around the habuku, he really sit around the habuku. GONG!"
>
> *(Cho 1992b)*

Within this joke, Cho directly questions and portrays what an essentialized Asian (Chinese or Korean) comedian would look like.

Though some audiences may perceive Cho's use of essentialized Asian identity as a method for reinforcing cultural stereotypes, audiences that can identify the irony within her humor understand the underlying, subversive significance of highlighting the ridiculousness of reducing an entire ethnic group to only a few exaggerated characteristics. Offering a completely essentialized depiction of Asian cultural identity allows Cho to point out the unfair expectations applied to this misrepresented group. Certainly, Cho capitalizes on the essentialist ideologies of Asians and Asian Americans in an effort to make audiences laugh, but she does so in such a way that utilizes irony as a means of veiled social critique.

Self- (and Culture-)Deprecating Humor

Self-deprecating humor is commonly utilized by stand-up comedians (Greengross & Miller 2009; Lowe 1986; Scarpetta & Spagnolli 2009). By highlighting personal flaws or embarrassing qualities, a comedian is able to put the audience at ease and create a sense of community while often remaining aligned with established social hierarchies (Gilbert 2004; Meyer 2000). This self-effacing style of humor is routinely utilized by members of cultural minority groups, and often, these types of jokes rely on socially constructed and accepted ethnic stereotypes (Gilbert 2004; Lowe 1986). Often, stereotypes aid the development and maintenance of personal identity among members of a cultural minority group (Chu & Kwan 2007), particularly within self-deprecating jokes. This style of humor allows performances within a social minority group to simultaneously support and rebel against social norms and stereotypes.

When told among members of the same cultural group, this style of humor can be utilized as a coping mechanism, or as a means of creating a sense of community between the joker and the audience (Chun 2004; Davies 1993). However, if the joker implicates his or her own cultural group among members of various other groups, the results can be unconstructive and lead to the perception of inferior social status (Greengross 2008). Though many of these stereotypes are not necessarily negative, with regard to Cho's humor, she utilizes well-known stereotypes regarding the Asian culture in a way that places the entire cultural group – and not necessarily just herself – as the object of the joke. Regardless of the nature of the stereotypes utilized within self-deprecating humor, when used to create social boundaries between cultural groups, the stereotypes have a negative functionality (Maddux et al. 2008). Though self-deprecating humor appears to provide a momentary source of entertainment, the ultimate effects can be much more detrimental. In fact, humor that directly or indirectly implicates an entire cultural group can serve to further separate the cultural group from the dominant majority through the reification of social stereotypes, a common risk of this style of humor (Lin et al. 2005). If used before audience members who do not have regular contact with the social group being highlighted, the performer may, in fact, offer a seemingly acceptable way to refer to the social group that reinforces limiting stereotypes. The way in which Cho utilizes self-deprecating humor typically encompasses all Asians instead of solely focusing on her own personal flaws.

Cho's particular style of self-deprecation is a bit subtle. Rarely does she solely mock herself. Instead, she resorts to highlighting "absurd" stereotypes associated with Asians or Koreans. During the filming of her sitcom, Cho was met with a wide variety of criticisms and compliments and she discusses these experiences in her stand-up comedy performances. Among the Korean American community, Cho's television persona was not well received, and to respond she utilized two distinct stereotypical and humorous expectations of Asian American women:

> Then there was the Asian American aspect. That there had never been a star of a sitcom before. And this was really discussed everywhere. I opened up my newspaper at home to the editorial section and they had printed a letter from a little Korean girl named Karen Kim, 12 years old, who wrote in saying, "When I see Margaret Cho on television, I feel deep shame." Why?! Why?! I guess this was because they had never seen a Korean American role model like me before. You know, I didn't play violin. I didn't fuck Woody Allen.
>
> *(Coleman 2000)*

Though the expectation that all Asians play the violin is not a particularly negative or demeaning stereotype, it is a common assumption. Additionally, considering the fact that Woody Allen divorced his wife to marry her adopted Asian daughter, the second "stereotype" Cho mentions is certainly meant as more of an exaggerated joke. However, her use of humor allows Cho to remove herself from the cultural expectations of Asian Americans and attempt to gain approval from the dominant social group by continuing to poke fun based on assumed stereotypes (Lin et al. 2005; Lwin, Stanaland, & Williams 2010). Cultural expectations can impact the way in which members of outside cultural groups perceive and, subsequently, behave toward a person (Saucier 2000). In Cho's case, the cultural expectations of Asian Americans seem to aid in her use of self-deprecating humor as a means of rebelling from the norm.

Poking fun at one of the oldest and most well-known stereotypes associated with the Asian culture, Cho introduces herself during a performance early in her stand-up comedy career, saying, "Hi. I'm Margaret Cho, I'm Korean. I don't have a store or anything" (Cho 1992b). In the same vein, Cho introduces another well-known stereotype associated with the Asian culture:

> I go on auditions constantly. And they stress me out. You know, I have nightmares that I'm going to be cast in a horrible sitcom, and I wake up screaming, [singing in a stereotypical announcer voice] "She's not wearing a wedding veil, because she's the kind of bride that comes in the mail. AHHHH!"
>
> *(Cho 1992a)*

Once again, relying on cultural expectations and stereotypical categorizations, Cho attempts to disassociate herself from her Korean American heritage by subtly effacing it. Implementing this more direct style of self-mocking, Cho creates humor that is aligned with Americanized cultural hierarchies (Gilbert 2004; Meyer 2000). Further, in light of these jokes, Cho seems to be attempting to "pass" as a member of the dominant social group among her audience, which is primarily comprised of European American men and women (Shugart 2003). Individuals who attempt to "pass" often assume qualities of the desired social group while still maintaining a clear position as an outsider (Shugart 2003). Because Asian Americans are physically distinct from European Americans, they are socially granted an "American" identity less frequently than other cultural groups (Devos & Heng 2009; No et al. 2008). In a humorous attempt at "passing," Cho, as a Korean American, offers humor that denotes her affiliation with the "American" culture, though she is unable to completely remove herself from her Korean heritage.

Finally, though not necessarily a negative trait, many Asians are stereotyped as being unable to drink excessive amounts of alcohol. Highlighting this stereotype while poking fun at her cultural group, Cho explains her experiences with alcoholism:

> I did what [is] really hard for Asian people to do. I became an alcoholic, and that's not easy because we can't drink. We get all red. [In a stereotypical "white girl" voice] "Do you have a sunburn?" "No, I'm fucked up."
> *(Coleman 2000)*

Though alcoholism is publicly perceived to be a negative affliction, the ability to drink provides a level of unofficial social credibility among the younger American population. Cho includes an example of members of other cultural groups finding her lack of ability to drink confusing. Once again, in pointing out that she is a cultural exception, Cho seems to exclude herself from an additional stereotypical categorization.

Among all the humorous styles that Cho implements throughout her various stand-up comedy performances, self-deprecation may not be the most obvious. However, the way in which she subtly mocks herself along with her cultural group serves to highlight several stereotypical expectations associated with Asians. While none of Cho's humorous self and cultural degradations are particularly hateful, through her use of this style of humor she attempts to create a sense of belonging among the dominant culture within her audience.

Conclusions and Implications

Over the course of her more-than-20-year career as a stand-up comedian, Margaret Cho has made quite a name for herself. In light of the fact that Cho is the only widely known woman Korean American comedian performing today, her use of cultural identity has a significant impact of the public's perception of not only Cho herself but also the entire Korean culture for some audiences. Through her unique style of stand-up comedy, Cho offers her opinions and insights regarding her family, the Asian American representation in the mass media, and the ways in which people communicate with each other. Her humor provides direct and covert perspectives regarding serious social issues while maintaining a unique level of entertainment. While Cho may not be widely supported by her Korean American contemporaries, her thought-provoking humor is unmistakably socially influential. When analyzing several of her early stand-up comedy performances, along with the 2000 stand-up comedy special, *I'm the One That I Want*, Cho's rhetorically significant use of humor emerges. Through the theoretical lenses of bicultural "otherness," ironic essentialism of Asian identity, and self- and culture-deprecating humor, it is clear that Cho offers an original perspective with regard to developing, maintaining, and communicating cultural identity in a unique and humorous way.

Certainly, stand-up comedians are able to discuss social issues in a way that is unique to their profession (Greenbaum 1999). This public forum grants people the ability to widely disperse opinions regarding social issues in an entertaining and enjoyable manner (Shouse 2007; Sturges 2010). Through the veil of humor, stand-up comedians can offer social criticism that might otherwise be deemed inappropriate or met with aggressive resistance (Mintz 1985; Scarpetta & Spagnolli 2009). Cho is a great example of the advantages that exist for stand-up comedians considering the aggressive and opinionated manner in which she offers her opinions regarding cultural stereotypes, expectations, and discrimination. As such, humor proves to be a rhetorically significant method for communicating crucial aspects of a person's social and cultural identity. Rather than simply consuming information, stand-up comedy allows an audience to participate more directly in the development of a message. An individual's sense of humor offers a glimpse into his or her values, intelligence, and interests, all integral aspects of personal identity (Murstein & Brust 1985).

Unlike African Americans or Hispanic Americans, Asian Americans have yet to occupy a predominant facet of the social spotlight in American culture. Not only has Cho become a pioneer within the world of stand-up comedy, she also remains one of the few members of an Asian community in any part of the American entertainment industry, offering representation to audiences that may otherwise not have had access to this cultural group. Because Cho is one of the few voices for the Korean American community, it bodes well that stand-up comedy is a popular form of entertainment because her messages are able to be received by a wide audience. Cho's willingness to offer a perspective on an otherwise underrepresented or misrepresented cultural group allows many people to learn more about Asian Americans in a humorous way. Because Asian Americans in general and Korean Americans in particular are able to identify with multiple cultural backgrounds, they often face the negative effects of bicultural "othering." Considering their dual cultural identification, the likelihood for these individuals to struggle for acceptance among each group increases. With humor as her primary communicative method, Cho is able to shed light on this potentially difficult process for bicultural individuals while developing and communicating her own cultural identity. The way in which Cho uses humor to address potentially sensitive social and cultural issues highlights the role that humor plays for all comedians when attempting to address – and possibly reduce – social tensions, stereotypes, and problems.

Further, the ways in which Cho utilizes exaggerated and well-known cultural stereotypes allows her to point out the ridiculousness of these types of unfair categorizations. The use of exaggerated stereotypes can serve to point out their absurdity (Colston & O'Brien 2000). Additionally, because Cho's cultural jokes are meant to be viewed through the lens of humorous entertainment, audiences are more likely to excuse potentially offensive messages (Park et al. 2006). Because of Cho's identity as a Korean American, it is more likely that her use of exaggerated Asian stereotypes is done in a playful, satirical, and ironic manner, and not as aggressively or hatefully. Ironic displays of culture and hyperbolic exaggerations of stereotypical characteristics allow a comedian to subtly and subversively offer a social critique while maintaining a positive, light-hearted atmosphere. However, because stand-up comedy is not necessarily meant to be taken seriously, Cho's use of irony and hyperbole run of risk of losing their intended meaning for audiences who do not share Cho's frame of reference (Booth 1974). Audience members who are unable to detect the irony within an essentialized or stereotypical depiction of the Asian culture may perceive Cho's style of humor as offensive or, conversely, they may support the reinforcement of this cultural categorization. Basically, with regard to ironic and hyperbolic humorous messages, author's intent is irrelevant, as it is the audience's responsibility to comprehend the meaning within the underlying messages. Of course, in light of the irrelevance of author's intent, it is possible that Cho does not mean for her essentialized depictions of Asian identity to be perceived ironically. However, it is to be assumed that because Cho is a stand-up comedian and because her primary method for communication is humor, she intends for her messages to be light-hearted and ironic, not culturally harmful.

Theoretically, Cho's use of self-deprecating humor highlights an influential aspect of this type of comic communication. When utilized among members of the same cultural group, self-deprecation can serve as a coping mechanism or community building device (Chun 2004; Davies 1993). However, because Cho's primary audience is comprised of European Americans, in the process of casting herself as the object of the joke Cho effectively implicates her entire culture based on her use of stereotypical cultural attributes and possibly subtly reinforces social segregation and limiting cultural stereotypes. Throughout Cho's performance, her style of self-deprecation is more subtle. In fact, her unique style of humor seems to be more "culture" deprecating as she points out undesirable aspects of her Korean heritage instead of personal flaws. Therefore, in this situation, self-deprecation serves to separate the joker from the cultural group she is humorously degrading. Individuals who utilize this type of humor run the risk of communicating a disdain for their cultural heritage despite the light-hearted nature of humor. Cho seemingly attempts to place herself among the cultural in-group while simultaneously castigating the out-group, of which she is also a member

(Lwin, Stanaland, & Williams 2010). In other words, Cho's humor momentarily attempts to bypass certain aspects of her Korean cultural identity and transition from being the cultural minority to being a part of the in-group through mocking her own culture.

Now in her forties, Margaret Cho shows no signs of slowing her stand-up career any time soon. Her bicultural identity certainly draws attention from audiences, but it is ultimately her humor that has allowed her to establish a successful and groundbreaking career as the first woman Korean American comedian to gain notoriety in the United States. Through her use of humor, Cho has offered a glimpse into an otherwise unknown, misunderstood, and mistaken sector of society. Her use of stereotypes, impressions, and humorous criticism offers a unique perspective that has the ability to deconstruct stereotypes or reinforce them depending on the audiences' perspective. Hate her or love her, Cho certainly makes people think and react, all while making her audience laugh.

References

Bernstein, M.J., Sacco, D.F., Young, S.G., Hugenberg, K., & Cook, E. (2010). Being "in" with the in-crowd: The effects of social exclusions and inclusion are enhanced by the perceived essentialism of ingroups and outgroups. *Personality and Social Psychology Bulletin, 36*, 999–1009.

Boone, R. (2002, May/June). Margaret Cho's I'm the one that I want. *Off Our Backs*. Retrieved from Academic Search Premier Database.

Booth, W.C. (1974). *A rhetoric of irony*. Chicago, IL: The University of Chicago Press.

Brewer, M.B. (1999). The psychology of prejudice: Ingroup love or outgroup hate? *Journal of Social Issues, 55*, 429–444.

Cho, M. (1992a). *Margaret Cho – Asian American*. Retrieved from www.cc.com/video-clips/t0p9sk/stand-up-margaret-cho – asian-american

Cho, M. (1992b). *Margaret Cho – Being Korean*. Retrieved from www.cc.com/video-clips/9g2urk/stand-up-margaret-cho – being-korean

Chu, T., & Kwan, V.S.Y. (2007). Effect of collectivistic cultural imperatives on Asian American meta-stereotypes. *Asian Journal of Social Psychology, 10*, 270–276.

Chun, E.W. (2004). Ideologies of legitimate mockery: Margaret Cho's revoicings of mock Asian. *Pragmatics, 14*, 263–289.

Coleman, L. (Director). (2000). *I'm the one that I want* [Motion picture]. USA: Cho Taussig Productions.

Colston, H.L. & O'Brien, J. (2000). Contrast of kind versus contrast of magnitude: The pragmatic accomplishments of irony and hyperbole. *Discourse Processes, 30*, 179–199.

Davies, C. (1993). Exploring the thesis of the self-deprecating sense of humor. In A. Ziv & A. Zajdman (Eds.), *Semites and stereotypes: Characteristics of Jewish humor*. Westport, CT: Greenwood Press.

Devos, T., & Heng, L. (2009). Whites are granted the American identity more swiftly than Asians. *Social Psychology, 40*, 192–201.

Esther, P. (1999, August 2). "I am all about rebellion." *Newsweek*. Retrieved from Academic Search Premier Database.

Fowler, G.A. (2000, August 21). Making a Cho-full noise. *U.S. News & World Report*. Retrieved from Academic Search Premier Database.

Fung, D.B. (2010). Interview with Asian comedian pioneer Margaret Cho. *Soompi.* Retrieved from www.soompi.com

Gianettoni, L. & Roux, P. (2010). Interconnecting race and gender relations: Racism, sexism and the attribution of sexism of the racialized other. *Sex Roles, 62,* 374–386.

Gilbert, J.R. (2004). *Performing marginality: Humor, gender, and cultural critique.* Detroit, MI: Wayne State University Press.

Gong, L. (2007). Ethnic identity and identification with the majority group: Relations with national identity and self-esteem. *International Journal of Intercultural Relations, 31,* 503–523.

Greenbaum, A. (1999). Stand-up comedy as rhetorical argument: An investigation of comic culture. *Humor, 12,* 33–46.

Greengross, G. (2008). Dissing oneself versus dissing rivals: Effects of status, personality and sex on the short-term and long-term attractiveness of self-deprecating and other-deprecating humor. *Evolutionary Psychology, 6,* 393–408.

Greengross, G. & Miller, G.F. (2009). The big five personality traits of professional comedians compared to amateur comedians, comedy writers, and college students. *Personality and Individual Differences, 47,* 79–83.

Haslam, N., Bastian, B., Bain, P., & Kashima, Y. (2006). Psychological essentialism, implicit theories, and intergroup relations. *Groups Processes & Intergroup Relations, 9,* 63–76.

Holden, S. (2000, August 4). Beyond Asian stereotypes, this comic settles scores. *New York Times.* Retrieved from www.nytimes.com

Iwamoto, D.K. & Liu, W.M. (2010). The impact of racial identity, ethnic identity, Asian values, and race-related stress on Asian Americans and Asian international college students' psychological well-being. *Journal of Counseling Psychology, 57,* 79–91.

Kashima, Y., Kashima, E., Chiu, C.-Y., Farsides, T., Gelfand, M., Hong, Y.-Y., & Yzerbyt, V. (2005). Culture, essentialism, and agency: Are individuals universally believed to be more real entities than groups. *European Journal of Social Psychology, 35,* 147–169.

Kelly, P. (2000). Cho, Margaret. *Current biography, 61,* 11–14.

LaFromboise, T., Coleman, H.L.K., & Gerton, J. (1993). Psychological impact of biculturalism: Evidence and theory. *Psychological Bulletin, 114,* 395–412.

Lee, R.C. (2004). "Where's my parade?" Margaret Cho and the Asian American body space. *The Drama Review, 48,* 108–132.

Lin, M.H., Kwan, V.S.Y., Cheung, A., & Fiske, S.T. (2005). Stereotype content comedy explains prejudice for an envied outgroup: Scale of anti-Asian American stereotypes. *Personality and Social Psychology Bulletin, 31,* 34–47.

Lowe, J. (1986). Theories of ethnic humor: How to enter, laughing. *American Quarterly, 38,* 439–460.

Lwin, M.O., Stanaland, A.J.S., & Williams, J.D. (2010). American symbolism in intercultural communication: An animosity/ethnocentrism perspective on intergroup relations and consumer attitudes. *Journal of Communication, 60,* 491–514.

Maddux, W.W., Galinsky, A.D., Cuddy, A.J.C., & Polifroni, M. (2008). When being a model minority is good … and bad: Realistic threat explains negativity toward Asian Americans. *Personality and Social Psychology, 34,* 74–89.

Marin, R., & Lee, C.S. (1994, September, 19). Too much sitcom, not enough Seoul. *Newsweek.* Retrieved from Academic Search Premier Database.

Meyer, J.C. (2000). Humor as a double-edged sword: Four functions of humor in communication. *Communication Theory, 10,* 310–331.

Mintz, L.E. (1985). Standup comedy as social and cultural mediation. *American Quarterly, 37,* 71–80.

Mok, A., & Morris, M.W. (2010). An upside to bicultural identity conflict: Resisting groupthink in cultural ingroups. *Journal of Experimental Social Psychology, 46*, 1114–1117.

Mok, A., Cheng, C.-Y., & Morris, M.W. (2010). Matching versus mismatching cultural norms in performance appraisal. *International Journal of Cross Cultural Management, 10*, 17–35.

Murstein, B.I., & Brust, R.G. (1985). Humor and interpersonal attraction. *Journal of Personality Assessment, 49*, 637–640.

No, S., Hong, Y.-Y., Liao, H.-Y., Lee, K., Wood, D., & Chao, M.M. (2008). Lay theory of race affects and moderates Asian Americans' responses toward American culture. *Journal of Personality and Social Psychology, 95*, 991–1004.

Palmer, J.D. (2006). Negotiating the indistinct: Reflections of a Korean adopted American working with Korean born, Korean Americans. *Qualitative Research, 6*, 473–495.

Park, J.H., Gabbadon, N.G., & Chernin, A.R. (2006). Naturalizing racial differences through comedy: Asian, Black and White views on racial stereotypes in *Rush Hour 2*. *Journal of Communication, 56*, 157–177.

Partington, A. (2007). Irony and reversal of evaluation. *Journal of Pragmatics, 39*, 1547–1569.

Pexman, P.M. & Olineck, K.M. (2002). Understanding irony: How do stereotypes cue speaker intent? *Journal of Language and Social Psychology, 21*, 245–274.

Rotella, M. (2001, May 7). I'm the one that I want. *Publishers Weekly*. Retrieved from Academic Search Premier Database.

Saucier, G. (2000). Isms and the structure of social attitudes. *Journal of Personality and Social Psychology, 78*, 366–385.

Scarpetta, F., & Spagnolli, A. (2009). The interactional context of humor in stand-up comedy. *Research on Language and Social Interaction, 42*, 210–230.

Shouse, E. (2007). The role of affect in the performance of stand-up comedy: Theorizing the mind-body connection in humor studies. *Journal of the Northwest Communication Association, 36*, 34–49.

Shugart, H.A. (1999). Postmodern irony as subversive rhetorical strategy. *Western Journal of Communication, 63*, 433–455.

Shugart, H.A. (2003). Performing ambiguity: The passing of Ellen DeGeneres. *Text and Performance Quarterly, 23*, 30–54.

Strauss, G. (2008, August 21). Cho returns to TV – on her terms this time. *USA Today*. Retrieved from Academic Search Premier Database.

Sturges, P. (2010). Comedy as freedom of expression. *Journal of Documentation, 66*, 279–293.

Tafarodi, R.W., Kang, S., & Milne, A.B. (2002). When different becomes similar: Compensatory conformity in bicultural visible minorities. *Personality and Social Psychology Bulletin, 28*, 1131–1142.

Wei, M., Liao, Y.-H., Chao, R.C.-L., Mallinckrodt, B., Tsai, P.-C., & Botello-Zamarron, R. (2010). Minority stress, perceived bicultural competence, and depressive symptoms among ethnic minority college students. *Journal of Counseling Psychology, 57*, 411–422.

2

IF LAUGHS COULD KILL

Eddie Izzard and the Queer Art of Comedy

Christopher J. Gilbert

> Not drag – drag means costume. What I do is just wearing a dress.
> (Eddie Izzard, interview with *Vanity Fair*, 2010)

Lofty laughter. Such was the queer pursuit of Russian writer, Nikolai Gogol, whose impressionistic caricatures of everyday life captured the vulgarity in beatific visions of the 19th century. The same might be said of British stand-up comedian, Eddie Izzard, whose surrealistic depictions of both the banal and the elevated aspects of our human condition seem to proclaim: "Onward! onward! away with the wrinkle that furrows the brow and the stern gloom of the face! At once and suddenly let us plunge into life with all its noiseless clatter and little bells …" (Gogol 1997, p. 135). And this amidst the clink and clunk of high heels as Izzard struts across a stage.

Izzard has made a career of performing in "heavy eye shadow, glittery shirts and sometimes skirts and fishnet stockings" while "delivering riffs about culture, history, and language – routines that are literally loopy as they swoop and circle back on themselves" (James 2008). Indeed, his comedy thrives on free association such that any performance could feature him flying through lines from Old Testament parables or Greek mythology to pet behaviorism, evolution, dinosaur clerics, Church politics, militarism, grammatical oddities, commercial advertising, osteopathy, bullying, bees, Wikipedia, baseball, the U.S. American national anthem, and so on seemingly *ad infinitum*. Or perhaps *ad absurdum*, given that Izzard performs a comic logic that laughs at the prescribed standards used to shape common perspectives on reality. Co-founder of the revered comedy troupe Monty Python and self-proclaimed "writer, actor, and tall person," John Cleese, famously dubbed Izzard "the lost Python." This is an apt judgment. Izzard admits Monty

Python's influence, and exercises it by inventing dialogues within outlandish one-man sketches (i.e., a conversation between God, Jesus, and the Holy Ghost that turns into an imagined episode of Scooby-Doo) and producing wild malapropisms (i.e., "'Why the big pause?' as the man in the pub said to the bear," which sets up a joke based on an historical time lapse between Earth's creation and human arrival). In other instances, he practices historical revisionism. "We had pagans [in Britain]," Izzard recounts in one joke. "They were into sex, death, and religion in an interesting, nighttime telly type of way. And we had the druids. Long white robes, long white beards, early transvestites, didn't get their shaving together." The perpetuation of gender confusion is important here, namely because Izzard relates it to a well-known and obscure architectural monument in the mystical area of Salisbury, England – Stonehenge – at the same time as he maps it onto popular folklore. "No one knows what the fuck a henge is," he proclaims. "Before Stonehenge there was Woodhenge and Strawhenge. But a big bad wolf came and blew them down, and three little piggies were relocated to the projects." Izzard's own transvestitism embodies this ostensibly methodized madness insofar as his surreal blend of the sublime and the ridiculous folds into a Pythonesque aesthetic "of cross-dressing, parody and camp" (Aronstein 2009, p. 116). Yet, for Izzard, this is not simply part of the gag.

In interviews Izzard identifies as a "card-carrying transvestite." On the one hand, this affirms his membership in a legitimate social group. On the other, it mocks "official" membership itself, calling out the potential harm of classifications. The notion of "mistaken identity," after all, is central to persistent remonstrations against alternative sexualities and marginalized identities more broadly. In fact, as recently as 2013, Izzard had to proclaim again – namely to American audiences – that he is *still* a transvestite, because in some of his appearances in film and on stage he seemed to be in "boy mode." This is no doubt why Izzard's stand-up comedy has also been a vehicle of civic education, an angle I accentuate throughout this chapter in order to contend that he has combined a comic history of ideas with a sort of gender politics that demonstrates how certain normative viewpoints influence broader sociopolitical orientations. Over and again, Izzard's absurd logic strings audiences along with anachronistic references that he combines with common sense to provide deep readings of the surface effects of, say, evolutionary time or dressing in drag. Nowhere is this more apparent than in his Emmy Award winning performance *Dress to Kill* (*DTK*), which was filmed at the Orpheum Theatre in San Francisco in November 1998 and distributed on video in June 1999.[1]

This chapter engages *DTK* as exemplary of Izzard's queer art of comedy, which interrupts common sense through ridiculous bits about the absurdity in conventional thought, speech, and action. Specifically, I argue that Izzard exemplifies stand-up comedy as a means of embellishing the proximity of so-called "queerness" to the norm in order to re-dress heteronormative images of civic identity and, in a 21st-century argot, neoliberal discourses. Or, better, Izzard articulates some of the ways in which oddities and curiosities can predominate the center stage, sometimes most tellingly in the latent judgments that circulate in and adorn those dominant cultural orders that seem to determine certain claims to public selfhood. Many stand-up comedians are celebrated for their comic irruptions and incongruous jokes, not to mention their seeming surrealism. Izzard, however, exhibits stand-up as a mode of "queer rhetoric" that "asks society to confront … the place of identity issues in politics" (Foss 2007, p. 77). To do so, he situates himself as characteristic of a strange fixation on stubborn interpretations of civic identity. Surrealism, in this sense, is a comic *poros*: a "passage" or "place" for approaching logical impasses and the rhetorical impact of contradictions in malleable constructions of reality. Izzard negotiates these aporia in a male-dominated, if not masculine, genre.[2] His stand-up performances are therefore important for their interruptions of the tyranny of gender, which characterizes and codifies normative views of human conduct that Izzard uses to portray the failure of normativity (Fausto-Sterling 2000; Halberstam 2000; Munoz 2009). Beyond gender per se, Izzard reassembles and disarticulates popular discourses by tracing the ways in which certain rhetorical vestiges reify social injustice through the cruel exercise of power. The comic reconfigurations in *DTK* are thus *trans-* in the literal sense, moving across contexts, through images and ideas that "clothe" reality, and over the "lofty origins" of truisms in order "to laugh at the solemnities of the origin itself" (Foucault 1984, p. 79). That Izzard is himself a transvestite, or one who traverses (*trans-*) categorizations of dress (*vestire*), only makes the extent to which he "kills" commonplaces through comedy that much more pronounced – especially since he does so by exploiting the comic stage as a relatively "safe" space to embellish just how bizarre the familiar seems when compared to the strange.

To demonstrate the rhetorical artistry in Izzard's queer comedy, this chapter examines how *DTK* troubles prescribed social standards and the folly in conventional wisdom. I begin with a brief discussion of its historical context at the turn of the 21st century wherein concerns for material security, cultural voluntarism, and political polarization seemed rampant in the U.S. (Fischer 2010). In addition, a so-called "crisis of masculinity" typified Western culture such that the end of the century signaled an odd publicity of chauvinism in so-called "lad culture." The rise of "deep-seated religious and moral divisions" further crystallized the culture wars, eventually growing contiguous with both figuratively and literally violent interactions between warring ideologies and public claims to civic identity (Layman 2001, p. 3). *DTK* provides a counter-narrative to these developments along two interanimating thematics: gender confusion and queer militancy, which together orient Izzard's performance of how personal character emerges through its decidedly public consequences. These thematics are important to U.S. American social politics because, even though he is a British comic, Izzard broaches topics that transcend geographic boundaries and touch on more widespread problematics of human sufferance. These topics also appear time-tested given that, while *DTK* is 15 years old, they remain relevant and even find their way in to Izzard's more recent shows, such as *Force Majeure* (2013). And considering that he harps on many touchstones of contemporary Eurocentrism, Izzard persistently serves as a sort of outsider looking in on many of the images and ideas that permeate American public life. Here again queerness is as much a way of seeing public culture as it is a personal or collective marker of civic identity.

Izzard's comedy, I argue, ultimately upends the values inherent to these inhabitations, declaiming nonsense as a means of overthrowing "good/common" sense to make sense anew.[3] In making my case, I attend in particular to his wide-ranging use of *metalepsis*, or the expression of outrageous causal relationships aimed at "changing sense." I also highlight his digressions, or ludicrous (yet "logical") departures from linear reason, to show how Izzard revises sociopolitical realities through rhetorical resources not readily available off the comic stage. Considering certain tropes as the stock-in-trade of Izzard's comedy enables me to evaluate how he "kills it" by toeing the line of taking perspectives on persons, images, ideas, and historical events too far. Important in this orientation is just how much the "clothing of rhetoric" itself plays in to Izzard's comic politics (Chaney 1996, pp.157, 163) insofar as his fustian witticisms and fantastical chronicles animate the vulgarity of the "natural" and the ordinary. It also allows me to approach the risibility in his performance as a sartorial sort of recourse for sociopolitical change (Brouwer 2010). As such, I close with a rumination on how Izzard transforms a personal aesthetic into "real" world politics, which he has increasingly folded into an interest in officialdom with his gestures toward shifting "from high heels to high office" (Dougary 2013).

One of the Lads

The video of *DTK* opens with an odd documentary of people riding the iconic tram in San Francisco. Through voice-over and views of Alcatraz spliced into footage of the Golden Gate Bridge and hilly city streets, Izzard talks blithely of Bay Area iconography only to peg the passengers as convicts on their way to prison. The tram operator is introduced as a prison guard, passengers are perpetrators of "hellish crimes" (i.e., stealing hubcaps), and tourists are forensic photographers – all of whom comprise a picture of the "criminal element." The comic clash in this prologue plays on conventional images of Alcatraz as a particularly touristic place while San Francisco is depicted as a rather dull dwelling for its residents, who live so close to the architectural remnants of incarceration, now a tourist trap. A contrast is thus established between a "paradise" and a "penitentiary," with the implication that people are imprisoned by both the accouterments and the ordinary ideas of their civil society. For some, this milieu is hospitable, even enticing. But looks can be deceiving. In the span of a few minutes Izzard crafts a nonsensical narrative about a reality that is otherwise readily recognizable. Then viewers are told: "Tonight's show is brought to you by the prisoners of Alcatraz."

It is telling that Izzard's prelude proclaims sponsorship not simply from "prisoners" – that is, from his actual audience – but also from misrepresentations. Consider that *DTK* was recorded and released at a time when identity cultures were carved out of calls for diversity and concomitant claims to uniformity. While no time period is homogeneous, one story of the 1990s emphasized an emergent "lad culture," or a reaction to male homosociality and the perceived rise of feminist sympathies that fostered chauvinistic appeals to heteronormativity and consumerist attitudes for dividing socioeconomic and sociopolitical groups along lines of shared beliefs and interests. Following Izzard, to buy in to conventional wisdom is to be "one of the lads," which is to say, one of the *guys*. Policing gender boundaries with traditional ascriptions of societal roles means valorizing certain appearances as true and good cultural signifiers. Such signifiers then collapse into the mainstream, with all of its prevailing opinions and popular tastes. (How jarring, then, are the decidedly humanistic words of a "prison guard," whom Izzard calls Freddie Dingo, declaring that people are people despite appearances.) British broadsheet, *Loaded*, and American magazine, *GQ*, are often identified as signposts for mainstream revivals of hardline masculinity in the 1990s. The consequences of the resurgence are central to Izzard's performance.

One consequence was a cultural reinstitution of binary logics in the widespread use of gender-specific language. Izzard frequently says that he does not wear women's clothes; he wears *clothes*. He does not wear *women's* makeup but rather makeup. Nevertheless, "a strange, manic kind of gender nostalgia" subtended popular appeals to manliness versus gayness (Harrison 2010, p. 70; see also Hatty 2000). Within them were commercialized identities that could be found in film portrayals (i.e., *Lock, Stock and Two Smoking Barrels* [1998]), music (i.e., gangsta rap and glam metal), and attire (i.e., "blue collar" working class). Beyond them were attempts to evaluate divergent gender identifications as psychogenic afflictions (that is, cognitive or emotional disorders rather than physiological predispositions) or, at the extreme, as matters of military offense (recall "Don't Ask, Don't Tell"), and thereby a reassertion of the mainstream in the quasi-acceptance of marginalized identity groups as illegitimate yet niche markets. Figures like Rush Limbaugh and Howard Stern, not to mention then President Bill Clinton, typify a masculinity that "wavered erratically between vulnerable child, loutish adolescent and grown cynic, mediating some of the contradictory demands placed on men at a time of changing gender roles while giving relief from the obligations of political correctness" (Harrison 2010, p. 69). The license to heterosexist lewdness was largely a response to the instability of the very tenets of lad culture, especially considering that traditional masculinity was often featured alongside male cosmetics, fashion, and grooming tips (Hodkinson 2011, pp. 236–237). The contradictions are evident in films like *Fight Club* (King 2009), in ad campaigns for male grooming, and in widespread appeals to "metrosexuality." In sum, traditionalism in the mainstream led some cultural stakeholders to shore up conventional wisdom with *lads* as the "foot soldiers" of masculinity. But as Izzard is quick to point out, they were also the fools.

The fervor and folly in demands for gender conformism were also played out in religious cum cultural institutions (Hunter 1991, p. 184). To begin with, there was in the 1990s a palpable reinstantiation of orthodoxy and progressivism (Thomson 2010, p. 2). This is most notable in Conservative pundit and social commentator Patrick Buchanan's infamous declaration of a "religious war" in the U.S. at the 1992 Republican National Convention. This war collapsed into what Kenneth J. Meier calls "morality politics," or attempts to influence both policy and public opinion in order to institutionalize social values. Buchanan, in this regard, was not too dissimilar from Stern and Limbaugh in that he was a jack-the-lad type raising hell in seeming *dis*regard for any position that went against his own view of convention. On top of this climate was the increased capitalization of religious commitments to cultural values as principles to be peddled through commercial media (Miller 2005). Commercialization thus begat the mass politicization of religion, or the mass consecration of cultural politics, allowing voluntarism to become a vulgar philosophy for cordoning certain civic identities. From gender politics to political creeds, the 1990s had been defined in a culture war idiolect as a time for "speaking in the name of core values and national traditions" (Harrison 2010, p. 18).

Hijacking Jack the Lad

In steps Eddie Izzard. Throughout the 1990s, Izzard utilized stand-up to reimagine the ways in which "pseudo-bodies" become conscripted into bodies politic through a comedy of errors in judgment.[4] This means, primarily, that he has long put his own body forth as a self-styled byproduct of absurd, never mind abusive, rhetorics of gender normativity, which are ironically drawn from "the kind of pretend-neutral, old-fashioned, nostrils-flared appraisal that women get and men almost never do" (Williams 2010). In demonstrating the ways particular bodies are "attired," he gave voice to embodied forms of judgment by laughing at and laughing off stereotypes while lashing out against the common sense in cultural knowledge structures. So, for instance, a half-hour in to *Unrepeatable* (1994), Izzard recounts an experience in the streets of Leicester Square wherein a laddish cabal of "dickhead men" harassed him, shouting: "Bloke in a dress! Bloke in a dress!" Such idiotic protestations were, for Izzard, actually code for declaring "I'm a wanker!" and utterly antithetical to what should be a contemporary enjoyment of "clothing rights." Given this brief example, it is easy to see why some might say that Izzard combines the intensely ironic insensitivity of Don Rickles with the frenzied energy and frenetic reasoning of Robin Williams, and then again with the deadpan and paraprosdokian style of Steven Wright. The apparent ease of his humor almost makes "it seem as if the transvestitism was no big deal" (Williams 2010), especially since Izzard's own abrasive speech betrays a more fundamental will to acceptance. This deeper motive makes sense given his interest in grander narratives, not just one-offs and one-liners; and his irony is far more built on *catachresis*, or the misuse and misapplication of images and ideas, than on a sort of propriety that would not allow so many turns on a logic that pretends to deny (or affirm) what is really affirmed (or denied).[5] A few primers therefore stand out here.

First, Izzard approaches stand-up as a comic modality of dressing up, undressing, and/or redressing discourse. He is eloquent, to be sure, and his rhetorical prowess reveals a real facility with language. But if elocution is at base about "the clothing of ideas in language," Izzard also makes it about how those ideas impact the clothiers and the wearers alike. Second, then, Izzard engages language as a means by which individuals and collectivities are fashioned into or out of shape, and also altered through exchange. Third, and perhaps most importantly, Izzard's queer comedy is a rhetorical form for interrupting misunderstandings, hence his circular and circuitous practice of mocking personal traits as tokens of collective identity claims that are fitted to broader ways of seeing (Richards 1936, p. 3). Still, whereas bits like the one from *Unrepeatable* were once momentary and episodic in Izzard's performances, in *DTK* they constitute a framework for clueing audiences in to the trials and tribulations of "trans–" identifications. They are also part and parcel of a much more surrealistic engagement with sociopolitical realities that often clarifies the absurdity in meanings through the very types of confusion that seem to foster misunderstanding or intolerance in the first place. Izzard's performance in *DTK* brings attention to his identity as a transvestite while shedding new light on particular issues and the cultural logics they evoke, and this while crafting new ways of seeing the impacts of everyday interactions as attractive alternatives to conventional wisdom.

Before delving into *DTK*, though, it is worthwhile to lay out the stakes in appreciating stand-up as a *poros* for showing how we clothe cultural categories, both rhetorically and materially, and thus how we approach popular judgments that circulate in and adorn dominant cultural orders. There is an ancient lineage to the metaphor of rhetoric as "clothing," or in Kenneth Burke's words as "equipment for living" (Burke 1967, p. 293–305). Cicero, in *De Oratore*, writes that "just as clothes were first invented to protect us against cold and afterwards began to be used for the sake of adornment and dignity as well, so the metaphorical employment of words was begun because of poverty, but was brought into common use for the sake of entertainment" (III.38.155). By "entertainment" Cicero probably means something akin to activity or exhibition of various points of view. Along with this he brings in his sense of rhetoric as an art for teaching, delighting, and persuading in accordance with a culture's civic virtues. And his metaphor makes rhetoric much more than figures of speech or thought; it is something to "try on." Just as we can clothe, denude, and redress our discourses, so can we give voice to bodily forms and the vestments and vestiges that describe them.

It is not too much to say that clothing is foundational to rhetoric, nor is it a stretch to suggest that rhetoric, well before Cicero, contributed to the formation of civic identities – specifically as they relate to the sorts of public appearances that make or break sociopolitical bonds, encourage or discourage, how people know themselves in relation to others, and allow some ways of seeing to remain in or out of view. As Robert Hariman (1986) contends:

> [C]lothes create meaning by concealment, for they cover the body to disclose its intention, and in covering identify the individual in respect to the social body. They reveal, only by suggestion, yet when they are removed, the 'interior' or 'hidden' meaning disappears, and a person's identity can be reconstructed only by reference to the 'external' society.
>
> *(p. 50).*

With such a vantage on the "clothing of rhetoric" (Chaney 1996, p. 157), Izzard's transvestitism might seem a convenient gimmick. But, as mentioned above, it is a lifestyle, not a tactic for inspiring "subversive laughter in the pastiche-effect" of dressing in drag (Butler 1990, p. 146). As Izzard has repeatedly said, he knew he was a transvestite when he was four years old and, after coming out at 23, worked hard "to walk around in heels and nails and not give a monkey's blok about it" (Garrison 2013). In other words, he struggled to stand in for abstract stereotypes and to withstand the sometimes-brutal reactions they might incite when materialized. Furthermore, Izzard's clothing as at once a verbal rhetoric and a visual display stands out for its codification of gender and given full view when flown in the face of normativity (Brummett 2008, p. 47). *DTK* is therefore as much about transforming "foreign" sexualities as it is about refiguring the "image-clothing" of dominant discourses (Barthes 1990, p. 3). The laddish context of *DTK* has been widely recognized for its over-emphasis on public displays of normative bodies. The political culture, too, has been noted for its dualistic organization of bodies politic. Certainly, Izzard's own "gender bending" performance disrupted the "phantasmatic constructions" of power and privilege that are so predicated upon looks and the collective will to police appearances.[6] Yet, insofar as he advances his stand-up as itself a queer art of making the familiar strange, he converted the "transvestite imagery" into a sociopolitical critique of powerful discursive formations and their supporting institutions, which seem to separate "the *naked* (real) truth" from "*clothing* (decoration)" (IJsseling 1976, p. 126; Tanke 2009). Even today, popular references to queers (let alone transvestites, in particular) tend to crop up when criminal acts are committed against them – or, conversely, when they are accused of committing illicit and/or scandalous offenses, like public indecency. Izzard utilizes stand-up as a transversal mode of performance for "becoming criminal" such that to unthinkingly be "one of the lads" is to be a wrong 'em boyo (Reynolds 2002). Or, in Burke's terms, it is to be stupid (1959, p. 41).

A Comedy of Nonconformity

Gender nonconformity has seen various historical stages of either exaggerated masculinity or overdone femininity. In fact, gender exaggeration both draws attention to the problems of variance and makes normative claims to (fe)maleness seem ridiculous. A "jack the lad" is generally a braggadocio – a figure defined by hyperbolic displays of self-aggrandizement. He is also a rogue thinker and actor, refusing to conform to societal proscriptions for behavior. Izzard, in many ways, fits this bill. However, instead of affecting a politics of self-display that refuses responsibility, Izzard acts with all the confidence of a man who throws off convention in order to inflate its consequences. *DTK* is so outstanding because it "dramatizes the problematization of the boundary between fiction and reality" (Malina 2002, p. 2). Izzard's comedy of nonconformity amplifies the absurdity in sticking points between these two stances, namely through surreal juxtapositions that purposefully "preserve certain forms of the real in order to devalorize its content" (Chenieux-Gendron 1990, p. 92). More specifically, it reformulates how audiences make sense of rhetorical constructions of public identity in society and politics. This begins with Izzard's provisional self-presentation.[7]

From the first, Izzard revaluates and revises common conceptions of transvestitism. The show opens with portraits of Izzard in the style of Andy Warhol appearing on large television screens beside the stage. Izzard walks out of the shadows sporting a Jean-Paul Gaultier dress (that had been shortened into a jacket), glistening black pants, red lipstick, eyeliner accompanied by blue eye shadow, and cropped blonde hair. Amidst applause, Izzard bows then hops around before announcing, "in heels as well," teeing up the numerous turns to gender that he will make throughout the show. "I am a *professional* transvestite," he declares, "so I can run about in heels and not fall over," which is significant because "if women fall over wearing heels, that's embarrassing. But if a bloke falls over wearing heels then you have to kill yourself." Straightforward as it seems, this simple assertion orients the entire gig. First, it legitimates transvestitism in suggesting that a transvestite only makes a fool of himself when he misuses accessories, not when he fashions himself as a woman in the first place. Second, and by extension, Izzard mocks public tolerance of his appearance in proclaiming that it is fit for a man to wear women's clothing but only until he does so in an unfitting manner. Finally, he exaggerates the sociality of gender norms by overstating the punishment for shame, not to mention the common sense that states of disgrace are self-inflicted. These threads are so significant because they typify the sort of "irruptive extensions" that Izzard affects in his reapplication of categorical judgments.[8]

Consider his immediate passage to a lesson on gender and sexuality. "If you're a transvestite," says Izzard, "you're actually a male tomboy. That's where the sexuality lies." This is a catachretic construction: the notion of a "male tomboy" borrows from connotations of girls dressing up and behaving as boys in order to craft a contrastive image of a boy who is girlish versus a girl who is boyish. The masculine qualifier juxtaposes two seemingly incongruous concepts. Nevertheless, when Izzard links his own apparent girlishness to heterosexuality, it makes sense. And he goes on: "It's not drag queen. No, gay men have got that covered." Here, after acknowledging that people can mistake transvestites for drag queens, he highlights the fact that transvestitism tends to be a way of life rather than a theatrical performance of flamboyance for comic effect. Then he ups the ante: "It's male *lesbian*. That's really where it is, okay?" In moving from the image of a tomboy to the image of a lesbian, Izzard stretches his association from gendered predispositions to sexual attractions. "It's true," he pronounces as the audience laughs, "because most transvestites fancy girls ... fancy women, so that's where it is. So running, jumping, climbing trees, putting on makeup when you're up there."

This reorganization of gender classifications by way of conventional characteristics establishes Izzard's fantastical take on a general impropriety that tends to animate judgments about alternative sexualities. Much of his comedy – and, to be sure, much of its rhetorical force – comes from digressions. As Heinrich F. Plett (2001) states, *digressio* allows for disruptions of narrative flow "in favor of exuberant subplots, authorial comments, and so on" (pp. 225–226). Cicero, Plett notes, went so far as to argue that digressions are often more important than the central topic (p. 257). This is likely because digressions are also rhetorical tactics of amplification. That is, in disconnecting from a topic to explore a thematic relation, a rhetor can emphasize a particular point through the elaboration and aggregation of referents, thereby garnering understanding and even goodwill. So, too, can clothing function like a "visible garment" for disclosing particular dispositions, even as it can serve "as both clarification and obfuscation, speech and silence, publicity and secrecy" (Burke 1969, p. 120). For Izzard, digression has the comic effect of displacing meanings through a sort of *amplificatio ad absurdum*, and it explicitly sustains his interest in upsetting common notions by transforming their usual vesture. Consider, in the first instance, that Izzard uses catachresis as a figure of abuse in order to disabuse his audience of the "proper" way to envision transvestitism. He sets right the very idea that gender bending, for whatever reason, is wrong. Izzard then pushes this toward the absurd when he converts impropriety into a comic congeries of well-ordered setups and punchlines – or, in this case, when he strays into a tale about how, as a kid, he kept his makeup in a squirrel hole.

According to Izzard, a male squirrel enabled his transvestitism, storing his stash of cosmetics beside a stockpile of nuts. "And sometimes," he relayed, "I'd get up that tree and that squirrel would be *covered* in makeup!" Here, Izzard pretends to be a squirrel applying lipstick while holding a pocket mirror. When a juvenile Izzard catches him, the squirrel acts as if he was just eating a nut, and then taunts: "'What? Fuck off." Izzard goes further still. From his childhood interaction he moves to the nature of squirrel behavior (i.e., they always eat nuts with two hands, chew their food frantically, and pause at odd moments to observe their surroundings). He then applies anthropomorphic qualities to squirrels, acting as though, when they pause, they are actually wondering, "Did I leave the gas on? No! No, I'm a fucking squirrel!" Sometimes, however, they tire of an all-nut diet and pine "for a grapefruit." Such a digression is significant to Izzard's general comic art insofar as it epitomizes his capacity to craft vividly absurd images of whatever topic he is engaging. Additionally, it actualizes the extent to which surrealism is tied to his revisions of sociopolitical realities, and to which clothing becomes a site for sexual demystification. Surrealism is a type of art that "undercuts the representation of the world" (Chenieux-Gendron, 1990, p. 88). Moreover, in such outlandish comic tales, it expands both verbal and visual rhetorics of clothing by "making fashion an important site for … cultural and individual expression" (Lusty 2007, p. 99). As a comic art in Izzard's stand-up, it reinforces the artfulness in his regroupings. It also allows Izzard to bring transvestitism out of the trees, so to speak, and into public culture with a defiant expletive that affirms the potential civic virtue in nonconformity. To be squirrelly here is to be appropriately fidgety in identity categories. This is not comedy as the conventional deviation from a norm via the surreal; it is a transformation of the norm itself.

Take as another example Izzard's establishment of a transvestite typology. Following Burke, a change of identity can be signaled by a change of name (1967, p. 27). Izzard's sense of the morphology in transvestitism is introduced early when he defines himself as a "professional" transvestite. This implies, on the one hand, a certain combination of skill, dexterity, and competency that comes with practice and experience while also signifying a measure of distinction, refinement, and sophistication. Izzard elaborates on these qualities when he situates himself outside of the common placement of transvestites in a "weirdo grouping," which he delineates with a story about a man in the Bronx who lived in a cage and emerged only to shoot geese. When the man was caught and arrested, it was discovered that he collected women's shoes. But if he was actually a transvestite, Izzard suggests, he was "a fucking *weirdo* transvestite." Then, with an eloquent gesture of pride and a nod to cosmopolitanism, he proclaims: "I'm much more in the *executive* transvestite area." Izzard locates complexity in seemingly straightforward classifications and even reveals the contradictions that actual bodies introduce to abstractions. This is evident later when he describes himself as an "action transvestite" who, like a squirrel, is fond of running, jumping, and climbing trees.

But Izzard's "action" orientation also comes from military aspirations he had as a kid, making the "running, jumping, climbing trees" bit a play on gender stereotypes. Izzard develops this by turning to militarism as a masculine predilection, and war as something for which he could have been well equipped. Still, it is the reason he gives for not enlisting that is most significant for his irruption of gender categories: military uniform codes. "I didn't join … because there's not much makeup in the army, is there? They only have that nighttime look and that's a bit slapdash." Here Izzard mimics a sloppy application of war paint, which makes soldiers "look a mess." Tellingly, he implies an artfulness to transvestitism that clashes with an identifiable combat aesthetic. This is in part a self-referential joke; Izzard has mentioned in numerous interviews that much of his self-consciousness as an out transvestite stemmed from his lack of fashion sense. But it is an appeal to public judgment as well when he brings up the politics of "Don't Ask, Don't Tell." The policy was implemented in 1993 as a means for the U.S. military to discipline and even discharge (never mind disgrace) openly gay service members. Izzard mocks its logic. "If you're a bloke wearing a lot of makeup … I don't think they *need* to ask, really." Izzard and others like him are obviously identified vis-à-vis the visual rhetorics that seem to signify alternative sexualities. Then again, the audience knows Izzard is straight. Furthermore, as he argues, the real fiction lies in policies for keeping up appearances. "No, you can't join," says Izzard in a hyper-masculine voice as he pretends to be either a policymaker or an army recruiter. "Wrong shade of lipstick for the army, I'm afraid." The implication here is that, in policy and practice, camouflage is paramount.

Izzard's turn to gender in the armed forces is also significant because, at the time, the European Court of Human Rights was in the process of shoring up non-discrimination laws for gay and transgender individuals in the British military. The U.S. would not do so until 2011. Through the use of *prosopopoeia* – or the rhetorical device of speaking and/or acting as if you are another person – Izzard renders ridiculous the public judgment of U.S. citizens, showing forth the prejudiced and collective will of a country to keep queer identities "outside the charmed circle" of "positive images" for gayness writ large (Sender 2003, p. 355). In addition, he demonstrates the potential damage done by forgetting that looks can be deceiving. "And you're missing a *huge* opportunity here," Izzard laments, "because we all know that one of the main elements of attack is the element of *surprise*." Then he asks the rhetorical question: what could be more surprising than the Airborne Wing of the First Battalion Transvestite Brigade? Just imagine a throng of transvestites "parachuting into dangerous areas," each "with *fantastic* makeup." Then imagine the stupor that might befall opposing forces. Izzard impersonates their reaction, standing in awe and uttering, "fucking hell, look at these guys." The made-up men are ludicrous, until it is realized that "they've got guns!" The onlookers pay for their chauvinism. And the U.S. suffers from its own prejudice when it holds fast to an olden notion of masculine national identity.[9] Here, Izzard reimagines warfare as a flight of fancy, which brings me to a final way he troubles gender conformity.

Izzard turns his attention to the 1963 film, *The Great Escape*. The film features American actor Steve McQueen and details the exploits of Allied prisoners attempting to flee a Nazi prisoner of war camp in Silesia by disguising themselves as Germans in plainclothes then fleeing the country. Unsurprisingly, Izzard is quick to point out his personal affinities given that most of the prisoners are British ("link up there") and it is an action film (and Izzard is an "action transvestite, link up there"). He opens his bit by proclaiming that the British play bad guys in American movies "because of the Revolutionary War." For those unconvinced, consider that the French get to play "esoteric characters" that are fawned over for their erotic exoticism. The reason: America has an historical debt to General Marquis de Lafayette. Izzard digresses here to reinforce his earlier points about American exceptionalism by insulting the audience members for not knowing their own history. "You don't know who he is, do you?" Izzard taunts before mimicking their cultural privilege. "The Spanish-American War? The French-Banana War?" Then Izzard corrects: "The Revolutionary War. Hung out with Washington. Street named after him in New York. Forget it." Importantly, Izzard instructs his audience in an unmentioned aspect of U.S. public culture by making fun of the strangeness that comprises common senses of American exceptionalism. General

Lafayette was a prominent figure during the American Revolution; Izzard uses him as a cudgel for mocking a U.S. audience that seems to have relegated him to the margins, perhaps because he was a foreigner.

From here Izzard recounts the plot of the film, detailing the British efforts to build elaborate tunnels, craft true-to-life costumes of German officers, and forge identifying documents. "On the day of the escape," he says, McQueen has met up with the other escapees who have "trilby hats on, overcoats, briefcases, canoe, bit of a rabbit. [...] And Steve's just there in *jeans* and a *t-shirt* ... disguised as an American man." That is, the British are forced to change their identities, while McQueen plays a white American male dressed up as himself. Not only does this epitomize a sense that Americanism has no need to hide itself, even in the direst of circumstances, but it also reinforces the relative invisibility of normative identities (see Nakayama & Krizek 1995). Evidence of this is contained in the film's outcome, wherein the British escapees are held up at a train station where they are fumbling the German language and getting hassled by the Gestapo while McQueen strikes out on his own and gets to the border of Switzerland by way of a motorbike. "This is from Poland," Izzard remarks. "And if you don't know the geography, it goes Poland, Czechoslovakia, Holland, Venezuela, Africa, Beirut ... the *Hanging* Gardens of *Babylon*, and then Switzerland." If the absurdity of Izzard's geographic layout does not do enough to expose the absurdity in *The Great Escape* as a "true story," the climax does. McQueen is the only one who "lives to tell the tale. Meanwhile, the British are all round up and shot in the head." For Izzard, this is the individualistic articulation of Manifest Destiny to a T, made even more so by the fact that he, a transvestite Brit, identifies more with the "damn cool" American than his own brethren. What is more, the damn Yankee actually upends revolutionary depictions of American men as enfeebled dandies by juxtaposing the manliness of individualist, prideful pursuits with the inefficacy and effeminacy of dressing up.[10]

I indicated above that much of Izzard's comedy relies on *metalepsis*, or the rhetorical force of changes in perception or perspective. Digressions, catachretic compositions, and *prosopoeic* arrangements all fill out Izzard's peculiar associations. More to the point, metaleptic rhetoric refers "to something by means of another thing that is remotely related to it, either through a farfetched causal relationship, or through an implied intermediate substitution of terms" (Metalepsis n.d.). The rhetorical and transformative effect, as illustrated above, is a comic expression that enables audiences "to experience new ways of being" (Malina 2002, p. 9). Put simply, Izzard's comedy opens up a space for his audience to see the consequences of gender identifications by making them ridiculous, and yet reasonable. So when he inflates the (martial) fallout from gender typecasts and their categorical failings, when he distorts the gendered nature of national identity, or when he travesties portrayals of hyper-masculine American exceptionalism, he actually amplifies the real-world merit of "queer" mockeries. This happens when he disrupts stereotypical narratives as much as when he interrupts the sociopolitical construction of subjects. Moreover, it happens when Izzard reveals the difference between fiction and reality as a *"mimetic* relation" *in actu* (Malina 2002, p. 9). In the end, Izzard demonstrates the transhistorical consequence of historiographical gender classifications by utilizing queer comedy as a rhetorical style of performance that bends the rules for coming to collective judgments about cultural conditions. And his comic absurdity perpetuates a politics of redressing ways of seeing when it educates his audience not on what is new but on what is taken for granted (Butler 1997, p. 50).

Conclusion: Comedic Radicalism

Transvestitism, for Izzard, is a way of life. But it is also a resource for a comic rhetoric of trans-vesture insofar as it provides a way to redress the historical shortcoming in gender (and other forms of) politics. Izzard is an everyday student of history. In addition to his advocacy for reconsiderations of transgender categorizations are career-long engagements with classical antiquity, historiographies of the Christian Church, and surrealistic myths of origins – all of which rely on his clever use of *allœosis*, or the exchange of conventional images and ideas with alternatives in order to amplify the paradoxes embedded in the norm.

It is little surprise, then, that Izzard refers to himself as a radical liberal, especially since the word "radical" carries connotations of both "going to the root or origin" and departing from the norm, or from orthodoxy. Izzard's radicalism crops up in his comedy when he wraps his political leanings in outlandish interpretations of sociopolitical problematics and their peculiar pedigrees. His surreal sense of humor leads him to advance a progressive politics that makes the commonplace appear nonsensical. By playing out the consequences of certain ways of thinking, speaking, and acting, Izzard enacts an *amplificatio ad absurdum* that exaggerates alterations of sense. In *DTK*, he stretches the sensibilities and perspectives of his audience so that when they snap back they might not return to the same place they started, whether in terms of their own self-image of civic identity or their situation of "others" in public culture.

For my part, Izzard seems most interested in how images and ideas impact the particular treatment of people in certain bodies politic. Hence why the form and function of clothing is endemic to the rhetorical artistry of his use of gender confusion as a more complex appeal than straightforward explanation, and as a means making nonsense a route to transformations in collective judgments. Nevertheless, and despite Izzard's worldwide popularity, transvestitism today "remains something to be discouraged and/or hidden" (Suthrell 2004, p. 174). Even though there is much to be said for what has been called "America's transgender moment," there is still a powerful feeling that this moment (and other similar moments) of increased visibility of marginal identities "tap into pre-existing panics about gender or sexuality, not necessarily spawning new ones" (Griggs 2015). In *DTK*, however, gender deviance and sexual nonconformity is presented as at once a comedic and a public good, and the fantastical moments that Izzard creates set up a sort of re-envisioning whereby the audience is moved by an insinuation that seems to emanate from the stage: it's not me (Izzard), it's you. Pushing back against incorrect and even unstated assumptions about transvestite lifestyles, as well as presumably common beliefs that it is only "appropriate" at certain times and in specific spaces (i.e., drag performances or gay burlesques – or on a stand-up comedy stage!), Izzard performs the very stereotypes that constitute artifactual constructions of femininity and masculinity, and that therefore get inscribed on particular bodies. Furthermore, in advocating a sort of masculine femininity,[11] Izzard posits stereotypical judgments about personal appearance – not to mention sexual preference – as so many perversions of cultural impulses and shared prejudices rather than aberrances of either will or instinct. This is why his comic turn to the ridiculous affects a "change of surroundings" in a "change of clothes" (Burke 1967, p. 27). Or, following Berlant (2008, p. 242), it is why *DTK* grapples with the import of sociopolitical membership by dressing up misconceptions in order to "kill" normative assumptions.

It is therefore appropriate that Izzard closes with a peroration on puberty and the psychosociality of bodily change, which in itself mocks his rationale for remaining in the closet throughout school (as he did not want to be killed with sticks by ignorant classmates). It is also fitting that he finishes by relaying a rather mundane tale of how he lost his virginity only to reaffirm his sexuality and leave the audience, as he says, with an "Oh" feeling. In this way, Izzard embodies dissonance, and the queer possibility that comes with it, especially given that "[n]othing in man – not even his body – is sufficiently stable to serve as the basis for self-recognition or for understanding other men" (Foucault 1984, p. 87). Or, as he has asserted for years now, Izzard does not wear women's dresses; he wears his own dresses that he buys, even if they were meant for a woman. Izzard makes this wobbly logic that there is necessarily something wrong with a "bloke in a dress" most discernible when he cycles the extra-ordinary back into the everyday.

Of course, as I have implied throughout this chapter, Izzard's stand-up is also about civic education and the sociopolitical potential of change through exchange. The long and winding yarns about his gender nonconformity add complexity to otherwise simple-minded explanations for deviation writ large. Histories are contradictory. Individuals are always multiple people. Yet conventional wisdom crystallizes ways of seeing the world even as it organizes what can or should even be seen. In *DTK*, comedy serves as a metaleptic *poros* for revealing through ridiculousness that ways of seeing are also ways of *not* seeing. Importantly, Izzard's Pythonesque skits craft new images and ideas out of olden principles. Just as he inhabits "women's" clothing, so too does Izzard display the inhabitation of other perspectives. Once again he does this literally when he invents dialogues and makes absent bodies present through "prosthetic embodiment" (Berlant 2008, p. 107), and figuratively when these presentations provide rhetorical shifts in position. This has civic virtue when one considers that such inhabitations imply that struggles for a common good have a direct relation to personal welfare. In addition, it suggests that Izzard's own rhetorical posture relies on the triumph of wit in the body of a wise fool. His wisdom seems undeniable when he comes back on stage for an encore that he ends up delivering mostly in French, highlighting his own status as a *travesti exécutif* while reminding his audience that *DTK* is nothing if it is not about the importance of shared vocabularies for understanding shared realities. Significantly, because of his English set-ups and his performative imitations, one need not speak French to understand the *farce française* in his finale.

Even with all of this, the question remains as to whether or not *DTK* actualizes change. One could argue that Izzard simply preaches to the proverbial choir when, as he admits, his audiences are primarily comprised of educated, socially conscious, center-right/center-left liberals (Robb 2013). Moreover, one could argue that stand-up comedians in general take advantage of a certain comic license to perform without "real world" consequences. But a few points stand out for consideration.

First, Izzard is by now widely recognized in both the publicity of his comedy and his roles in a handful of popular films. At the time of *DTK*, which remains his most decorated performance, he was praised for turning his own recognizability into recognition for transvestitism in public culture. Interestingly, communication scholar and rhetorical theorist Edward Schiappa discovered that *DTK* in particular has actually proven to decrease audience prejudice toward transvestites and other minority groups (Schiappa 2008, p. 111). The proof of its endurance is in the popularity of successive recordings of his stand-up as well as in his broad acclaim and worldwide attention beyond the stage. In the summer of 2009, for instance, Izzard ran 43 marathons in 51 days (charting a 1,105-mile course from London, through Liverpool, Belfast, Edinburgh, Leeds, and back again) to raise £200,000 for Sport Relief, a charitable affiliate of Comic Relief that donates money and services to impoverished people around the globe. In 2013, he received the seventh annual Cultural Humanism Award from the Humanist Community at Harvard University, which is co-sponsored by the American Humanist Association and the Harvard Community of Humanists, Atheists, and Agnostics. Izzard has also long been a Labour activist and has even expressed interest in converting his comedic activism into a 2020 run for mayor of London (which seems appropriate given the idiomatic indications of visual acuity in the calendar year). And as I write, he is carrying out a world tour, *Force Majeure*, from which he took a "break" in June 2014 to fly from the U.S. to Normandy in order to perform a trilingual show on the anniversary of D-Day in commemoration of those who fought for democracy. I mention all of these things not because it is necessary to prove how audience reception surpasses performance situations, but rather to acknowledge that part of Izzard's rhetorical force stems from his ethos *as a comedian*. In other words, it is his queer disposition and surrealistic temperament that dispose audiences to grant the good sense in his comic nonsense.

Second, as a stand-up comedian, Izzard is uniquely situated to act out potentially tragic consequences of misguided perspectives. While demonstrating rhetoric itself as a queer art of comedy, which of necessity places so much importance in the play of appearances, he also cautions audiences against losing sight of the depths that are brought to the surface in rhetorical play. In his circuitous and circular commentaries on transvestitism, Izzard models a logic for approaching even the severest bigotry with a humane sense of humor – a logic, that is, which relocates deeply "offensive" circumstances and discourses to the comic space of stupidity. Traditional oratory in the category of the serious is not nearly as attuned to the lofty nonsense that often emerges in such a queer "art of surfaces" (Deleuze 1990, p. 9). Moreover, Izzard's comedy is unrepentantly oriented toward cultural histories as resources for explaining why we are certain ways, and so he diminishes his own need to persuade per se in order to play up his collection of available means of persuasion that are travestied as *topoi* for habits of thinking, speaking, and acting. In this way, Izzard simultaneously commends and maligns his audiences' capacity to reason. He also manipulates reason itself through a metaleptic process that recalls a catchphrase of *Monty Python's* John Cleese, which speaks directly to Izzard's promotion of sociopolitical change: "And now for something completely different."

DTK therefore offers a comedic politics of establishing difference in the visibility of tacit images and ideas about public life. As a sort of meta-parody of a popular skit from *Monty Python's Flying Circus*, Izzard revises gender confusion and common practices of relegating alternative sexualities and gender deviants to the margins from a civic education in "How Not to Be Seen" to an absurd yet auspicious tutorial on "How (Not) to See." One need not be an Izzard initiate, or even a fan of Monty Python, to appreciate the gesture to collective stakes in personal ways of seeing in this reference. Consider that one of Izzard's main incentives to comedy was his own experience coming out as a transvestite (i.e., of being seen). Consider, too, his general sense that the Golden Rule is the only necessary civic tenet, which bespeaks a wider concern for what stereotypes and blind faiths can do for or against public relationships. Arguably, the comic stage is a "safer" space than a more seriously construed bully pulpit to tease out some of the tensions that lead to violent public interactions. It is less dangerous for Izzard because, with him, the outré is expected. In fact, it is the unconventional that ultimately enables him to make the "strange" familiar. *DTK* is therefore an exemplar for laughing at how we dress ourselves and others in order to redress public ills – or not.

Notes

1 *Dress to Kill* won two Primetime Emmy Awards for writing and performance. It also stands as the fifth of nine video recordings (spanning from 1993 to 2013). The title seems to be a send up of Brian De Palma's 1980 erotic thriller of the same name, which is replete with lascivious sex and bloodlust perpetuated by a cross-dressing killer. Additionally, the title retools an affirmative idiom for dressing up in order to be noticed: "if looks could kill."
2 See Gilbert 2004; Horowitz 1997; Kohen 2012; and Stebbins 1990.
3 Note that this is a decidedly Deleuzian logic of nonsense. See Deleuze 1990.
4 I borrow this term from Berlant (2008). Butler (2004), too, discusses such interpellations in terms of "cultural conscriptions."

5 Note, too, that Izzard's use of *catachresis* shares affinities with a comic deployment of what Kenneth Burke calls "casuistic stretching," or the conscious introduction of new principles of judgment that mystifies in order to clarify social standards. Indeed, Izzard advances absurdly comic demonstrations as a means of moving from strict categorical groupings to categories of association. See Burke 1959, pp. 229–231.
6 I borrow the phrase "phantasmatic constructions" from Judith Butler (1990; 2004). See also Halberstam 1998 and Devor 1989.
7 See Halperin 2012.
8 According to Derrida (1982), an "irruptive extension" of a sign, or of any representation, is not simply a substitution of one idea for another but rather a disruption of the very notion that a particular representation or idea is necessarily proper, or that the meaning it conveys is ineludibly correct. Derrida ties such an extension to the concept of *catachresis*, mentioned earlier as the comic misuse of social knowledge (p. 255).
9 Elsewhere, I have evaluated this predisposition in terms of representations of abject soldier bodies (Gilbert 2014).
10 A digression early in the bit only exaggerates Izzard's point. Before recounting the film, he tells a story about doing a gig in Memphis, Tennessee, and meeting a stereotypical hillbilly who asked him to "talk British" for his kids. Izzard mimicked the man, pretending to round up the children – "Jimmy Sue, Bobby Will, Fishy Bob" – then reminding them all that he speaks English. Obviously the accent is of interest, but the kids would still rather watch a man emasculate a donkey then gawk at a foppish Brit.
11 Note that Halberstam defines androgyny as the "movement back and forth between femininity and masculinity" (1998, p. 294).

References

Aronstein, S. (2009). "In my own idiom": Social critique, campy gender, and queer performance in *Monty Python and the Holy Grail*. In K.C. Kelly & T. Pugh (Eds.), *Queer movie medievalisms* (pp. 115–128). Burlington: Ashgate.
Barthes, R. (1990). *The fashion system*. Ed. by M. Ward and R. Howard. Berkeley: University of California Press.
Berlant, L. (2008). *The female complaint: The unfinished business of sentimentality in American culture*. Durham: Duke University Press.
Brouwer, D.C. (2010). Risibility politics: Camp humor in HIV/AIDS zines. In D.C. Brouwer & R. Asen (Eds.), *Public modalities: Rhetoric, culture, media, and the shape of public life* (pp. 219–239). Tuscaloosa: University of Alabama Press.
Brummett, B. (2008). *A rhetoric of style*. Carbondale: Southern Illinois University Press.
Burke, K. (1959). *Attitudes toward history*. Berkeley: University of California Press.
Burke, K. (1967). *The philosophy of literary form: Studies in symbolic action*. Berkeley: University of California Press.
Burke, K. (1969). *A rhetoric of motives*. Berkeley: University of California Press.
Butler, J. (1990). *Gender trouble: Feminism and the subversion of identity*. New York: Routledge.
Butler, J. (1997). *Excitable speech: A politics of the performative*. New York: Routledge.
Butler, J. (2004). *Undoing gender*. New York: Routledge.
Chaney, J. (1996). The revolution of a trope: The rise of the new science and the divestment of rhetoric in the seventeenth century. In S. Barker (Ed.), *Signs of change: Premodern → modern → postmodern* (pp. 155–174). Albany: State University of New York Press.
Chenieux-Gendron, J. (1990). *Surrealism*. Trans. by V. Folkenflik. New York: Columbia University Press.
Cicero (n.d.). *De Oratore*. Cambridge, MA: Harvard University Press.

Deleuze, G. (1990). *The logic of sense*. Trans. by M. Lester. New York: Columbia University Press.
Derrida, J. (1982). *Margins of philosophy*. Trans. by A. Bass. Chicago: University of Chicago Press.
Devor, H. (1989). *Gender blending: Confronting the limits of duality*. Bloomington: Indiana University Press.
Dougary, G. (2013). Stand up and be counted: Eddie Izzard interview. *The Telegraph*. Nov. 22. Retrieved from www.telegraph.co.uk/culture/comedy/9969289/Stand-up-and-be-counted-Eddie-Izzard-interview.html
Fausto-Sterling, A. (2000). *Sexing the body: Gender politics and the construction of sexuality*. New York: Basic Books.
Fischer, C.S. (2010). *Made in America: A social history of American culture and character*. Chicago: University of Chicago Press.
Foss, K.A. (2007). Harvey Milk and the queer rhetorical situation: A rhetoric of contradiction. In C.E. Morriss, III (Ed.), *Queering public address: Sexualities in American historical discourse* (pp. 74–92). Columbia: University of South Carolina Press.
Foucault, M. (1984). Nietzsche, genealogy, history. In P. Rabinow (Ed.), *Foucault reader* (pp. 76–100). New York: Pantheon Books.
Garrison, B. (2013). Eddie Izzard on atheism, transgender, and "the invisible bloke upstairs." *The Advocate*. March 8. Retrieved from www.advocate.com/comedy/2013/03/08/eddie-izzard-atheism-transgender-and-invisible-bloke-upstairs
Gilbert, C.J. (2014). Standing up to combat trauma. *Text and Performance Quarterly, 34*, 144–163.
Gilbert, J.R. (2004). *Performing marginality: Humor, gender, and cultural critique*. Detroit: Wayne State University Press.
Gogol, N. (1997). *Dead souls*. Trans. by R. Pevear & L. Volokhonsky. New York: Vintage.
Griggs, B. (2015). America's transgender moment. *CNN*. April 25. Retrieved from www.cnn.com/2015/04/23/living/transgender-moment-jenner-feat/
Halberstam, J. (1998). *Female masculinity*. Durham: Duke University Press.
Halberstam, J. (2000). *The queer art of failure*. Durham: Duke University Press.
Halperin, D.M. (2012). *How to be gay*. Cambridge: Harvard University Press.
Hariman, R. (1986). Status, marginality, and rhetorical theory. *Quarterly Journal of Speech, 72*, 38–54.
Harrison, C. (2010). *American culture in the 1990s*. Edinburgh: Edinburgh University Press.
Hatty, S.E. (2000). *Masculinities, violence and culture*. Athens: Ohio State University Press.
Hodkinson, P. (2011). *Media, culture and society: An introduction*. Thousand Oaks: Sage Publications.
Horowitz, S. (1997). *Queens of comedy: Lucille Ball, Phyllis Diller, Carol Burnett, Joan Rivers, and the new generation of funny women*. London: Routledge.
Hunter, J.D. (1991). *Culture wars: The struggle to define America, making sense of the battle over the family, art, education, law, and politics*. New York: Basic Books.
IJsseling, S. (1976). *Rhetoric and philosophy in conflict: An historical survey*. Netherlands: The Hague.
James, C. (2008). Eddie Izzard's master plan. *New York Times*. March 16. Retrieved from www.nytimes.com/2008/03/16/arts/television/16jame.html?pagewanted=all&_r=0
King, C.S. (2009). It cuts both ways: *Fight Club*, masculinity, and abject hegemony. *Communication and Critical/Cultural Studies, 6*(4), 366–385.
Kohen, Y. (2012). *We killed: The rise of women in American comedy*. New York: Sarah Crichton Books.

Layman, G. (2001). *The great divide: Religious and cultural conflict in American party politics.* New York: Columbia University Press.
Lusty, N. (2007). *Surrealism, feminism, psychoanalysis.* Burlington: Ashgate Publishing.
Malina, D. (2002). *Breaking the frame: Metalepsis and the construction of the subject.* Columbus: Ohio State University Press.
Metalepsis. (n.d.). *Silva Rhetoricae.* Retrieved from http://rhetoric.byu.edu
Miller, V.J. (2005). *Consuming religion: Christian faith and practice in a consumer culture.* New York: Continuum.
Munoz, J.E. (2009). *Cruising utopia: The then and there of queer futurity.* New York: New York University Press.
Nakayama, T.K., & Krizek, R.L. (1995). Whiteness: A strategic rhetoric. *Quarterly Journal of Speech, 81,* 291–309.
Plett, H.F. (2001). Digressio. In T.O. Sloane (Ed.), *Encyclopedia of rhetoric* (pp. 225–226). New York: Oxford University Press.
Reynolds, B. (2002). *Becoming criminal: Transversal performance and cultural dissidence in early modern England.* Baltimore: Johns Hopkins University Press.
Richards, I.A. (1936). *The philosophy of rhetoric.* New York: Oxford University Press.
Robb, P. (2013). *Ottawa Citizen.* Nov. 8. Retrieved from www.ottawacitizen.com/health/wacky+world+Eddie+Izzard/9143946/story.html
Schiappa, E. (2008). *Beyond representational correctness: Rethinking criticism of popular media.* Albany: State University of New York.
Sender, K. (2003). Sex sells: Sex, class, and taste in commercial gay and lesbian media. *GLQ: A Journal of Lesbian and Gay Studies, 9,* 331–365.
Stebbins, R.A. (1990). *The laugh-makers: Stand-Up comedy as art, business, and life-style.* Montreal: McGill-Queen's University Press.
Suthrell, C. (2004). *Unzipping gender: Sex, cross-dressing and culture.* New York: Berg.
Tanke, J.J. (2009). *Foucault's philosophy of art: A genealogy of modernity.* London: Continuum.
Thomson, I.T. (2010). *Culture wars and enduring American dilemmas.* East Lansing: University of Michigan Press.
Williams, Z. (2010). Eddie Izzard: Straight but not linear. *The Guardian.* Nov.19. Retrieved from www.theguardian.com/culture/2010/nov/20/zoe-williams-eddie-izzard-saturday-interview

3

"NO DAMN MAMMY, MOMS!"

Rhetorical Re-invention in the Stand-up Comedy of Jackie "Moms" Mabley

Abbey Morgan

Before Eddie Murphy was "Raw," Bill Cosby was "Himself," or Richard Pryor hit "The Sunset Strip," there was Jackie Moms Mabley. Adorned with toothless smile, floppy hat, oversized shoes, and floral-print housecoat, Jackie Moms Mabley would produce a stand-up variety stemming from early 20th-century vaudevillian traditions well into the mid 20th century. She would set the prototype for those notable entertainers aforementioned, participating in the cultivation and transformation of U.S. entertainment, ultimately positioning herself as the first black female comedian. Honing her monologue, weaving song and her famous softshoe shuffle, Mabley would do more than just stand-up; she would carve a space of a new variety. Using anachronistic references to the stereotypical mammy figure, as Elsie Williams notes in her seminal work on the comedienne, *The Humor of Jackie Moms Mabley*, Mabley would use the limits of racial, gendered, and sexual representation as a way to reinvent black female identity, speaking loudly, unabashedly, and acerbically within a public space not readily accepting of black female voices.

But to know Mabley, would be to know her simply as Moms. Her 1969 introduction on the *Ed Sullivan Show* affirms this as she presents herself to her television audience: "For the benefit of some you children now that don't know Moms, that's the name: Moms. M.O.M. frontwards, M.O.M. backwards, upside down, W.O.W., WOW!" By the time Mabley delivered this introduction to her "children," she had already amassed a career spanning nearly 40 years, touring the country, playing Carnegie Hall, and performing regularly at the world famous Apollo Theater in Harlem. Black, female, and lesbian – a social trifecta of representational limitation – Mabley would use these public confines to her rhetorical prowess, making audiences laugh, holding few political punches.

This chapter looks behind the laughter and into the rhetoric of Mabley's comedy. Marked as the first black female comedian, Mabley would use her rhetorical skill within roles traditionally deemed to confine. Emerging during the height of the Jim Crow Era, Mabley's comedy, through anachronistic references to the stereotyped figures like the mammy, would voice highly politicized agendas over the course of her career. In her stand-up routines issues concerning race, sexuality, politics, and contemporaneous social conditions often took center stage.

Joining the vaudeville circuit in 1921 under the mentorship of husband and wife duo Butterbeans and Susie, Mabley developed the Moms persona. Her costume, floppy hat, housecoat, oversized shoes and missing teeth – deliberately distinct from her off-stage characteristics – play into the limited roles permitted for black female performers as mammy, servant, or tragic mulatto. Yet Mabley's framing of herself as Moms displays her ability to manipulate facets of a representational black female identity. Through the performance of an old black grandmother she makes available the potential for rhetorical agency in spite of and within conventionally oppressive frameworks. In her acts she structures herself as a mother speaking to her "children" as she always called her audience. Using the stage, Mabley relies heavily on what could not be said historically (by blacks or by women) in public (in front of whites and in front of men). She takes up the tools to construct new images of black identity, consciously within the public eye. Jackie Mabley's comedic presentation as Moms rhetorically subverts oppressive limitation on sociopolitical agency by employing stereotypically racialized and gendered roles and consciously re-inventing and inscribing new representation of black female identity.

This chapter explores Jackie Moms Mabley's performative rhetorical work through three sections. I have divided the chapter into these three sections conceptually with the aim of looking at Mabley's connection to larger African American traditions of humor, linking Mabley's brand of comedy to a distinct collective consciousness. Looking at Mabley's stand-up (Mabley 1961a; 1961b; 1963a; 1963b) within this framework makes available a conversation on the wide-reaching impact of African and African American slave traditions. I then aim to connect Mabley's dialectic with an African American collective consciousness through her rhetorical staging of oppressive limitations. Here, I examine what Elsie Williams suggests is an anachronistic reference to the mammy stereotype as it operates in Mabley's rhetoric. I look to tie this larger context of African American humor, established in the first section, to Mabley's rhetorical framing through her costume and maternal persona as it extends and participates in these traditions. With this exploration of the Moms persona, I hope to make an intervention that suggests Mabley's rhetoric provides new grammar for addressing black female identity by claiming the body, making sexual choice visible and narratively crossing out old representations of identity to write new ones.

The first section observes trends in African American humor and the ways in which Mabley's humor connects to these trends. Invoking the Duboisian "double consciousness," black humor (which I am using to reference here as African American humor rather than a type of gallows humor) engages a subculture reminiscent of hush harbors,[1] employing the guise of the merry slave often necessary for survival, obscuring the private uncensored exchanges between slaves from the white tyrannical public gaze. Mabley's routines would draw heavily from these traditions also evident in minstrelsy and vaudeville, traditions that also deeply influenced Mabley's work.

The second section examines the Moms persona and the rhetoric of the grandmother. Mabley's calculated appearance – no teeth, knit hat, floppy, oversized shoes, and floral print housecoat – play to the stereotyped parameters for women as mother and black women as mammy. Further, the universal figure of the grandmother, which Mabley frequently referenced as part of her self-deprecating humor, produces rhetoric through a grandmother's authoritative wisdom, but it also acknowledges an intimate racially traumatic U.S. history. As the black grandmother closely references the mammy, Mabley crafts her routines with a familiarity, reminding us that under slavery and well after it the black female slave raised the white children as well as the black children. Compounding this sense of maternal authority and political wisdom, Mabley keenly constructs a narrative to black audiences and later in her career for a broader, white audience, addressing both as "all [her] children." This section then moves to an analysis of several of Mabley's jokes as she uses the rhetorical frame of the grandmother. I have chosen to look at a range of Mabley's jokes rather than focus on one specific routine to highlight Mabley's continued thematic throughout her career. With this move I hope to emphasize, through a variety of jokes, the staying power of Mabley's stand-up as well as her stronghold on this particular representation. While Mabley had a significant film career, extensive work through the 1920s and 60s in theaters across the U.S., roles on television (in most of which she plays the Moms character) and published work as a playwright with Harlem Renaissance figure Zora Neale Hurston, I am specifically concerned here with her stand-up comedic routines as a form of rhetorical power.

The third section suggests that Mabley's stand-up writes a new type of "American Grammar." I borrow the phraseology from scholar Hortense J. Spiller's seminal 1987 essay "Mama's Baby, Papa's Maybe: An American Grammar Book," to explore the ways in which Mabley inscribes symbolic power by reclaiming the black female captive body, working to reconfigure the gap between what Spillers calls the "body" and the "flesh." As Mabley imparts a persona that intentionally takes up a universally matriarchal role, she not only problematizes the limitations for black female identity through this hackneyed figure, but she also writes new symbolic order, humorously re-gendering the historically "un-gendered" black female body. Taking control of her sexual choices through her "old man" jokes, Mabley troubles hegemony while claiming black female sexuality. In this section, I underscore ways Mabley's appropriation of the guise of a black grandmother yields space to grammatically and subsequently symbolically re-invent new black female identity ultimately navigating a strategic sexual agency.

Lastly, as I conclude, I glance at Mabley's enduring impact in the stand-up routines of contemporary comedians as testament to her rhetorical influence. I offer that Mabley's use of restrictions for blacks and for women, predicated on her own racialized, gendered and sexualized identity, exemplifies avenues of resistance and access available in unlikely roles of confinement. As we see other contemporary comedians like Eddie Murphy assembling manifestations of their own personal homage to the comedienne, we can see ways Mabley's stand-up endures. This endurance is worth articulating for its continued dialectic with African American traditions of humor.

By dividing the text this way, I aim to view Mabley in relation to larger contexts of African American humor, as she specifically consults oppressive frameworks to write new narratives for black female identity.

"We Wear the Mask that Grins and Lies": African American Traditions of Humor

> We wear the mask that grins and lies,
> It hides our cheeks and shades our eyes, –
> This debt we pay to human guile;
> With torn and bleeding hearts we smile,
> And mouth with myriad subtleties.
>
> Why should the world be over-wise,
> In counting all our tears and sighs?
> Nay, let them only see us, while
> We wear the mask.
> We smile, but, O great Christ, our cries
> To thee from tortured souls arise.
> We sing, but oh the clay is vile
> Beneath our feet, and long the mile;
> But let the world dream otherwise,
>   We wear the mask!
>   *(Paul Laurence Dunbar, "We Wear the Mask," 1895 [1993])*

The sentiment expressed in Dunbar's 1895 poem speaks to the "two-ness" at work in the collective consciousness of black Americans. By 1903, W.E.B. DuBois's *Souls of Black Folk* would coin the term "double-consciousness," furthering this notion and illuminating the subculture prevalent in black American identity. The metaphor of the mask that "grins and lies" in Dunbar's poem seems a most fitting one to reflect the roots of African American comedy.

Mel Watkin's On The Real Side: A History of African American Comedy from Slavery to Chris Rock (1994/2004) provides one of the most comprehensive critical studies of African American humor to date, noting the necessity of an African American subculture as means of survival and a tool for adaptation. Watkins marks the inception of a unique African subculture on the slave ships as they traversed the Atlantic during the treacherous trek of the Middle Passage[2] between the 1600s through the 1800s. The subculture operates simultaneously as a private sphere for blacks with its own collective cultural codes of engagement while creating a guise from the white tyrannical gaze. Watkins writes,

> Maintaining the appearance of the naïve was crucial as a survival technique, providing the perfect guise for aggressive humor and wit whereas a "sullen slave" might merely cause discomfort for a master, an "impudent" slave would most likely force slaveholders to inflict quick and severe punishment.
> (p. 66)

The development of verbal wit and rhetorical devices typified in African and African American storied traditions like trickster tales, survivalist humor, and accommodationist humor[3] facilitated the facade of the happy, docile, jovial slave, pacifying the master while developing a private culture for blacks to speak amongst each other.

The blackface, minstrel traditions evident in films like D.W. Griffith's *Birth of a Nation* metaphorically reference the duality emergent in black American consciousness while showcasing the limitations of representations of black identity. Whites, adorned in burnt cork or blackface, took the stage in minstrel shows during the late 1800s and later in vaudeville beginning at the turn of the 20th century through the 1960s, popularizing monolithic representations of blacks. The white performers readily relied on parody, gags, and stereotypes of black Americans for entertainment. Yet, white performers were not the only ones taking the stage with painted face. Unlike their white counterparts, however, the black performers could parody no one else but themselves. In the documentary *Vaudeville* (Garner, Palmer, & Vereen 1995), Watkins notes that while blacks were limited to their roles on stage they were only allowed to portray the racist stereotypical figures like Uncle Tom, Zip Coon, Sambo, the Pickaninny, and the black mammy. It was these black performers, marked as "real Negro delineators," who moved vaudeville from merely a variety show where whites parodied blacks, to what would soon develop into an original sense of African American comedy.

Almost all black performers before the 1950s wore blackface, as a rule, even for black audiences. But some chose to remain "masked" after these rules subsided. Black blackface performers like Bert Williams, who became in his day the highest paid minstrel performer playing the character of Sambo, and Dewey "Pigmeat" Markham, noted in the documentary *Vaudeville* as "one of the last of the [vaudeville] performers to take off the mask" (Garner, Palmer, & Vereen 1995), exemplify the literal use of the mask in performance to connect to their audiences while following the scripts of racist restrictions. Williams, starting the minstrel in 1893 and dubbed by director and actor Robert Townsend as the "Jackie Robinson of show business" for his unprecedented crossover into white mainstream audiences, reached both black and white audiences with his ability to render the stereotypical

Sambo character, as Mel Watkins suggests, "more human." Commenting on William's actual sadness beneath the paint, W.C. Fields notes the contingent duality for the blackfaced performer: "he was the funniest man I ever saw … and the saddest man I ever met." His acts demonstrate the skill with which black performers don comedic guise against the backdrop of racial hatred.

Although performers like Bert Williams set a precedent for his billing in all-white casts in white theatres, other black entertainers honed their craft through the Theatre Owners Booking Association (TOBA), also known as the chitlin' circuit, a series of theatres owned by white booking agencies designated for black performers and black audiences. In 1921, Jackie Mabley joined the vaudeville circuit under the guidance of husband and wife duo Butterbeans and Susie. The stories behind the exact reason for Mabley joining show business have varied. However, one version of a story Mabley tells is recalled by Elsie Williams in her seminal text, *The Humor of Jackie Moms Mabley* (1995). Williams notes "[Mabley] was nearly snatched […] by a white woman who so admired her ability to handle a surly youngster in a department store that the woman (the boy's mother) wanted to take her home" (p. 70). Mabley's response: "I don't do no domestic!'" (p. 70). Despite her resolution that she "don't do no domestic," Mabley would use her own grandmother – her "granny" – as her inspiration, crafting a domestic on-stage caricature.

Her name change from Loretta Mary Aiken to Jackie Mabley is also subject to its own versions of story, but one story remains that she took the name of a boyfriend, Jack Mabley at the time. Williams cites Mabley joking that he "'took a lot off her,' so at least she could take his name" (p. 42). Her nickname "Moms" came from her fellow performers who acknowledged Mabley's maternal tendencies off the stage. Adding the "s" as Elsie Williams states, "in the African American community […] commonly suggests endearment, respect, and familial or group bonding" (p. 48). With this, Mabley sharpened her stage persona using remnants of minstrel traditions and vaudevillian variety.

Just as those performers who came before her, Mabley would specifically engage African and African American traditions like the trickster takes, modernizing them to reach her various audiences. Conscious and aware of her limits as black and as a woman, particularly within the real context of whites lynching blacks by the hundreds, Mabley's performance as matriarch allows for a rebellious discourse within the presumably harmless granny, trickster frame. In her 1965 stand-up recording *Now Hear This* (1965), Mabley takes her audience through the story of Willie who has the job of driving a white woman to her home after she has had too much to drink. As Willie arrives at the woman's home, Mabley narrates the scene:

> So he took her home and got her to the door. She say, "Pull off my coat." So Willie pulled off her coat. "Pull off my dress, Willie." Willie pulled off her dress. "Willie, pull off my girdle," and she say, "And NEVER let me catch you with them on again. *YOU UNDERSTAND?!*"

The scene acquaints the audience with a familiar scene of a black male driver and white female passenger/client. But Mabley plays into the audience perception of the taboos surrounding black male and white female sexual relations. She allows the scene to escalate and then in true trickster-like fashion pulls the rug from under her audience. As a cross-dressing man, Willie is rendered harmless to the white woman. Mabley's play with words aligns with the African and African American trickster storytelling traditions, and as Williams states, "[he] is no longer a threat, and the trickster's deception allows Moms to back away from the racially controversial and taboo to the safety of accommodationism" (1995, p. 97). Further, Mabley's use of this trickster mask allows her space to imagine and reinvent old narratives. While the white woman is still in charge of Willie, indicated in her directives and in her authoritative stance as Willie's passenger, Mabley imagines different identities for the black male. The presupposed representations of black male as predatory, rapist are subverted while simultaneously inviting an otherwise privatized discourse on male sexualities. Williams states, "Mabley's trickster's antics provide us with […] three possibilities: to laugh at the trickster, at the tricks he plays on others, and most of all, at the implications his activities and behavior have for us" (p. 97). Within African and African American traditions and the seemingly restrictive gendered grandmother role, Mabley makes us consider sociopolitical possibilities while we laugh.

Beyond her trickster guise, Mabley's connections to African American comedic traditions emerge out of the troubles of her personal story. In a world where women are not supposed to be funny, Mabley would wear the mask that grins, hiding the realities of her real life challenges. Mabley's presumed, double silence as black and as woman – a notion Sojourner Truth's 1851 rhetorical proclamation "Ain't I A Woman?" addresses – surfaces in fragmented stories. The facts around Mabley's early life remain unconfirmed, but many reports indicate that Mabley's father died when she was 11 and soon after she was raped twice, by an older black man and later by a white town sheriff, both resulting in pregnancies. Many scholars of African American humor offer that Mabley's tragic and dismal background systemically align with African American traditions of "making a way out of no way," and the collective use of humor or the sorrow song[4] to cope with tragedy. And while we may struggle nailing down the details of Mabley's life – even her birth date is tenuous as some reports indicate it as 1894, while others, including Moms herself, at times note it as 1897, paralleling many slaves who could not pinpoint their exact date of birth – we can link her story to a collective African American experience. The imprecision surrounding Mabley and her upbringing again offer the metaphor of the mask that grins and lies. On stage, Mabley developed singing acts, a soft shoe routine (which later in her career became known as the "Moms shuffle"), monologues, and stand-up comedy eliciting laughter through the pain often linked to the realities of racial and gendered hatred.

All Mr. Moms' Children: Making Moms, Telling Jokes, and Engendering Change

> Kris Kristofferson: I think we got to get down to business. They're making motions.
>
> Jackie Mabley: Is they? Well wait a minute wait a minute wait a minute. I never could work with my teeth. [turns to remove teeth]
>
> *(1974 Grammy Awards)*

By the time Mabley delivered these lines, she was a well-established performer with a career spanning six decades, whose audience had grown accustomed to her grandma antics. This 1974 Grammy Awards ceremony would be Mabley's final live television appearance, but the comedy and rhetorical devices at play would endure. For Mabley, her comedy takes shape before she even utters a word. Recognizable by her floppy hat, her floral housecoat, her oversized shoes, and, of course, her missing teeth, Moms' costuming rhetorically renders her a harmless grandmother. Taking out her teeth, mumbling her words and playing into difficulties hearing align with this figure of the grandmother. Mabley's jokes rely on the miscommunication often prevalent due to the physical shortcomings of getting older, as she would often direct her audience in her routines with comments like "you know Moms can't see good." Aligning herself with this inability to see or to hear well, Mabley's physical incapability – presumably due to her old age – grants her an excuse to carry on with what we may deem inappropriate topics of conversation.

Using the attributes that stereotypically characterize an old woman, Mabley looks like your mother and makes the audience laugh while broaching lascivious content in one dose and political wisdom in another. Her "jaw jokes" demonstrate this trope of having difficulty hearing while delivering sexually suggestive material. In Mabley's concert, *Live at the Greek Theatre* (1971), she delivers one of the many versions of this joke:

> I was going to Seattle, I will never forget as long as I live – I got on the plane to New York, got as high as the Empire State, somp'n went "clink 'em" in my head. And my head stopped up. "BOP!" I couldn't hear nothin'! [the flight attendant] say, "Moms chew this chewing gum; maybe that will help you!" I chewed it; it didn't help me none. Oh, my head kept on turning 'round when we flew over the Great Rockies! My head was hurting … I say, "Honey, do something for me, I feel like I'm dyin'.'" She say, "Moms, drop your jaws!" And I misunderstood her, you know? [laughter] I caught a terrible cold, I did. [laughter]

Here, through enthymeme, Mabley plays on her ears being clogged from the air pressure of the flight but also on the idea that the character of the old woman may be hard of hearing. In other renditions of this joke, Mabley plays specifically on her old age as result of her difficulty hearing. The phrase "drop your jaws," for Mabley and her audience, becomes "drop your drawers." Mabley thus evokes a sexually suggestive image of her dropping her "drawers" or underwear without having to say so explicitly (Mabley never used direct obscenities in her comedy routines). Furthermore, the physical clogging of the ears as a result of the air pressure and Mabley's continued play on being hard of hearing permits a type of vulgarity through the grandmother frame. The old woman get-up facilitates the guise of the fool and allows the audience to gather the sexual suggestiveness of the joke.

The drastic distinction between her on-stage costume and her off-stage character further signals Mabley's calculated use of the grandma persona as a form of rhetoric predicated on sexual and gender restriction. "Well, we all called her Mr. Moms," Billy Mitchell notes during our 2014 phone conversation. Billy Mitchell, more aptly known as "Mr. Apollo," was Mabley's former errand boy when he was 15 years old. He currently serves as the historian at the world famous Apollo Theater in Harlem, giving tours of the theatre every day. Without any initial prompting and upon hearing my project on Mabley, Mitchell begins our conversation with this particular characterization of Mabley. Throughout our exchange, Mitchell insists that Mabley's on-stage persona may have been Moms, but off-stage, he asserts, she was "Mr. Moms." "She loved women," he continues, "and she had lots of them."

Correspondingly, many of her fellow performers note that, off the stage, Mabley was like "one of the guys." In the 2013 HBO documentary *Whoopi Goldberg Presents Moms Mabley*, Norma Miller, a dancer and fellow performer who shared a dressing room with Mabley and Mabley's girlfriend, notes that "she was Moms on that stage, but when she walked off that stage, she was mister Moms." Miller continues, "There was no question about it. She really was mister Moms. We never called Moms a homosexual [...] we never called her gay; that would never fit her [...] we just called her Moms." Similarly, photographs of off-stage Mabley with fellow performers show her wearing predominantly men's clothing with short, almost tapered hair. Other performers recall that Mabley off-stage always had women hanging from her arm, supporting Mitchell's anecdotes. And while the politics of Mabley's sexual identity is not an area currently studied at length or one that I engage at length here, its implications speak to her rhetorical savvy. Enough can be said, based on this peer observation, to note Mabley's on-stage and off-stage distinction present rhetorical guise to reach an audience who recognize women in limited terms as maternal.

"By choosing the guise of the grandmother," Elsie Williams writes, "Mabley honors the matriarchate, described by E. Franklin Frazier's *The Negro Family in the United States* as 'the guardian of the generation'" (1995, p. 75). The universal sense of recognition of the grandmother figure is furthered as we consider the black female identity in America. As a black woman emergent in the U.S., Mabley's public identity is always connected to a racial history. Williams cites Frazier's study noting his emphasis on the intersections of Mabley's identity with the racial history of slavery:

> The grandmother's prestige and importance were as great among slaves on the plantation as her influence and services were in the master's house. Being the oldest head in the maternal family, the grandmother was on hand for the birth of both black and white children and functioning as parents for the orphaned and abandoned children as well.
>
> (p. 75)

Thus, the rhetorical stage-effect invokes a complex familiarity rooted in the historical roles for black women. Audiences can recognize the grandmother and more specifically the black grandmother as kin-like or familial. Mabley plays on this history and the social restrictions for black women addressing black and white audiences alike as "all Moms' children" in her stand-up routines. She assumes a sense of maternal authority through this framework. Addressing her audience as her children as their grandmother, she explicitly takes up the task, as she puts it in her 1969 appearance on the *The Merv Griffin Show*, of delivering "nothin' you ain't gone hear in the street." Connecting this maternal authority to "the streets" Moms supplies a type of bawdy humor that merely serves to teach or to "hip" her audience, as she would term it.

In *Black Macho and the Myth of the Superwoman,* Michelle Wallace (1999) highlights four positions slave women were permitted to occupy: physical laborers, house servants, sex partners for their masters, and mammies. Assessing the roles of black women in film, Donald Bogle's *Toms, Coons, Mulattoes, Mammies, and Bucks: An Interpretive History of Blacks in American Film* (1973) notes that black women were relegated to the mammy or servant roles. The mammy figure, Bogle describes, "is distinguished by her sex and her fierce independence. She is usually big, fat, and cantankerous" (p. 9). Yet Moms Mabley would use the limited racist imaging of the black female and traditions of slave systems to deliver political messages in her comedic performances. Elsie Williams proposes that this Moms persona "represents a kind of virtuosity of the mammy anachronism" (1995, p. 99). Her use of this figure is not to replicate, but to reinvent it using its reference. Through it, Mabley establishes a familiarity engendering a sense of agency that allows her to speak on topics in the public space of the stage on issues women traditionally cannot address without confronting patriarchal vitriol.

The thematics of Mabley's jokes often took on real issues concerning the politics of sex, gender, and race. In *Moms Mabley at the White House Conference* (1966), Mabley constructs an imaginative space on stage that speaks to political authority and voices immediate political concerns:

> Just come back from the White House Conference. Oh, I was there, baby, I was there! [laughter] Me and LBJ [more laughter] He said, "Mom I'm glad to see ya!" […] I said, "Daddy I been wanting to ooze down here for

a long long long time." He said, "Well I can say that you welcome." I said, "Oh thank ya very much." 'Bout that time some ole big mouth senator come up with that ole bushy hair [...] [Mabley mumbles imitating his speech] I say, "SHUT YO MOUTH!" [laughter] "Please, if you will. All I want you to do is sign that President's Civil Rights Bill! That's all I want you to do." [applause]

On the stage, Mabley uses the imaginative space through her narration to speak back to oppressive institutions through the frame of the grandmother. Her meeting with President Lyndon Johnson constructs a platform for her character to speak directly to political issues, specifically within the context of civil rights. But off-stage political figures like John F. Kennedy, Martin Luther King Jr., and Adam Clayton Powell Jr. would meet with Mabley, inviting her to conferences to speak on such issues. Mabley's rhetorical posture on-stage as the harmless yet authoritative grandmother gains her access to tell political figures to "shut up" and do what she says to do, reminiscent of mothers telling children to eat their vegetables because she said so. Further, Mabley is able to harness the real-life black sociopolitical rage within the context of the civil rights movement and the black power movements of the 1960s. Yet this sense of rage is palatable for white audiences, despite Mabley yelling, "SHUT YO MOUTH," presumably because it comes from Moms.

If we think of Mabley as incongruously playing into the mammy while simultaneously critiquing an outmoded U.S., we can consider her stand-up comedy as participating in what Kimberly Wallace-Sanders calls for in her 2008 text, *Mammy*. Wallace-Sanders's book looks to reconfigure conceptions of the mammy as a static figure, arguing, "It might be most useful to think of the mammy as a multifaceted prism used to illuminate a continuous spectrum of American views and attitudes about racial hierarchy" (p. 12). Mabley's stand-up does this most directly, giving voice to black female identities previously rendered static, silent, and subservient.

"No Damn Mammy, Moms!": An American Grammar Lesson and Rhetorical Re-Invention

Let's face it. I am a marked woman, but not everybody knows my name. "Peaches" and "Brown Sugar," "Sapphire" and "Earth Mother," "Aunty," "Granny," God's "Holy Fool," a "Miss Ebony First," or "Black Woman at the Podium": I describe a locus of confounded identities, a meeting ground of investments and privations in the national treasure of rhetorical wealth. My country needs me, and if I were not here, I would have to be invented.

(Hortense J. Spillers)

This opening paragraph to Hortense J. Spillers's 1987 "Mama's Baby, Papa's Maybe: An American Grammar Book," addresses the phenomenon that is the black female body. But more aptly for Spillers, this excerpt reveals the phenomena happening upon the black female body. In this seminal article, Spillers surveys the "ungendering" of the black female captive, delineating the "flesh" from the "body" – with flesh coming before the body – to highlight the rupture between the two at the moment of captivity. The black female captive body, for Spillers undergoes the violence of ungendering as she becomes a body for reproduction of cargo rather than a woman reproducing children. Thus motherhood and matrilineal connections are for Spillers a "misnaming" of relation; when we speak of the enslaved person, we perceive that the dominant culture, in:

> a fatal misunderstanding, assigns a matriarchist value where it does not belong; actually *misnames* the power of the female regarding the enslaved community. Such naming is false because the female could not, in fact, claim her child, and false once again, because the female could not, in prevailing social climate as a legitimate procedure of cultural inheritance.
>
> (p. 80)

This misnaming for Spillers reproduces a cycle of violence as it refuses to address the calculated rupture of a dominant, symbolic, familial structure as a material trauma of slavery. And while Mabley's comedy happens after slavery, we can argue that her rhetoric dwells in slavery's direct history and its stinging trauma. Here, it is appropriate to note that: in addition to Mabley modelling her Moms persona after her own grandmother, her grandmother was also a slave. Through her maternal guise, Mabley's stand-up works to rename and reconfigure this "misnaming" that Spillers addresses. Just as Kimberly Wallace-Sanders's *Mammy* calls for an exploration of the dynamics of the stereotypical mammy figure as a way to explore national perspectives, Mabley's comedy offers a distinct brand of dynamism. I argue that Mabley's stand-up produces a new American grammar concerning black female identity. While Spillers negotiates a landscape pre-dating Mabley's antics, I suggest that Mabley is doing the linguistic and rhetorical work, redressing the ruptures between the body and the flesh while mobilizing static representations of black women. In this section, I look to ways Mabley actively writes a new identity distinct from previous inscriptions on black female identity.

Mabley's reinvention takes place at the physical level in her maternal costuming and in the imaginative storytelling of her jokes. In her stand-up routine recorded on the comedy album *Moms Mabley at the White House Conference* (1966), Mabley narrates an encounter in the south with the Ku Klux Klan. She often encounters the Klan in her jokes, re-imagining the oppressive group. Acting as narrator, she asserts an authority and also resituates the Klan in her jokes as inferior through her language:

> Come right back from the conference and had to go back down home. Had to go back down there [...] them people down there terrible [...] Rough down there, baby [...] it's impossible down there. Man, I swear them people think we still have to mind them, do what they say *do!* Some ole

Klan come talkin' about: "Mammy." I said, 'no damn mammy, *Moms,* I don't know nothin' 'bout no log cabin; I aint never seen no log cabin – split level in the suburbs, *Baby!*"

Mabley constructs this dialogue with the Klan figure as both a reference to prevalent racist imaging of the black female, and scratches out this labeling, staging a reinvention, declaring it's "Moms!" This grammar lesson for the Klansman operates twofold; it asserts previous, historical assumptions while it performs a renaming. Mabley stresses an antiquated sensibility connected to the Klansman with her use of the word "ole" to mean "old," but also makes visible a moment of reclamation and reinvention. Her assertion of the word "Moms" as her proper name, inscribes a new name where Spillers suggests was a previous misnaming. Not necessarily "Mom," but instead "Moms," Mabley inserts a new brand of maternity through this linguistic variation. Mabley uses this restricted representation of black female identity to strike one anew. The fact that she "ain't seen no log cabin," furthers this detachment, and the declaration that she lives in a "split-level in the suburbs," re-imagines and resituates black female identities in new spaces. Addressing the Klan as "baby," speaks to the vernacular of the time, but also infantilizes the patriarchal, oppressive, violent figure of the Klansman within mother-child dialectic. Mabley takes the previous passivity of black female identity, which Spillers highlights as one that "would have to be invented," and actively writes her own identity. While she does not eradicate the history of oppression, her reinscription and self-writing gain political agency through her stand-up.

Anyone who knows Mabley knows her "old man jokes." These jokes take on a distinctly active role in re-imagining black female identity, asserting sexual choice and sexual agency. Elsie Williams suggests that this "feminist position […] challenges the double standard which society has traditionally respected in allowing the male to choose a marital partner often much younger than himself, while holding the female in contempt who exercised the same freedom" (1995, p. 80). Through this storyline of wanting "no old men," Moms constructs a feminist discourse that subverts and resists patriarchal hegemony. Further, this narrative that refuses prescribed relationships incites a narrative of choice concerning black female sexuality. Whereas the black female body is historically a site of sexual violence, representing the very lack of consent or even personhood, Mabley, through her brand of humor, subverts this passive position. These "old man jokes" strategically gender and sexualize the black female body in ways that garner authority. Mabley continually jokes that she does not want an old man repeatedly stating, "Anytime you see me with an old man, I'm holding him for the police." Here, this outright refusal of an old man, not only inserts consent and authority, historically denied from black women, but she also furthers her control as she holds him for the police. Mabley's stand-up creates a space for the police as a form of penalty for the old man, redressing a history of male sexual aggression and violation toward black women.

In a 1969 live television performance on the *Merv Griffin Show*, Mabley delivers a stand-up routine referencing this old man who frequents her jokes. She says, "Childrens always askin' me, they say, 'Moms what is it like to be married to an old man?' I say, 'honey the only way I can explain it: it's like pushin' a Cadillac … up a steep hill … with a rope.'" Mabley as Moms, addressing her children, takes on the taboo topic of male impotency and female sexual needs. The substitution for the impotency of the old man's genitalia for the image of pushing a Cadillac up a hill with a rope, not only works to comedic affect, but it also invites a public dialogue around a topic traditionally off-limits for women on the stage. Mabley's continual revocation of this old man, a man who in previous jokes she says that her father picked, so he should marry him, engenders a sense of choice for women.

Mabley's reinvention takes place both as grammar lesson for the fictitious Klansman and through an assertion of sexual choice. Not merely a passive receptacle "to be invented," Mabley actively becomes the inventor. Spaces for new black female identities emerge through Mabley's rhetoric. Crossing out previous, limited prescriptions of identity, Mabley's stand-up speaks from the silences to re-imagine, re-invent, and assert agency.

Conclusion

… At seventy-some odd, bind my tongue and bind my feet?

[…] Thus did Miss Mabley stand
real and risqué
to do her do
to say her say
and let her seventy blessings sway …

          didn't lose
          the
              beat.

(Julia Fields, "Cue," 1976)

Using the "seventy-some odd" costume of grandmother, Jackie Moms Mabley demonstrates how roles designated to confine can engender avenues for voice and possibility. Snubbing those old men, dropping her "jaws," and refusing to work with her teeth, Mabley would show a generation that looks can be deceiving. Her politically laced jokes often hit the hardest concerning issues of race and sexuality. The harmless facade of our little old grandmother facilitated a discourse that would reinvent and reimagine black identity on and off the stage.

We can see the influence of Mabley in successive comedians. Eddie Murphy's grandmother character in the 1996 film *The Nutty Professor* takes up Mabley's persona. With similar deep voice and familiar no-holds-barred demeanor, Murphy's grandmother, as he notes in a 2013 interview for the HBO documentary on Mabley (Goldberg 2013), invokes Mabley directly. Nearly 75 years after Mabley crafted Moms, Murphy's performance emphasizes Mabley's rhetorical endurance and her continued dialectic with African American traditions of humor.

Occupying what seems limited representation for black women, offers Mabley space to speak. By directly invoking the stereotyped figure of the mammy, Mabley rewrites narratives of oppression evidenced in the Klansman sketch. Further, Mabley's stand-up becomes a space for redress. While we cannot eradicate the brutal incidents of slavery, Mabley makes visible the capacity to reclaim and recuperate identities rendered passive and inert. Mabley's participation within traditions of African American humor furthers a dialectic of collective resistance that can take shape in unlikely spaces. On the public stage in historically private registers, Mabley's politics harness a racialized dissatisfaction with concomitant Jim Crow politics and assert a sexual agency for women denied such choice.

For Mabley, her comedic savvy played into social restraint in order to make social change. Her impact remains viable in contemporary comedic performances and still influences a discourse that stirs political engagement in issues of sexuality, gender, and race. As Moms, Mabley could say it plain. And, just as Fields's poem notes, Miss Mabley "[stood] real" against the pressures for women, and she "didn't lose [her] beat."

Notes

1 Hush harbors were spaces slaves gathered to practice religious traditions in secret away from the white slaver owners as many of the practices were forbidden. These harbors allowed slaves to speak freely and uncensored.
2 Maria Diedrich, Henry Louis Gates Jr., and Carl Pedersen (1999) note, "The most comprehensive (and to date accurate) work has been carried out by Philip Curtin, who estimated that a total of 10 to 11 million slaves were brought to the Americas from Africa. Of that number, more than 85 percent were brought to the Americas from Africa" (p. 6).
3 Williams (1995) notes "Survivalist humor provides innumerable stories of slaves using their wit as barter for some advantage or gain […] By becoming amusing darkies who entertained the master and their guests, [the slaves] found themselves a new identity and a way out of the field, assuring themselves […] elevated status […] Whereas the humor of the plantation survivalist was characterized by the masking of mores and developed out of a conscious effort on the part of the slaves to direct the course of their lives in a potentially hostile environment, accommodationist humor was first directed by the slavemasters themselves and only later appropriated by the slaves themselves" (pp. 13–15). Minstrelsy is an example of accommodationist humor.
4 Frederick Douglass, in his 1845 *Narrative of the Life of Frederick Douglass, An American Slave*, addresses the misconception of slaves singing as a mark of their happiness, noting, "it is impossible to conceive a greater mistake. Slaves sing most when they are most unhappy" (1960/1845, p. 28). These "sorrow songs" as W.E.B. DuBois later terms them (1961) emphasize a coded culture, obscured from white gaze and convoluted with communal stories.

References

Bogle, D. (1973). *Toms, coons, mulattoes, mammies, and bucks: An interpretive history of blacks in American films.* New York: Viking Press.

Diedrich, M., Gates, H.L. & Pedersen, C (Eds.). (1999). *Black imagination and the middle passage.* New York: Oxford University Press.

Douglass, F. (1960/1845). *Narrative of the life of Frederick Douglass: An American slave.* Cambridge, MA: Belknap Press.

DuBois W.E.B. (1961). *The souls of black folk.* New York: Fawcett Publishing.

Dunbar, P.L. (1993). *The collected poetry of Paul Laurence Dunbar.* J.M. Braxton (Ed.). Charlottesville: University Press of Virginia.

Fields, J. (1976). *A summoning, a shining.* Charlotte, NC: Red Clay Books.

Garner, R., Palmer, G., & Vereen, B. (1995). *Vaudeville* [Motion picture]. New York, NY: Thirteen WNET.

Goldberg, W. (Director). (2013). *Whoopi Goldberg presents Moms Mabley* [Motion picture]. HBO Docs.

Mabley, J. (1961a). *Moms Mabley at the Playboy Club* [Sound recording]. Chicago: Chess.

Mabley, J. (1961b). *Moms Mabley at the UN* [Sound recording]. Chicago: Chess.

Mabley, J. (1963a). *I got somethin' to tell you* [Sound recording]. Chicago: Chess.

Mabley, J. (1963b). *Young men, si, old men, no* [Sound recording]. Chicago: Chess.

Mabley, J. (1965). *Now hear this* [Sound recording]. Universal City, CA: Mercury Records.

Mabley, J. (1966). *Moms Mabley at the White House Conference* [Sound recording]. *Chicago: Chess.*

Mabley, J. (1971). *Moms live at the Greek Theatre* [Sound recording]. Universal City, CA: Mercury Records.

Spillers, H.J. (1987). Mama's baby, papa's maybe: An American grammar book. *Diacritics, 17*(2), 64–81.

Wallace, M. (1999). *Black macho and the myth of the superwoman.* New York: Verso.

Wallace-Sanders, K. (2008). *Mammy: A century of race, gender, and Southern memory.* Ann Arbor: University of Michigan Press.

Watkins, M. (1994). *On the real side: Laughing, lying, and signifying: the underground tradition of African-American humor that transformed American culture, from slavery to Richard Pryor.* New York: Simon & Schuster.

Williams, E.A. (1995). *The humor of Jackie Moms Mabley: An African American comedic tradition.* New York: Garland Publishing.

RESPONSE: STAND-UP AND IDENTITY

LAUGHING AT OTHERS

The Rhetoric of Marginalized Comic Identity

Joanne Gilbert

When asked why I left stand-up comedy in order to be a college professor, I responded that once I had played to inebriated crowds at three in the morning, there was very little that 18-year-olds could do at three in the afternoon to faze me. Surprisingly, it turns out that they can, a fact that has caused me to view students as potential hecklers. My favorite high school teacher once said, "A classroom is like a comedy club; in both places, the audience is saying, 'Entertain me. If I learn something, that's O.K., as long as I'm having a good time.'" And as those of us who make our home in academia know all too well, our students can be a very tough crowd. We claim to focus on critical thinking, and yet we will try anything to capture and maintain our students' attention. Indeed, we often simultaneously lament a lack of student engagement and offer up *infotainment*[1] in hopes that our students might learn while laughing.

    I approach the study of humor from the dual perspective of educator and former practitioner. My work on marginal performance focuses on the way female comics rhetorically construct and perform their marginality onstage, educating audiences with their distinctive brand of cultural critique. A unique discourse, as an *antirhetoric*,[2] humor simultaneously advances agendas and disavows its own impact; consequently, the comic frame liberates even as it labels incisive social criticism "just a joke." In the hands of skilled comics – especially those whose identities relegate them to society's margins – humor is an epistemological lens, one that affords a critical perspective otherwise unavailable to mainstream audiences. The three chapters in this part explore marginal comic identities, deepening our understanding of the complex and nuanced cultural critique these comics provide. In order to elaborate on the way comedic performance of marginality simultaneously educates and entertains, this chapter offers a response to the three previous chapters by first considering the authors' contributions, next, discussing the shape-shifting rhetoric of a fourth comic, Wanda Sykes, and finally, suggesting the importance of communal laughter.

The "Bicultural Otherness" of Margaret Cho

Scholars of humor have long been fascinated with the way comic identities perform a deft rhetorical feat in the public sphere, scrutinizing taboo topics with a unique rhetorical lens and license for social criticism (Gilbert 1996; 2004; 2014; 2015; Mintz 1987; Zijderveld 1982). The preceding three chapters explore precisely this phenomenon, featuring performers who leverage their marginal subject positions in order to expose the hypocrisy, bias, and taken for granted assumptions that characterize much public discourse. Although the stand-up comics examined in each chapter differ from one another markedly in terms of both demographic markers and rhetorical style, all three serve as exemplars, performing their marginality in innovative and powerful ways.

Focusing on Margaret Cho, Lowrey and Renegar explain that as the only female Korean American comic working in the United States, not only is Cho the first Korean American comic many audiences have seen, but also the first popular Asian comic to command a sizable fan following in the U.S., a fact emphasized by her recently bestowed title, "Number One Asian American Comedian of All Time." Navigating the vicissitudes of a career spanning over two decades, the authors maintain, has allowed Cho to create a distinctive comedic persona who engages in cultural critique through performing bicultural otherness, ironic essentialism, and stereotypical self-deprecating humor. Although a substantial body of humor scholarship analyzes the strategic self-deprecation routinely employed by marginal comics (Barreca 1991; Boskin and Dorinson 1987; Fraiberg 1994; Gilbert 2004; 2014; Horowitz 1997; Mintz 1987; Walker 1988), and stereotypes certainly are the de facto "currency of stand-up comedy" (Gilbert 2004, p. 151), Lowrey and Renegar argue that Cho's use of these comic resources is distinct due to her unique position, living between two cultures. Indeed, this notion of "bicultural otherness" contributes significantly to our understanding of Cho's particular marginal performance.

Transforming the simultaneous criticism of being *too* Korean and not Korean *enough* from a liability into an asset, Cho uses her "outsider within" (Collins 1986) status to critique both Korean and U.S. culture. As Lowrey and Renegar note, Cho engages only in mild self-deprecation, preferring to deride cultural targets such as U.S. media bias and traditional Korean gender roles. Additionally, she uses ironic essentialism – that is, hyperbolic stereotypes – to explode the types, themselves, as in her lampooning of traditionally submissive Asian women in order to expose the inherent ethnocentrism in U.S. media. Cho herself acknowledges, "What I do ... is I take a stereotype and I enlarge it to the point where it seems ridiculous" (Fraiberg 1994, p. 324, as cited in Willet, Willet & Sherman 2012, 236–237). As Willet et al. (2012) point out, "By overplaying the stereotype, Cho asserts her agency and undermines the stereotype" (p. 237).

Although Lowrey and Renegar do not situate Cho within the historical context of female comics in the U.S. (other than a passing reference to Joan Rivers, Brett Butler, and Roseanne Barr), the tradition of successful comedic performers exaggerating stereotypes in service of critiquing those very types is well established. Jackie "Moms" Mabley, Phyllis Diller, and countless other U.S. female comics have employed this technique since vaudeville (Gilbert 2004). Consequently, it is not Cho's use of either ironic essentialism or self-deprecation that distinguishes her from numerous other marginal comics. Rather, it is her ability to straddle two distinct cultures and, in so doing, articulate a unique perspective, informing an inimitable critique. At times, Cho (2000) departs from this persona, as when discussing her performance on a lesbian cruise ship: "I had sex with a woman on the ship. And I went through this whole thing, ya know – I was like, 'Am I gaaaaay? Am I straight?' And I realized – I'm just slutty. Where's my parade?" Even when foregrounding her bisexuality rather than her biculturalism, however, Cho's performance of marginality offers trenchant social critique – this time, of the political left's typical strategy when celebrating under-recognized identities and communities.

Perhaps comics who perform bicultural otherness might serve as intercultural "change agents" (Imahori 2006) as they immerse themselves in two different cultures, reporting back to each about the other, and utilizing their "outsider within" status to the fullest possible extent. Perhaps through their humor, these comics can help bridge the gap between cultures, creating identity and community in audiences able to laugh at their own frailty and foibles. Ultimately, as Lowrey and Renegar suggest, featuring her otherness allows Cho to communicate her hybridized and complex cultural identity in a manner both instructive and entertaining. Willing to take risks and champion underrepresented groups, Cho is a critical comedic voice in contemporary culture.

The Strange Familiarity of Eddie Izzard

Like Cho, Eddie Izzard performs a marginal comic identity. As Christopher Gilbert notes, Izzard is distinct not so much because he is a self-acknowledged "card-carrying transvestite" who identifies as a "male lesbian" – a heterosexual male attracted to women – but because he uses his queer status to redress heteronormativity and critique neoliberal discourse. Gilbert argues that by using clothing rhetorically, Izzard exemplifies Burke's notion of rhetoric as "equipment for living"; foregrounding his transvestite identity via his stand-up, Izzard engages in the "queer art of making the familiar strange."

By situating marginalized gender identities within mainstream culture, "making them ridiculous, and yet reasonable," Izzard features taken for granted assumptions, exposing them as constructions. In this sense, Izzard's rhetorical clothing becomes a sort of "equipment for wearing," as he uses the accoutrements and "made up" mask of femininity to critique a culture of hyper-masculinity, engaging in "a comic modality of dressing up, undressing, and/or redressing discourse."

By literally re-dressing the wrongs perpetuated through heteronormative discursive practices such as U.S. American exceptionalism, Izzard fashions a unique comic identity extremely popular with diverse audiences.

Gilbert's rich discussion furthers our understanding of the subversive potential inherent in marginal comedic performance. By positioning his marginality as mainstream, his flamboyant dress as quotidian, Izzard performs as a member of the hegemonic group, a straight white male who is attracted to women and just happens to like wearing makeup and heels. By his own admission, Izzard is an "executive transvestite" (as opposed to a "weirdo transvestite"), a persona at once amusing and nonthreatening to heterosexual audiences. Adopting the rhetorical posture of a "reporter" (Gilbert 2004), Izzard entertains audiences with running commentary on a range of cultural phenomena. Not confrontational or aggressive like Cho and other female "bitch" or male "rebel" comics (Gilbert 2004),[3] Izzard presents his critique as just, Gilbert notes, "one of the lads." By offering cultural criticism in an appealing manner, one that renders the strange familiar, even ordinary, Izzard accomplishes something extraordinary; he evokes goodwill from an audience not predisposed to accept cross-dressing as a normative practice. Indeed, as Gilbert points out, for Izzard, transvestitism is not simply his lifestyle, but also "a resource for a comic rhetoric of transvesture insofar as it provides a way to redress the historical shortcoming in gender (and other forms of) politics."

Although metalepsis, "the rhetorical force of changes in perception or perspective," is key to much successful humor, particularly of the absurd or incongruous sort, Gilbert's assertion that Izzard's use of this device is distinct bears up when we consider the significant performative achievement Izzard delivers. In the tradition of countless successful comics whose performance of marginality grants them a license for cultural critique (Gilbert 2004), Izzard adroitly offers his audience a fundamentally new experience – one of acceptance, even admiration, of a marginal, often maligned identity in all its sartorial splendor.

The Master's Tools of Moms Mabley

Neither Margaret Cho nor Eddie Izzard could offer the marginal performances they do without comedic forerunners like the trailblazing Jackie "Moms" Mabley. As Abbey Morgan cogently argues, Mabley is a critical figure in the comic tradition not only because she was the first African American female comic to gain celebrity stature in the U.S., but also because she forged a new conception of black female identity through her subversive use of the iconic Mammy stereotype. As an early practitioner of the kind of cultural criticism that Cho, Izzard, and countless other marginal comics provide, Mabley employed the particularly pernicious persona of the docile, submissive Mammy figure in order to critique the dizzying inequalities in U.S. culture. Asserting that Mabley's singular accomplishment was "not to replicate but to reinvent" the Mammy as empowered and empowering, "giving voice to black female identities previously rendered static, silent, and subservient," Morgan underscores the key importance of Mabley's contribution.

Gaining political and sexual agency for African American women through her comedic critique of Jim Crow politics, Morgan maintains, Mabley produced "a new American grammar concerning black female identity." Situating Mabley's career within the historical context of African American humor traditions such as minstrelsy, Morgan illustrates Mabley's unique rhetorical merit. Indeed, adopting the classic "bawd" persona (Gilbert 2004), Mabley broke barriers of both race and sex; she achieved this in a manner not only palatable, but also endearing to audiences by inhabiting the guise of a lovable granny. Although known to be a lesbian ("Mr. Moms"), a good deal of Mabley's material centered upon lusting after men – hardly surprising given the cultural constraints of the mid-20th century in which she performed. It is precisely this conflation of the maternal and the hypersexual that distinguished Mabley, and these were characteristics she would help establish as common depictions of African American women in popular culture (Gilbert 2004). Simultaneously adopting the emblematic Mammy persona and critiquing the system of racial inequality it represented, Mabley deftly employed the "master's tool" to interrogate racist practices, "using the type to explode the type" (Gilbert 2004, p. 151). At once homespun and subversive, Mabley created substantial inroads for the many successful marginal comics who succeeded her.

Building upon and extending prior discussions of Mabley, Morgan emphasizes Mabley's artistry and connection to the robust tradition of African American humor. Further, Morgan elaborates the reasons Mabley is widely regarded as a comedic pioneer. Through her distinctive use of subversive rhetorical strategies, Mabley created language to name her experience, an experience shared by generations of African American women. And through naming, Mabley legitimized that experience, entertaining audiences as she educated them. Clearly, Moms Mabley is a central figure in the history of stand-up comedy; her ability to engage the dominant culture while deriding its significant political and ethical flaws even before the dawn of civil rights in the U.S. was nothing short of remarkable, and her rich legacy is evident in the acts of every marginal comic performing today.

Wanda Sykes as Rhetorical Shape-shifter

Ever since Mabley's groundbreaking work, generations of African American female comics have performed their marginality for diverse audiences, emphasizing and capitalizing upon their difference in order to launch subversive cultural critique. Primarily adopting bitch, bawd, or reporter personas, these comics have claimed a rhetorical space in the public sphere, ensuring that the dominant culture literally pays a price to be lampooned and upbraided (Gilbert 2004). On a continuum of performers from beloved *Saturday Night Live* alumna-turned academic Ellen Cleghorne[4] to the bombastic and mercurial Monique, one comic emerges as a unique blend of bitch, bawd, and reporter, a performer who has been entertaining and educating audiences with her distinctive brand of stand-up since 1987: Wanda Sykes. Employing stereotypes, making the strange familiar, and creating a new incarnation of black female sexual agency, Sykes' comic identity serves as a synthesis of the rhetorical strategies enumerated in the preceding three chapters.

In her early stand-up performances, Sykes relied on fairly traditional material, even trafficking in "dick jokes,"[5] long the standby of male comics, as illustrated in the following bit from 1998:

> My last show I did a benefit for a feminist organization … So I walk out there and I'm like, "Hey look – uh, I can't stay here too long with you broads cuz I got to get home and cook my man a nice hot dinner. And he likes oral sex by 9:45." I'm glad y'all laugh – they didn't. They didn't find anything funny. I got scared, I was like, "Oh Lord, I have made these women mad – I stepped over the line." So I was like, "Ladies, calm down – I'm just jokin' – he likes oral sex *any* time!"
>
> (Sykes 1998)

Unlike male comics, however, by using exaggerated stereotypes of humorless, man-hating feminists and submissive, subservient non-feminists, Sykes actually critiques a culture that defines women by the services they provide to men in the kitchen and bedroom. More subtle is Sykes' acknowledgment of the tension between second and third wave feminists, groups often at odds about whether women's sexualization leads to empowerment or objectification.

Like Cho and many other successful comics, Sykes also has long featured the character of her mother as the butt for a number of her jokes as evident in the following bit from 1998:

> I get a divorce … I can see my mother now: "What? Oh, oh, oh – oh, you gonna get a divorce, huh? It's just that easy, huh? Things get hard, things get rough, you just wanna throw in the towel, it's just like that. Lemme tell ya something – that's a bunch of bull – lemme tell ya something – your father and I had a *shootout*, okay? He took one in the *arm* – Harry, show her where I shot you. Now see, that's *love* right there – gotta learn how to work these things out. He was *wrong*, I shot him – you move *on*."
>
> (Sykes 1998)

Like the first bit, this material succeeds not only because of the stereotypes employed (in this case, the long-suffering, overbearing mother), but also due to the element of surprise or incongruity – the use of metalepsis.

By 2003, Sykes had developed both her bitch and reporter personas, engaging audiences with her inherent likeability. Still including a focus on sex differences as a primary source of her humor, Sykes created material with which her legions of female fans could identify, such as the following:

> For guys, sex is like goin' to a restaurant and no matter what you order off that menu, you walk outta there goin', "Damn, that was good!" …

For women, you know, we go to the restaurant, you know, you order somethin' – sometimes it's good, sometimes you gotta send it back. Sometimes, you might get food poisoning. But you have those hit and misses, you gonna wanna skip a few meals, right? "Oh, I'm not hungry today …" Or you might go, "Ya know? I think I might cook for myself today" … Guys wonder why we fake it. It's called *time management* … I don't need to be up all night workin' on somethin' I know ain't gonna happen – you just cuttin' into my sleep time now. Shoot – I'm tryin' to do us both a favor.

(Sykes 2003)

Although orgasm jokes are a staple of stand-up comedy for both male and female performers, Sykes puts a new spin on a common female complaint; through her use of metaphoric language regarding food, and her paralinguistic virtuosity portraying the cunning and cajoling female partner, she both surprises and delights her audience.

In 2006, Sykes' first HBO special (nominated for an Emmy Award in 2007), *Wanda Sykes: Sick and Tired,* brought edgier material to thousands of viewers. Her now classic "detachable pussy" bit begins with a description of "pussyless" women able to inhabit previously unsafe spaces such as a "professional ballplayer's hotel room at 2 o'clock in the morning," and moves to the testament of a friend's loyalty as Sykes calls her from a date, asking, "Look, do me a favor. Run by my house and grab my pussy. It's in the shoebox on the top shelf." The final punchline in this bit, however, serves as a critique of rape culture in its depiction of Sykes' male partner. After his entreaty, "You, uh, going out with your girlfriends, uh … guess you can, uh … leave your pussy at home. I'll watch it," and Sykes' subsequent horror, noticing upon her return the "pussy all bent out of shape," he sheepishly admits, "Uh … some of the fellas came by." Although this punchline refers to a gang rape scenario, female fans howl with laughter, apparently appreciative of Sykes' larger cultural critique, one that lambasts patriarchal structures of violence and oppression (Gilbert 2015).[6] As she does in the earlier orgasm joke, in this bit, Sykes positions her marginalized identity strategically, turning the tables on her hapless male partner as she undermines his power and privilege.

For 20 years, Sykes honed her comedic chops, following in Mabley's footsteps as she employed her race and sex in service of social criticism. As a contemporary analogue to Mabley's hypersexualized Mammy persona, Sykes' conflation of bitch, bawd, and reporter postures has allowed her to engage audiences in a nonconfrontational and nonthreatening manner. Most notably, Sykes' persona has remained consistent despite the major shift in her rhetorical focus since coming out publicly as a lesbian in 2008. In her much-celebrated 2009 HBO special, *I'ma Be Me,* Sykes performs material about her wife and kids, aging, and politics. Trebly marginalized as an African American lesbian, Sykes nonetheless succeeds in engaging her audience through marginal performance that is not only palatable, but also irresistible. Like Izzard, she makes the strange familiar; in one bit, she discusses her constant state of exhaustion as a parent:

> I'm always tired … I don't understand how people cheat, ya know, especially when they … have new kids and they cheat. Where the fuck do you get the energy to cheat? Shit … I told my wife, I said, "Look – if you *ever* catch me in another woman's bed, you know I'm just there for a *nap*."
>
> (Sykes 2009)

Like Izzard, Sykes accomplishes a significant rhetorical feat, presenting her own domestic life as unexceptional, and in so doing, defusing the stigma of difference.

In perhaps the most famous bit from this particular performance, Sykes explores the topic of coming out to her parents, turning a fraught interaction into a humorous critique of homophobia (Gilbert 2014):

> It's harder being gay than it is being black. It is because there's some things … that I had to do as gay that I didn't have to do as black. I didn't have to come out black! I didn't have to sit my parents down and tell them about my blackness. I didn't have to sit them down – "Mom, Dad – I gotta tell ya'll something – I hope you still love me – I'm jus' gonna say it – Mom, Dad – I'm black." (In her mother's voice) "What? What did she jus' say? Oh Lawd, Jesus – she didn't say black. Lawd, did she say black?" "Mom, I'm black." "Oh no, Lawd Jesus … anything but black, Jesus – give her cancer, Lawd, give her cancer – anything but black Lawd." "Mom … I'm black … that's just how it is." "No – you know what – you been hangin' around black people … and they got you thinkin' you black – they twisted your mind." "No, Mom … I'm black – that's just … how it is." "What did I do? What did I do? I knew I shouldn't have let you watch Soul Train."
>
> (Sykes 2009)

In this bit, Sykes adopts the reporter posture, peppering her narrative with the impression of her hysterical mother. In so doing, she upends heteronormativity, and presents homophobia as ridiculous. As Willet et al. (2012) note:

> her humor works to alter specific clusters of social ties and make possible new ones no longer based so sternly on taxonomies of race, class, gender, or sexuality and the toxic emotions of fear and resentment that can reinforce their normalizing power. The contagious laughter of Sykes' black lesbian humor jolts white heteros from their normative scripts.
>
> (p. 236)

Indeed, the evolution of Sykes' marginalized comic identity reveals her as a rhetorical shape-shifter, a protean figure who delivers acerbic social criticism with charm and authenticity – one who mines her own experience for the universal truths with which all audiences can identify.

Laughing at and with Others

When I was performing stand-up comedy in the mid-1980s in New York City, the "comedy boom" was in full swing as clubs proliferated and even novice comics had opportunities to perform in both urban showcase clubs and road clubs throughout the country. Ironically, cable television, the very medium largely responsible for exposing even small-town U.S. communities to live comedy, also played a factor in the "comedy bust" of the 1990s as the market became saturated and cable TV sometimes featured decidedly mediocre performers (Vanderknyff 1992). The 2010s have spawned a resurgence, however, as live comedy is, once again, a growth industry, and comics are playing arenas and stadiums around the world in what has been termed a "golden age" of comedy (Waddell 2014). In fact, business insiders are ebullient; as head of the Creative Artists Agency comedy department, Nick Nuciforo notes, "The comedy business has never been stronger" (quoted in Waddell 2014, n.p.). Despite the substantial online consumption of comedy via YouTube, it seems that there is still a place and a desire for live comic performance; although there are times for solo enjoyment of stand-up comedy via smartphone or tablet, being part of a live audience is a fundamentally different experience, one that involves membership in a community of laughers. Because the genre of stand-up comedy is inherently interactive, and because humor is the only discourse that requires an audience in order to be legitimized through laughter (Gilbert 2004), this community is vital to the very existence of live comedy, a unique medium that continues to be a viable and popular form of entertainment, interaction, and, thus, social engagement and reflection.

Indeed, stand-up comedy is big business. But "Stand-up comedy is serious political and cultural business" as well (Thomas 2015, p. 105). Ever since the deformed fools of ancient times parlayed their marginal status into a propitious form of social criticism masked as entertainment, comics have performed a critical cultural function. Within the shifting sands of identity politics, the contemporary marginal stand-up comic serves as "part time bomb and part time capsule" (Gilbert 2004, p. 176), at once preserving cultural memory and containing potentially incendiary critique. And although when comics like Cho, Izzard, Mabley, and Sykes use humor strategically and subversively, inverting power dynamics as they elicit laughter, "the subversive effect of marginal humor is *primarily* rhetorical" (Gilbert 2004, p. 178), all political action must necessarily begin with critique. As Willet et al. (2012) maintain when discussing Sykes' work, "When the ironist confronts the powers-that-be, she does not challenge this power directly but she does engage, subvert, and obliquely oppose it" (p. 236). Ultimately, then, the performance of comic marginal identity is "an exercise in power negotiation" (Gilbert 2004, p. 179), one that enlightens as it entertains, transforming public spaces through communal laughter.

Notes

1 Although Postman (1985) coined this term referring to television news and educational programming, it certainly applies to the myriad ways we use visual stimuli such as presentation software and video clips in order to attract and hold student attention.
2 See Gilbert 2004, p. 12.
3 See Gilbert 2004, Chapter 4, for a full description of Gilbert's taxonomy of female comedic postures (the kid, bitch, bawd, whiner, and reporter), as well as a brief discussion of analogous male postures, such as the rebel.
4 See Bellino 2015.
5 A "dick joke" is a joke with sexual or scatological content (Gilbert 2004, p. xiv).
6 See Gilbert 2015 for an extensive discussion of YouTube comments from Sykes' fans regarding this bit.

References

Barreca, G. (1991). *They used to call me Snow White ... but I drifted: Women's strategic use of humor*. New York: Penguin.
Bellino, D. (2015). 'SNL' alum Ellen Cleghorne on black women in comedy and what she's been up to since the show. [Web log comment]. *VH1.com*. February 16. Retrieved from www.vh1.com/news/89549/ellen-cleghorne-snl-40-black-women-in-comedy/
Boskin, J., & Dorinson, J. (1987). Ethnic humor: Subversion and survival. In A.P. Dudden (Ed.), *American humor* (pp. 97–118). New York: Oxford University Press.
Cho, M. (2000). *I'm the one that I want*. Retrieved from www.youtube.com/watch?v=183l-qkr2_w
Collins, P.H. (1986). Learning from the outsider within: The sociological significance of black feminist thought. *Social Problems*, 33(6), 514–532.
Fraiberg, A. (1994). Between the laughter: Bridging feminist studies through women's stand-up comedy. In G. Finney (Ed.), *Look who's laughing: Gender and comedy* (pp. 315–335). Amsterdam: Gordon & Breach.
Gilbert, J. (1996). Last laughs and final words: Humor and power in the Hill/Thomas hearings. In P. Siegel (Ed.), *Outsiders looking in: A communication perspective on the Hill/Thomas hearings* (pp. 107–127). New York: Hampton Press.
Gilbert, J. (2004). *Performing marginality: Humor, gender, and cultural critique*. Detroit: Wayne State University Press.
Gilbert, J. (2014). Lesbian stand-up comics and the politics of laughter. In P. Dickinson, A. Higgins, P.M. St. Pierre, D. Solomon & S. Zwagerman (Eds.), *Women and comedy: History, theory, practice* (pp. 185–197). Lanham, MD: Farleigh Dickinson Press, co-published with Rowman & Littlefield.
Gilbert, J. (2015). Members of the tribe: Marginal identities and the female comedy fan community. In A. Trier-Bieniek (Ed.), *Fan girls and the media: Creating characters, consuming culture* (pp. 57–71). Lanham, MD: Rowman & Littlefield.
Horowitz, S. (1997). *Queens of comedy: Lucille Ball, Phyllis Diller, Carol Burnett, Joan Rivers, and the new generation of funny women*. Amsterdam: Gordon & Breach.
Imahori, T. (2006). On living in between. In M.W. Lustig & J. Koester (Eds.), *Among us: Essays on identity, belonging, and intercultural competence*, 2nd ed. (pp. 270–282). Boston: Pearson Education, Inc.
Mintz, L.E. (1987). Standup comedy as social and cultural mediation. In A.P. Dudden (Ed.), *American humor* (pp. 85–97). New York: Oxford University Press.
Postman, N. (1985). *Amusing ourselves to death: Public discourse in the age of television*. New York: Penguin.

Sykes, W. (1998). *Comedy Central presents Wanda Sykes Hall*. Retrieved from www.cc.com/episodes/usyhgp/comedy-central-presents-cc-presents – wanda-sykes-season-1-ep-101

Sykes, W. (2003). *Tongue untied*. Retrieved from www.cc.com/video-clips/nqgm92/wanda-sykes – tongue-untied-always-thinking

Sykes, W. (2006). *Wanda Sykes: Sick and tired*. Retrieved from Wanda Sykes, www.youtube.com/watch?v=Jv5pjSRSLGQ

Sykes, W. (2009). *I'ma be me*. Retrieved from Wanda Sykes, www.youtube.com/watch?v=1_wWJ-_4uSY

Thomas, J. (2015). *Working to laugh: Assembling difference in American stand-up comedy venues*. Lanham, MD: Lexington Books.

Vanderknyff, R. (1992, December 16). Stand-up downfall?: Comedy: decline in club attendance in O.C. and nationally tied to recession, glut of cable shows and mediocre performers. *Los Angeles Times*. Retrieved from http://articles.latimes.com/1992–12–16/entertainment/ca-2002_1_comedy-club

Waddell, R. (2014, May 16). Comedy issue: Live comedy becomes a $300 million punchline. *Billboard*. Retrieved from www.billboard.com/articles/events/live/6091827/live-top-arena-comedy-tours

Walker, N. (1988). *A very serious thing: Women's humor and American culture*. Minneapolis: University of Minnesota Press.

Willet, C., Willet, J., & Sherman, Y.D. (2012). The seriously erotic politics of feminist laughter. *Social Research*, 79(1), 217–246.

Zijderveld, A.C. (1982). *Reality in a looking-glass: Rationality through an analysis of traditional folly*. London: Routledge & Kegan Paul.

PART II
Stand-Up, Race, and Culture

> White folks get a ticket, they pull over, "Hey officer, yes. Glad to be of help. Here you go." Nigger got to be talking about, "I AM REACHING INTO MY POCKET FOR MY LICENSE because I don't want to be no motherfucking accident!"
>
> (Richard Pryor)

4

RHETORIC OF RACIAL RIDICULE IN AN ERA OF RACIAL PROTEST

Don Rickles, the "Equal Opportunity Offender" Strategy, and the Civil Rights Movement

Raúl Pérez

> It appears that the most crucial element in the dissemination and use of ethnic humor is the perceived ambiguity of the speaker's intentions and motives by those who are its targets ... Unless the humorist or the joke-teller makes it explicitly clear that he or she is not using humor to express prejudicial attitude, bigotry, and racial and/or ethnic superiority, he or she is likely to be accused by members of ethnic groups of having such attitudes.
>
> (Mahadev L. Apte 1987, p. 27)

> That's all the Jews do, sit in their underwear, belch and watch TV [audience laughs]. The Irish guys are staggering around. The colored guys are going "glory, glory hallelujah" [audience laughs]. The Mexicans "I'm goin to da toilet I don't care what the colored guys do" [audience laughs]. And the queers are going "let's go in the park and have a love out!" [audience laughs]. These are the jokes lady. If you're waiting for Billy Graham to come in here forget about it [audience laughs].
>
> (Don Rickles 1968)

Introduction

The first half of the 20th century consisted of numerous campaigns against racial and ethnic ridicule in the U.S. Various efforts by ethnic whites – including Italian, Irish, and Jewish groups – to end the circulation of denigrating and insulting stereotypes occurred during the early part of the century (Mintz 1996; Kibler 2009). African Americans succeeded these campaigns during the early part of the civil rights movement as they contested the legacy of blackface minstrelsy and a century's worth of racist and insulting portrayals of blacks (largely by whites) as uncivilized and buffoonish (Boskin 1979; 1986). By challenging blackface comedy shows like *Amos 'n' Andy*, one of the longest running and most popular shows on radio and television until the civil rights period (Von Schilling 2003), groups like the NAACP sought to improve the public image of African Americans (Boskin 1986; Ely 1991; Haggins 2007). During the latter part of the civil rights period, Latinos continued this wave of public protest against racial and ethnic ridicule by challenging anti-Latino caricatures and stereotypes, like Frito-Lays' "Frito Bandito," a corn-chip stealing bandit, and comedian Bill Dana's Latino minstrel character "José Jiménez," a dim-witted and inarticulate buffoon (Bender 2003; Pérez 2014). The Polish American Congress would follow suit as they challenged the circulation of "Polack jokes" in media that ridiculed Polish immigrants as "stupid," "crude," and "brutish" people (Pula 1996). This wave of protests signaled a turning point in American comedy (Apte 1987; Berger 1998), one in which ethnic and racial minorities would no longer sit passively by as Anglo Americans engaged in the "pleasure of racist laughter" (Lott 2013) at their expense.

Comedian Don Rickles was able to rhetorically circumvent this growing wave of protest against racial ridicule by creating a more "ambiguous" form of racially insulting comedy (Apte 1987; Weaver 2011). In contrast to his contemporary "ethnic" humorists who targeted a particular group in their performances or careers, Rickles delivered a style of public racial ridicule that was conscious of *diversifying* the targets of ridicule in his performance. During the civil rights movement, escalated racial unrest significantly weakened the country as a "racial dictatorship," a society in which whites subordinated non-whites culturally, politically and economically (Omi & Winant 2014). Yet, at a time when fellow comedian Bill Dana was being targeted by Chicano civil rights groups for his racist portrayal of Latinos as inarticulate buffoons, comedian Don Rickles can be heard delivering a wide range of racist insults, stereotypes, and dialects in his 1968 Grammy-nominated performance *Hello Dummy!*

In this chapter, I analyze Rickles' performance as the emergence of the "equal opportunity offender" strategy. The rhetorical impact of this strategy worked to frame his insults as carrying, more or less, *equal weight* in the eyes and ears of the audience. This rhetorical strategy allowed Rickles to engage in racial ridicule during a period of intense social and political transformation of a deeply stratified U.S. society.

The goal of my analysis is not to suggest that Rickles *is* a racist or to somehow uncover his "true intentions," but rather to illustrate the rhetorical mechanisms that Rickles used to perform racial ridicule while circumventing the kind of opposition faced by his contemporaries. The "equal opportunity offender" strategy worked rhetorically, I contend, to veil Rickles' comedy as ambiguous rather than racist and helped preserve his status as a revered stand-up comic from the civil rights era to the present. Rickles would come to face some criticism for his comedy, and would later "tone down" his act, but he largely escaped the kind of public scrutiny, boycott and protest faced by fellow comedians and comedy shows. That is, Rickles' comedy illustrates the rhetorical efficacy of the "equal opportunity offender" strategy to veil racial insult and ridicule as palatable and "just a joke," even during periods of intense ethnic and racial conflict.

An analysis of Rickles' comedy points out *how* comedic racial ridicule changed from the pre-civil rights period to the present. In recent years this influential rhetorical strategy has been increasingly incorporated, among white comedians in particular, as a way to make racial and ethnic ridicule once again acceptable in the eyes and ears of an audience.

White Comedians and Race

The general strategy employed by whites to produce ethnic and racial "humor" during the pre-civil rights era largely consisted of overt racial ridicule (Boskin and Dorinson 1985; Lott 2013). Until the civil rights movement, white performers typically built their routines around racial and ethnic ridicule and insult targeted at a particular racialized group. Blackface minstrelsy was the most prominent example as it was one of the most popular forms of entertainment in the U.S. from the pre-civil war period until the civil rights era (Boskin 1986). In this comedic genre, white performers, including ethnic whites, painted their faces black and portrayed African Americans as inferior, buffoonish, child-like and un-assimilable (Lott 2013; Rogin 1998; Roediger 1999). While ridicule of working class European immigrants was also a part of this discourse of "othering" through comedy (Kibler 2009; Mintz 1996), by the early 20th century the boundaries between white and non-white were more rigidly defined as white ethnic minorities were increasingly "becoming white" (Brodkin 1998; Ignatiev 2008; Jacobson 1998; Roediger 1999), and their ethnic identity became an "option" they could celebrate or hide (Waters 1990). Blackface minstrelsy greatly contributed to this assimilation process by allowing ethnic whites, like the Irish and Jewish, to hide their ethnic identity behind a painted black face while ridiculing African Americans (Roediger 1999; Rogin 1998). By mid-20th century, white ethnic performers gained popularity through routines that targeted other non-whites.

This form of "comedy" reflects the *superiority theory* of humor, which highlights the capacity for humor to function as an oppressive discourse (Billig 2005). Racial ridicule reinforced ethnic and racial stereotypes and inequality by supporting a racial hierarchy via a "white racial frame" (Feagin 2014). Indeed, as Feagin suggests, over the last few centuries this powerful racial frame has provided a lens through which whites produce, interpret, and defend "racial stereotypes, images and emotions" that help secure "white privileges and advantaged conditions as meritorious" at the expense of non-whites (2014, p. 26).

According to Weaver (2011), this kind of racist comedy, in which a particular racial minority group was continually targeted by racial ridicule, can also be seen as a *monosemic* form of racist discourse that contained one dominant meaning or interpretation. That is, during pre-civil rights era comedy whites ridiculed non-whites. As a *uni-directional* form of ridicule that flowed down the racial hierarchy (Pérez 2014), it was later easier for targeted groups to interpret and challenge such comedy as "racist" during the first half of the 20th century, as the racist insult in these comedy routines was often overt rather than ambiguous. The difficulty of *monosemic* and *uni-directional* forms of racist comedy to "succeed" in public discourse in contemporary society,[1] when produced by whites in particular, illustrates that the rules for public race-based comedy have changed (Pérez 2013).

While a "sense of humor" is a core cultural value in the U.S., the post-civil rights period created a context in which "greater constraints" were placed on public use of racial/ethnic jokes, insults, and caricatures than at any other point in U.S. history (Apte 1987). The emerging "emphasis on cultural and ethnic pluralism," Apte contends, rendered "ethnic humor" as a controversial topic, where deployment of racial/ethnic humor by non-group members was generally disavowed.

This shift in the consumption of comedy was also reflected in its production. As Littlewood and Pickering (1998) argue, the emergence of an anti-sexist and anti-racist shift in the "alternative" British stand-up comedy scene during the early 1980s raised important questions about whether the comedy "kicked up or down" the social hierarchy (p. 295).

The vigilance of racist comedy among comedians is also apparent in the U.S context. For instance, by 1970 comedian Bill Dana abandoned his widely popular Latino minstrel character, José Jiménez, following protests by Chicano civil rights activists (Pérez 2014). Similarly, comedian George Carlin, famous for his liberal use of obscenities, legal battles over free speech in comedy, and overt criticism and ridicule of religion and American culture, expressed his refusal to do "ethnic humor" in the early 1970s, saying, "There isn't a lot that outrages me ... except racial jokes, ethnic jokes. I find nothing funny about that – just tasteless" (Ford 1974).

By the early 1990s humor scholars took notice of this shift and began to suggest it was now nearly impossible for whites to perform ethnic and racial humor in public (Apte 1987; Berger 1998). The continued difficulty for white comedians to perform offensive racial comedy in public was also evident in such examples as white comedian Ted Danson's 1993 flop when appearing in (ostensibly ironic) blackface at the New York City Friars Club (Ebert 1993) and the public apology by comedian Michael Richards following his racist rant against black audience members at the Hollywood *Laugh Factory* in 2006 (Farhi 2006). This contestation against ethnic and racial ridicule and the struggles for racial equality drastically changed the public sense of humor for white Americans in particular.

However, while true that it became increasingly difficult for whites to engage in racial ridicule during the civil rights era, comedian Don Rickles illustrates that it was not rhetorically impossible to do so. While Rickles' comedy was certainly controversial, the rhetorical ambiguity of his performance allowed Rickles to continue to perform racial insults. As Epstein (2001) notes, "[t]hese kinds of jokes drew criticism, of course. But Rickles succeeded because audiences knew he was kidding and meant no harm, though the words themselves cut deeply" (p. 224). While Epstein does not describe *how* Rickles' comedy works, he suggests that the ethnic "middle man" position of Jews in the U.S. placed Jewish comedians as "important mediators between Jews and American culture." That is, Jewish performers remained simultaneously "inside" and "outside" the Anglo

American mainstream. He contends that Jewish comedians gained "acceptance from an alien Gentile culture and did so in a way that was not threatening to middle America" (p. xi).

One way in which such comedy was not threatening to "middle America" was by continuing the tradition of racial insult, rather than redirecting ridicule up the racial hierarchy towards whites. According to Gillota (2013), this mediator position among Jewish performers created a complicated history between Jews and racial ridicule. Gillota suggests that while their status as "outsider" allowed them to continue to identify with the plight of African Americans, they remained prominent blackface performers through the first half of the 20th century. However, largely considered white following WWII, the blackface mask "began to wear thin" as Jewish performers faced increased opposition to blackface and other forms of ethnic and racial ridicule. Such contestation contributed to the distancing of Jewish performers from this genre (p. 53). Yet, Rickles' brand of racial ridicule proved that audiences were not only willing to continue laughing at offensive racial ridicule, but that they were being relieved by it.

Cathartic Racial Humor

Studies conclude the civil rights movement drastically changed public race-talk and that it is no longer publicly acceptable – for whites in particular – to make overt and offensive racist claims in public (Bobo, Kluegel & Smith 1997; Bonilla-Silva 2013). This shift in the logic of public racial discourse is illustrated by the emergence of coded or covert forms of race-talk in public and the appearance of "semantic moves" (e.g. "I'm not racist, but …") that were unnecessary in the pre-civil rights era (Bonilla-Silva 2013; Mendelberg 2001). Correspondingly, the logic of race comedy in public has changed. Comedians have learned to utilize distancing strategies in order to persuade an audience that they are not racist even as they tell racially offensive jokes (Apte 1987; Pérez 2013). Together, these changes in the acceptability of serious and humorous public racial discourse, which resulted from a mass movement for racial justice, have generated a context in which offensive race-talk in public has become socially unacceptable and increasingly taboo.

Yet, conventional theories of humor suggest that what is socially taboo tends to be an ideal candidate for humor. For instance, *relief theories* of humor suggest that laughter works as a social and psychological "safety valve" by providing release for socio-cognitive tension when expressing unacceptable discourse as a joke (Berger 1997; Morreall 2009). As Berger (1997) suggests, "however deplorable the sentiments expressed in these jokes may be from a moral standpoint, they may nevertheless be perceived as funny; indeed the very fact that such jokes may be deemed morally offensive may enhance their attractiveness as a forbidden pleasure" (p. 52). Using this approach, one way to read Rickles' performance in 1968 is as a form of cathartic comedic relief over the racial anxiety and tensions of the period.

However, who tells certain jokes and the context in which they occur is also important for the public acceptance of unacceptable public discourse. That is, the social role of "the comic" is not unlike the role of "the jester" – it provides special permissions to the individual to violate established social norms. In this way, the comedy club can be seen as an extension of Bakhtin's medieval carnival, where the rules of ordinary social discourse are temporarily inverted (Gilbert 2004, p. 59).

But again, the public scrutiny faced by comedians like Bill Dana, Ted Danson, and Michael Richards also indicate that simply being a comedian and being on a comedy stage is not a license to tell or perform racist jokes, characters, and/or commentary freely. Jokes, however offensive, must be crafted appropriately in accordance with prevailing social norms (Pérez 2013). Therefore, while the perceived identity of the joke teller and the context in which jokes are shared are significant, *how* such jokes are told is just as, if not more, important.

In order for an audience to "accept" offensive racial jokes in the post-civil rights era, there needs to be a perceived "incongruity" (Burke 1959; Gilbert 2004) between the performer as a "person" and the jokes being told. A public audience needs to believe that there is a "non-racist" person underneath the "racist comedian" (Pérez 2013). As Apte (1987) suggests, "the most crucial element in the dissemination and use of ethnic humor is the perceived ambiguity of the speaker's intentions and motives by those who are its targets" (p. 27). The ethnic and racial humor of the pre-civil rights period did not need the presence of such ambiguity or intentionality, as the subordination of non-whites during this period of "racial dictatorship" did not require their approval. However, this *monosemic* form of humor is no longer possible in public without opposition from targeted groups. Apte concludes that, in the post-civil rights period, comedians must make "it explicitly clear that he or she is not using humor to express prejudicial attitude, bigotry, and racial and/or ethnic superiority," otherwise "he or she is likely to be accused by members of ethnic groups of having such attitudes" (p. 27).

The civil rights movement created a context in which a more "ambiguous" form of racist comedy could take form. During a period in which the state responded to the victims of racial injustice with the promise of "equal opportunity," humorists like Rickles borrowed this notion and turned it on its head by seemingly *democ(k)ratizing* the targets of racial and ethnic insult. The *democ(k)ratization* of racist comedy, via the "equal opportunity offender," allowed for greater *polysemia*, or multiple interpretations and ambiguity (Weaver 2011), to take root in such discourse in the post-civil rights era, where racism generally become more elusive (Bonilla-Silva 2013). According to Weaver, this shift created a context in which there is greater ambivalence and confusion in interpreting this kind of race-based comedy as *monosemic* racist discourse. Comedians, such as Rickles, have increasingly worked to exploit this semantic-slippage, while audiences and critics attempt to decipher the "authorial intention" of such performers (p. 149).

Therefore, it is important to look at the mechanisms in operation that allow comedians to make use of racist discourse that is generally disavowed in contemporary public discourse (Lockyer & Pickering 2005; Weaver 2011). This approach will allow critical observers to highlight the special rhetorical strategies in operation that allow comedians to access offensive racial discourse in a way that is otherwise inaccessible to most other speakers in most other public contexts.

Goffman (1959) observed that individuals tend to reserve the derogation of others for when they are not present (pp. 170–175). The "backstage," he argued, provides a safe space for individuals to voice their insults and contempt of absent members. This "treatment of the absent" is sharply inconsistent with the way people generally engage with others in face-to-face "frontstage" settings. In contrast, a comedy club is a socially sanctioned space that gives license to individuals on stage to violate these social norms in public (Gilbert 2004). Comedians routinely mock, insult and derogate audience members in their performances. In what follows, I analyze the "treatment of the present" by insult comic Don Rickles in his 1968 Grammy-nominated performance *Hello Dummy!* in order to illustrate the rhetorical efficacy of stand-up comedy to breach boundaries of acceptable racial discourse in public. To my knowledge, no in-depth attempts have been made to analyze Rickles' comedy or to situate it in the context of the civil rights movement.

Methods

I use Critical Discourse Analysis to analyze the rhetorical strategies used by Rickles to perform racial ridicule during the civil rights movement. I borrow from Bonilla-Silva and Forman (2000) and van Dijk (1992; 1993) and their examination of changes in public racial discourse in the post-civil rights and post-WWII era. These and other studies have focused on the strategies used by whites to (dis)engage in public race-talk. For instance, Bonilla-Silva (2013) illustrates a number of discursive strategies used by whites and contends that a central feature of the emergent "color-blind" ideology of the post-civil rights period consists of an active avoidance by whites in using direct racial language to express their racial views (p. 102).

Building on these studies, my approach illustrates how comedians use specific rhetorical strategies and techniques to say racist things instead of avoiding them. This is due, in part, to the social role of the comedian. In contrast to social scientists who are interviewing individuals about their racial attitudes, the comedian is looking to entertain and elicit a reaction (laughter) from the audience (Apte 1987; Mintz 1985). Shocking and taboo discourse is currency in the social world of stand-up comedy, in a way that is distinct from most other public settings, as individuals generally work to "manage their identity" (Goffman 1959) by avoiding offensive discourse in public.

I also borrow from Goffman's work on "keying" to examine Rickles' comedy (Goffman 1974; 1981). This approach allowed me to decipher the strategies and techniques that made Rickles' brand of racial ridicule more palatable, as he was careful not to misstep on a land mine during his waltz of insult in a period of racial protest. I will focus on four particular strategies in the following section: *Negative Self-Presentation, Negative Other-Presentation, Audience Homogenization via Insult,* and *Appeals to Humor.*

Negative Self-Presentation

According to van Dijk (1992, 1993), one of the ways in which racism is rhetorically and discursively maintained is through "positive self-presentation." This strategy allows dominant in-groups' members to omit negative qualities and characteristics of their own group, while engaging in "negative other presentation," which emphasizes negative stereotypes and characteristics of out-groups. By highlighting perceived deficiencies of minority groups, dominant groups maintain boundaries between "us" and "other." Yet, the civil rights movement created a context in which such discourse by non-group members would be perceived as racist in public (Apte 1987; Bonilla-Silva 2013).

The use of "negative self-presentation," or self-deprecation, is an important rhetorical strategy employed by comedians to circumvent this constraint (Pérez 2013). This strategy helps close the gap between audience and joke teller by allowing the performer to "manage" his or her identity (Goffman 1959) in front of the audience. As Apte (1987) observes, "self deprecating humor is not only about one's ethnic background, but also about one's sex, religion, language, social status, and so on … It appears that such jokes, when told by the ethnic groups themselves, are acceptable. Only when outsiders tell them, do the jokes become public and not tolerated" (p. 38). This strategy is one that is consistently employed by Rickles in his 1968 recording. Take the following example early in his performance:

> I'm a Jew. We're the chosen people. We don't have to do nothing. Pick up a couple of dollars and phone God. "Hello God" [audience laughs]. Jews, you gotta be like the Jews. Just sit in the house, in your living room, in your underwear. "Put on the TV, Shirley [belches]" [audience laughs]. That's all the Jews do, sit in their underwear, belch and watch TV [audience laughs].

Rickles invokes conventional stereotypes about Jews and money throughout his routine. This strategy allows the performer to reveal unflattering and commonly shared stereotypes regarding his ethnic background, and works rhetorically by helping the performer build rapport with the audience early on. Rickles also employs other standard Jewish stereotypes such as the "hook nosed Jew" and the "Jewish American Princess," a stereotype about materialistic and sexually repressed Jewish women (Booker 1991; Dundes 1985). Take the following example directed at a female audience member:

> You've gotta be a Jew, lady. You're the only one with a stole on and it's 105 for crying out loud [audience laughter, cheers and applause]. You're either a Jew or an old beaver in heat [audience laughs].

Rickles directs his attention at a female audience member that he believes to be Jewish. Rickles insults the audience member for her presumably expensive and inappropriate attire for the event, as well as her supposed repressed sexuality. This approach reinforces the negative self-presentation strategy by targeting an audience member that presumably shares the performer's ethnic identity. Towards the end of the show Rickles revealed to the audience that he is consciously and deliberately engaging in negative self-presentation, saying, "That's right! I make fun of my own people!"

By mocking his Jewish identity, and insulting Jewish audience members, Rickles employs the negative self-presentation strategy in order to "manage his identity" before the audience. By doing so, the strategy signals to the audience that Rickles is willing to target his own group and that he does not view his own ethnic group as exempt from ridicule or primarily from a positive perspective. However, the general tendency by Rickles was to ridicule Jewish women rather than men in the audience. This illustrates the intersecting racial and gender inequalities of how ridicule is often directed down the racial and gender hierarchy.

Nevertheless, in contrast to some of his contemporary Jewish "ethnic humorists" – like Dana, who omitted his Jewish identity while he engaged in Latino minstrelsy – Rickles placed his Jewish identity as a core part of his act and mocked it. By doing so, Rickles set the stage for engaging in "negative other-presentation" during a period of increased constraint on ethnic and racial ridicule by non-groups members (Apte 1987).

Negative Other-Presentation

A central feature of Rickles' brand of insult comedy is that he presumably targets everyone. He is an "equal opportunity offender." His style of comedy earned him nicknames like "The Merchant of Venom" and the ironic title "Mr. Warmth." Indeed, in his 1968 performance Rickles proceeds to insult a number of ethnic, racial and national groups, women, homosexuals, and heterosexuals alike. This strategy distinguished Rickles from his contemporary "ethnic humorists," particularly those that continued in the minstrel tradition. His consistent and effective use of being the "equal opportunity offender" during the civil rights era signaled a cultural shift in the style of racial ridicule that would be increasingly tolerated during and after the civil rights movement.

As mentioned earlier, during this period racial ridicule became more difficult for non-group members as a result of a growing emphasis on "cultural pluralism" and opposition to racism. Yet, by engaging in negative self-presentation, a certain degree of freedom was provided for comedians to engage in "negative other-presentation." According to Apte, by telling "ethnic jokes in which *all* extant ethnic groups are made the target … the idea here is that since all ethnic groups are ridiculed, no one should take offense" (1987, p. 38, emphasis in original). That is, the rhetorical effect of this strategy is that by "insulting everyone," Rickles is ostensibly insulting "no one." Take the following examples, which follow his self-deprecating Jewish jokes above:

> The Irish guys are staggering around. The colored guys are going [African American accent], "Glory, glory hallelujah" [audience laughs]. The Mexicans [Latino accent], "I'm goin' to da toilet I don't care what the colored guys do" [audience laughs]. And the queers are going [effeminate voice], "Let's go in the park and have a love out!" [audience laughs]

Rickles employs the negative-self presentation strategy to illustrate that Jews are also targets in his act before engaging in negative other-presentation to mock the Irish, blacks, Latinos, Arabs, Polish, Welsh, Mexicans, and homosexuals. By strategically establishing that his performance is one that seemingly targets all groups, Rickles takes the liberty to ridicule groups that are presumably "off limits" during this period of intense racial conflict, blacks and Latinos in particular, saying:

> I kid about the Negros. Be proud, be proud of your heritage. We need the Negros. For what? What the hell we need the Negros for? [audience laughs] Oh yeah, so we can have cotton in the drug store [audience laughs] … Why do I make fun of the Negros? Cause I'm not one of them! [audience laughs]

And:

> Mexicans, you never fool around with the wife, right? You're too busy laying on the floor fixing the mud so it don't cave in [audience laughs]. They never fool with the wives, the Mexicans, they're walking around the house yelling [Latino accent], "Turn on the television!" [audience laughs] … But, if it weren't for you people we'd never have filth. [audience laughs]

Throughout his performance, Rickles picks out audience members and ridicules them by using ethnic, racial, and national stereotypes, banter, mimicking and mocking their dialect, language and culture, and creates absurd scenarios and imagery to generate what Freud called "tendentious jokes," or jokes that focused on topics that are socially taboo (Gilbert 2004; Seshadri-Crooks 1998), all of which were intended as "play" (Goffman 1974, p. 48). That is, part of what makes his racist jokes and banter "playful" and appealing to the audience is that Rickles is using discourse that has become socially unacceptable during the civil rights movement. Rickles circumvents opposition to his racial insults by diversifying the targets of ridicule, a strategy that works to convince the audience that his insults carry *equal weight*.

However, it is difficult to see how racial insults carry equal weight in an unequal society. Therefore, Rickles was cautious in how his racial insults were deployed. For instance, while Rickles ridiculed Latinos and blacks using conventional stereotypes and imagery, he was careful to avoid using racial slurs and master signifiers like "wetback," "spic," or "nigger" in his act. By doing so, Rickles reveals the boundary of the "playful" racism that is central to his act. As Goffman (1974) suggests:

> [A]lthough individuals can playfully engage in an extremely broad range of activity, limits on playfulness are established in various groups … Among familiars, for example, there will be appeals to "taste."
>
> *(p. 49)*

One of the effects of the civil rights movement was to make racial slurs "distasteful" in public discourse. Therefore, Rickles works to provide "keys" (Goffman 1974; 1981) or cues to the audience that distance his racial insults from literal meaning and allow the audience to interpret or "frame" his racist discourse as "play," that he is only "kidding." As Goffman (1974) observes, a "key" refers to:

> [A] set of conventions by which a given activity, one already meaningful in terms of some primary framework, is transformed into something patterned on this activity but seen by the participants to be something quite else.
>
> *(pp. 43–44)*

In this case, racism is the "primary framework" and racist jokes, seemingly, are the "something quite else." Therefore, it is not merely that Rickles is *in* a "comedy club" that gives license to *what* he utters. But it is the strategic delivery of his banter (the *how*) that veils his racial insults as socially acceptable by denying racism (van Dijk 1992) in his performance. During this sequential process of "negative self-presentation" and "negative other-presentation," Rickles rhetorically and strategically delivers his content to the audience to produce a "community of laughter" (Mintz 1985) that can readily enjoy the "forbidden pleasure" of racial and ethnic ridicule during a period of racial and ethnic protest.

Homogenization via Insult

In his analysis of stand-up comedy, Mintz (1985) observes that certain rituals need to take place in a comedy club in order for an audience to "go along" with a show. The comedian, he suggests, "establishes his or her comic persona, discussing personal background, life-style, and some attitudes and beliefs. This allows the audience to accept the comedian's marginal status and to establish that the mood of comic license is operative. This mood is accentuated by encouraging applause and laughter, thereby establishing a tone of gaiety and fun. Then the comedy routine itself can begin" (p. 79). The goal, he suggests, is to "establish for the audience that the group is *homogeneous*, a community, if the laughter is to come easily" (p. 78, emphasis added).

Based on examples provided above, Rickles' comedy detracts from this goal as his style of comedy consists of fragmenting, rather than homogenizing his audience. In his brief commentary on Rickles, Mintz provides a similar observation by suggesting that "[s]o-called 'kamikaze' comedians such as Don Rickles make the insult banter a feature of their act, but that is a special brand of stand-up comedy not necessarily connected with the process of establishing a community" (p. 79). However, Mintz does not describe *how* Rickles' "special brand" of comedy works or *how* it operates to create a "community of laughter" during his spectacle of ethnic and racial ridicule as an "equal opportunity offender."

One consistent technique used by Rickles to produce a "community of laughter" was the use of the verbal cues or "keys" that signaled to the audience that they were a "group." As Goffman suggests, "[V]ocal cues can be employed to ensure that the boundaries and character of the quotatively intended strip are marked off from the normally intended stream" (1981, pp. 174–175). Rickles provides "parenthetical" or "bracketed" statements that are intended to signal to the audience that they are a homogeneous group. Take the following example in which Rickles targets a Latino audience member and a Jewish woman:

> Look at the size of him lady. He just lays on you and you die [audience laughs]. **Look at this, the lady went** [in a shrill feminine voice], "What? The Mexican lay on me? [audience laughs]. **Anyway gang** [audience laughs] … The old Jewish lady got in heat when she heard the fat Mexican was gonna lay on her [audience laughs]. **Anyway gang**. "The hell you think's gonna happen? You won't have any kids … a taco falls out!" [audience laughs]

As illustrated in previous sections, through the rhetorical strategy of negative self-presentation, Rickles is granted license to negatively present "others." Through this process of sequential degradation, Rickles creates a seeming community of the "collectively disparaged." Audience members share a laugh at the expense of targeted groups or individuals at hand, before Rickles moves on to a new victim. In order to signal a collective affinity, Rickles provides verbal cues to "key the audience" (e.g. "anyway gang") that they are a group. This creates a "community of laughter" during his focused banter, which the rest of the "gang" can enjoy. During this process, Rickles produces different combinations of "in-groups" and "out-groups" as he rapidly shifts his attention from one target to the next. However, it is important to keep in mind that what keeps this "community of laughter" together is the cathartic release provided by the racial (and gender) ridicule that Rickles' comedy provides.

Rickles also readily changes "frames" throughout his 1968 performance, as he rapidly weaves in "unserious" racial and ethnic insults with "serious" commentary on "bigotry." This strategy is also facilitated by "keying" the audience with changes in the tone, pitch and tempo of his voice:

> [Slow paced, declarative tone] Anyway folks, we enjoy though. **We kid around, right?** It's ridiculous. With bigotry, with the Negros, with summer,

with race riots. It's idiotic, I mean that. [Faster paced, joking tone] Didn't recognize the Negro gentleman in the back. How are ya baby? As far as I'm concerned sit up front, make trouble (audience laughs). **Anyway gang.** [laughs]. **That is a Negro guy isn't it**. Cause the way things are nobody wants to say what they are today. It's the truth. You walk up to the average Negro, what do all the bigots around here say, "Are you a Negro?" [Deep voiced Caribbean accent] "No, Mr. Rickles, I am a calypso singer [audience laughs]. I come from Saint Thomas. My name is Leroy" [audience laughs] … Ever since the war, they don't say they're **Negros**. Huh. Hawaiians [audience laughs]. **Anyway gang**.

His "unserious" racial and ethnic insults are generally accentuated by multiple higher or lower pitched voices or dialects that "speak from his mouth" and tend to be faster paced. When switching over to his "serious" frame to reveal the "real Rickles," he employs a slower paced and more declarative voice that "speaks from his chest." By doing so, Rickles is "keying the audience" that his racist jokes and insults are supposed to be interpreted as "play" (Goffman 1974, p. 48). This strategy multiplies the perceived ambiguity and *polysemicity* in his comedy, as it becomes more challenging to read his comedy as primarily a form of *monosemic* racist discourse (Apte 1987; Weaver 2011).

However, while this rhetorical strategy of fragmenting and insulting the audience in order to homogenize them suggests that "everyone" is the target of ridicule and that "no one" is spared from his "wrath," Rickles' comedy tends to disproportionally "kick down" (Littlewood & Pickering 1998) the racial/ethnic and gender hierarchy. Therefore, in order to minimize opposition to his brand of insulting racial ridicule, Rickles works to remind his audience that they are "just jokes."

Appeal to Humor

Viewing humor as a rhetorical tool, Gilbert (2004) observes that a joker can shield criticism by distancing a claim and renouncing its intent by declaring it was "just a joke" (p. 12). Rickles employs this strategy numerous times throughout his performance as a refrain. For instance, in his banter with the Latino audience member early on in his show about "filthy Mexicans," Rickles makes sure to remind the audience and the target that his jokes and comments are all in "good jest":

> **No, I kid,** Henry … you're a wonderful Mexican, really. **I'm a Jew and you're a Mexican**, and I say this from my heart. A Negro can move into my neighborhood. You can't. [audience laughs]

Rickles suggests he is only "kidding" and continues to mock the Latino audience member. The rhetorical impact of his "just kidding" disclaimers, therefore, are intended to "frame" his insults as "play" and deny racism in order to appease the targeted audience member and persuade the rest of the audience into accepting that his comments are "just jokes." In another instance, a female audience member sitting near the stage distracts Rickles. Rickles uses this as an opportunity to insult her and to continue mocking the Latino audience member:

> **Don't make it a rally you dummy broad** [audience laughs]. What the hell's a matter with you? Want the Mexican to come over to your table and get the runs [audience laughs]? **It's only a joke** Mexican, you're the chosen people, we're wrong [audience laughs].

Rickles insults the woman with sexist banter by referring to her as a "dummy broad" and continues to engage in "culturally racist humor" (Weaver 2011) by ridiculing Latinos and their "diarrhea-inducing-food" as dangerous. Yet, Rickles illustrates sensitivity to the sociopolitical context and mockingly suggesting that the woman is "making it a rally" during his show while he retorts to the Latino audience member that his insults are "only jokes." Presumably finding Rickles' banter humorless, Rickles responds to the Latino audience member and his lack of amusement, asking, "Don't you find this funny, Mexican?"

This deliberate effort by Rickles to remind the audience that he is "only kidding" and that his comments are "just jokes" can also be viewed as part of the rhetorical strategy of *prolepsis* (Richardson 2007). This strategy involves anticipating and reacting to potential criticism from the audience. As illustrated above, on a number of occasions Rickles invokes this strategy when audience members can interpret his comedy and banter as offensive. In order to highlight that his racial and ethnic ridicule is intended to be "framed as play," at the end of his performance Rickles switches from a "comedic frame" (Gilbert 2004) to a "lecture frame" (Goffman 1981) and states his position on his brand of humor in his closing remarks:

> [Slow paced, declarative tone] My humor, ladies and gentleman, is directed in a way to laugh at ourselves. If you accept it in that spirit, I am deeply grateful. If there be doubt, I hope you will see us another night … I am no rabbi, priest, or reverend. You know this. I stand here and speak of all faiths, creeds, and colors. And why not, really why not? Because in my experience in the Navy, when things were rough nobody bothered or cared to ask. Color, church, synagogue. Who cared? Frightened to death we stood together on the bow of the ship and said "please," and that is the truth, "please." When our time is up we will all be on one team. So why do we need bigotry and non-sense? Let's enjoy while almighty God gives us time. Will Rogers once said, "I never picked on a little guy. Only big people." May I say to this entire audience, on a hectic night, you are pretty big, and I do thank each and every one of you. [audience applause]

What Rickles attempts to provide with his closing remarks is a "framework" for how to interpret his comedy. That is, the function of such commentary can be viewed as a way to "stage his talk" and "manage his identity" (Goffman 1959) in order to create distance between his brand of racial and ethnic ridicule and "real racism." Rickles changes his voice from "unserious" to "serious" and invokes discourse about "our shared humanity." The rhetorical impact of such commentary by Rickles is that it creates further ambiguity and *polysemicity* in his performance and makes it more challenging to frame as *monosemic* racist discourse. In this way, the combination of strategies illustrated above show how Rickles' brand of stand-up comedy allowed him to make use of overt racial discourse inaccessible in most other forms of public talk.

Conclusion and Discussion

Rickles' performance during this period of social transformation can be seen as a strategic form of racial comedy that is "flirting with law" (Seshadri-Crooks 1998). According to Seshadri-Crooks, racist jokes in a "multiracial and 'liberal' democracy" work to re-channel aggression and hostility that has become taboo through changes in written and moral law (p. 362). The emergence of laws banning racial discrimination, along with the rise of cultural norms against public displays of racial intolerance and offensive racial discourse, created a context in which comedians like Don Rickles straddled the line of appropriate and taboo racial discourse (Littlewood & Pickering 1998). By paying attention to the rhetorical joking mechanisms at work, Seshadri-Crooks contends observers will be able to focus on "how variations in the dialectical pressure of aggression and inhibition – conditions of the joke – produce different joke situations indicating shifts in the history of racism and its common sense" (1998, p. 364).

The rhetorical strategies Rickles employed in his 1968 performance signal a shift away from the kind of racial ridicule in U.S. comedy that was prominent in the pre-civil rights era, a form of comedy that was reflective of U.S. "race relations" at that period in time. The use of the "equal opportunity offender" strategy became increasingly necessary as the emerging socio-political climate increasingly regulated offensive racial discourse in public, among whites in particular, comedic and otherwise. Negative self-presentation or self-deprecation, for instance, allowed comedians like Don Rickles to narrow the distance between joke teller and audience. Self-targeted insults work rhetorically by convincing the audience that the performer can "take a joke" at his or her own expense. The performer is then granted license to insult the audience, in this case through the use of racial and ethnic ridicule. Rickles also employed other rhetorical strategies and distancing techniques, such as verbal cueing and switching between comedic and serious frames, to persuade the audience that his insults were "just jokes." These strategies worked to homogenize the audience while insulting them, and created a "community of laughter" that would tolerate racial and ethnic ridicule during this period of racial unrest and protest.

Rickles' racial ridicule also provided a form of "cathartic release" for the audience during a period of intense racial conflict. His jokes provided relief during a time when white supremacy was unwilling to concede some equality to non-whites and people of color responded with mass protests and urban revolt. The rhetorical impulse of his humor attempted to re-channel some of the violence and conflict in the streets. The humor implied the notion that if we laugh at ourselves, we won't kill each other.

While it is tempting to view Rickles' comedy primarily as a "subversive act" against bigotry, his comedy can also be seen as actively combating the emerging norms against offensive racist discourse in public. To see the *polysemicity* in Rickles' comedy is to acknowledge the ways in which it is challenging bigotry at the same time that he is reinforcing it. As Gilbert (2004) suggests, citing Nilsen (1993):

> [J]okes based on … stereotypes become even funnier when we think that the stereotypes are being broken in the jokes, but we later discover that the stereotypes aren't being broken at all.
>
> *(p. 152)*

Weaver notes that while we may prefer to privilege the "reversal" in comic racial discourse, as one that ostensibly subverts racist meaning, there is a prior reliance on racist meaning that has the potential to be reactivated and rearticulated (2011, p. 120).

For instance, one way in which Rickles' comedy can be seen as a way of reactivating or re-articulating prior racist meaning is to see how it worked to publicly challenge the emerging norms of "racial etiquette" in the post-civil rights era. His comedy was an early form of opposition to what came to be derisively referred to as "political correctness." Littlewood and Pickering (1998) contend that "politically incorrect" comedy can also be viewed as one of "adaptation rather than subversion" (p. 301), as the strategies detailed above helped Rickles adapt his brand of racial ridicule to a changing sociopolitical and discursive environment. His comedy, therefore, can be understood as an early form of anti-PC discourse that has been increasingly embraced by those on the conservative right in particular (Fairclough 2003; Littlewood & Pickering 1998).[2] What protected people of color from overt racial ridicule in public in the post-civil rights era were the norms (both legal and social) that worked to enforce notions of civility between whites and non-whites in an ostensibly democratic society. These new norms were a result of the challenge posed by a mass movement for racial equality seeking to upend a "racial dictatorship" that viewed people of color not as people but as objects of ridicule.

Although Rickles did not receive the level of opposition faced by some of his contemporary comedians for his brand of strategic racial ridicule, the sociopolitical context did work to restrain his brand of comedy. As Littlewood and Pickering (1998) observe, comedians who relied heavily on ridicule and derogatory jokes began to "[tone] down their acts and [became] more self-conscious of their content, uttering disclaimers or resorting to narrative devices designed to shield the teller from the attribution of racism or sexism" (p. 299). This shift is apparent in Rickles' 1968 performance, as illustrated above, and continued into the post-civil rights period. As Smith (1988) notes, by the 1980s "Rickles toned down his ethnic insults and concentrated more on physical traits (fat people, tall people, dopey people, etc.)" (p. 533).[3]

However, while Rickles ostensibly diminished his use of racial insult, comedians who engage in racial ridicule have increasingly relied on the rhetorical strategy of the "equal opportunity offender." For instance, during the mid-1990s, comedian Jackie Mason was shaking up the comedy world with his hit Broadway show, *Politically Incorrect* (Brantley 1994). This performance closely followed Rickles' formula of diversifying the targets of ridicule and insult, and was seen as a "breath of fresh air" during the post-civil rights period.

More recently, non-Jewish white comedians like Jeff Dunham and Lisa Lampanelli have made racial and ethnic ridicule central features of their comedy, and they are conscious of employing the "equal opportunity offender" strategy in order to minimize opposition to their work. As Dunham, one of the highest grossing comedians in the world, observed when discussing his controversial comedy:

> I've skewered whites, blacks, Hispanics, Christians, Jews, Muslims, gays, straights, rednecks, addicts, the elderly, and my wife. As a standup comic, it is my job to make the majority of people laugh, and I believe that comedy is the last true form of free speech.
>
> *(Gell 2009)*

As such comedy deals centrally with issues that stem from a history of racial oppression, white comedians are often hypersensitive about criticism of their race-based comedy and adamant that such comedy is "not racist," "just a joke" and an exercise in "free speech."

Similarly, Lampanelli, a self-described "equal opportunity offender," defended herself against online backlash when making use of racial slurs on Twitter by emphasizing her "non-racism," as well as her deployment of this strategy. Lampanelli deflected online criticism by stressing this theme in her body of work:

> I've played every comedy club and every theatre across the country for the last 25 years and seen a lot of audience members from different ethnic persuasions ... I have always used in my act every racial slur there is for Asians, blacks, gays, and Hispanics. To me, it's acceptable if the joke is funny and if it is said in a context of no hate. It's about taking the hate out of the word.
>
> *(Shuter 2013)*

While Lampanelli implies that such jokes are "not really racist" and only "funny" when performed by a comedian in a multicultural context, Billig (2001) and Weaver (2011) highlight the "pleasure of bigotry" in their analysis of racist jokes among white supremacists on the Internet. In contrast to Lampanelli's suggestion that humor and racial hatred are incompatible, such examples illustrate that racism can also be practiced as something fun and entertaining among both multicultural and racist audiences.

Therefore, comedians tend to make deliberate use of the "equal opportunity offender" strategy in order to veil their commentary as "just jokes" and "not racist," and distance themselves from what they believe to be "real racism." The fact that non-Jewish white comics are increasingly using this strategy "successfully" to engage in racial ridicule further suggests that the previous constraints on racial ridicule among whites more generally are weakening. That is, we have entered a new era in the history of racism and racial ridicule.

Finally, I contend the emergence and continuity of the "equal opportunity offender" strategy in comedy corresponds to the current period of "race relations" that has been increasingly described as "color-blind" (Bonilla-Silva 2013). While it appears counterintuitive to view this brand of racially insulting comedy as "color-blind," the central tendency within the logic of this racial ideology is to "abstractly equalize" whites and non-whites in order to minimize the continued significance of race and racism in contemporary society (Bonilla-Silva 2013). From this perspective, the civil rights movement ended racism and racism is no longer a major issue that impacts the "life chances" of ethnic and racial minorities. Therefore, I contend this brand of racially insulting comedy falls in line with the logic of color-blind racism in at least three important ways:

1. By providing cathartic relief for the constraints on overt racist discourse in contemporary society, for whites in particular, racial ridicule by comedians becomes relegated to the realm of the "unserious" as it is viewed as "just a joke."
2. By asserting that racial ridicule is "just a joke," this current "common-sense" understating of racist humor, as it relates to racism more generally, reinforces the notion that racist jokes are "peripheral" and far removed from hate-filled *real* racism.
3. By suggesting that the insults, slurs, and stereotypes that target whites and non-whites carry *equal weight,* the continued significance of race and racism is minimized and trivialized.

Therefore, it is important that we consider not only how stand-up comedy has (positively) contributed to social and cultural transformation, but as an "agent of change" we must also *critically* focus on how comedy can simultaneously work to weaken and strengthen social inequalities and racial ideologies in an ostensibly "color-blind" and "post-racist" society.

Notes

1 It is worth mentioning that today extreme racist jokes are widely circulated in private settings or posted anonymously on the internet in both mainstream forums and far right website. See Billig 2001; Weaver 2011.
2 For example, as conservative radio talk show host Rush Limbaugh suggested following Ted Danson's blackface controversy at the Friars Club: "How come you can't have a

little fun about blacks? ... What protects them? Why are they immune from legitimate forms of humor?" (Baker 1993).
3 It is worth pointing out that Rickles recently received public scrutiny for jokes about Barack Obama that many viewed as racially offensive (Kilday 2012).

References

Apte, M.L. (1987). Ethnic humor versus "sense of humor." *American Behavioral Scientist*, 30(3), 27–41.
Baker, P. (1993). Now no laughing matter. *Washington Post*. March 21.
Bender, S. (2003). *Greasers and gringos: Latinos, law, and the American imagination*. New York: NYU Press.
Berger, A.A. (1998). *An anatomy of humor*. New Brunswick, NJ: Transaction Publishers.
Berger, P.L. (1997). *Redeeming laughter: the comic dimension of human experience*. New York: Walter de Gruyter.
Billig, M. (2001). Humour and hatred: The racist jokes of the Ku Klux Klan. *Discourse & Society*, 12(3), 267–289.
Billig, M. (2005). *Laughter and ridicule: Towards a social critique of humour*. London: Sage.
Bobo, L., Kluegel, J.R., & Smith, R.A. (1997). Laissez-faire racism: The crystallization of a kinder, gentler, antiblack ideology. *Racial attitudes in the 1990s: Continuity and change*, 15, 23–25.
Bonilla-Silva, E. (2013). *Racism without racists: Color-blind racism and the persistence of racial inequality in America*. Lanham: Rowman & Littlefield Publishers.
Bonilla-Silva, E., & Forman, T.A. (2000). "I am not a racist but...": Mapping white college students' racial ideology in the USA. *Discourse & Society*, 11(1), 50–85.
Booker, J.L. (1991). *The Jewish American Princess and other myths*. New York: Shapolsky.
Boskin, J. (1979). *Humor and social change in twentieth-century America*. Boston: Trustees of the Public Library.
Boskin, J. (1986). *Sambo: The rise & demise of an American jester*. New York: Oxford University Press.
Boskin, J., & Dorinson, J. (1985). Ethnic humor: Subversion and survival. *American Quarterly*, 37, 81–97.
Brantley, B. (1994). Jackie Mason; Politically Incorrect; It's Mason on being incorrect (no joke). *New York Times*. April 16. Retrieved from www.nytimes.com/1994/04/06/theater/review-theater-jackie-mason-politically-incorrect-it-s-mason-being-incorrect-no.html
Brodkin, K. (1998). *How Jews became white folks and what that says about race in America*. New Brunswick, NJ: Rutgers University Press.
Burke, K. (1959). *Attitudes toward history*. 2nd Edition. Los Altos, CA: Hermes Publications.
Dundes, A. (1985). The JAP and the JAM in American jokelore. *Journal of American Folklore*, 98(390), 456–475.
Ebert, R. (1993). Danson's racist "humor" appalls crowd at roast. *RogerEbert.com*. October 10. Retrieved from www.rogerebert.com/rogers-journal/dansons-racist-humor-appalls-crowd-at-roast
Ely, M.P. (1991). *The adventures of Amos 'n' Andy: A social history of an American phenomenon*. New York: Free Press.
Epstein, L.J. (2001). *The haunted smile: The story of Jewish comedians in America*. New York: Public Affairs.
Fairclough, N. (2003). Political correctness: The politics of culture and language. *Discourse & Society*, 14(1), 17–28.

Farhi, P. (2006). "Seinfeld" comic Richards apologizes for racial rant. *Washington Post.* November 21. Retrieved from www.washingtonpost.com/wp-dyn/content/article/2006/11/21/AR2006112100242.html

Feagin, J.R. (2014). *Racist America: Roots, current realities, and future reparations.* New York: Routledge.

Ford, S. (1974). Comedian Carlin's point is to make point. *Daily News.* November 24. Retrieved from http://news.google.com/newspapers?nid=1696&dat=19741122&id=O9seAAAAIBAJ&sjid=t0YEAAAAIBAJ&pg=6926,3488437

Gell, E. (2009). Another day, another doll(ar). *Forbes.* June 3. Retrieved from www.forbes.com/2009/06/03/forbes-100-celebrity-09-jeff-dunham-achmed-comedy-puppets.html

Gilbert, J.R. (2004). *Performing marginality: Humor, gender, and cultural critique.* Detroit: Wayne State University Press.

Gillota, D. (2013). *Ethnic humor in multiethnic America.* New Brunswick, NJ: Rutgers University Press.

Goffman, E. (1959). *The presentation of self in everyday life.* New York: Anchor Books.

Goffman, E. (1974). *Frame analysis: An essay on the organization of experience.* Cambridge, MA: Harvard University Press.

Goffman, E. (1981). *Forms of talk.* Philadelphia: University of Pennsylvania Press.

Haggins, B. (2007). *Laughing mad: The black comic persona in post-soul America.* New Brunswick, NJ: Rutgers University Press.

Ignatiev, N. (2008). *How the Irish became white.* New York: Routledge.

Jacobson, M.F. (1998). *Whiteness of a different color.* Cambridge, MA: Harvard University Press.

Kibler, M.A. (2009). Paddy, Shylock, and Sambo: Irish, Jewish, and African American efforts to ban racial ridicule on stage and screen. In M.H. Ross (Ed.). *Culture and belonging in divided societies: Contestation and symbolic landscapes* (pp. 259–280). Philadelphia: University of Pennsylvania Press.

Kilday, G. (2012). Don Rickles shocks Hollywood crowd with racial Obama joke. *The Hollywood Reporter.* June 8. Retrieved from www.hollywoodreporter.com/news/don-rickles-president-obama-shirley-maclaine-335308

Littlewood, J., & Pickering, M. (1998). Gender, ethnicity and political correctness in comedy. In S. Wagg (Ed.), *Because I tell a joke or two: Comedy, politics, and social difference* (pp. 291–312). London: Routledge.

Lockyer, S., & Pickering, M. (2005). *Beyond a joke: The limits of humour.* Basingstoke: Pelgrave Macmillan.

Lott, E. (2013). *Love & theft: Blackface minstrelsy and the American working class.* Oxford: Oxford University Press.

Mendelberg, T. (2001). *The race card: Campaign strategy, implicit messages, and the norm of equality.* Princeton: Princeton University Press.

Mintz, L.E. (1985). Standup comedy as social and cultural mediation. *American Quarterly, 37,* 71–80.

Mintz, L.E. (1996). Humor and ethnic stereotypes in vaudeville and burlesque. *MELUS, 21*(4), 19–28.

Morreall, J. (2009). *Comic relief: A comprehensive philosophy of humor.* Chichester, UK: John Wiley and Sons.

Omi, M., & Winant, H. (2014). *Racial formation in the United States.* 3rd Edition. New York: Routledge.

Pérez, R. (2013). Learning to make racism funny in the "color-blind" era: Stand-up comedy students, performance strategies, and the (re)production of racist jokes in public. *Discourse & Society, 24*(4), 478–503.

Pérez, R. (2014). Brownface minstrelsy: "José Jiménez," the Civil Rights Movement, and the legacy of racist comedy." *Ethnicities*. In print.
Pula, J.S. (1996). Image, status, mobility and integration in American society: The Polish experience. *Journal of American Ethnic History, 16*(1), 74–95.
Richardson, J.E. (2007). *Analysing newspapers: An approach from critical discourse analysis*. Basingstoke: Palgrave Macmillan.
Rickles, D. (1968). *Hello Dummy!* Warner Bros.
Roediger, D.R. (1999). *The wages of whiteness: Race and the making of the American working class*. New York: Verso.
Rogin, M. (1998). *Blackface, white noise: Jewish immigrants in the Hollywood melting pot*. Berkeley: University of California Press.
Seshadri-Crooks, K. (1998). The comedy of domination: Psychoanalysis and the conceit of whiteness. In C. Lane (Ed.). *The psychoanalysis of race* (pp. 353–379). New York: Columbia University Press.
Shuter, R. (2013). Lisa Lampanelli defends racial slur, says she won't stop using N-word. *Huffington Post*. February 19. Retrieved from www.huffingtonpost.com/2013/02/19/lisa-lampanelli-racial-slur-lena-dunham_n_2719639.html
Smith, R.L. (1988). *Comedy on record: the complete critical discography*. New York: Garland Publishing.
Van Dijk, T.A. (1992). Discourse and the denial of racism. *Discourse & Society, 3*(1), 87–118.
Van Dijk, T.A. (1993). Principles of critical discourse analysis. *Discourse & Society, 4*(2), 249–283.
Von Schilling, J.A. (2003). *The magic window: American television, 1939–1953*. New York: Haworth Press.
Waters, M.C. (1990). *Ethnic options: Choosing identities in America*. Berkeley: University of California Press.
Weaver, S. (2011). *The rhetoric of racist humour: US, UK and global race joking*. Farnham, UK: Ashgate Publishing, Ltd.

5

"WOULD YOU WANT YOUR SISTER TO MARRY ONE OF THEM?"

Whiteness, Stand-Up, and Lenny Bruce

Matthew R. Meier and Chad M. Nelson

Lenny Bruce may be the most influential stand-up comedian in the history of American comedy. Often cited as an inspiration for the comics that followed in his generation's footsteps, Bruce's no-holds-barred satirical style made a lasting impression on the form of stand-up comedy in America (Azlant 2007). In the early 1960s, that style landed Bruce a gig Carnegie Hall, a series of record deals, and recognition by *Time* as the "the most successful sicknik" – sick comic – of his comic generation (The sickniks 1959). It also landed him in the back of a few police cars, behind bars and, eventually, in the national spotlight at the center of debate about free speech and obscenity in the United States.[1]

The importance of Bruce's comic legacy – particularly in regards to his obscenity trials – is difficult to understate and the case for his cultural significance is well established. Bruce has been featured as the subject of a number of documentary films (Baker 1972; Weide 1998; Gale 2011), a Hollywood biopic starring Dustin Hoffman (Fosse 1974), several biographies (Goldman 1974; Bruce 1992; Collins & Skover 2002), and is an essential component to any number of cultural histories of comedy, satire, and stand-up in America (Nachman 2003; Zoglin 2008; Kantor 2009; Kercher 2010). Curiously, however, apart from Kevin Casper's (2014) essay on Bruce's 1967 performance film – which is one of the earliest full-length stand-up comedy concert films – rhetoricians have paid little attention to Bruce's comedy. His legacy looms large, to be sure, but his rhetoric, as Azlant (2007) suggests, deserves more attention than it has received.

In our contemporary moment, scholarly treatments of comedy and satire abound in the rhetorical studies literature. Taking on subjects such as *The Daily Show with Jon Stewart* (Baym 2005; Waisanen 2009; Jones 2010; Jones & Baym 2010), *The Colbert Report* (Baym 2007; Meddaugh 2010; Rossing 2012), and *The Onion* (Achter 2008; Waisanen 2011), scholars have demonstrated again and again the importance of satirical rhetoric to American public culture. Few scholars, however, have turned their attention to historical satire in the United States and fewer still to stand-up comedians. This absence ignores the impact of generations of satirical rhetors who cultivated the form, audience, and culture. By considering Lenny Bruce's satire, therefore, we hope to begin the process of filling in those gaps for future scholarly consideration.

With that in mind, however, we recognize that any contribution to such a project can only be partial. Bruce's comic oeuvre – preserved in performance recordings, documentary footage, and court transcripts – is a varied as it is extensive. It would be impossible, in any one chapter, to provide a comprehensive and nuanced analysis of his satire. Thus, we have chosen texts from his body of work that take race, racism, and whiteness as their primary subject. Our choice is motivated by three primary factors. First, Bruce's satire, "How to Relax Your Colored Friends at Parties" (1961) is often lauded as one of his most famous and important routines. Second, Bruce was one of the only comics in the civil rights era to dare to discuss the topic on stage, a point which is all the more significant because he was white.[2] Third, his satires on race and racism speak to both over-arching themes in his comedy – such as saying words that were unspeakable – and to the capacity of satire to engage in very specific discourses in American public culture.

In this chapter, we argue that Bruce's satire operates as a tactical challenge to what Nakayama and Krizek (1995) call the strategic rhetoric of whiteness, or the propensity of whiteness rhetoric to sustain its privileged discursive position. At the same time, rhetorical critique of Bruce's stand-up comedy in light of his socially privileged position as a comedian further reveals two key tensions relevant to any critique of whiteness emerging from within a white subjectivity and particularly those presented by stand-up comedians and satirists. First, his satire does well to reveal the invisible structures, assumptions, and discourses of whiteness by rhetorically translating those abstractions into more concrete terms and experiences for his audience. In so doing, however, Bruce's satire hides his own whiteness in order to maintain his centrality and power over the audience as the performer. Hence, it reaffirms the need for what Nakayama and Krizek refer to as critical reflexivity of one's own social privileges, other silenced voices, and institutional forms of whiteness. Bruce's satire creates moments wherein he and his audience can potentially engage in critical self-reflexivity and embrace meaningful social change by revealing concrete examples of white privilege and racism. But therein lies the second key tension that we identify in Bruce's rhetorical use of satire as a critique of racism; those moments of reflexivity tend to remain individualized for the performer and each member of the audience. For this reason, they are easily dismissed by the strategic rhetoric of whiteness as the result of isolated and particularized examples of "those other" racists and "their" racism. For these reasons, Bruce's stand-up is at once a productive critique of whiteness and a strategic means of reinforcing the centrality of the white subject. And consequently, our critique of Bruce's stand-up offers an opportunity for further understanding the political potentials and pitfalls for satirical approaches to critiquing racist discourses as well as points toward additional considerations for critical reflexivity practices of whiteness.

Of course, we both do so from our own positions of whiteness and privilege. The first author comes to Whiteness Studies through the critical rhetorical tradition and cultural studies, but tends to feature comedy, popular culture, and democracy as the primary focus on his scholarship. The second author writes specifically about whiteness, rhetoric, and issues of Latina/o identities and interests in urban educational politics. By no means do these realities legitimize our arguments in this chapter, and we consciously attempt to struggle through issues of racism and whiteness critically mindful of the relationships between our own subjectivities, our writing, and its consequences. However contradictory, we find affinity with John Warren (2003) in recognizing our limitations in speaking for others, our personal and professional implications in white privilege, and our common desires to work toward the undermining of those social positions upon which our privileges rest.

In constructing these arguments, we proceed by first engaging with Whiteness Studies in the rhetorical tradition. From that foundation, we extend Nakayama and Krizek's discussion of Michel de Certeau's (1984) concept of "strategies" and "tactics" in order to suggest that satire, and stand-up comedy more generally, can function as a tactical response to the oppression of strategic rhetorics (pp. 35–37). Turning to Bruce's satire, we then bring the concepts of the strategic rhetoric of whiteness and the tactical critique of satire to bear on three of Bruce's more prominent routines that address race, racism, and whiteness. Finally, we return to Nakayama and Krizek's call for critical self-reflexivity as one means of easing the tension present in the satirical treatment of race and racism hopefully rendering it a productive tactic for engaging the strategic rhetoric of whiteness, not only for Bruce's historical moment, but also for our own.

Whiteness and Rhetoric

In their work on whiteness as a strategic rhetoric, Nakayama and Krizek (1995) argue that whiteness is paradoxical. On one hand, whiteness avoids a definitive essence. When attempting to define whiteness, it finds a way to slip through the analytical grasp. And yet, whiteness persistently and subtly presents itself in everyday social relations as normative. Because whiteness has become naturalized and ostensibly universalized, it is often unknowingly perceived as the norm by which all others are to understand themselves (Nakayama & Krizek 1995). Within this paradoxical position, whiteness can be understood as a rhetorically constructed privileged position. By conceptualizing the construct in this manner, Nakayama and Krizek "avoid searching for any essential nature to whiteness. Instead, [they] seek an understanding of the ways that this rhetorical construction makes itself visible and invisible, eluding analysis yet exerting influence over everyday life" (p. 293).

In an effort to make whiteness subjectivities visible, Nakayama and Krizek identify six ways in which whiteness can function as a strategic rhetoric. For instance, at times, whiteness brazenly functions by rhetorically equating being white with social power. But at other times, the denial of color allows one's white subjectivity to remain invisible. Similarly, when "white" is solely treated as a biological category without discussion of the cultural significance of being white or whiteness, any critical attention to power relations is denied. Additionally, assuming that white simply means "Americans" subsumes all co-cultural others into the nationalist extension of the dominance of whiteness. Clearly expressing individualist values, the refusal to label one's self disregards the import of historical and social constructions of racial identities as well as the privileged position, only accessible to some, necessary to make such a claim. And lastly, acknowledging the historical influences on one's identity and constructions of whiteness does not necessarily imply an examination of related power relations thus allowing whiteness an escape. Consequently, several, including Nakayama and Krizek, have called for some form of critical self-reflexivity as a means to make whiteness visible and struggle against its discursive dominance (Moon & Flores 2000; Simpson 2008; Shome 2000). By making whiteness visible through critique, the necessary task of centering marginalized cultural identities and knowledges becomes possible. Such a process is political and intended to address the institutionalized oppression of racial identities (Frye 1983; Jackson, Shin, & Hilson 2000).

To summarize, whiteness invisibly produces and maintains social hierarchies, white privileges, institutional racism, and material inequalities (Warren 2003; Flores, Ashcraft, & Marafiote 2010). Whiteness extends beyond a particular race or ethnicity. It describes certain dimensions of power including normative race privilege; a privileged white standpoint from which to view others, one's self, and society; and a particular set of ill-defined, often invisible, but hegemonic cultural practices (Frankenburg 1993). Those who adopt this socially privileged position of "white" are often unaware of how complicit they are in maintaining and producing the very social and institutional privileges that not only protect their way of living, but also subjugate others to discursive and material forms of marginalization (Wander, Martin, & Nakayama, 1999). This represents the ideological nature of whiteness. One way that whiteness functions ideologically is to erect and protect institutional and everyday experiences of white privilege and the material interests of white people over the interests of people of color (Crenshaw 1997). This could be carried out in numerous rhetorical ways including the superimposing of racialized categories on people and experiences or through a rhetoric of colorblindness with its faulty assumptions that power and race can simply be transcended, and we just need to treat everyone as "individuals" (Crenshaw 1997). Colorblindness allows those in positions of whiteness to dismiss talk about race and turn a blind eye to practices of racial discrimination in social interactions and at the institutional level. Consequently, the task of an ideological critique of whiteness entails locating "interactions that implicate unspoken issues of race, discursive spaces where the power of whiteness is invoked but its explicit terminology is not" (Crenshaw 1997, p. 254).

Whiteness and Humor

In their discussion of whiteness, Nakayama and Krizek draw explicitly upon Michel de Certeau's (1984) conceptual distinction between what he calls "strategies" and "tactics" (pp. 35–37). For de Certeau, a "strategy" is only available to "a subject with will and power." A strategic rhetoric such as whiteness, therefore, operates *only* from a position of power and seeks to locate that power in an environment of its own making. In this way, a strategic rhetoric "postulates a *place* that can be delimited as its *own* and serve as the base from which relations with *exteriority* composed of targets or threats can be managed" (p. 36). By locating itself as the center of power, whiteness creates a relationship whereby all other racial identities are forced to the margins and defined, at least in part, by their *not*-whiteness. What is more, because it provides the center for our understanding of race in discourse, it tends to be invisible, an unspoken assumption that requires no justification.

Whereas a strategic rhetoric is the faculty of the powerful, a tactical rhetoric remains "the art of the weak" (de Certeau 1984, p. 37). As de Certeau explains, "A tactic is determined by the *absence of power* just as strategy is organized by the postulation of power" (p. 38). In relation to the strategic rhetoric of whiteness, tactics, therefore, emerge from the margins, the realm of not-white others. In this way, tactics are the "isolated actions" that marginalized racial groups use to counter the strategic oppressions that support and maintain the structures of whiteness (p. 37).

Tactics are a means of standing-up to power – of critiquing, challenging, and deceiving power. They are, however, constrained by and subject to power. In this way, a tactical rhetoric "must play on and with a terrain imposed on it and organized by the law of a foreign power" (p. 37). Thus, tactics rely upon incongruities, "cracks," and "opportunities" from within the discourse of the powerful (p. 37). Whereas strategy is a rhetoric concerned primarily with creating a location for power, tactic is a rhetoric of timing. Unable to delimit a location of power for themselves, the marginalized use tactics to capitalize on *moments* of weakness as they emerge from within the structure of power. Whiteness is concerned with maintaining its strategic centrality – its location – but the tactical critique of whiteness operates by taking the discourse of whiteness by surprise. The critique of whiteness requires "a clever *utilization of time*, of the opportunities it presents and also of the play that it introduces into the foundations of power" (p. 38).

The connection between de Certeau's conceptualization of strategies and tactics and the rhetoric of whiteness not only reveals, as Nakayama and Krizek indicate, how power strategically operates from behind the cloak of whiteness, but also how and *when* those structures of power can be tactically contested. One tactic for this contestation, we argue, is satirical critique. Satire, as Gilbert Highet (1962) explains, is a tactical rhetoric that attempts to combine laughter and derision in order to "tell the truth" (pp. 233–234).[3] However, the satirist cannot be indiscriminant in her or his truth telling. Satirical truths tend to ridicule powerful rather than marginalized subjects. They render invisible assumptions visible in order to challenge the power concealed by its invisibility. Satire aims up at the powerful because in doing otherwise it moves from comedy to cruelty (Dagnes 2012). From the satirist's perspective, strategic rhetorics, as locations of power, are ripe for critical treatment.

More to the point, because whiteness is characterized as a strategic rhetoric of "will and power" it is a subject more than appropriate for satirical derision. In fact, in his essay on former Comedy Central late night host Stephen Colbert's use of race humor in his satirical parody, Jonathan Rossing (2012) contends that the comedian "invites White audiences to face whiteness and its privileges" and to question the very foundations of what has been called a "postracial society" (p. 56). For this reason, Rossing argues that "humor functions as a critical cultural project and site for racial meaning making that may provide a corrective for impasses in public discourses on race and racism" (p. 45).

In the sections that follow, we outline and critique three of Lenny Bruce's satirical routines. Each routine prominently features a critique of whiteness vis-à-vis the everyday practices of racism in civil rights era American culture. In so doing, we argue that Bruce's satire operates as a tactic for challenging the center of whiteness, but does so without the critical reflexivity called for by Nakayama and Krizek. For this reason, his satire – like that of so many others – is self-sabotaging because although it appears to be critical on its surface, it nevertheless reinforces the centralization of power tacitly maintained by the strategic rhetoric of whiteness.

Are There Any Niggers Here Tonight?

As the very first track of the Lenny Bruce collection *Buyer Beware* (2004a), the otherwise unreleased cut from a live performance begins almost as an afterthought. "By the way," Bruce wonders, "are there any niggers here tonight?" At its start, it feels like a transition, but the harshness and nonchalance of his language leaves his audience appropriately stunned. After a long, sighing whistle, Bruce says what he's sure everyone is thinking: "What did he say? Is he really getting out of his nut? Are there any niggers here tonight! Is he that desperate for shock value? Would he scrape the bottom to be that cruel to say, 'Are there any niggers here tonight?'"

This opening operates on two fronts. First, by filling in the audience members' side of the exchange, Bruce "poaches" their response of righteous indignation (de Certeau 1984, p. 37). In this way, his mock exasperation steals away from his mostly white audience one means of strategically maintaining the centrality of whiteness by being offended on behalf of those people who are rightly offended by the slur. Bruce's momentary parody, therefore, functions as a tactic that externalizes one strategic maneuver typical of the rhetoric of whiteness rendering it visible and, therefore, open to critique.

Second, it establishes, for the audience listening to *Buyer Beware*, or re-establishes, for the live audience, Bruce's rhetorical posture. He says the words that people aren't supposed to say. His nonchalance and comfort with the epithet reminds his audience that he stands-up against linguistic taboo regardless of topic. He breaks rules. He violates expectations. And he does so deliberately.

Paradoxically, however, this rhetorical posture operates as Bruce's own strategic rhetoric. It marks him as a subject with "will and power" as de Certeau would suggest. It is Bruce alone who can, for whatever reason, say the words and break the rules. On the one hand, violation is an essential component of much comedy (see Lynch 2002) and linguistic taboos – or what Mikhail Bakhtin (1984) calls *billingsgate* – are a more than common topic for the comedian. On the other hand, it is a strategy that is available to Bruce, at least in part, because he already occupies the center of power. He is, after all, white and his white subjectivity affords him a racially innocent and largely uncontested position from which to speak for his audience. In this way, Bruce's strategic maintenance of his comic posture stands in contrast to his tactical critique of the strategic rhetoric of whiteness because it participates in and depends upon the very discourse of whiteness for its legitimacy. As Shome (2000) explains, whites can deploy rhetorical strategies of deflection and evasiveness to shift attention to individual performances of racism by others while hiding one's own complicity in whiteness and those nameless institutional forms of racism from which one ultimately benefits. These rhetorics defer "from acknowledging the larger issue of how the everyday organization of social and cultural relations function to confer benefits and systemic advantages to whites," whether they be sitting in the club or standing center stage at least they were not turned away at the door (Shome 2000, p. 367).

After waiting a beat, Bruce offers his rebuttal to the unwarranted umbrage of his audience: "Have I ever talked about the *shvartz* and they left the room? Or the *moulinjons* or the *yans*, or placated some Southerner by absence of voice when they rant and rave about the nigger, nigger, niggers?"[4] These rhetorical questions, to which the suggested answer is no, conclude Bruce's opening gambit by simultaneously reinforcing his authority and denigrating his mostly white audience – some of whom may have already walked out of the live performance. If Bruce's language use does not offend his black audience members and he is unwilling to remain silent in the face of the obvious racism of the stereotypical Southerner then his audience, he concludes, should not be permitted to take offense at his choice of words. Enthymematically, his argument seeks to mark him as morally superior to the members of his audience while at the same time marking them as deficient and blind to their own racist tendencies. This argument does tactically challenge the rhetoric of whiteness by revealing how offense taken by the powerful on behalf of the marginalized allows the powerful to maintain their centrality. As before, however, it robs the audience of that strategy by employing it on the comic's behalf. Bruce, himself, gets to determine who can be offended and what does or does not count as offensive. In this way, by externalizing his audience from the power afforded by its whiteness, Bruce can seize that power for himself and protect his own whiteness from critical interrogation.

Building momentum, Bruce moves into the body of the bit unleashing a barrage of epithets:

> Are there any niggers here? I know I'm working with a nigger. I think I see one nigger couple back there. Between those two niggers sit three kikes. [whistles] Thank God for the kikes ... and two spics and one mick. We have two spics, one mick, three kikes, and one spunky funky hunky. Any more boogies, three more sheenys, eight more guineas, six guineas, seven Wops, six grease balls ... six dykes, four kikes, and eight niggers.[5]

If his audience wasn't offended by the initial question, it almost certainly is by the end of his intentionally insensitive rant. The sheer accumulation and machine-gun delivery of the words ensures as much. The series of slurs, though, is not put forward purely for the purposes of shock and awe. It also carries the critical set-up of Bruce's satire. By including a series of slurs for whites – Jews, Irish, and Italians – as well as Hispanics and lesbians in his continued usage of epithets targeting blacks, Bruce equates slurs used against persons of color or LGBTQ individuals and those used against whites. This chain of equivalences, for Bruce, becomes the point upon which his satirical argument rests.

This argumentative claim, however, is particularly beneficial to Bruce's white subjectivity. Not only does it require his "will and power," but it also reinforces its centrality. To be fair, a slur is an insult and is usually intended to offend the represented person. For that reason, each epithet is offensive and, therefore, the words are all equal in their function. However, the slurs used against whites do not alter the access to the center of power afforded to them by their whiteness. An Irish, Italian, or Jewish person still benefits from their whiteness even in the face of an insult – a point underscored by Bruce's constant references to his Jewish identity, usage of Yiddish vernacular, and his relative authority over his audience.[6] An otherwise racially marginalized person, however, is not afforded the same access. For that reason, the slurs are not and cannot be understood as equal. The powerless are constantly reminded of their powerlessness whereas the powerful take offense, to be sure, but lose no standing over and against the marginalized. This equation of slurs used against whites with those against persons of color appears to be a satirical – or tactical – critique of the power given to the word "nigger," but it nevertheless carries consequences that benefit the strategic rhetoric of whiteness. Not only does it render that word accessible to whites by defining it as effectively inoffensive, but it also obscures the access to power available to whites by hiding it behind a series of false equivalences comprised of slurs that are not and cannot be equal.

In a way, this rhetorical strategy is comparable to what Nakayama and Krizek (1995) identify as whiteness's ability to transcend race while maintaining dehumanizing and stereotypical racial categories for co-cultural others. Although those using this strategy may profess equality and perhaps even anti-racist intensions, in this context, the rhetor actually reinforces systemic white privilege (Rothenberg

2007). The privilege of whiteness is thus paradoxically revealed and denied in the rhetorical acts of not only identifying what experiences can and cannot be spoken, but also in determining what racialized language can or cannot be offensive for all audiences.

The bit's payoff, if it can be referred to as such, comes a few beats later as Bruce offers:

> The point. If President Kennedy got on television everyday and said, "I would like to introduce all the niggers in my cabinet.'" And all of the niggers called each other niggers – they often times do, but not in front of the ofays.[7] And every day you heard, nigger, nigger, nigger, nigger. In the second month, nigger wouldn't mean as much as good night or God Bless you when you sneeze … Nigger would lose its impact and it would never make a four-year-old nigger cry when he came home from school. The *gornisht* gives it the power, Jim.

Bruce's argument hinges upon the idea that language is abstract, that the word is distinct from its referent. His conclusion, that the *gornisht* – the emptiness or nothingness – of the epithet is its source of power, however, misses the mark. If the word is empty – or emptied – then its emptiness is beneficial not to the marginalized persons who bear the brunt of its oppression but to those already located comfortably at the center of power.

In this way, Bruce's satirical critique of the epithet appears to be a tactical response to the rhetoric of whiteness, but nevertheless falls prey to the strategic nature of whiteness. In part, this is due to Bruce's inability – or perhaps unwillingness – to critique his own whiteness. The bit requires his power, his centrality, which is at least in part dependent upon his whiteness. So much so, in fact, that he externalizes his audience, sacrificing it at the altar of whiteness, in order to maintain his own position of centrality and undermine otherwise justifiable responses to oppression. In this way, the bit, which appears to be a critique of whiteness and racism, re-centers the power and privilege of whiteness over co-cultural others.

How to Relax Your Colored Friends at Parties

Without doubt, "How to Relax Your Colored Friends at Parties" was one of Bruce's signature bits. The routine first appears on the A-side of *American* (1961) and also on the 2004 *Buyer Beware* boxed set.[8] Like most of Bruce's material, the routine appears in a constant state of evolution and features more than a little improvisation. For that reason, each recording is slightly different even though they adhere to the same form and themes. The bit, which includes African American jazz guitarist Eric Miller as the "straight man" of the duo, is a loosely structured conversation between a white partygoer and one of the musicians hired by the host of the party. It represents, as Bruce explains in the introduction, "the typical white person's concept of how we relax colored people at parties." Making his satirical subject – white behavior in the presence of black people – apparent, Bruce takes a moment to remind his audience, "in the bit, I play the white guy" (Bruce 2004b). This tag, which gets one of the bigger laughs in the routine, functions as a subtle attempt to obscure Bruce's racial identity and the proximity to the center of power it affords. It strategically separates Bruce from the character he performs and, in so doing, renders his own whiteness invisible and safe from the critique that follows.

Following the brief introduction, the bit begins with two characters meeting and briefly exchanging pleasantries. As if at a loss for words, Bruce's character – introduced to the audience as Anderson – turns to Miller – who is playing a version of himself – and says, "You know that Joe Louis was a helluva fighter." Miller nervously agrees, "You can say that again, Joe Lewis was a helluva fighter." The joke, which occurs quite suddenly and without any additional context, is clearly made at the expense of the white character whose attempt to find a point of identification should be an obvious absurdity for the audience.[9] In the event that the audience might not get the joke, however, Bruce lingers on the theme name-dropping African American performers and characters. "That Bojangles," Bruce-as-Anderson says, "Christ, could he tap dance!" (Bruce 1991). Moments later he continues, "I used to watch him on the television all the time. Them show people are alright. I guess you know a lot of people in show business, eh?" (Bruce 2004b). Fumbling around to remember names, Bruce's character offers Aunt Jemima, "The guy on the Cream of Wheat box," and Stepin Fetchit as possible acquaintances of Miller. Of course, Aunt Jemima and Rastus, the chef depicted in Cream of Wheat advertisements, are completely fictional. And even though Stepin Fetchit was an actual person, his stage name and the excessively stereotypical character that made him famous was not a point of identification for much of the civil rights era African American community.

The satire, in this case, takes the form of Bruce's hyperbolic representation of the assumptions made by whites in their interactions with persons of color. He takes a fairly pedestrian idea about how a person should make small talk – attempting to find common ground or points of shared knowledge – and renders it absurd by referring to a series of characters and people with whom the only shared identification with his conversation partner is race. The spoof riffs on the underlying assumption that Miller should know the people because they are all black and, in so doing, externalizes that unspoken and unfounded assumption for critique. At the same time, it reveals the potential for latent racism in even the most well-intentioned interactions. Although Bruce's character may be drunk – in one recording he says he's "pissed to the ears" – he does not appear to be malicious (Bruce 2004b). In fact, he seems fairly well meaning even in light of his ignorance and racist insensitivity. This quality of the character is significant because it speaks to – and challenges – the role of *intention* in the discourse of racism. Operating comfortably from the center of power, a white person can claim to have not intended offense after making a racist remark and expect to remain safe from repercussion. Bruce's character seems to embody the "I'm not racist, but …" or "no offense" strategy for maintaining the centrality of whiteness. Externalizing and hyperbolically extending that strategic defense in his satire, therefore, Bruce's routine operates as a tactical response to that all too common, and often invisible, strategy of maintaining white centrality.

This tactical critique becomes even clearer a few beats later as Bruce-as-Anderson refers to the hosts of the party as "hebes" – a slur for Jewish people – and, catching himself, asks Miller, "You're not Jewish are you? No offense." In one rendition, he continues back-peddling adding, "Some of my best friends are Jews. We have them over to the house for dinner" (Bruce 1991). Drawing on his own identity and experiences with everyday racism, as a secular Jew, Bruce holds these quotidian statements up for critique. Although they speak to Jewish identity rather than African American identity, the statements made by Bruce's character are equally applicable as strategies for reestablishing the centrality of whiteness regardless of which co-cultural other is marginalized by the offending comment. Here again, Bruce's satire works by tactically poaching discourse from the everyday rhetoric that supports the structures of racism that maintain the strategic position of whiteness.

In his review of Eric Goldstein's *The Price of Whiteness: Jews, Race, and American Identity*, Steinman (2008) identifies a similar tension in the historical evolution of the Jewish identity in the United States. Although many Jewish immigrants and their decedents have historically held anti-racist values and sympathized with the marginalized experiences of African Americans, economic survival and success entailed embracing the subjectivities available to them because of their whiteness. In the process, their newly privileged positions, afforded in part by whiteness, alienated many Jewish people from the experiences of the African American community and ultimately played a part in shoring up the centrality and social privilege of the white subjectivity. Although Bruce cannot be considered a stand-in for all Jewish people, this may help toward reconciling the tensions created by his personal desire for comedic success, his ability to rhetorically take advantage of both his Jewish identity and his whiteness, and the anti-racist motives underlying his satire.

As the bit progresses, Bruce's character continues this theme of awkwardly relocating whiteness at the center of the exchange and forcing co-cultural others to the margins. For instance, his character contends, "Yeah, the way I figure is no matter what the hell a guy is, if he stays in his place, he's alright." The spatial metaphor in this statement is particularly notable. Strategic rhetorics such as whiteness, as de Certeau explains, first seek to centralize power and carve out a territory where it can reside comfortably. The notion of "staying in one's place" maintains the centrality of already existing relations of power because everyone's place is determined in relation to the subject that can delineate its own space – that is, the white subject. Spoken by the white character in the exchange, this line re-establishes his authority over both his imagined Jewish hosts and his African American conversation partner. However, Bruce's ability to speak this line – even through character that he performs – is granted in part by his whiteness. Thus, as Bruce's character exercises his power to define those at the margins without fear of recourse, Bruce himself acts in kind due in part to his access to power.

The definitional capacity of whiteness becomes apparent moments later when Bruce's character actively redefines Miller's saying, "You're a white Jew, you sonofagun. I like you. You're okay" (Bruce 2004b). This joke externalizes and satirizes the strategic use of naming to support the rhetoric of whiteness. Naming, or nominalism as Raymie McKerrow (1989) suggests, is one of the primary means of exercising rhetorical agency. Giving names or labels to marginalized people, therefore, is a strategic demonstration of power because it eliminates the possibility for the marginalized to name themselves. In giving the name, the agent of power also eschews the names or labels already assumed by the marginalized. What is more, the giving of a label also reinforces the implicit hierarchical relationship between those labels by marking them as closer to or farther from the center of power. In this way, when Bruce's character identifies Miller's as a "white Jew" he subsequently divorces Miller from any identity which he might choose to claim for himself while at the same time reinforcing the implication that the label "Jew," because it is associated with whiteness, is better or more desirable than the label "black." From this perspective, Miller's character seemingly has no choice but to accept the new label given to him and thereby submit to the authority granted by Bruce's (and Anderson's) whiteness.

As the bit draws to a close, Bruce's character offers to have his new friend over to his house. His invitation, however, is not without conditions. He explains, "Look, you can come over to my house if you promise you won't do it to my sister." Playing on the sexual mystique associated with black masculinity, Bruce's joke externalizes a stereotype of the marginalized group often mobilized to justify keeping them "in their place." In one performance, Bruce dwells for a moment on the topic posing, "I hear you got some perfume you put on and make them do it to you." In a rare moment of direct address, Miller's character flatly denies the query (Bruce 1991). Bruce's character then responds, "That's not true? There's no perfume you put on them? They just do it to you?" Emphasizing the notion of the magical perfume rather than the hyper-sexualized stereotype of black men, Bruce's character's response is typical of the strategic rhetoric of whiteness. Although Miller denies the entire claim outright, Bruce's character chooses to associate Miller's rejection with the perfume rather than the stereotype because it permits him to leave his otherwise unfounded assumption about black male sexuality – and its capacity to justify marking black men as different or dangerous – unquestioned. As before, this satirical maneuver tactically reveals not only the assumptions that would attempt to justify whiteness, but also the strategies used to rhetorically maintain its centrality. This rhetorical maneuvering parallels what Rachel Griffin and Bernadette Calafell (2011) identify in the rhetoric of NBA Commissioner David Stern because Bruce's joke, ever constrained by the strategic rhetoric of whiteness, reproduces rather than challenges a stereotypical and demeaning image of black masculinity.

For his parting shot, Bruce's character returns to the issue of his invitation. "Hey listen, I'd like to have you over to the house, I was telling you," he says, "but, uh, wait till it gets dark" (Bruce 1991). The joke, in this case, hinges on the obvious absurdity of telling a person to wait until dark to visit for fear the neighbors might see. At the same time, however, it draws that absurdity out into the open where it can be critiqued. Satirizing the white character's desire to maintain his access to the power associated with whiteness, the joke highlights the absurd notion that having a black friend is somehow threatening to white identity. Like many of the jokes in this bit, this line tactically critiques the discourse of whiteness by saying aloud the often unspoken assumptions that support it as a dominant discourse. At the same time, like much of the routine, the joke obscures Bruce's own white identity in order to critique not whiteness, but *a certain kind of whiteness*. Bruce's oafish Anderson character is as easily dismissed as he is recognized for his racist tendencies. For this reason, as is the case for his other routines, Bruce's satire does well to tactically challenge certain components of the strategic rhetoric of whiteness, but it does not, and perhaps cannot, challenge the center of that discourse because Bruce himself occupies that space.

The Ku Klux Klan and Would You Want Your Sister To Marry One of Them?

Near the middle of his first set in his now famous 1960 concert at Carnegie Hall, Bruce offers a satirical take on an imagined interaction with a Ku Klux Klan member (Bruce 1995). The bit also appears, in nearly identical form but for a clearer set-up, in the *Buyer Beware* collection.[10] Riffing on the charged question, "would you want your sister to marry one of *them*?" Bruce challenges the validity of such a proposition. "The trouble with all of that" he suggests, "is that it is a generality. It's for dummies. You got to tell me which sister, which one of them!" (Bruce 2004c). Using the hypothetical marriage as his backdrop, Bruce demonstrates how by moving between general and specific terms the racist assumptions that support the offending question are strategic constructs that are particularly susceptible to tactical critique.

The question, "would you want your sister to marry one of them?" operates comfortably from within the locus of power carved out by the strategic rhetoric of whiteness. The conclusion of the argument that the question carries, that "they" are somehow dangerous to "us" and "our" families, depends upon capacity of the powerful subject to define the marginalized. It requires the rhetorical authority of whiteness to externalize the co-cultural other. In exercising that power, the question argues for the construction of a racial dichotomy that clearly marks white as good and not-white as bad. In this way, the question strategically centers whiteness and uses its power to maintain, re-establish, and justify that power.

Turning the rhetorically strategic question on its ear, Bruce asks the same question of an imagined Ku Klux Klan member. He muses, "I'm going to give you a choice, [your] own free will of marrying a black woman or a white woman. Two chicks of about the same ages, same economic level, and you make the choice" (Bruce 1995). On its face, this seems like an identical proposition to the one commonly used to elicit racism in defense of one's sibling. As Bruce continues, however, it becomes clear that the question is not as it seems. "You've got to marry her," he says, "whatever marriage means to you – kissing and hugging and sleeping in a single bed on hot nights. Fifteen years with a [harshly] *black, black* woman, or fifteen years with a [softly] white, white woman. Kissing and hugging that *black, black* woman or the white woman" (Bruce 1995). Given the Ku Klux Klan's position on interracial marriage – or persons of color in general – the choice would seem obvious. Complicating the matter, however, Bruce explains, "the white woman is Kate Smith [laughter], the Black woman is Lena Horne." The joke transforms the question by emphasizing one component of physical appearance – normative beauty represented by Horne – over another – race – and thereby renders the question itself ridiculous.[11] The question's answer, after Bruce's satirical treatment, seems no less obvious.

Returning to the question about a person's sister, he offers, "If I give your sister the choice between a Charles Laughton and a Harry Belafonte, you're into the toilet."[12] Moving from the general, "one of them," to the specific, Harry Belafonte or Lena Horne, reveals how the abstract language of the question obscures the choice presented therein. It also marks the criterion race as less important than the criterion attractiveness. This implied hierarchy of criteria, however, is nevertheless constructed from the white subject's perspective. That is, the concept of attractiveness used to render the question ridiculous – embodied by Harry Belafonte and Lena Horne – is dependent upon images of the co-cultural other that are pleasing to the white subject. What is more, even though the satirical twist rearranges the hierarchy of criteria, it *does not eliminate* race as a criterion for choosing a spouse. Paradoxically, therefore, it seems to suggest that given similar marks for attractiveness, race would be an appropriate criterion for evaluating a potential love interest.

In one rendition, Bruce recognizes and attempts to respond to these problems with his satirical logic. He says, "Then if you say, Harry Belafonte isn't a very good thing because he's kind of an ofay with a tan. He's been assimilated and it's only one. I'll come up with twelve million for you. I'll come up with twelve million black keisters, twelve million *black, black* Sidney Poitiers" (Bruce 2004c).[13] His rebuttal addresses the issue of skin color and shade, but does nothing to challenge the centrality of the white subject. His new example, Sidney Poitier, though darker skinned than Belafonte, nevertheless appeals to the white subject's sense of what is or is not attractive. For this reason, even though Bruce attempts to tactically subvert certain negative connotations of race, he reinforces a hierarchical understanding of a different aspect of marginalized people – beauty. Unintentionally, therefore, Bruce marks certain black subjects as closer to or farther from the center of power because they are more or less appealing to the white subject. In this way, even though Bruce is critical of one aspect of the strategic rhetoric of whiteness, his satirical critique of that discursive fragment cannot escape the capacity of whiteness to move and adapt even in the face of a direct challenge.

Conclusion

Lenny Bruce thought of himself as a "surgeon with a scalpel for false values" (quoted in Zoglin 2008, p. 10). If he was a surgeon, he likely preferred the sledgehammer to the scalpel. This is particularly true of his satirical treatment of race and racism. His satire was biting, provocative, and, at times, productive. As Kenneth Tynan suggests, when at its best, Bruce's material "demolishes" his targets (Bruce 1992, p. xii.). At the same time, however, his satire left a fair amount of collateral damage in its wake. In his attempt to take down the powerful, Bruce often unintentionally added to the burden of the marginalized. His inability to divorce his comedy from the centrality of whiteness and model meaningful self-reflexivity render his material useful for both a tactical critique of certain aspects of the rhetoric of whiteness and a strategic re-centering of that very discourse.

These successes and shortcomings of Bruce's satire, however, offer important lessons to critics of whiteness regardless of whether they prefer the stand-up stand's mic or the scholar's pen. First, his routines suggest a capacity for satire to function as a tactic that renders visible strategic discourses that benefit from their invisibility. As Bruce exemplifies, the everyday discourses of racism and white privilege are easily undermined when their assumptions are spoken aloud and externalized for critique. Speaking the unspoken, in this way, is a powerful tool for realizing a robust and productive critique of whiteness.

Second, as we have illustrated, simply speaking the unspeakable does not constitute productive critique. In fact, as argued in this chapter, when the powerful use language that is offensive to the marginalized in an attempt to strip the language of power, the powerful reassert their position as the powerful. That is, by arguing that a slur should not be offensive or that a certain behavior is or is not racist, the powerful exercise their power over the marginalized by suggesting how they ought to respond to their oppression. Speaking the unspeakable productively requires consideration of how language becomes unspeakable, for whom it is unspeakable, and how it does or does not benefit those who speak it. This last point is key. Failure to recognize how a critique benefits one group over another creates a possibility whereby satirizing racism actually works to benefit racists.

Third, at least for comedy, the potential for social change is easily lost – and perhaps just as easily gained – in relation to the comic's willingness to engage in and model self-reflexivity for his or her audience. On the one hand, the desire to avoid critical reflection of oneself is unsurprising because of the power dynamic present in stand-up performance which requires the comic to establish his or her centrality in order to effectively maintain an audience's attention. On the other hand, in so far as satirical critique is a tactical response, comics and critics alike have much to gain by situating their criticism in terms of their own subjectivity and experience. Bruce's marginality as a Jew, for instance, was a powerful contributor to his comic *ethos* and, as we have suggested, helped legitimize his critique of power. What his satirical routines and commentaries lacked, however, was any discussion of how that marginality does or does not affect the critic's capacity to see the invisible structures of whiteness and, notably, how access to both the center and the margins creates a privileged position for the critic. As Lawrence Mintz (1985) argues, the stand-up comic is presented as "defective" in some way, but that defect, at least when paired with a white subject position, is a source of power that can be used to elevate or oppress the marginalized depending upon the comic's willingness to reflect upon his or her subjectivity.

As authors implicated in similar privileged positions of whiteness, we struggle, alongside scholars such as John Warren (2003), with the reality that we professionally benefit from writing about whiteness and racism. While this chapter may represent another professional accomplishment for us, for "others" it may stand as a reminder of all too familiar and personal experiences of marginalization and everyday racial oppression, experiences that we can only understand as filtered by our positions of privilege. Further, as white critics, we recognize that this chapter, its critique, and our interpretive lenses are saturated by our own privileges and, therefore, make certain rhetorical phenomena visible to us, but also obscure other voices, perspectives, and experiences. Thus, for us, this chapter signifies an opportunity to publicly struggle with these realities and their consequences; even as that opportunity is afforded to us in part because of our racial, socioeconomic, and educational privileges.

In sum, although Bruce's satire reveals and critiques whiteness, it is nevertheless contained by the strategic rhetoric of whiteness. In tearing down whiteness, therefore, Bruce's satire builds it back up and protects it from further criticism. A more productive critique of whiteness, satirical or otherwise, requires careful consideration of how arguments benefit those in power over and against the marginalized and how the subject position of the rhetor reorients even the most vicious critique in such a way as to benefit subjectivities available to the rhetor him or herself.

Notes

1 *The People of New York vs. Lenny Bruce* remains a landmark first amendment case in regards to obscenity law. Bruce was convicted on obscenity charges and sentenced to serve time at Riker's Island. He died in 1966 awaiting appeal. In 2003, he was posthumously pardoned by then Governor George Pataki.
2 African American stand-up/activist Dick Gregory, of course, was noted for using race as a subject for his satire, but Bruce's earliest race satire is recorded before the beginning of Gregory's career. For more on Gregory's comedy and activism, see Rossing 2013.
3 The quote "tell the truth, laughing" here is a translation or, at the very least, paraphrase of the Roman satirist Horace.
4 Shvartz, Moulinjon, and Moulinyan are derogatory slang terms for black people. The former is Yiddish, the latter two Italian.

5 Kike and sheeny are derogatory terms for Jewish people, spic for Spanish speaking people, mick for Irish people, Boogie for black people, Guinea, greaseball, and Wop for Italian people, and dyke for lesbians.
6 On this point, Bruce's inclusion of slurs that for Jews works, at least in part, to bolster his ethos and underscores his argument that words, as words, should not be considered offensive.
7 Derogatory slang for a white person.
8 *American* was re-released in digital format with *Togetherness* (1960) as *The Lenny Bruce Originals Volume 2* (1991). Although the recordings are identical, we should note that our transcriptions are derived from the 1991 release, rather than the original vinyl, and the *Buyer Beware* recording. For the sake of clarity, we only provide citations for quotations that are unique to either recording in our discussion of this routine.
9 It is worth noting that Joe Louis was a particularly charged historical figure for the African American community because he was one of the first World Champions of color (Jack Johnson was the first) and his seemed to transcend the racial divide in pre-civil rights American culture. For this reason, a white man staking claim to the legacy of Joe Louis would have been particularly offensive in Bruce's and Miller's historical moment. What is more, Louis had been retired from boxing for nearly a decade when Bruce and Miller produced the first recording of the bit and, therefore, name-dropping Louis would have been especially awkward for the audience.
10 The track listing on the Carnegie Hall Concert calls the bit "Ku Klux Klan," because it appears more or less without an introduction. The previously unreleased recording in the *Buyer Beware* set is titled, "Would You Want Your Sister to Marry One of Them?"
11 Kate Smith had an incredibly successful career as a singer in radio and television, but because she was tall and heavyset she was not the conventional image of female beauty. African American actress, singer, and activist Lena Horne, however, was the stereotypical Hollywood starlet.
12 Like Smith and Horne, the white Laughton was wealthy and heavyset whereas the Harry Belafonte was dapper.
13 Ofay is a derogatory slang term for a white person, and keister is slang for buttocks.

References

Achter, P. (2008). Comedy in unfunny times: News parody and carnival after 9/11. *Critical Studies in Media Communication, 25*(3), 274–303.
Azlant, E. (2007). Lenny Bruce again: "Gestapo? You asshole, I'm the mailman!" *Studies in American Humor 15*(3), 75–99.
Baker, F. (Director). (1972). *Lenny Bruce without Tears* [Motion Picture]. United States of America: Fred Baker Films.
Bakhtin, M. (1984). *Rabelais and his world*. Bloomington: University of Indiana Press.
Baym, G. (2005). The Daily Show: Discursive integration and the reinvention of political journalism. *Political Communication, 22,* 259–276.
Baym, G. (2007). Representation and the politics of play: Stephen Colbert's Better Know a District. *Political Communication, 24,* 359–376.
Bruce, L. (1961). *American*. USA: Fantasy.
Bruce, L. (1991). How to relax your colored friends at parties (feat. Eric Miller). On *Originals Volume 2* [CD]. USA: Fantasy.
Bruce, L. (1992). *How to talk dirty and influence people*. New York, NY: Fireside.
Bruce, L. (1995). Ku Klux Klan. On *The Carnegie Hall Concert* [CD]. USA: World Pacific.
Bruce, L. (2004a). Are there any niggers here tonight? On *Buyer Beware* [CD]. USA: Shout.

Bruce, L. (2004b). How to relax your colored friends at parties (feat. Eric Miller). On *Buyer Beware* [CD]. USA: Shout.

Bruce, L. (2004c). Would you want your sister to marry one of them? On *Buyer Beware* [CD]. USA: Shout.

Casper, K. (2014). "I didn't do it, man, I only said it": The asignifying force of the *Lenny Bruce Performance Film*. *Rhetoric Society Quarterly, 44*(4), 343–362.

de Certeau, M. (1984). *The practice of everyday life*. Steven Rendall (Trans.). Berkeley: University of California Press.

Collins, R.K.L. & Skover, D.M. (2002). *The trials of Lenny Bruce: The rise and fall of an American icon*. Naperville, IL: Sourcebooks.

Crenshaw, C. (1997). Resisting whiteness' rhetorical silence. *Western Journal of Communication, 61*, 253–278.

Dagnes, A. (2012). *A conservative walks into a bar: The politics of political humor*. New York: Palgrave MacMillan.

Flores, L.A., Ashcraft, K.L., & Marafiote, T. (2010). We got game: Race, masculinity, and civilization in professional team sport. In T.K. Nakayama & R.T. Halualani (Eds.), *The handbook of critical intercultural communication* (pp. 417–445). Malden, MA: Blackwell Publishing.

Fosse, B. (Director). (1974). *Lenny* [Motion Picture]. United States of America: Marvin Worth Productions.

Frankenberg, R. (1993). *White women, race matters: The social construction of whiteness*. Minneapolis: University of Minnesota Press.

Frye, M. (1983). *The politics of reality: Essays in feminist theory*. Freedom, CA: The Crossing Press.

Gale, E. (Director). (2011). *Looking for Lenny* (Motion Picture). United States of America: Borderline Films.

Goldman, A. (1974). *Ladies and gentlemen Lenny Bruce!!* New York: Random House.

Griffin, R.A., & Calafell, B.M. (2011). Control, discipline, and punish: Black masculinity and (in)visible whiteness in the NBA. In M.G. Lacy & K.A. Ono (Eds.), *Critical rhetorics of race* (pp. 117–138). New York: New York University Press.

Highet, G. (1962). *The anatomy of satire*. Princeton: Princeton University Press.

Jackson, R.L., Shin, C.I., & Hilson, K.B. (2000). The meaning of whiteness: Critical implications of communicating and negotiating race. *World Communication, 29*, 69–86.

Jones, J.P. (2010). More than "fart noises and funny faces": *The Daily Show's* coverage of the U.S. recession. *Popular Communication, 8*(3), 165–169.

Jones, J.P. & Baym, G. (2010). A dialogue on satire news and the crisis of truth in postmodern political television. *Journal of Communication Inquiry, 34*(3), 278–294.

Kantor, M. (Director). (2009). *Make 'em laugh: the funny business in America* [Motion Picture]. United States of America: Rhino.

Kercher, S. (2010). *Revel with a cause: Liberal satire in postwar America*. Chicago: University of Chicago Press.

Lynch, O. (2002). Humorous communication: Finding a place for humor in communication research. *Communication Theory 12*(4), 423–445.

McKerrow, R.E. (1989). Critical rhetoric: Theory and praxis. *Communication Monographs, 56*, 91–111.

Meddaugh, P.M. (2010). Bakhtin, Colbert and the center of discourse: Is there no "truthiness" in humor. *Critical Studies in Media Communication, 27*(4), 376–390.

Mintz, L.E. (1985). Stand-up comedy as social and cultural mediation. *American Quarterly 37*(1), 71–80.

Moon, D., & Flores, L.A. (2000). Antiracism and the abolition of whiteness: Rhetorical strategies of domination among "race traitors." *Communication Studies, 51*(2), 97–115.

Nachman, G. (2003). *Seriously funny: The rebel comedians of 1950s and 1960s.* New York: Pantheon.

Nakayama, T.K., & Krizek, R.L. (1995). Whiteness: A strategic rhetoric. *Quarterly Journal of Speech, 81,* 291–309.

Rossing, J.P. (2012). Deconstructing postracialism: Humor as a critical, cultural project. *Journal of Communication Inquiry 36*(1), 44–61.

Rossing J.P. (2013). Dick Gregory and activist style: Identifying attributes of humor necessary for advocacy. *Argument & Advocacy 50*(2), 59–71.

Rothenberg, P.S. (2007). *Race, class, and gender in the United States* (7th ed.). New York: Worth Publishers.

Shome, R. (2000). Outing whiteness. *Critical Studies in Media Communication, 17*(3), 366–371.

Simpson, J.L. (2008). The color-blind double bind: Whiteness and the (im)possibility of dialogue. *Communication Theory, 18,* 139–159.

Steinman, C. (2008). The price of whiteness: Jews, race, and American identity, by Eric L. Goldstein. *Political Communication, 25*(3), 336–338.

The sickniks (1959). *Time 74*(2), 44.

Waisanen, D.J. (2009). A citizen's guide to democracy inaction: Jon Stewart and Stephen Colbert's comic rhetorical criticism. *Southern Journal of Communication 74*(2), 119–140.

Waisanen, D.J. (2011). Crafting hyperreal spaces for comic insights: The *Onion News Network's* ironic iconicity. *Communication Quarterly 59*(5), 508–528.

Wander, P.C., Martin, J.N., & Nakayama, T.K. (1999). Whiteness and beyond: Sociohistorical foundations of whiteness and contemporary challenges. In T.K. Nakayama & J.N. Martin (Eds.), *Whiteness: The communication of social identity* (pp. 13–26). Thousand Oaks, CA: Sage.

Warren, J.T. (2003). *Performing purity: Whiteness, pedagogy, and the reconstitution of power.* New York: Peter Lang.

Weide, B. (Director). (1998). *Lenny Bruce: Swear to tell the truth* [Motion Picture]. United States of America: Whyaduck Productions.

Zoglin, R. (2008). *Comedy at the edge: How stand-up in the 1970s changed America.* New York, NY: Bloomsbury USA.

6

TEASING THE FUNNY

Native American Stand-up Comedy in the 21st Century

Amanda Morris

"Three Indians walked out of a bar sober …" Vaughn Eaglebear looks around at the reservation casino audience, scanning the room amidst the hesitant half-giggles, amused murmurs, and one shout of "That's right!," biding his time to complete the punchline. After a full 15 seconds, he delivers: "It could happen."

Contemporary Native American stand-up comedians like Eaglebear often deploy trickster strategies in their sets to simultaneously reassure and unsettle the audience. These strategies are playfully subversive and/or taboo, flirting with or outright embracing the socially inappropriate to disrupt expectations. Arguably, all stand-up comics use trickster tactics to some extent. However, Native American comics in particular take these tactics one step further; acting as trickster allows them to share real stories about contemporary Native communities, practices, and ideas that directly counter stereotypes about Native peoples that may not otherwise be well-received in another venue.

This chapter builds from personal fieldwork with the Powwow Comedy Jam (PCJ), an intercultural/intertribal comedy group of four comics from across Native America. The PCJ has performed all over the country, on reservations, in mainstream comedy clubs, and on college campuses. When I conducted a Google search for "Native American comedians" and "American Indian stand-up comics" back in 2008, the results were mostly references to history. The only two contemporary Native American comics to arise (on the second results page, no less) were the Powwow Comedy Jam and Charlie Hill (Oneida).[1] Further, the Powwow Comedy Jam seemed to be the only major Native American stand-up comedy troupe actively working that also had a significant public presence at the time, including a website, press photos, clips on YouTube, and a list of upcoming performances. Charlie Hill may have initiated the first generation of contemporary Native American stand-up comics working in the 1960s and 70s, but it wasn't until the 21st century that the second generation took up the comic effort. By

2010, the PCJ was so successful in their efforts to gain public attention that they inspired the Showtime network to produce the *American Indian Comedy Slam*,[2] a special featuring the PCJ troupe, their comic forebear, Hill, and others.

Drawing on my fieldwork with the PCJ, in this chapter I present a detailed analysis of a single set from one PCJ team member, Ojibwe comedian Jim Ruel, in order to demonstrate the rhetorical function of the trickster strategy in Native American stand-up. Native comedians frequently transcend the base purpose of stand-up comedy, which is laughter, and rise to a new level of teasing inquiry and engagement with one of the most difficult objects to change: the stereotype-laden and misinformed American mind. The dichotomy of reassuring and unsettling their audiences is embedded in the stories and moments created and re-created by many Native American comedians in order to challenge deeply held beliefs and assumptions about indigenous peoples, including conceptions that indigenous peoples aren't funny, humorous, joyful communities with individual and evolving cultures.

Trickster Strategies and Native American Stand-Up Comedy

The trickster, in worldwide storytelling traditions, is a clever hero or antihero – a character who breaches the rules of proper behavior and disrupts the status quo. Tricksters feature prominently in most, if not all, Native American nations' stories. According to John Zerzan (2012), "Trickster tales reach back from a time of a world that was once whole, but was already in fragments when the first attempt to record these stories took place … the trickster's elemental, amoral energy does not recognize boundaries … it is not so easy to get a fix on this character, who fairly often displays contradictory elements" (p. 130). In this respect, trickster is not real; it is a powerful idea that drives change. In this light, Native American stand-up comedians are more than just stand-up comics; they delight and play with the audience in ways that uphold the trickster idea of change. Tricksters are often represented in stories as creatures who compassionately and humorously subvert social and cultural norms, "illustrating the fact that laughter can open doors and allow us to see reality differently" (Zerzan 2012, p. 131). Although contemporary Native comedians are not themselves tricksters, per se, they do use trickster strategies of humor, compassion, and subversion in order to help audiences see their realities differently. To this end, these comedians are also intellectuals and storytellers, sharing experiences and theories about contemporary Native realities with audiences that may or may not be receptive to this information.

Anishnabeg scholar Gerald Vizenor (1995) provides the best theoretical and practical guidance on tricksters as applied to Native cultures. He writes, "Tricksters only exist in a comic sense between two people who take pleasure in a language game and imagination, a noetic liberation of the mind" (p. 83). As an important imaginative figure in many cultures, tricksters subvert the rules and evade easy definition. Contemporary Native American comedians are not themselves the mythical tricksters, but they are borrowing some tricksters' tactics in order to invert audience expectations, teach about living Indigenous peoples, and shatter the boundaries that keep non-Native peoples from seeing Native peoples as alive and vital communities. Some of these tactics include teasing about both American and Native American cultural norms, sharing the mistakes they've made in order to teach the audience how not to behave, and celebrating the duality and flexibility of contemporary Native cultures through humorous anecdotes and stories.

By deploying these tactics throughout their comedy sets, Native American stand-up comedians create new stories on stage, stories about contemporary Indigenous peoples for their audiences. These poetic tactics exemplify the power of performance in changing minds about troubling issues. Jill Carter (Anishinaabe/Ashkenazi) writes about the theatrical experience on the urban stage as a space of opportunity for Native artists:

> It is a site through which we might continue the oral tradition and remember our histories, but also chronicle recent events, struggles, preoccupations, and victories. Each theatrical event engineered by Native artists in urban settings affords the opportunity to unite a scattered body politic and to engage in relationship-building as histories, languages, lifeways, and philosophical principles are embodied and shared. The theatrical event, regardless of the culture from whence it springs, carries the promise of transformation for performer and spectator alike: the urban stage, then, becomes the site upon which Native artists also come together with their communities to negotiate the luminal interstices between those who we were (pre-colonization), those who we have been told we are (colonization), and those who we will become (decolonization). Such healing and transformative ritual "acts," engendered to aid in the formation of the new, decolonized human being, require, as they always have, the intervention and ministrations of our nations' models-and-agents of transformation – our trickster-figures.
>
> *(2010, p. 265)*

While Carter writes about how Native trickster figures are brought to life in plays on the stage, the principle and overall outcome remains the same when applied to the Native comedians performing in a contemporary space.

Powwow Comedy Jam: "Trail of Laughs"

When I met the PCJ team in Everett, Washington, in February 2009, Vaughn Eaglebear did not use the "three Indians walk out of a bar sober" joke because there were six people in the audience for their 10:30 show at Marson's Comedy Club and only two were Native Americans. The "Indians walked out of a bar" joke only seems funny with an insider audience – Native Americans who understand the realities of alcoholism in their midst and who can likewise be self-referential about it and laugh at themselves. This joke doesn't work the same way with a primarily non-Native audience. In fact, the offense level increases when the teller is white. I use myself as a case in point. After my Everett trip, I prepped my students that I was about to tell them a joke that is a "not-joke" simply because I'm the one telling it. Then I told them this well-known "Indians walked out of a bar" joke and the response was as predicted – some nervous giggles followed by hands covering mouths and widened eyes. Could this discomfort with such a painful subject prevent the necessary acceptability level for more non-Native audiences to find Native comedians funny? When I asked the Powwow Comedy guys about this during an interview after one of their performances, Marc Yaffee (Navajo) first pointed to the fact that there are only three million Native Americans, so the built-in audience is smaller. But when I pushed him on this, he said that the content or subject matter they deal with, particularly the topics that are specific to Native experiences in this land, are sometimes difficult for mainstream audiences to hear and understand.

In his oral "foreword" to the PCJ's DVD, *Joke Signals* (Holiday 2005), Charlie Hill expresses his appreciation for what these "young fast guns" are doing and also sets up the important potential of Native comedians to change how we see ourselves, our nation, and how we talk and think about Native peoples:

> I think what they're doing is wonderful even though everyday to Native people, it's new to America simply because they don't know who we are. And when you laugh at people and you understand people and that's where it is ... you get people to laugh ... I like that these guys get you to laugh with us and not at us ... These guys bring a lot of intelligence and different, distinctive points of view ... It's nice to see these guys are out and being together from four different cultural backgrounds is like an alliance of Indian nations, it's alliance, and together, you know, we've tried before, we've fought the government and they beat us because we got their diseases, we've signed treaties and they broke every one of them, we've tried peace negotiations but there's no such thing as peace in this land. We've tried everything, we've cajoled them, we were nice to them when they got here, but now these four guys, the new Powwow Comedy Jam, they're gonna take this land back one joke at a time, something we've never tried before.

J.R. Redwater, the former Standing Rock Sioux member of the PCJ, cares a great deal about increasing cross-cultural understanding. In a follow-up e-mail interview after our first interaction at their show in Everett, he wrote me about the importance of understanding the contemporary Native perspective and expressed gratitude to Showtime for broadcasting and recording the *American Indian Comedy Slam*. "Indian Humor exists in every Native culture," Redwater said, "but most people do not know that we are funny. Most of the time, our perspective is injected directly into our sets." He went on to explain that words like "snaggin'," "ayyeeez," "enit," "frybread," and "rez" are slang terms that he often tries to quickly explain to audiences to increase their knowledge and get them into a shared comedic space.

In fact, during the set I had the privilege to see, Vaughn Eaglebear (Colville) used "Ayyeeez," and asked those of us in the audience if we knew what he was talking about. The one Native couple in the audience nodded assent and the rest of us were visibly clueless. So he paused his set to quickly explain this is equivalent to "psyche" or "just kidding" in White American traditions and then proceeded to use the term liberally throughout his set, knowing that we all now understood what he meant.

Furthermore, in response to a query about how important cross-cultural education is to the group, Marc Yaffee (Navajo) responded by email, "Cross cultural education is very important to us. Comedy lets us connect with non-natives in a humorous setting where they are more likely to accept the points we make as they're done in a humorous way." Jim Ruel (Ojibwa) said that almost anything he says on stage about Native Americans "is a teaching moment because in general folks know pretty much nothing about us." He said that most people are surprised that a Native American can do comedy because of the "serious and stoic" stereotype. Knowing this, Ruel purposely takes these stereotypes and misconceptions and inverts them for audiences so they "would still be able to laugh along and not feel attacked."

These educational moments, wanted or unwanted, expected or unexpected, are an opportunity for trickster strategies. They allow the comedians, through the cultural tool of language, to directly engage audiences that may not be familiar with the terms, ideas, and perspectives unique to Native American experiences. However, according to Kristina Fagan (2005), in the only scholarly collection to date that deals exclusively with American Indian comedy, "To read Aboriginal humor only in terms of its relationship to white society is limiting" (p. 24). As she evaluates Native author Greg Sarris's humorous purpose in *Keeping Slug Woman Alive*, Fagan discovers that his story "tells us a great deal about how he wants us to see him and his own community" (p. 24). Therefore, in considering Native American comedians' perspectives and performance strategies, it is important to recognize the multi-purposed approach and understand that each comedian has different priorities in relation to their white audiences, but all Native comics seem to share this tactic of telling non-Native audiences how they want them to understand their Indigenous communities. This tactic is vital to building cross-cultural understanding and reducing racism. It is also a form of activism that can benefit these comedians' home communities, although there are no guarantees this positive outcome will result. Ideally, when non-Native audiences are able to connect to a Native cultural perspective through shared laughter with the PCJ, the chances of that audience continuing to buy into the mainstream belief that Native peoples don't exist and even if they do, they don't have a sense of humor, is greatly reduced. The small opening that this shared laughter creates may inspire people to self-educate about contemporary Native populations, or seek out knowledge that they would otherwise be unaware of, or, at the very least, lean toward acceptance and away from bald ignorance.

Indigenous Studies scholar Jace Weaver (Cherokee) engages the continuing existence of American Indian intellectual traditions, addresses the question of what "distinguishes written product by Natives from that of non-Natives," and offers a new methodology and framework for this type of study, writing in his introduction to *That the People Might Live*, "It is important that Native cultures be seen as living, dynamic cultures" (1997, p. 8) as opposed to the colonialist assumptions of cultural stasis and death: "By viewing the Indian as vanishing and Indian cultures as disintegrating, it was possible to view 20th century Indians who refused to vanish as degraded and inauthentic … It is a vision of the 'Indian as corpse,' and the stasis box is only a thinly disguised coffin. An extinct people do not change. Their story is complete" (p. 18). In America especially, we have become disturbingly comfortable with this idea. Perhaps this comfort is one of the reasons why, when confronted with Native American comedians exploring issues that touch on such assumptions, we're not quite sure how to react. Surely, not with laughter!

Lawrence Gross (San Manuel Band of Mission Indians) contributed a significant article on "Humor in American Indian Cultures" to the 2014 *Encyclopedia of Humor Studies*. Gross opens with the admonishment not to generalize American Indian humor because of the large number of existing nations in North, Central, and South America. "However," he then adds, "even though American Indians are stereotypically seen as being stoic, in actuality, humor is an extremely important part of most American Indian traditions," before launching into his focus: trickster tradition and teasing (2014, p. 24). While the trickster traditionally appears "in the oral tradition of most American Indian nations," he writes, the character also focuses on the wider contemporary world, specifically helping to "shape a preexisting world into its present form" by using its wits to survive (p. 24). The stories told on the stage by the PCJ comics not only invert audience expectations about "stoic" Indians, they also use wit to shape a new and better world for the comics and their communities.

According to John Limon (2000), "stand-up is uniquely audience dependent" (p. 12). In particular, he argues that a two-second laugh is "respectable," a four-second laugh "greets the best joke of a standard *Tonight Show* monologue," and to get a laugh up to six seconds – an extraordinary occasion – "you generally need two distinct waves of laughter, as in the case of jokes that are immediately funny and funnier (they are usually self-reflexive) upon reprocessing" (p. 16). This plays into his theory that the audience creates, or co-creates, the joke. Otherwise, the comedian is left with either a bad joke, or worse, a non-joke. When I suggested this theory to Ruel and Yaffee, though, their responses were both firm and humorous. Yaffee responded:

> I don't agree with the theory that the audience creates the jokes as much as it measures a joke's effectiveness in that given environment when it's delivered. It is amazing how a joke will work so well with some crowds. For instance, an Indian joke told in front of an all white audience could bite the

dust while in front of an Indian audience, it might get a four to six second response – it's where the joke is being delivered. A joke in my opinion is still a joke when it is created and enjoyed in the mind of its creator. Now the joke may never be validated and liked by anyone else but it still exists at least on paper or in the writer's memory.

(Powwow Comedy Jam 2009)

Concurrently, Jim Ruel wrote a bit more extensively about why he disagrees with Limon's theory, saying, "I prefer to think of standup as an art form. To me that means it should be personal, creative and original. You are saying something." The question of whether theory and art can go together is an argument for another day, but Ruel's point is well taken. While theories such as Limon's (or Vizenor's, or Carter's) can certainly provide scholars a new way of considering the artistic and intellectual output of particular groups and subgroups of people, practical application in tangible and real locations may also require a different lens and perspective. Not all theories can comfortably survive the transition into the world of practitioners.

Jim Ruel: "What are you into? Concrete?"

For the sake of space, I will only analyze one of the PCJ team's performances. However, Jim Ruel's performance at the Isleta Casino (see Holiday 2005) provides ample evidence for building my case. Ruel's set is a particularly good example of trickster strategies because his humorous anecdotes celebrate the duality and flexibility of contemporary Native cultures, reshape the audience's conception of contemporary Native peoples, and reveal the absurdity of any embedded stereotype about Native Americans that audience members may have. When considering the possible communal purpose and potential cross-cultural impact of such stories, one is prompted to ask: which is the more important second element, a complication or a moment of reflection? Or, are they both vital to helping the comedians' achieve their purpose?

In the case at Isleta Casino, it is important to note that Ruel is Ojibwe from Minnesota and his audience is primarily Isleta Pueblo (one of the 19 Pueblo groups of the Southwest), which does create a contact zone of cross-cultural tension. For instance, at a few points in his performance, Ruel lightly mocks the audience's misunderstanding about what he is saying. In one moment, something as seemingly banal as climate becomes the complication upon which Ruel and his audience can build a moment of reflection in which mutual understanding and laughter can be the result. Specifically, one minute and 22 seconds into his set, he draws on the sympathies and knowledge of his Native audience by talking about identity problems, "The thing about bein' half is people don't know what you are. They see you and try to guess, they're like, 'Oh, pothead!' [laughter] No, I'm Native American. Oh, you must have the good shit, hook me up! [bigger laugh] That's not my thing, okay. It'll be a cold day in Canada before you see me smokin' a joint."

At this point, the audience is almost completely silent for several seconds, to which Ruel responds by pausing and making a face that indicates his disbelief that they don't get the joke. What makes the audience laugh is Ruel's facial expression and body language as he physically, but silently, censures their incomprehension. Granted, his delivery of this last line is pure deadpan, delivered with absolute conversational seriousness, but Ruel's tonal reversal is so fast that it leaves his audience in the witticism's wake. Addressing the missed punchline, he thus follows up his humorously scolding looks by explaining, "It's cold up there. Some of you are like, 'Oh, wow, he's a like a role model to his people, good for him.'" At this point, the audience realizes they have been censured for their lack of understanding and good-naturedly laughs as the comedian laughs at them. But none of Ruel's set is mean-spirited – all the teasing is delivered gently and, in this case, brings people in line with his perspective. Gross writes about such teasing in American Indian humor and cultures, writing, "Whatever rules govern teasing behavior, the social expectation among traditional societies was and is that one should accept teasing gracefully … there is a continual social dynamic in which teasing goes back and forth. When done properly, teasing acts to cement social relations and strengthen the bond within the group" (2014, p. 25). When applied to Ruel's performance, evidence of strengthened social relations and graceful acceptance of teasing exists in the audience's good-natured and appreciative reactions.

In fact, a majority of Ruel's set would fall under Ian Ferguson's (2005) definition of "In Jokes," or "jokes told by Indians when non-Natives (and this again refers primarily to White People) are in the room":

> These jokes tend to be a little self-deprecating, and they often have a political edge … The whole point of In Jokes is their accessibility. Everyone is allowed to laugh, and everybody is supposed to get the joke. Despite the social commentary of the subject matter or point of view, no one is meant to feel uncomfortable. If there is a little teasing going on, it's supposed to be gentle, not mean-spirited.
>
> *(pp. 125–126)*

From former girlfriends, edible long underwear, and New Agers to Thanksgiving, dreamcatchers, and "authentic" representations of Indians in Hollywood films, Ruel tackles a wide variety of familiar surface content through personal stories that resonate with anyone comfortable in contemporary America, while simultaneously revealing deeper problems about how Native people are perceived in mainstream America by non-Natives. By performing a set that includes such a heavy emphasis on misperceptions and the outright skewering of those misperceptions, Ruel's set targets white people explicitly. Take his bit on New Agers, who, upon finding out he is Native American, make the judgment that he "must be so into nature." Ruel's comeback to this is, "What are you into? Concrete?" Somehow his explicit censure of non-Natives' false assumptions also plays with audience expectations, which keeps people off-guard and, thus, more open to laughing at themselves and each other in this new space. The jokes can be funny to both Native and non-Native people despite the clear one-sided targeting. Why? If I was to point to Ruel's laid-back, relaxed on-stage persona that is more academic, intricate, and well-planned than it might first appear, it may be an adequate explanation. I could also point out that he tells good stories. Funny stories. And funny stories appeal to everyone within earshot. However, the transcultural construction and flow of his set allow Ruel to traverse dangerous territory that borders on bold accusation in a way that many white folks find as charming and laugh-out-loud funny as his Isleta reservation casino audience did. Perhaps the inversion of audience expectations, lessons about living Indigenous peoples, the clear challenge to both Native American and broader American cultural norms, combined with the sharing of humorous anecdotes that celebrate the duality and flexibility of Native cultures and playing on audience members' beliefs in certain ideas about Native peoples, ensure Ruel's cross-cultural comedic success. This particular combination also provides evidence of his strategic trickster performance.

Combining physical gestures (such as making up a ridiculous "rain dance" that includes mainstream dance moves from "YMCA" and "I'm a Little Teapot" in perfect timing with his words), Ruel coaxes his audiences along a path of intellectual decolonization and helps them laugh at themselves, at their misperceptions about Native peoples, and at their potentially misguided ideas about American history and education. In short, Ruel helps his audiences feel Thomas King's advice, that "we are at our best when we laugh at ourselves" (2005b, p. 55), and experience Don Kelly's wisdom, "I can laugh at myself. And we can laugh together, and at one another" (2005, p. 181).

Most importantly, as Gross points out, "In order to tease someone from a specific nation, one has to know the traditions and practices of that nation well enough to engage in teasing behavior" (2014, p. 25). Ruel clearly understands Ojibwe *and* broader American cultural traditions and practices, which gives him the ability to tease effectively. Two excellent examples of this attack occur during Ruel's Thanksgiving and urban Native stories. The Thanksgiving bit immediately follows the edible long underwear bit, after the audience has warmed up with the "Canada-is-cold" censure, and the introductory knowledge that Ruel self-identifies as "a half-breed." Ruel transitions into talking about moving to LA and being invited by a friend for Thanksgiving dinner:

> He was being all very sensitive. He was like, "Oh my gosh, do you guys celebrate that?" [mild laughter] I was like, "Yeah, we do … but we call it You're Welcome Day." [laughter] Little different. [Ruel begins gesturing with his free arm] "Anytime! [arm wave forward to indicate "no problem"] Don't worry about it! [pats himself on the back] Have some squash!" [holds hand out front, palm up, and fingers spread wide in a large bowl formation – this gesture quickly turns into an upraised middle finger; this rude gesture is followed by a fairly long and appreciative laugh from the audience].

On one hand, Ruel is sharing a story of experience – the awkwardness of being the lone Native American invited to Thanksgiving dinner and all the politically correct baggage that experience carries. On the other hand, Ruel is also telling a metastory about a common experience and sentiment likely shared among Indigenous peoples that has both historical and contemporary resonance. Hence, it is both a moment of complication *and* a moment of reflection. Historically, his brief comedic tale of 39 words linked to several meaningful physical gestures calls on the audience's awareness and knowledge of the traditional Thanksgiving story in which Native peoples help the white Pilgrims survive their first winter on this land. Yet the tale further relies on the audience's shared assumption that the Pilgrims' subsequent invasion and land theft was wrong and no holiday can make up for that, no matter how good the mashed potatoes and stuffing. Essentially, the joke implies that by reducing the struggle of Native populations' adaptation and adjustment to their European invaders to a trivialized national holiday on which people "celebrate" this unequal and imbalanced historical relationship, anyone who celebrates this "holiday" is just as guilty and complacent as the federal government is and was in the metatrivialization of entire Indigenous cultures and belief systems. Ruel's Native audience is not only aware of this history, they also share in its pain. For white audiences to find this story funny, they must have a certain level of awareness and compassion for the truth, which diverts from the stories many white Americans were taught in grade school about the Indians saving the Pilgrims and feasting together in happy brotherhood. Ruel's seemingly simple story places this official government tale on a platter and then roasts it thoroughly to the enjoyment of all who accept that the official white American story is a lie.

Another official story lambasted in Ruel's personal tales involves being an urban Native kid growing up in Minneapolis:

> Thing about being an urban Native, people are always, you're, like, always on display. Even in kindergarten. I was the only Native in my class. Teacher'd have storytelling time. She'd be like, "Alright everyone, sit Indian style." [murmured giggles] Everyone's checkin' me out. [points toward audience with a straight arm and pointing index finger] "Hey, look! Jim's got a style there!" So I put my legs behind my head [pulls one leg up as if to put it over his head] "Come on, everybody, let's go!" [laughter] Teacher gets all pissed off. [mimes teacher's accusing stance] "Hey! That's not Indian style!" "Hey, who's the Indian here?" [laughter] "This is the new style, lady!" [murmuring laughter] "Catchin' on at all the strip clubs!" [more murmuring laughter] Even my friends, man, they go hunting in the fall and want to bring me along as their tracker. [laughter] I'm like, "Dude, I grew up in the city, I'm more of a stalker" [hunches down and stalks across stage, laughter ensues]

The first part of this bit should be understandable and recognizable to anyone who survived the American education grade school system. Sitting "Indian style" in school as a child is as familiar to my own experiences growing up in in

Pittsburgh as it was painful and humorous for Ruel. By turning the tables on his teacher, though, even if in exaggerated terms, Ruel also turns the table on the ridiculous idea and existence of the phrase "Indian style." As he does with the official national Thanksgiving tale, Ruel takes stereotyped assumption and cuts it apart for all to enjoy.

Finally, Ruel's comedy works to support communities. Ruel can claim membership to several communities, including the greater Ojibwa community, the stand-up comedy community, the broader Native American community, and others. How do these communities benefit from his trickster storytelling performances? The short answer might be that Ruel, as a stand-up comic, proves that Ojibwas and other tribal peoples can make a living in a creative performance field and brings different stories and experiences to the table of stand-up comedy. However, his comedy is also a source of personal and communal healing for the Native audiences who hear and laugh at Ruel's stories. According to Gross, "Trickster stories teach American Indians how to live in this world just as it is, with all the nobility and weaknesses that make up the human character. Trickster stories instruct American Indians to maintain a positive attitude in the face of even the most severe suffering … the importance of having a sense of humor is something that is taught by the trickster stories of American Indians, and as a result, humor is an important part of their cultures" (2014, p. 25). For Ruel's white American audiences, misperceptions are overturned and hopefully minds are opened a bit wider, which may lead to improvements in cross-cultural understanding, one of the morally educative outcomes that this type of comedy offers multiple audiences. Just as Vine Deloria, Jr. was "an uncompromising advocate of the personhood and humanity of Indian peoples" (Weaver 1997, p. 125), so, too, is Jim Ruel. Expressing his rhetorical sovereignty by telling personal stories that perform a double philosophical and psychological duty, as well as by creating laughter among disparate audiences, Ruel actively takes a stand on how his Native communities' stories are told in the public domain. He engages his non-Native audiences with experiences, stories, and perspectives that often include difficult and uncomfortable ideas, yet Ruel has mastered the art of making people laugh at themselves and each other. And shared laughter in the contact zone between peoples can be the thread of commonality that allows for potential cross-cultural communication and education to take place.

"You've Heard It Now" (or, Implications and Conclusions)

As a scholar and writer who overtly uses humor to delve into serious social, economic, and political issues, Thomas King provides a solid bridge between academic and non-academic Native worldviews. In an essay for Drew Hayden Taylor's collection *Me Funny*, King (2005a) criticizes the recent increase in academic attention to Native American humor, writing, "One, we've decided that Native humor exists, and two, we've come up with a general definition. Or description. Or good guess" (p. 170). Clearly, King is not a fan of defining Native people or Native humor and argues, rather, that Native humor leans toward the indefinable: "The definition may lie in and change with performance … it's like the wind. We can't see it. We don't know where it comes from. And the only time we feel it is when it's blowing in our face" (p. 171). Remaining indefinable preserves the power, authority, and joyfulness of Native humor and preserves the sacredness of trickster stories. Clearly, to define Native humor too narrowly would sap its strength to persuade, cajole, and comfort. The academy's love of defining and categorizing people and ideas into neat, easily managed compartments can constrain study and may de-value the insights potentially available with interdisciplinary approaches. To deny our interconnectedness, whether across academic disciplines or across ethnic divides in comedy, would be to deny our commonality. King says it well: "There are probably cultural differences in humor, but I suspect that what makes Native people laugh is pretty much what makes all people laugh … We are at our best when we laugh at ourselves" (p.181).

Lawrence Gross's discussion of trickster stories likewise states, "The ability to laugh at oneself and not take oneself too seriously is another important lesson garnered from trickster stories. By being able to laugh at oneself, trickster stories also teach the importance of forgiveness of self and others" (2014, p. 25). Darby Li Po Price (1998) makes a similar observation. Writing about the challenges in performing identities and the choice Native comedians must make in choosing an identity, Price concludes, "Establishing common grounds across ethnic groups creates a collective sense of we-ness" (p. 263).

King definitely has a point that Native American humor should not be narrowly defined. Furthermore, Price's assessment that "Indian standups perform as intercultural mediators … to entertain and educate their audiences" (p. 269) is a powerful reminder that performance can be as persuasive as writing. However, I would like to suggest that there are some stark differences between Native American-generated humor and other comedians' stories. That difference is the content and subject matter of their performances and historical context that is unique to Native peoples in North America.

Simply put, most Native American comedians refer to or deal with, in minor or major ways during their performances, land, treaty, and reservation issues. No other group can claim to have these same historical pains and wrongs. These subjects are unique to Native American experience in this land. One of my favorite Charlie Hill jokes is when he relates to the audience the tale of the heckler one night who told him, "Why don't you people go back to where you belong?" So Hill says he went and camped in the man's backyard. The point of his teasing is clear. Native people were here before the Europeans came and stole the land and non-Natives are still benefiting from this early theft. This painful fact will not go away and is prevalent in all of the Native comedians I have observed thus far, just as ongoing colonialism is an issue with the American Indian scholars.

Ultimately, though, Native American stand-up comedians are important actors operating outside the academic world to cajole, comfort, tease, influence, and affect how their audiences see and understand contemporary Native American experiences. Many audience members, such as those who experience Ruel's performances, may be open to acceptance and tolerance, but may have no understanding about the differences in experience between white and Aboriginal peoples. Ruel and other Native comics teach through laughter by using trickster strategies of teasing and self-deprecation in order to confront their Native and non-Native audiences with the audiences' own assumptions, expectations, and misperceptions about themselves and each other. Laughter results and a greater humanistic understanding grows as a new narrative takes hold.

In one of Charlie Hill's sets, for instance, First Nations actor Graham Greene introduces him by stating, "Back when he started, Aboriginal people struggled to achieve equality and justice and he vowed to perform until that day came along. Well, looks like the poor guy will never be able to retire! [laughter]" (Charlie Hill on The Comedy Network n.d.). Greene's introduction draws attention to the still problematic inequality that exists between Native and non-Native peoples. This inequality is something that new and different perspectives can fix in the short and long term. It all starts with sharing stories and laughter and, as King writes, "Just don't say in the years to come that you would have lived your life differently if only you had heard this story. You've heard it now" (2005a, p.167). Of course, the implication is that once we've heard the story, we can't go back to not knowing. As with the contact zone of the stage environment, this liminal state we inhabit straddling two different planes of knowledge once we've heard a story is the opening through which that new perspective can instigate ideas of tolerance and understanding, which may ideally lead to action on behalf of Native American communities.

Examining contemporary Native stand-up comedy through the trickster rhetorical lens in order to determine how this comedy benefits the comedians, their audiences, and their various communities results in some interesting outcomes. First, my brief look at one comedian's individual set sheds the merest glimpse into the effectiveness of this lens and approach, which cries out to be used again on a broader scale, with more depth and more comedians. Second, the acceptance level of the audience and their willingness to participate in the inversion cycle, as well as their acceptance to go beyond their own mental boundaries into an intellectual consideration of the pressing social problem of Native peoples' stereotyped existence in the mainstream may be an unusual situation. In a standard Friday night comedy club, the audience may not realize they will be hearing from a particular cultural perspective. The names of these comedians have no particular "Native American" identity markers, except, perhaps, for the group name, "Pow-wow Comedy Jam."

Finally, this comedy that incorporates trickster tactics can benefit both the comedians' indigenous communities and their audiences by acting as a bridge between two worldviews. The hope is that this type of comedy opens minds to more acceptance, understanding, and, frankly, less racism and misinformed assumptions about Native peoples. These comedians are modern day intellectuals weaving trickster tales in a volatile contact zone on a nightly basis to make us laugh at each other and, most importantly, at ourselves.

Notes

1 When I met with the PCJ comics, they called Hill "the godfather of Native American stand-up."
2 The American Indian Comedy Slam can be viewed for free in its entirety on hulu. com, zimbio.com, or dailymotion.com.

References

Carter, J. (2010). Trickster in the first person. In D. Reder & L. Morra (Eds.), *Troubling tricksters: Revisioning critical conversations* (pp. 21–58). Waterloo, ON: Wilfrid Laurier University Press.
Charlie Hill on The Comedy Network (Winnipeg Comedy Festival). (n.d.). *YouTube*. Retrieved from www.youtube.com/watch?v=QOf-3TShBio
Fagan, K. (2005). Teasing, tolerating, teaching: Laughter and community in Native literature. In D.H. Taylor (Ed.), *Me funny* (pp. 23–50). Vancouver, BC: Douglas & McIntyre.
Ferguson, I. (2005). How to be as funny as an Indian. In D.H. Taylor (Ed.), *Me funny* (pp. 123–132). Vancouver, BC: Douglas & McIntyre.
Gross, L. (2014). Humor in American Indian Cultures. In S. Attardo (Ed.), *Encyclopedia of humor studies* (pp. 24–27). Thousand Oaks, CA: Sage Publications.
Holiday, B. (Director). (2005). *Joke signals* [DVD]. H2F Comedy Productions, Inc.
Kelly, D. (2005). An now, ladies and gentlemen, get ready for some (ab)original stand-up comedy. In D.H. Taylor (Ed.), *Me funny* (pp. 51–66). Vancouver, BC: Douglas & McIntyre.
King, T. (2005a). Performing Native humour: The Dead Dog Café Comedy Hour. In D.H. Taylor (Ed.), *Me funny* (pp. 169–186). Vancouver, BC: Douglas & McIntyre.
King, T. (2005b). *The truth about stories: A native narrative*. Minneapolis: University of Minnesota Press.
Limon, J. (2000). *Stand-up comedy in theory, or, abjection in America*. Durham, NC: Duke University Press.
Powwow Comedy Jam (M. Yaffee, J. Ruel, V. Eaglebear, J.R. Redwater). (2009/2010). Personal interview and email. February 2009 – May 2010.
Price, D.L.P. (1998). Laughing without reservation: Indian standup comedians. *American Indian Culture and Research Journal, 22*(4), 255–271.
Vizenor, G. (1995). A trickster discourse: Comic and tragic themes in Native American literature. In M. Zanger & M. Page (Eds.), *Buried roots and indestructible seeds: The survival of American Indian life in story, history, and spirit* (pp. 67–83). Madison: University of Wisconsin Press.
Weaver, J. (1997). *That the people might live: Native American literatures and Native American community*. New York: Oxford University Press.
Zerzan, J. (2012). *Future primitive revisited* [ebook]. New York: Feral House.

RESPONSE: STAND-UP, RACE, AND CULTURE

FROM INSULT TO REFLECTION
Stand-Up Comedy and Cultural Pedagogy

Alberto González

The chapters in this part focus on the uneasy intersection of stand-up comedy and race. Involved in the case studies are questions such as: What special latitude does the comic have in performing offensive material about race? What larger social discourses help us to understand how comics mitigate or intensify reaction to their offensive material? What are the possibilities for progressive social engagement between comic and audience?

The responses to these questions draw from whiteness and ethnic studies, discourse analysis, and rhetorical criticism. Collectively, the chapters describe an evolution of sorts in comic purpose. Don Rickles represents the unapologetic voice of white superiority that now must be cautious due to the successes of the civil rights movement. Lenny Bruce represents the initial counter-cultural reaction to post-WWII modernity with a direct assault on whiteness. Finally, the Powwow Comedy Jam represents a new comedic pedagogy that seeks to unsettle the centrality of whiteness in most acts.

In this response, I will offer observations on each case study and then conclude with several implications for intercultural and interracial communication studies and instruction.

The Myth of Color-Blind Comedy

On occasion, I will still meet a person who expresses pride in their own irascibility. "I don't discriminate," they say, "I offend everyone." This statement is usually meant to establish the person's unvarnished individualism and the absence of bias in the judgment of others. I have never met anyone who said this who didn't occupy white positionality and who didn't go on to say offensive things from the "white racial frame" (Feagin 2014) and in so doing proved that, indeed, they do discriminate and they are biased. Don Rickles might have presented an "equal opportunity" rationale, but his jokes were hardly equal injury.

Informed by the early work of van Dijk (1993) on racist communication and more recent work by Bonilla-Silva (2013), Peréz persuasively shows how performers adjusted their material in light of increasing social rejection of racist speech. Rickles was able to create enough "ambiguity" between his material and racism by diversifying the ethnic and social identities that were the subjects of his bits, by engaging in self-deprecation, and by avoiding the most taboo subjects and epithets.

Van Dijk provides an additional possibility for explaining how Rickles was able to deflect criticism. This relates to class identity. As a child, I would look forward to watching *The Merv Griffin Show* each afternoon. I remember watching Don Rickles and I viewed him as a working class, mean-spirited bully – what Archie Bunker would be like if Archie did stand-up. To me, he was a contrast to the more refined and affluent class comics such as Bob Hope, and Jerry Lewis and Dean Martin. Van Dijk argues that the working class and marginalized groups are the actual sites of racism in the elite imaginary and this attribution allows dominant interests to deny racism even as elites "prepare" racist scripts for popular consumption (van Dijk 1993, p. 10). By adopting the persona of the crude, down-on-his-luck comic, Rickles played upon the low expectations of audiences.

This also helps to explain the difference in treatment between Rickles and Ted Danson and Michael Richards, whom Peréz also mentions. When donning blackface for a comedy roast of Whoopi Goldberg in 1993, Ted Danson was known from the popular television series *Cheers* (as well as several movie comedies). When cellphone video of his racially-laden, slur-filled outburst at a heckler went viral in 2006, Richards was known for his character on the series *Seinfeld*. Both TV shows were wildly successful. Audiences expected both actors to "know better" than to show poor judgment (like Danson) or lose composure during a set (like Richards). Danson and Goldberg, who were romantically involved at the time of the blackface incident, argued that they had intended the blackface routine to be ironic and to call attention to racism after the hate mail they had received opposing their interracial romance (Williams 1993). Most observers concluded that their choice was a poor and unfunny way to address that problem given their access to the media. Richards claimed that he just "flipped out" (Associated Press 2006) and that he had never used racial slurs before. He sought public forgiveness from the Rev. Jesse Jackson and other Black leaders.

These events, however, did weaken the claim that all is easily forgiven in the service of a punchline and that audiences and club owners have a role in determining what is acceptable language (Salkin 2006). Despite these comics' efforts to explain their actions, they reinforced the claim that invoking the most hateful and harmful racial epithet in the U.S. was a readily available option. Richards "flips out" but the hateful language was ready and waiting. Danson and Goldberg wanted to lash out at critics but the hateful language was ready and waiting. What should be remembered and stressed here is that the white positionality that these comics occupied meant *always* having access to the most damaging language strategies in their society.

However, Rickles' mediator role (due to his Jewish "outsider status") between African Americans and the dominant white society seems tenuous. There were increasing numbers of Jewish entertainers during this time – Mort Sahl, Shelly Berman, Mike Nichols and Elaine May, and Jerry Lewis – not to mention already established and influential writers and directors like Mel Brooks and Carl Reiner. As Meier and Nelson note in their use of Goldstein's (2006) work, rather than capitalizing on an outsider status, Rickles might have been buying acceptance into the dominant class. If anything, I view Rickles less as a mediator and more as a proxy for white expressions of racism.

What Meier and Nelson observe about Lenny Bruce can also be said of Rickles: "the slurs used against whites do not alter the access to the center of power afforded to them by their whiteness." In going only for the laugh, the diversity of groups attacked ultimately works to once again expose the vulnerable and direct attention away from Jewish acceptance into whiteness during that time and mask the increasing privilege that attended to the new status.

While Don Rickles mined for laughs the stereotypes of the stereotypes that the civil rights movement wanted to move beyond, Lenny Bruce – the beat poet of stand-up – confronted the stereotypes and attempted to unmask white positionality in ways that could occasionally make audiences uncomfortable, forcing them to wonder if this was really an act. These were the "cringe-worthy" jokes and scenes before comics like Andy Kaufman invented and perfected the cringe-worthy bit.

In their case study of Bruce, Meier and Nelson note that, unlike Rickles, "Bruce's satire creates moments wherein he and his audience can potentially engage in critical self-reflexivity." Although Bruce (as a white Jewish American) "already occupies the center of power" his comedic perspective "operates as a tactic for challenging the center of whiteness."

The transition toward social consciousness and moral awareness in stand-up comedy that Bruce pioneered cannot be underestimated. Bruce truly was dangerous because he was a voice *from within*. Because he was disaffected and because he exposed the self-serving practices of the very institutions that supported and ultimately undermined him, he was labeled the "sick comedian." Another Jewish American artist who expressed alienation and alternative interpretive frames was Bob Dylan. In 1981, Dylan wrote a song dedicated to Bruce that said in part: "Maybe he had some problems, maybe some things that he couldn't work out. But he sure was funny and he sure told the truth and he knew what he was talking about" (Dylan 1985, p. 455). Whether one considers him a savior or a martyr of the genre, it is clear that Bruce helped create a new paradigm for stand-up comedy.

Though their careers were essentially contemporaneous, Rickles was a throwback to Jim Crow sensibilities while Bruce reflected the disaffected and oppositional sensibilities that would inspire and define the 1960s counterculture. In the old paradigm, as represented by Rickles, the comic's *raison d'être* was the laugh. With Bruce, it was also the laugh but it was more, as well. At least in part, the goal was a new awareness – it was a different kind of relationship with the audience. While Rickles was content to keep invisible what everybody knew – that marginalized people had no chance – Bruce explored the contours of power and the ignorance and neglect that facilitates domination. Chidester (2008) has examined the "presence of absence" in relation to whiteness and power. In an examination of how the "absence" of racial and ethnic others in the TV show *Friends* signals their presence, Chidester notes, "if whiteness consistently affirms and reinforces its claims to racial centrality and superiority in part through a distinctively visual discourse, then the absence of such symbolic markers might also communicate distinctive meanings" (p. 159). In the case of stand-up comedy, the *absence* of a critical interrogation of race relations during the Civil Rights Era emphasizes its *presence* in the larger society and the corresponding need for inclusion among comics. In the realm of race relations, Bruce worked to make the absent present.

Finally, while Rickles invoked identities simply to become the object of his insult, Bruce showed people *in interaction*. "How to Relax Your Colored Friends at Parties" works almost like sketch comedy as Bruce sets a particular scene with characters and dialog. Bruce has created an intercultural context to critique white positionality.

Toward a Dialogic Awareness through Comedy

Amanda Morris moves us beyond the 1960s and 1970s, to considerations of contemporary comic approaches. She describes how the Powwow Comedy Jam accomplishes "intellectual decolonization." Here, Native American comics use humor to "reach a new level of teasing inquiry and engagement." Traditionally, the sacred clown or trickster facilitates "group unification through humor" (Bradley 2012, p. 136). The Native comic is in a position to approximate the trickster role and bring new realizations to audiences.

At this point, I have to digress. A friend, Charmaine from the Acoma Pueblo, and I were co-authoring a book chapter and during one meeting we had to walk from one building to another when a downpour occurred. I took out my umbrella and offered to share. "No," she said, "I come from a desert culture. It is against my religion to shield myself from the sacred rain." "Okay," I thought and kept the umbrella to myself. But I didn't feel good about the people looking at me accusingly, thinking that I was selfish with the umbrella. "However," she said as the rain continued, "That doesn't mean we can't run"! So we started running to the next building. At this moment, I understood that Native cultural sensibility was playful and creative.

Meier and Nelson would say that the Powwow Comedy Jam operates as a tactical response to oppression because it emerges from the margins. Because they utilize local meanings and stories, tactical responses tend to be vernacular expressions (Ono & Sloop 1995; Enck-Wanzer 2011) that emphasize particularity and difference and work to de-center the white interpretive frame. Morris also notes the "potential cross-cultural impact of such stories."

The intercultural pedagogy of the Powwow Comedy Jam is reminiscent of the *Axis of Evil Comedy Tour* (Hartmann et al. 2006). Four comics of Middle Eastern descent – Ahmed Ahmed, Maz Jobrani, Aron Kader, and Dean Obeidallah – performed routines that described life in the United States, post-9/11. Beginning in 2005, they toured the U.S. and the Middle East and a concert was shown on *Comedy Central*; the concert was later released as a DVD.

It was clear in the aftermath of the 9/11 attacks that Muslim Americans and persons from the Middle East (Arab or otherwise) were a little-understood population. One goal of the performers was simply to illustrate the diversity of Middle Eastern identities. The comics themselves were Egyptian American (Ahmed), Iranian American (Jobrani), and Palestinian American (Kader and Obeidallah). A second goal of the performers was to bring to the surface the perspectives of heritages that had undergone intense social transformation. Obeidallah described the difference this way: "Before 9/11, I'm just a white guy living a typical white guy life. All my friends have names like Monica and Chandler and Joey and Ross. I go to bed September 10th white and September 11th, I'm an Arab." The routines were designed to allow the audiences to empathize with the performers and critically examine social changes in the U.S. and the treatment of people of Middle Eastern heritage.

Jim Ruel's routine, like the sets performed by the *Axis of Evil* comics, depicts examples of intercultural interactions. Through Ruel, we hear how the stereotypes sound to him – whether it is an assumption that he is "into nature" or that he "must have the good shit, hook me up!" We can imagine him attending a Thanksgiving Day dinner and telling someone that Native Americans call it "You're Welcome Day" before he serves a dinner guest with middle finger extended. Morris' analysis that the stories follow a complication-reflection dialectic suggests that stand-up comedy has reached a new level of intimacy and thematic balance when compared to Rickles and even to Bruce.

Conclusion

Together the chapters in this part illustrate how vulnerability is embraced or mitigated and how productive reflection is facilitated or avoided. The chapters reveal how stand-up comics are implicated in rhetorical discourses that advance or hamper social change. The chapters also provide a succinct backdrop for understanding the multitude of current performers who include race and ethnicity in their acts.

Whether we call them tricksters, jesters, clowns, or comics, making people laugh allows the performers to break social rules. Making people laugh about observations on serious social tensions surrounding race and inviting audiences to reflect on their own complicity in privilege and discrimination becomes more challenging with each new social crisis. When comic Sarah Silverman (2005), for instance, says, "I don't care if you think I'm racist. I just care if you think I'm thin," she invites audiences to imagine the competing interests of white dominance and patriarchy. She calls attention to the social friction created by whiteness and the male gaze. It may be that comics like Sarah Silverman and Jim Ruel are unlikely rhetors. However, they provoke social change by performing rhetorical acts, namely by revealing contradicting values, questioning traditional assumptions, and re-centering perspectives in marginalized identities.

In intercultural communication courses, we often show recordings of stand-up comics and sketch comedy as a way to discuss intercultural and interracial relations and their representations. We always struggle with the question: Does showing this routine in class help or hurt intercultural and interracial relations? After all, a stereotype needs to be revealed before it can be problematized. At times the presentation of the stereotype can overshadow its critique. In one class after I showed the *Axis of Evil Comedy Tour*, a student remarked, "Arab people shouldn't be making fun of 9/11." It took a long time to have the student realize that the concert was not about the terrorist attacks but about the instant transformation of human relations. Who better to hear this from than those who experienced it firsthand? The chapters in this part have allowed me to realize that when we teach communication courses and treat racialized discourses, strategic rhetorics of whiteness, oppositional tactics by marginalized groups, and related topics, the instructor faces the same vulnerability as the comic who includes race in his or her routines.

Drops mic. Walks off page

References

Associated Press. (2006). Richards still sorry, goes into therapy. *USA Today*. November 27. Retrieved from http://usatoday30.usatoday.com/life/people/2006–11–25-richards-radio_x.htm

Bonilla-Silva, E. (2013). *Racism without racists: Color-blind racism and the persistence of racial inequality in America*. Lanham: Rowman & Littlefield Publishers.

Bradley, C. (2012). Native American communication and culture through humor. In A. González, M. Houston, & V. Chen (Eds.), *Our voices: Essays in culture, ethnicity, and communication* (pp. 134–138). New York: Oxford University Press.

Chidester, P. (2008). May the circle stay unbroken: *Friends*, the presence of absence, and the rhetorical reinforcement of whiteness. *Critical Studies in Media Communication*, 25, 157–174.

Dylan, B. (1985). Lenny Bruce. *Lyrics: 1962–1985*. New York: Alfred A. Knopf.

Enck-Wanzer, D. (2011). Race, coloniality, and geo-body politics: *The Garden* as Latin@ vernacular discourse. *Environmental Communication*, 5(3), 363–371.

Feagin, J.R. (2014). *Racist America: Roots, current realities, and future reparations*. New York: Routledge.

Goldstein, E.L. (2006). *The price of whiteness: Jews, race, and American identity*. Princeton University Press.

Hartmann, R., Brown-Marmel, J., Schreiberg, S., Tate, R. & Jobrani, M. (Executive Producers). (2006). *The axis of evil comedy tour* [Concert DVD]. United States: Levity Productions.

Ono, K.A. & Sloop, J.M. (1995). The critique of vernacular discourse. *Communication Monographs, 62*, 19–46.

Salkin, A. (2006). Comedy on the hot seat. *The New York Times.com*. Retrieved from www.nytimes.com/2006/12/03/fashion/03comedy.html?ref=style&_r=0

Silverman, S. (2005). *Jesus is Magic* [Concert DVD]. United States: Black Gold Films (II).

van Dijk, T.A. (1993). *Elite discourse and racism*. Newbury Park: Sage.

Williams, L. (1993). After the roast, fire and smoke. *The New York Times.com*. Retrieved from www.nytimes.com/1993/10/14/garden/after-the-roast-fire-and-smoke.html

PART III
Stand-Up and Politics

Now [John F.] Kennedy's elected and people are coming up to me and saying, "You're a bright young guy, it's amazing that you're not in the government!" I won't be connected with a government that would have me in it!

(Mort Sahl)

7
THE COMEDIC PRINCE
The Organic Intellectualism of Bill Hicks

Aaron Duncan and Jonathan Carter

> Folks, it's time to evolve ideas. You know, evolution did not end with us growing thumbs. You do know that, right? Didn't end there. We're at the point now where we're going to have to evolve ideas.
>
> (Bill Hicks 2004, p. 205)

This statement from comedy legend Bill Hicks summarized both his philosophy in life and comedy. He wanted push the envelope, to question dogma, to force people to consider alternative viewpoints in hope that we could evolve to create a more just society. Hicks was one the greatest comedic minds of his generation. He rose to fame in the late 1980s and early 1990s through a dozen appearances on *The Late Show with David Letterman* and a series of televised comedy specials. A native of Houston, Texas, he began writing jokes at the early age of 13. Three years later, in 1978, he gave his first professional performance at the newly opened club Comedy Workshop in San Felipe with his partner Dwight Slade. Although shortly after the performance Slade would move away to Portland, Oregon, Hicks continued to write and perform. Because he was still in high school Hicks often had to sneak out of his parents' house in order to perform. As he grew, he became a tireless comic. From 1988 to 1993, he averaged 265 performances a year. Although they would later have a falling out, Hicks' popularity was boosted by his numerous appearances on Letterman's show and by a series of HBO specials. Sadly, just as he was reaching the peak of his fame, Hicks was diagnosed with stage four pancreatic cancer and given only months to live. He passed away at the age of 32 years old in 1994.

Despite dying young. Hicks is considered by many to be among a handful of truly great comedic thinkers. Comedian Brett Butler stated, "Bill was right up there with Lenny Bruce and Richard Pryor. He was easily the best comic of my generation" (qtd. in Hicks 2004, p.1). Speaking on the enormity of his loss,

Tonight Show host Jay Leno (2014) stated, "For a comedian, it was like losing John Lennon." Senior drama critic for the *New Yorker* John Lahr (2014) concluded, "Hicks was a cunning comedian, probably the best informed and articulate one I've encountered in a quarter century of writing about entertainers. He made unacceptable ideas irresistible, and reminded viewers that the best entertainers are the unelected legislators." Although Hicks died 20 years ago, his comedy has undergone a dramatic resurgence in popularity. In the last five years Bill Hicks has been the subject of three books and a feature-length documentary. At the time of this writing, YouTube videos featuring his comedy have over 12.5 million views. Hicks' style of comedy crafted a type of cutting pessimism and humor that has been imitated by countless others. Lahr noted that Hicks' comedy was the predecessor to shows like *Politically Incorrect* and *The Daily Show* and he referred to Hicks' style as "comic civic disobedience" (qtd. in Hicks 2004, p. xxvi).

Comments such as these demonstrate that Hicks was more than a comedian. His comedy provides a template for alternative political subjectivities. Based on this insight, this chapter explores how Hicks' brand of humor functions as an example of Antonio Gramsci's (1971) concept of the "Modern Prince" and in doing so serves as an artistic remedy to the political spectacle that has besieged American politics. By considering Hicks' work through the lens of Gramsci's concepts of the Modern Prince and organic intellectual, we examine how comedic rhetoric can be effectively deployed to combat the dominant hegemonic discourse present in a society.

Constructing the Political Spectacle

Murray Edelman (1988) in his book *Constructing the Political Spectacle* painted a bleak picture of the modern political landscape. He explained that events, language, and media construct a political spectacle in a way that works to maintain the status quo and perpetuate social, economic, and political inequalities. "The critical element in political maneuver for advantage is the creation of meaning," Edelman wrote, explaining this leads to "the construction of beliefs about events, politics, leaders, problems, and crises that rationalize or challenge existing inequalities" (p. 104). Burke (1969) agreed that creation of meanings was central to politics when he stated the chief focus of rhetoric is "the manipulation of men's beliefs for political ends" (p. 41). Edelman's observations are more than 25 years old, but they remain as important and evident as ever. Cheng (2006) argued that the political spectacle has continued to thrive in modern conditions and has spread around the world. Throughout history, societies have continued to create systems of inequalities that deprive some groups of basic necessities and provide others with lavish excesses. The desire to keep this system of inequalities functioning creates a continual need for the political spectacle (Hershey 1993). Gramsci (1971) offered the concept of the Modern Prince as means for challenging the dominant discourse and countering hegemonic systems that perpetuate inequalities. We utilize Gramsci's work as a means of supplementing Edelman's discussion of the political spectacle because it offers us greater praxis for determining how and when dominant discourses, like the political spectacle, can be most effectively deconstructed.

Gramsci and the Modern Prince

Whereas many scholars have evaluated Machiavelli's *The Prince* as a manual for political action, Italian theorist Antonio Gramsci (1971) asserted that the text has greater value as a myth that illustrates how a powerful narrative – within a specific historical moment – can lead a divided and oppressed people to political action. Specifically, Gramsci asserted that the real power of *The Prince* had little to do with its specific propositions or theory, but rather that in context of its historical position the theory allowed the "creation of a phantasy [sic] which acts on a dispersed and shattered people to arouse and organizes its collective will" (p. 126). It is through intellectuals, especially organic intellectuals, utilizing the narrative style of the Modern Prince that a successful resistance to dominant power structures can be created. It is important to note that we are not contending that Bill Hicks represented the incarnation of the Modern Prince. As we discuss later, we contend that Hicks was an organic intellectual. We believe that the Modern Prince is a rhetorical product, which in this case takes the form of comedy, in order to challenge the political spectacle. In this capacity, while not every construction of the Modern Prince may lead to immediate political action, understanding the formation of such rhetorical products is still important as they provide inventional resources and theorization of praxis that can be mobilized for future political struggle.

Gramscian Praxis

Gramsci argued that the best philosophy is one of praxis, believing that the combination of theory and action leads to the most comprehensive and effective counter-hegemonic philosophy. His concept of praxis can be broken into two component parts, negative and positive mediation. In many ways these mediations function similarly to Burkean identification and division; negative mediation is the creation of an identifiable gap between the audience and a privileged other. This is the element of pure theory in the praxis. It identifies the problems in the system, and the roots of those problems, in an effort to motivate the complacent within the system toward action. Conversely, positive mediation works to create rhetorical identification with the action that can rectify this gap (Aune 1994). By constructing the problems identified via negative mediation as solvable, and by providing the means to do so, this stage of mediation gives resistance direction of action and hope of success. Gramsci explained:

> The philosophy of praxis had two tasks to perform: to combat modern ideologies in their most refined form, in order to constitute its own group of independent intellectuals; and to educate the popular masses.
>
> *(1971 p. 392)*

Thus, the best theorization will not only work to deconstruct disparate power relations, but also to formulate that deconstruction in a way that the masses can access it to motivate action. To emphasize one task of praxis at the cost of the other undermines any potential utility in theorization by denying the theory either substance or action.

The Organic Intellectual

For Gramsci, the organic intellectual is the realization of the intellectual potential that resides in all people. Specifically, he asserted that because all people have a more direct connection to the politics of everyday life, they are in a unique position to create rhetorical action that responds to their lived experience. This stands in stark contrast to traditional intellectuals who exist in the social structure as professional "experts" or "academics." Strine (1991) notes that interrogating the discourse of such lived experience is essential, as rhetorical critics – as products of traditional intellectualism – have the potential to ignore rich insight that the lived experience provides in favor of mass media and official political discourse. Only when we turn to non-traditional political discourses, such as comedy, do we gain the best insights criticism can offer.

Hicks existed outside the traditional expert culture and outside the class of individuals normally considered to be experts. Hicks had little in the way of formal education. He did not attend college and possessed no degrees or certifications that would qualify him as an expert or intellectual in a traditional sense. From this position of an outsider of American political culture, he embodies the localized experience of American politics for the working class. Furthermore, he never had a career outside of being a comedian. He started working as a comedian at the age of 16 and did so until his death at the age of 32. As such his intellectualism came primarily through his lived experience with the world and his observations about its inner workings. Hicks (2004) explained that majority of his comedy in early years came from his life growing up in Texas with his parents. For example, his religious views were shaped by his interactions and fights with his parents. Biographer Cynthia True (2002) described how these fights would play out. The elder Hicks would say:

> "I believe that the Bible is the literal word of God." And Bill would counter, "No it's not, Dad." "Well, I believe that it is." "Well," Bill replied, "you know, some people believe that they're Napoleon. That's fine. Beliefs are neat. Cherish them, but don't share them like they're the truth."
>
> (p. 25)

Religion would end up being a continual theme of his comedy throughout his life, but he would trace his origins back to his childhood experiences with it.

Landy (1994) explained the importance of the organic intellectual by noting that traditional intellectuals tend to alienate the masses in favor of reinforcing the structures of power that gave them their intellectual privilege. Organic intellectuals are able to use their "specialization" to challenge directly the hegemonic ideologies sustained by traditional intellectuals. Hicks' specialization in comedy provided him a unique tool for challenging dominant social ideologies. Moreover, because organic intellectuals have a direct connection to the group that they are theorizing about, they are able to identify with them. Whereas traditional intellectuals often speak in complex terms and with uncommon vocabulary, comedians do not. Hicks' frequent use of profanity and his veracious love of the word "fuck" demonstrated how his comedy rejected the rhetoric of the traditional intellectualism. Part of his appeal was his imperfection. He drank, he smoked, used drugs, and talked about all of this on stage. One his most famous bits involved his discussion of smoking. Hicks (2004) stated:

> The only good thing about smoking now is every cigarette pack has a different Surgeon-General's warning. That's kinda neat. Mine was: "Warning: Smoking may cause fetal injury of premature birth." Fuck it. Found my brand. Just don't get the ones that say "lung cancer," you know. Shop around.

Through his discussion of smoking Hicks makes it clear that he is imperfect. In doing so, he does not set himself apart from or above his audience, but rather identifies with them. Such identification with their audiences gives organic intellectuals authority because they demonstrate their understanding of the groups' language and thus they are better able to engage in the process of mediation.

The organic intellectual also draws on the power of self-reflection in a way that those participating in the spectacle of normal society cannot. Zompetti (1997) argued that a self-reflexive moment is necessitated by the individual to create genuine praxis. This reflexivity allows organic intellectuals to find their position within the hegemony and to locate the power disparities in their society. "Furthermore, in conjunction with the identification of cultural and historical elements, it also permits the location of a political space for resistance" (p. 77). Therefore, through self-reflexive development of philosophy, the organic intellectual creates ground for strong positive and negative mediation. The open access to mediation places the organic intellectual in a position of full potential for rhetorically based change.

The Modern Prince as Collective Will and Intellectual/Moral Reform

If the organic intellectual creates the full potential of change, the idea of the Modern Prince is the manner in which this potential is realized. Initially, the Modern Prince must be built around some notion of collective will or a desire of the many subalterns to unify against the dominant authority (Landy 1994). The position of the masses as the protagonist serves a dual function of situating them in the struggle and moving them to resistance. The collective will is further entrenched through the negative mediation of organic intellectuals. Because the organic intellectual has undergone a self-reflexive moment, their theorization will establish that the problems their own subaltern experiences are linked to other subaltern groups. Because the organic intellectual is able to communicate in the language of the masses, their negative mediation will link oppression to the collective will.

Beyond merely bringing people together, the Modern Prince must also give them a plan to continue their movement. Specifically, it must create a new moral/intellectual system that contests the dominant authority (Gramsci 1971). This completes the process of positive mediation by providing instruction for resistance. While this instruction may not be explicit, the process of valuing resistive constructs means that the new truths/morals must be placed above the old. Ultimately, it is the combination of the negative mediation of the organic intellectuals, with the positive mediation of the Modern Prince that creates a full philosophy of praxis. This challenges the dominance of the status quo, and allows the masses to participate – because it is of them, about them, and for them.

We contend that comedian Bill Hicks was an organic intellectual whose comedy functioned, and continues to function, as a Modern Prince working to deconstruct the political spectacle. In the words of the back cover of *Love All the People*, a collection of his works, "He attacked the lies that justified and prettified the carnage of the First Gulf War. He attacked the easy surrender of art to commerce, the demeaning cynicism of the marking culture and the power of the media to confuse and corrupt." His potential power as an organic intellectual is noted by political commentator Keith Oberman, who stated, "With his clarity of vision and gift for words, if Bill Hicks had had any more time he might have started a revolution" (quoted in Hicks 2004, p. 1). Hicks pushed the boundaries of traditional comedy and the use of humor not merely as form of entertainment but as vehicle for enlightenment.[1] With this statement, Oberman observed Hicks' comedy's potential to become the Modern Prince. We contend that comedian Bill Hicks was an organic intellectual and his comedy provides a road map for deconstructing the political spectacle.

Comedian as Organic Intellectual

Comedians have long played the role of observer and interpreter for the public and functioning as a sort of organic intellectual. Successful comics derive their humor from explaining their lived experience in a way that resonates with diverse audiences. Hicks described how he viewed the role of the comedian when he stated, "To me, the comic is the guy who says 'Wait a minute' as the consensus forms. He's the antithesis of the mob mentality. The comic is a flame – like Shiva the Destroyer, toppling idols no matter what they are. He keeps cutting everything back to the moment" (quoted in Lahr 1993).

While all art can be useful in demystifying the political spectacle, we argue that comedy is an especially valuable form of art in need of greater investigation and attention. Burke (1937) argued that when done properly comedy has the power to serve as a "comic corrective." Comedy offers a unique method to connect with audiences because "jokes make us laugh ... any viewers are likely to seek out parody, and few of us are likely to feel imposed upon in the way we might react to overtly didactic messages" (Gray 2005, p. 234). The success of this type of humor is that it does not attack its audience because it allows its audience members to see themselves as the "informed insider" and does not position them as members of the "ignorant outside" (p. 234). Todd (2002) discussed the power of this type of comic framing by noting that it "constructs a position of semi-detachment, where one is able to reflect and comment on human foibles without guilt, shame, or other negative emotion, or without undue involvement in the human comedy" (p. 66). In the case of the political spectacle, comedy is most effective when it allows audience members to see the flaws in the functioning of the spectacle, without drawing attention to how audience members work to maintain the spectacle.

Hicks' self-reflexive nature was exemplified in his views on smoking. On the one hand, Hicks saw his smoking as a form of resistance, a rejection of the dominant health discourse of the need for us to attempt to defeat or control death. Hicks noted that famed runner Jim Fixx died young while noted drinker and smoker Yul Brynner lived a longer life. Imitating the deceased Fixx, Hicks stated, "I jogged every day, ate nothing but tofu, swam five hundred laps every morning; I'm dead. Yul Brynner drank, smoked, and got laid every night of his life; he's dead ... shit" (2004, p. 39). However, Hicks eventually changed his views on smoking, reflecting that the money he was giving to tobacco companies eventually ended up in the hands of politicians he disliked, like Jesse Helms. His awareness of his participation in his own oppression demonstrated his ability to be self-reflexive and to adapt changing circumstances.

The Power of Negation

Hicks used his comedy to question the status quo, especially the nature of capitalism and the role of the news media in promoting hegemony. Edelman (1988) argued that the system oppresses the lower class and retrenches its own hegemonic authority and, through the use of spectacle, trains lower classes to be inactive. However, the privileged are very politically active and engaged, because the system works to benefit them. Moreover, the system ignores those most disadvantaged and focuses attention in narratives that do nothing to highlight the problems of the system. It places little attention on systemic issues that plague American society like the widening wealth gap and chronic homelessness. Conversely, Hicks engages in a negative mediation to counter these dominant conceptions. Specifically, he used his comedy to draw attention to chronic problems like the homeless population plaguing New York City. Hicks stated:

> First thing I noticed when I came up here was of course the homeless situation. Now, I'm no bleeding heart, OK? But ... when you're walking down

the streets of New York City and you're stepping over a guy in the sidewalk who, I don't know, might be dead ... does it ever occur to you to think, "Wow. Maybe our system doesn't work?" Does that question ever bubble up for ya?

(2004, p. 11)

At the time, few mainstream comics would dare, or even think, to use the homeless situation in a major city as a source for humor, but Hicks did, in a manner that not only makes a joke but also raises an important question: "Is our society broken?" Hicks raises a question that ought to have been raised by the news media and other members of society. In doing so, he provides an organic theorization. In addition to drawing attention to the city's chronic homelessness problem, his negative mediation put the blame for the problem not on individual political or business leaders but on "our system" and asked the audience to question the value of a system that could allow us to ignore an entire class of individuals. Considering that Edelman argued that one of the flaws of most criticism is that it puts the focus on leadership and individuals, deemphasizing the importance of institutions and social forces, Hicks' mediation based on his organic experience allows him to confront the political spectacle in a way Edelman argues few critics (traditional or organic) would.

Hicks also used his comedy to draw attention to the ways that news coverage works to maintain the dominant forces of the status quo. According to Edelman, the news, a form of traditional intellectualism, promotes narratives that serve a specific purpose. The main purpose of these stories is to convince the audience to focus their attention on destroying a specific evil or enemy in order to protect their future. The main purpose of these perceived "enemies" is to be attacked and to allow for a cathartic bloodletting. Edelman continued, "To burn heretics, destroy their careers, or publicly humiliate them is to save the social order from contamination and to cure a pathology in the antagonist" (1988, p. 76). Such maintaining of dominance positions the media as traditional intellectuals, theorizing the world in a way that reifies the existing hegemony. Individual scapegoats are sacrificed but the system itself remains unchanged.

The construction and the cathartic slaying of enemies was something that Hicks was both aware of and critical toward. For example, Hicks was extremely critical of the First Gulf War and, particularly, the news media's coverage of it. Hicks said:

The media: once again, watching too much news really bummed me out. Remember how it started? They kept talking about the *Elite* Republic Guard? You know, the *Elite* Republican Guard. These were the bogeymen of the war, the first couple of months ... Well, after two months of bombing and not one reaction from these people they became simply the Republic Guard. Ha ha ha ha ah! Not nearly as elite.

(2004, p. 43)

Here he illustrates the problematic discourse fostered by the news. In highlighting the word "elite," Hicks foregrounds how traditional intellectuals framed Saddam Hussein and his Republic Guard as serious threats to the American way of life. His subsequent mocking and laughter draws attention to how this did not turn out to be true in the early 1990s or when the United States attacked Iraq again a decade later. As an organic intellectual, Hicks used his observations to dispute the social construction of the Republican Guard as elite and to place blame on the media for accepting and propagating this construction.

Using the tool of negative mediation, Hicks also worried about a country that needed a war to feel good about itself. "Who are the people with such low self-esteem they need a war to feel better about themselves? I saw them on the news, waving their flags" (2004, p. 43). He offers a suggestion on how we can feel better about ourselves: "sit ups, maybe a fruit cup, or a walk around the block at dusk – I always find that cheers me up" (p. 43). This routine by Hicks is interesting because it is equally critical of the construction of a perceived enemy and critical of the emotional high Americans felt from vanquishing that enemy. Here we also see the beginning of his proposed method of resistance to hegemony fostered by the current system. In proposing exercise and fruit cups rather than war, Hicks suggests that rather than looking to others to improve our self-esteem we should focus on ourselves. Here he begins to build the collective will by framing his arguments in a way that plays upon the American cultural values of individualism and personal responsibility.

Outside of his criticism of American wars, Hicks also troubles the larger trend of the news media to create ever new enemies for the viewing public. The media not only constructs enemies to be vanquished but it also continually provides us with new threats. By focusing our attention on these cycle threats, attention is taken away from the spectacle. Hicks was all too aware of how the news media operated. Hicks demonstrated this when he stated:

> I watch too much news, man. It's depressing. You ever watch CNN for longer than say … twenty hours in one day? I gotta cut that out. Watch CNN: It's the most depressing thing you'll ever see, man. "WAR, FAMINE, DEATH, AIDS, HOMELESS, RECESSION, DEPRESSION, WAR, FAMINE, DEATH, AIDS." Over and over again. Then you look at your window. Where is all this shit going on, man?
>
> *(2004, p. 41)*

Here Edelman and Hicks agree on two important aspects of contemporary news coverage. First, through his list cycle of threats, Hicks notes that news is almost always negative, focusing on a never-ending stream of threats and problems. Second, in his reference to the window, Hicks highlights how the majority of stories on the news do not impact our daily lives. Kellner (2004) explained that the news media aids in the construction of "spectacles of terror" which work to dramatize events and terrify citizens. Hicks challenged the "spectacle of terror" by pointing out that most of us are unaffected by the events focused on in the media. Such spectacles help to create the trained inaction that Edelman observed because the problems are framed as too large and scary to be solved by average people. By juxtaposing his experience as an organic intellectual against the traditional intellectualism of media, Hicks used his comedy to undermine the terror spectacle and to show his audiences that they do not need to live in a state of fear.

According to Edelman, it is important for the media to construct stories that follow a predetermined plot. In doing so the news media often construct and reconstruct the same problem over and over again. Hicks pointed to the War on Drugs as one of these constructed stories. Hicks mockingly stated:

> We are losing the war on drugs. You know what that implies? There's a war being fought, and people on drugs are winning it … What does that tell you about drugs? Some smart, creative people on that side.
>
> *(2004, p. 20)*

He argued that drug addicts are not criminals but, rather, at the very worst they are sick people who should be treated, not sent to prison. More than anything, he took issue with the news media's reporting about drugs. Hicks stated:

> You never see positive drug stories on the news, do ya[?] Always that same LSD story, you've all have seen it. "Young man on acid jumped out of building thought he could fly, what a tragedy." What a dick, fuck him he's an idiot. If thought he could fly what didn't he take off from the ground? … [Wouldn't it be nice] to base your decision on information instead of scare tactics, superstition, and lies[?] I think it would be newsworthy. "Today, a young man on acid realized that we are all one consciousness experiencing itself subjectively … Here is Tom with the weather."
>
> *(2004, p. 20)*

Here, Hicks points out that news media often only show viewers one side of an issue. The notion of a positive drug story is powerful because it created what Kenneth Burke (1945) called a "perspective by incongruity" (p. 69), a new understanding prompted by its break from "piety," the "sense of what goes with what" (p. 74). Hicks' version of the news upsets the social order and challenges the piety of narratives surrounding drugs. Society has been taught that all drug stories end badly and that nothing positive can come from the use of them. Hicks' concept of the positive drug story presents an incongruous viewpoint that draws attention to the way the dominant discourse functions to suppress alternative narratives.

Hicks' narrative of the positive drug story is also powerful because of the irony embedded within it. Burke (1945) identified irony as one of the four master tropes of rhetoric. He noted that irony often functions in the process of the dialectic by providing the antithesis to the viewpoints held by the dominant members of a society. The juxtaposition that irony provides is capable of pointing out the hypocrisies and absurdities present in American politics. For example, during Operation Desert Storm, Hicks stated:

> The war was a very stressful time for me, the war. Yeah. I was in the unenviable position of being for the war but against the troops.
>
> *(2004, p. 41)*

This statement is ironic because it plays upon the common refrain of dissenters that they were "for the troops, but against the war." On the highly contentious issue of flag burning he stated:

> Flag-burning really brought out people's true colors. People were like, "Hey, buddy, my dad died for that flag." Well, that's weird, 'cause I bought mine.
>
> *(2004, p. 7)*

Hicks' goal was to demonstrate the absurdity of these statements and highlight the odd way the political spectacle frames issues. In doing so, he provides a clear vision of the gap between political elites and lived experience, setting the stage for the mobilization of collusive will to challenge hegemonic values and structures.

The Comedic Demystification of Spectacle

The comedy of Bill Hicks functions as a modern embodiment of the prince, but his life also demonstrates the downside of challenging the dominant discourse. Hicks believed that resistance to domination is accomplished through the creation of art and he often used negation to accomplish this task. Hicks believed that commerce is the enemy of art and this makes it difficult for art to remain true to its purpose. Discussing the challenge of getting creative ideas on television, for instance, he complained, "Everything is run by accountants and demographics and marketing" (2004, p. 288). His contempt for capitalism's role in degrading art and truth was evident by the way he began the majority of shows. He often began his show by stating, "By the way, if anyone here is in advertising or marketing … kill yourself … Kill yourself. Seriously, though if you are, do. Aaaah, no really, there's no rationalization for what you do, and you are Satan's little helpers" (p. 124). According to Hicks the subjugation of art to the desires of marketers and advertisers was ruining it. Today, for example, even prominent political satire and commentary like that on the *The Daily Show* has advertisers whom writers and producers must consider. According to Hicks, for art to become successful it must "sell out" to the marketplace and thus lose all meaning.

Edelman likewise claimed that "kitsch" promotes a single established meaning, whereas true art creates ambiguous space for liberation. It draws our attention to multiple ways of seeing. Unfortunately, the marketplace has a vested interesting in promoting kitsch. Hicks believed that capitalism is the main cause of the problem and this is one reason we feel it was important to incorporate the work of Gramsci into our analysis of his comedy. Hicks referred to the U.S.A. as the "United States of Advertising" and television as "Lucifer's dream box." He called advertisers and marketers the "ruiners of all things good" in sets, stressing, "Seriously, no, this is not a joke" (p. 13). Like many things Hicks did, this probably seemed odd to many people and audiences. At first glance, it may seem like Hicks' rhetoric is problematic. He is drawing attention to the way that members of the audience maintain the spectacle. Such a move would not allow detachment because he has positioned his audience as members of the "ignorant outside." However, although a few members of the audiences at each show may work in the field of marketing, Hicks knew that most would not. By calling attention to marketers, he labeled them as the "ignorant outside" and implicitly labeled everyone else in the audience as members of the "informed inside." It also worth remembering that Hicks' greatest success came outside the United States. This was likely because members of foreign audiences felt less alienated by his criticism of American society.

Hicks' own career is also an example of the problems that true art encounters when it has to function in a capitalist marketplace. On October 1, 1993, Bill Hicks became the first performer since Elvis Presley to be censored at CBS's Ed Sullivan theatre. Presley was famously not shown below the waist in an effort to censor his gyrating and suggestive hips. After doing his twelfth appearance on David Letterman's talk show, Hicks thought everything with the performance went fine. Letterman even complimented him on the performance. However, CBS executives later told Hicks that they would not air the performance. They deemed Hicks' material, which contained no obscenities, too controversial for television (Hicks 2004). His material covered topics like religion, government, and capitalism. One subject in particular that censors felt was too controversial to air on television was Hicks' discussion of abortion. He stated, "You know who's really bugging me these days? These pro-lifers … You know what bugs me about them[?] If you're so pro-life, do me a favor – don't lock arms and block medical clinics. If you're so pro-life, lock arms and block cemeteries" (pp. 250–251). Hicks also proposed creating a television show that would feature him hunting and killing pop country musician Billy Ray Cyrus and discussed the double standard in which we treat female versus male homosexuality. These topics and viewpoints all threatened the status quo and the establishment, and so the establishment attempted to silence him. Thus, although art may be the antidote to the political spectacle and the key to a new intellectual revolution, it does not appear that such a revolution would be televised.

Additionally, Hicks highlights a flaw with all art, which is that in order for it to be relevant it must criticize the political spectacle and in doing so it often puts the focus back on leaders and individuals. For example, much of the comedy about the Second War in Iraq focused on President George W. Bush's individual ineptness. Comedian Will Ferrell popularly portrayed Bush on *Saturday Night Live*, but the basis of the comedy was in his depiction of Bush as bumbling idiot incapable of correctly pronouncing words like "nuclear" and making up words like "strategery." Similarly, Hicks' criticism of the first Gulf War focused on George

H.W. Bush's individual flaws. Unintentionally, art may reinforce many of the same values and misconceptions that the political spectacle does.

Hicks' career also highlighted the potential drawbacks of challenging the political spectacle. In addition to being censored on Letterman's program, Hicks' career suffered domestically. The Hicks biography, *American Scream: The Bill Hicks Story* (True 2002), explained that Hicks was labeled as "criminally unpatriotic" at home and that his success was stymied in America. Hicks did not find large-scale success until he started traveling internationally, first to Canada and then to Great Britain. It was in the latter that he found a large and enthusiastic fan base willing to accept his message. The forces of capitalism and politics marginalized Hicks in his home market and forced him to go elsewhere in order to become successful. Only years after his life ended did Hicks' comedy garner mainstream attention.

Positive Mediation and the Power of Art

When discussing the power of art to combat the dominant discourse Edelman concedes that the construction of true art is hard to achieve and that its impact is usually temporary. However, Gramsci contended that it was possible to unify people from divergent groups to challenge dominant discourses. Hicks embraced the potential power of art conveyed through the organic intellectual to become a unifying force. Although Hicks' and Edelman's views of American politics and society might be equally pessimistic, Hicks offers us a far more hopeful view of the future. Edelman asserts that one of the problems of the dominant political discourse is that it teaches people they are powerless to overcome it. "In subtle ways the public is constantly reminded that its role is minor, largely passive, and at most reactive" (Edelman 1998, p. 97). Such discourse makes people hopeless and robs them of power by showing us our irrelevance. Edelman argues, "An individual vote is more nearly a form of self-expression and of legitimation than of influence and that the link between elections and value allocations is tenuous" (p. 97). Hicks countered the political spectacle by not only demonstrating its flaws but by providing positive mediation by demonstrating a method for opting out of the spectacle. Hicks' solution to the problems facing society is also the title of his book, *Love All the People*. Hicks compared the spectacle to a roller coaster ride and stated:

> When you choose go on it you think it's real, because that's how powerful our minds are. The ride goes up and down and round and round and it has thrills and chills, it's very brightly colored and its loud, and it's fun, for a while ... It's just a ride, and we can change it anytime we want ... It's a choice, between fear and love. The eyes of fear want you to put bigger locks on your door, buy guns, close yourself off. The eyes of love instead see all of us as one.
>
> *(2004, p. 20)*

Love is the key for Hicks. Edelman tells us that art can demystify the spectacle by creating ambiguous areas for the construction of multiple meaning. Hicks' view of art is by contrast much simpler. Art succeeds because it demonstrates to us that we are all one. Rather than create ambiguous meaning, it reiterates a specific and important message. Hicks argues that by deconstructing the political spectacle we deconstruct the appearance of difference between us. He states:

> Here's what we do. You know all that money we spend on nuclear weapons and defense every year? Trillions of dollars. Instead, if we spent that money feeding and clothing the poor of the world, which it would pay for many times over, not one human being excluded ... not one ... we could as one race explore outer space together in peace, forever.
>
> *(2004, p. 36)*

Now it's important to note that Hicks did not think this would be easy, but he does appear to think it's possible. The key to overcoming the political spectacle is to, in the words of Hicks, "Love all the people." While it would be easy to dismiss Hick's positive mediation as pure sentimentality, Hardt and Negri (2011) remind us that "love is a material, political act" (p. 184). Both they and Hicks argue that the spectacle of capitalism focuses on difference which works to separate us and keep people from coming together. Through the eradication of the difference and focus on the essential elements that bind us together, we are capable of embracing love and working harmoniously to create better systems and institutions. It is with this strong unifying positive mediation that Hicks finishes the construction of his Modern Prince, providing a solution that unifies subalterns as a singular expansive hegemony,[2] able to challenge the problems highlighted through his negative mediation.

Conclusion

The political spectacle that Edelman observed over 25 years ago remains as evident and ongoing as ever. The news media continues to construct threats and reassurances and rehash the same stories without critically examining the ongoing systematic flaws that allow these problems to continue. Ironically, this is one of the facets that has helped Bill Hicks' popularity continue to grow. In the foreword of the book *What Would Bill Hicks Say?*, author Ben Mack noted the impetus for writing the book was the recognition that Hicks' comedy was as relevant now as ever (Mack & Pulkkinen 2006). He was inspired to write the book after he played a YouTube clip for a friend that showed Hicks ranting about George Bush's involvement in the Iraq War. Mack's friend was shocked to learn the video was over ten years old because his commentary appeared to be so contemporary. Decades after his death, Hicks' comedy remains alive and relevant with millions of hits on YouTube and media of all types proffering his message. In 2009, David Letterman invited Hicks' mother, Mary Hicks, on his show to formally apologize for censoring her son over 15 years before. Hicks addressed numerous problems in his comedy that continue to plague American society, such as the War on Drugs, homelessness and poverty, religious extremism, conspicuous consumerism, and the role of the media and government as a system of inequalities. Sadly, none of the problems that Hicks observed have been solved and the ongoing nature of the political spectacle has helped to make his comedy timeless. This teaches us both the power of the spectacle to endure but also the power of princely art to endure as well.

Our analysis of Bill Hicks' comedy has also helped to reaffirm the relevance and importance of Gramsci's work to the field of rhetoric. We believe that Gramsci's work provides a unique tool for the analysis of popular texts and that his work has been underused – or, at the very least, under-cited – by rhetorical scholars. Gramsci's writing is especially valuable given the emphasis he placed on praxis and its overlap with Burkean concepts, such as the comic frame. The concept of the organic intellectual remains an enduring concept that not only describes politically minded comedians like Bill Hicks but could be used to examine people from a variety of disciplines who embody the will of the people. This project highlights the unique ethos and power of the organic intellectual as an agent of change and challenger of hegemony.

There little doubt that Bill Hicks was an organic intellectual and this along with his fervent distrust of market capitalism allowed him to embody not merely the collective will of a growing number of people during his own life, but through the use of technology, the collective will of people decades later. Hicks' continued relevance reflects not only the continued existence of the political spectacle but the continual need for organic intellectuals to combat the spectacle. Gramsci believed that the Modern Prince succeeded because of his unique connection to a specific historical context, but such is not the case with Hicks, whose message has continued to outlive the messenger.

As with all great comedy, Hicks' message was timeless. Long after Bill Hicks died, his comedy continues to motivate people to seek change. Edelman argued that the political spectacle is rooted in the present but art is timeless. True art offers an enduring critique of the spectacle and this speaks to possibility of the Modern Prince to serve as both a historical and ahistorical agent of action. It also reflects the double-edged nature of technology as a tool of the Prince. Technology, primarily the Internet, has allowed Hicks' message to live on and succeed because of a large grassroots following outside the traditional capitalist system that comedians normally participate in to become successful. At the same time, it has allowed people to profit off of his message. YouTube generates advertising dollars, authors and producers sell books and DVDs, and one can even buy a Bill Hicks' iPhone cover, the irony of which is doubtlessly lost on its user. This highlights the inability of even organic intellectuals to fully resist the forces of the market.

Despite the continued dominance of capitalistic forces, comedy serves as a potentially revolutionary means of creating a new incarnation of the Modern

Prince. This is especially true in the case of the comedy of Bill Hicks because it offers a solution to the spectacle. It tells us the spectacle can only be solved when we embrace the demystifying concept of love. The power of this argument is part due to the fact Hicks relied upon the comic frame to make it and, thus, avoid the pitfalls of the tragic frame. Our work indicates that comedy is especially powerful when it not only critiques the spectacle but also brings together divergent groups that make enacting change possible. Hicks offered us a message of hope through the creation of princely art that exposed a message that simultaneously critiqued the spectacle and erased the differences that hold us back. And, perhaps more importantly, his comedy allows us to hope that one day we will create a society that does indeed "love all the people."

Notes

1 Profiling Hicks for *The New Yorker,* critic John Lahr (1993) wrote, "His comedy takes an audience on a journey to places in the heart where it can't or won't go without him. Through laughter, Hicks makes unacceptable ideas irresistible. His is particularly lethal because he persuades not with reason but joy."
2 Hardt and Negri (2011) would call this the "Multitude."

References

Aune, J.A. (1994). *Rhetoric & Marxism.* Boulder, CO: Westview Press.
Burke, K. (1937). *Attitudes toward history.* Berkeley: University of California Press.
Burke, K. (1945). *A grammar of motives.* Berkeley: University of California Press.
Cheng, M. (2006). Constructing a new political spectacle: Tactics of Chen Shui-bian's 2000 and 2004 inaugural speeches. *Discourse & Society, 16,* 583–608.
Edelman, M. (1988). *Constructing the political spectacle.* Chicago: University of Chicago Press.
Gramsci, A. (1971). *The prison notebooks.* New York: International Publishers.
Gray, J. (2005). Television teaching: Parody, The Simpsons, and media literacy education. *Critical Studies in Media Communication, 22,* 223–238.
Hardt, M., & Negri, A. (2011). *Commonwealth.* Cambridge, MA: Harvard University Press.
Hershey, M.R. (1993). Election research as spectacle: The Edelman vision and empirical study of elections. *Political Communication, 10,* 121–140.
Hicks, B. (2004). *Love all the people: Letters, lyrics, routines.* London, England: Constable & Robinson Ltd.
Kellner, D. (2004). 9/11, spectacles of terror, and media manipulation. *Critical Discourse Studies, 1,* 41–61.
Lahr, J. (1993, November 1). The goat boy rises. Retrieved from www.newyorker.com/archive/1993/11/01/1993_11_01_113_TNY_CARDS_000365503?currentPage=all
Lahr, J. (2014). *Famous fans.* Retrieved from www.americanthemovie.com/?page_id=313
Landy, M. (1994). *Film, politics, and Gramsci.* Minneapolis: University of Minnesota Press.
Leno, J. (2014). *Famous fans.* Retrieved from www.americanthemovie.com/?page_id=313
Mack, B., & Pulkkinen, K. (Eds.). (2006). *What would Bill Hicks say?* Berkeley, CA: Soft Skull Press.
Strine, M.S. (1991). Critical theory and "organic" intellectuals: Reframing the work of cultural critique. *Communication Monographs 58,* 195–201.

Todd, A. (2002). Prime-time subversion: The environmental rhetoric of The Simpsons. In M. Meister & P. Japp (Eds.), *Enviropop* (pp. 63–80). Westport CT: Praeger.

True, C. (2002). *American scream: The Bill Hicks story.* New York: Harper Paperbacks.

Zompetti, J.P. (1997). Toward a Gramscian critical rhetoric. *Western Journal of Communication, 61,* 66–88.

8
WHAT'S THE DEAL WITH LIBERALS?

The Discursive Construction of Partisan Political Identities in Conservative Stand-Up Comedy

Ron Von Burg and Kai Heidemann

> Q: How many liberals does it take to change a light bulb?
> A: At least ten, as they will need to have a discussion about whether or not the light bulb exists, and even if they can agree upon the existence of the light bulb they still may not change it in order to keep from alienating those who might use other forms of light.
>
> *(Retrieved from www.biblebelievers.com/LightBulb.html)*

Introduction

Within the social and political sciences, pluralist theories of governance typically theorize the political process in liberal democratic societies as based upon continual conflict and competition between distinct social groups vying for increased influence and control of the State (Faulks 2000, pp. 44–47). The concerted struggle to win over the long-term loyalty and dedication of large groups or "blocks" of voters is conceived in this perspective as integral to the work of political parties.[1] In their quest to "get out the votes" and "mobilize the base," political party activists and constituents devote tremendous time and resources to the cultivation of collective or group-based identities, which ideally function to motivate people to support party-based agendas and interests. Part of the work taken up by the constituents of political parties in their quest for electoral leverage is not simply to "rally the base," but also to define who exactly "the base" might consist of, and what precisely they stand for. This process involves the discursive construction of partisan-based identities and interests; that is, who we are and what we (don't) want. The constitutive function behind such discursive labor places identification and division at the center of any persuasive appeal articulated by political actors. However, this emphasis on identity construction can trouble the prospects for effective democratic dialogue across such ideological differences.

While the discourse of partisan politics often plays out in serious, sober and rational registers, humor can play an important rhetorical role in bridging or expanding the gaps that divide partisan identities by disarming opponents as well as shaping in-group identities and loyalties (Fine & de Soucey 2005; Hariman 2008). Humor offers an inventory of tropes and figures that enable discourses of identification for actors to engage in political deliberation, positioning and argumentation. By looking at the ways in which humor is deployed by specific actors for political purposes, much can be learned about the practices of collective identity-making that underlie the political process within representative democracies. Moreover, a look at the role of humor in identity construction can tell us a great deal about how political actors from opposite sides of the proverbial aisle perceive each other as well as their willingness and capacity to engage in the forms of inter-partisan negotiation and compromise which functioning democracies typically rely upon to solve public problems and crises (Dahl 2000). As Burke (1969) argues, identification lies at the heart of rhetoric, but the prospects for persuasion and dialogue rest on the ability to cultivate identification over an emphasis on division.

Within the contemporary United States, the political deployment of humor is typically associated with a liberal or "left of center" bent (Dagnes 2012). The bulk of scholarship (and media attention) treats comedic performances as primarily a tool of the left, crafting identities through the mockery of conservative policies and politicians. Popular programs such as *The Daily Show* and *The Colbert Report* as well as the acclaimed comedic stylings of Louis C.K. and Sarah Silverman demonstrate close associations with humor and liberal identities. With the exception of a few notable examples, such as Dennis Miller and P.J. O'Rouke, conservatives lack comedic champions, political jesters whose incisive wit offers a trenchant corrective to liberal discourse. Dagnes (2012) argues, for example, that comedic performance as a political tool is largely at odds with a conservative ideology that privileges tradition and order. Therefore, studying the rare breed of a self-proclaimed conservative comedian in the context of partisan politics provides significant insight into the role humor plays in the (re)production of conservative identity as well as the (re)production of liberal identity from the conservative standpoint.

The comedic performances of Brad Stine, the self-anointed "God's Comic," highlight how humor functions in the construction of conservative and liberal identities. We argue that Stine's comedic act illuminates a burlesque tenor in conservative humor that thwarts any rapprochements between liberal and conservative identities. Specifically, we consider how Stine's stand-up comedy act at the 2012 meeting of the Conservative Political Action Committee (CPAC) contributes to the reproduction of partisan political identities on the eve of the 2012 Presidential election. Burlesque, as Kenneth Burke argues, frames the object of derision as fundamentally flawed, a villainous opponent unworthy of redemption or reconciliation. Appel (1996), expanding on Burke's concept of burlesque, argues "burlesquers do not slap the wrist of the 'idiots' only to then embrace them, like comedians. Nor do they kill their enemies dead, like tragedians. They do, though, want them gone from the featured scene of activity. They scapegoat them" (p. 272). Likewise, Carlson (1988) notes that "[t]he writer of burlesque is uninterested in the motivation of the actors; the object is merely to make them look as ridiculous as possible. There is no sense of identification with the clownish figure here, for that would be to admit that we have a share in the folly" (p. 317).

To be sure, burlesque is not the sole province of conservative humor. Liberal comedians, such as Bill Maher, often traffic in the burlesque, belittling conservative opponents as ignoramuses incapable of rational deliberation. Stine's burlesque, however, constructs *both* liberal and conservative identities to articulate an irreconcilable division, placing the conservative identity within an epic struggle against imperialistic liberal forces. We argue that Stine's humor constructs the conservative identity as the victim of liberal oppression, struggling against an opponent fundamentally opposed to the essence of America. Merging the literature on humor and political communication from the field of rhetorical studies with sociological scholarship on ideology and identity, we demonstrate how Stine's aggressive and sardonic rhetorical stylings construct ideological boundaries that demarcate a mythical community of conservative Republicans as a superior, yet threatened Protagonist Self engaged in an epic struggle with an inferior and menacing Antagonist Other: liberal Democrats.

In his comedic moves, Stine relies heavily upon the tropes of both satire and burlesque – juxtaposition and parody specifically – to articulate rigid political identities. Drawing on Burke's poetic categories of satire and burlesque, we find that a primary effect of Stine's act is geared toward eliciting sentiments of superiority and authority for the Protagonist Self ("Us") through ridicule, mockery and derision of the Antagonist Other ("Them"). Despite his putative attempts at satire, positioning liberals as the oppressors in need of chiding, Stine's specific rhetorical gestures are best read as burlesque, an unreflexive otherization that barters in disillusionment. By way of conclusion, we ask whether such identity-making processes harm the political process by entrenching sentiments of conflict and division among actors in civil society at the expense of striving for the forms of collaboration and deliberation needed to make democratic systems of governance work.

Satire, Burlesque, and the Conservative Comedic Voice

In *Attitudes Toward History*, Kenneth Burke (1984) identifies how attitudes of acceptance and rejection, grounded in various literary genres, frame the process of community formation and disarticulation. Rooted in his study of literary criticism, Burke argues that "frames of acceptance" (epic and tragedy) articulate cohesive symbolic systems of meaning that enable one to find a place in the world, whereas the "frames of rejection" (satire and burlesque) relish in challenges to the dominant symbols of authority and "throw the emphasis stylistically upon the partiality of rejection rather than the completeness of acceptance" (p. 22). These symbolic systems provide the vocabulary necessary for articulating community, naming celebrated characteristics as well as scripting attitudes toward such characteristics. Burke notes:

> these names shape our relations with our fellows. They prepare us *for* some functions and *against* others, *for* or *against* the persons representing these functions. The names go further: they suggest *how* you shall be for or against. Call a man [sic] a villain, and you have the choice of either attacking or cringing. Call him [sic] mistaken, and you invite yourself to attempt setting him [sic] right.
>
> *(Burke 1984, p. 4, emphasis original)*

As poetic categories, satire and burlesque share many of the same tropes: irony, juxtaposition, and parody. However, as a process of attitude formation, satire and burlesque possess subtle, yet important differences as discourses of community formation. According to Burke, "the satirist attacks *in others* the weaknesses and temptations that are really *within himself* [sic]" (p. 49). Satire thrives in projecting strategic ambiguity, reflexively performing internal as well as external critique. In this light, satire often builds identity boundaries by focusing humor inward on the Self in a critical manner so as to get people to laugh at themselves. Such self-effacement offers a disarming discourse of identification. As the preferred comedic device of underdogs, satire "speaks truth to power," mocking the hypocrisies and insincerities of the dominant political discourses. As Dagnes (2012) suggests, satire is rooted in anger, an expressed distaste for a putatively unfair system. Although offending others is an occupational hazard for the satirist, this anger invites audiences to participate in the particularized rejection of the current power structure.

Burlesque, however, is purely an external assault, forgoing the introspective virtues of satire. Burke suggests "the writer of burlesque makes no attempt to get inside the psyche of [the object of ridicule]," instead opting to reduce the external actions of the ridiculed to absurdity. Burke continues: "the method of burlesque (polemic, caricature) is partial not only in the sense of *partisan*, but also in the sense of *incompleteness*" (1984, p. 55). The reduction to absurdity ignores subtleties in reasoning and behavior, distilling the actions and beliefs of the Other into one-dimensional objects of derision. Burke (1984) notes "the methods of caricature do not equip us to understand the full complexities of sociality – hence they warp our programs of action and, by identification, humiliate the manipulator of them, thereby making cynical self-interest the most logical of policies" (p. 93). Burlesque celebrates caricature of the Other without the inconvenience of critical introspection of the Self. Carlson (1988) explores the role of humor among 19th-century women noting that feminist efforts moved from satire to burlesque and away from a comic framing, thwarting opportunities for social change. She argues that in order to change the social order, "[t]here must be identification among the members of the out group, the members of that group with the social order, and the social order with the members" and "there must be clear alternatives to the unacceptable practices of the hierarchy" (p. 319). The descent into burlesque, however, undermines such an effort by foreclosing both identification across different members in the social order and the openings to altering the social order.

The frames of comedy, satire, and burlesque move along a continuum, from mocking transgressors mistaken in their ways, but not beyond redemption, to vilifying them as fundamentally flawed threats in need of expulsion. As Gring-Pemble and Watson (2003) note, "the move from the comic to the burlesque highlights the moment when audiences are no longer laughing with the characters but at them … the burlesque frame encourages readers to view their world through polarized lenses" (p. 150). The polarizing effect of burlesque, as Carlson suggests, thwarts any chance for identification with the transgressors and undermines discussion of serious political issues. Kline (2010) explores how the burlesque framing of midwifery in primetime television comedies stymies serious dialogue on alternative birthing practices. Likewise, as Gring-Pemble and Watson (2003) discuss in Garner's satirical send-up of the political correctness debate, when the comedic frame blends with the burlesque, "the discouragement of communication characteristic of the burlesque overshadows the open communication sanctioned by the comic frame" (p. 150). While humor can be disarming, and invite an opportunity for identification and further dialogue, it also can sow the seeds of division, creating new identities for in-groups and out-groups (Meyer 2000). Most extant scholarship attending to the rhetorical dynamics of burlesque explores the characterizations and identities of those subject to scorn; however, there is less attention to how the burlesque frames create the identity of the burlesquer.[2] We expect burlesque to employ *reductio ad absurdum* to characterize the object of derision as irredeemable and unworthy of dialogue, but to foreclose future attempts for communication requires that rejection to become fundamental to the identity of the burlesquer. It is this dynamic we identify as most salient in Stine's burlesque performance.

Partisan Identities Through the Other

In *A Conservative Walks into a Bar*, Alison Dagnes (2012) reflects on the well-worn bromide that conservative comedians are unwelcome in the liberal entertainment industry. While she concludes that there is a dearth of conservative comedians, specifically satirists, this scarcity is rooted not in some nebulous liberal bias but a fundamental tension between the goals of satire and conservative ideology. Political satire challenges power and institutional order. As a frame of rejection, satire revels in destabilizing the existing order, magnifying inconsistencies that a satirist identifies as an abuse of power. The conservative penchant for social order and stability highlights an uneasy relationship with satire. This is not to suggest that conservatives are unmoved by institutional hypocrisy and abuses of power or that liberals have little interest in social order, rather conservative humor relies on framing dominant structures and trends as articulations of liberal ideology. For example, to the conservative humorist, the oppressiveness of political correctness and the interminable "War on Christmas" demonstrate how ascendant liberal power requires a satirical corrective.

The rhetorical process of framing liberal ideologies as hegemonic forces that stifle individual liberty is certainly satirical in spirit but is burlesque in practice. At present, one rarely finds political satirists directing their invective at the truly poor and the disempowered. Not only would such quips lack humor, but also the satire possesses little social value. Likewise, burlesque's mockery trained at the powerless would be unseemly and unfunny, a process of ridicule that does little to understand the reasons for such conditions. It is, therefore, incumbent on the comedian to frame the object of scrutiny as the dominant powerful force, even if such structures and ideologies are generally not hegemonic demonstrations of power. For satire to work, the comedic point of articulation must come from a position of less power, even if the satirist is not a disadvantaged outsider taunting obtuse and narcissistic hegemons. In the comic frame, the fool is mistaken, warranting the opportunity for a corrective that opens the space of dialogue and engagement, an opportunity not afforded with burlesque. When navigating the differences between satire and burlesque, critics must examine how the comedic voice articulates the object of mockery as an instantiation of power deserving of satire. To that end, it is important to understand how the same rhetoric juxtaposes the identities of the mocker and the mocked. We do not wish to suggest that burlesque is the primary feature of the conservative comedic identity – though it is notable that many recent scholarly treatments of political burlesque engage conservative rhetors (Appel 1996; 2003) – rather, that Stine's burlesque rhetoric co-constructs conservative and liberal identities as inherently incongruous, and attempts to reconcile difference violates such an identity.

There is perhaps no greater example of a conservative commentator using humor, namely burlesque, to articulate rigid political identities more than Rush Limbaugh. In *Cracking Up*, Paul Lewis (2006) notes how Limbaugh's humor relies on incessant mockery and ridicule to articulate various political attacks. Limbaugh's harsh invectives, from his mockery of Janet Reno to Robert Reich to Sandra Fluke, traffic in burlesque forms of rejection that find no common ground or opportunity for correction with the subject of derision. Limbaugh only relents when public (economic) pressure threatens his sponsors, and he retreats into labeling such attacks as merely jokes. As Lewis notes, Limbaugh uses "a veneer of comedy to lower resistance to his arguments and provide cover when they are assailed" (p. 167). However, presenting the attack under the guise of humor does little to identify common ground with the assailed, rather it affirms the separate and incommensurate identities of the mocker and the mocked.

Partisan identities, as with other forms of social identity, are articulated by constructing an imagined community of sympathetic insiders who constitute the party and who represent its various aims and agendas. A central element of this for the Republican Party, for example, is a claimed commitment to 'austerity', i.e., low tax rates and reduced public spending. As noted on the official website of the Republican Party:

> Taxes, by their very nature, reduce a citizen's freedom. Their proper role in a free society should be to fund services that are essential and authorized by the Constitution, such as national security, and the care of those who cannot care for themselves. We reject the use of taxation to redistribute income, fund unnecessary or ineffective programs, or foster the crony capitalism that corrupts both politicians and corporations.[3]

Here, a key element in the construction of a partisan identity is defined by the taking up of a stance against progressive models of taxation and redistributive forms of economic planning. The tropes of freedom and individualism, measured by economic liberty, inflect notions of conservative identity and are understood to be in stark contrast to more liberal economic policies.

Partisan-based political identities also necessitate an identification of those unsympathetic outsiders who are perceived as variously hostile, skeptical, or ambivalent toward the party faithful and their platform. In addition to developing and drawing upon ideological repertoires so as to construct group-based notions of "the Self," the constituents of political parties must also develop and nurture narratives which establish the identity of "the Other," that is, their opponents. Indeed, ideas and beliefs about the threatening and antagonistic nature of the Other are often at the very core of how partisans construct solidaristic and empowering notions of the Self. In other words, within-group identities are formed in great part by drawing an exclusionary boundary to outsiders (Fine & de Soucey 2005).

For Charland (1987), this boundary drawing is a process of constitutive rhetoric. Grounded in the Burkean theories of identification and Althusserian notions of interpellation, constitutive rhetoric calls audiences into being by articulating the "always-already" narrative markers of a group identity. Within the United States, for instance, recent identity markers of the Republican Party have come to rely heavily upon the demonization of members of the Democratic Party as misguided and untrustworthy when it comes to promoting national economic output, stability, and productivity. Hence, one's ability to properly identify as Republican resides in the negative characterization of all things Democrat. This difference goes beyond mere party identification. The recent ideological move to purge liberal Republicans, Republicans-In-Name-Only or RINOs, from the conservative ranks has become a common invective for conservative Republicans who feel the electoral losses in 2008 and 2012, specifically, are products of political impurity. Republican candidates tacking to the right in various primaries demonstrate, specifically from incumbents, a noticeable shift in the ideological composition of the Republican Party electorate.

In the process of defining their own identities as protagonists in the electoral struggle, party actors produce discourses and viewpoints regarding the antagonistic identity and interests of their opponents. The antagonism of "the Other" may be perceived as being rooted in nefariousness and an explicit intent to do wrong on the one hand, or as stemming from naiveté and false consciousness on the other. Either way, the primary trope at work is that partisan outsiders should not be confided in to steer the reins of government. The process of competing for votes thus often takes shape through the development of narratives that portray a sympathetic and solidaristic community of protagonists fighting against an unsympathetic and threatening group of outside antagonists. While the rhetorical form of these narratives can take on many shapes, humor can often play a key role in uniting the party faithful (Boskin 1990).

Stine and Conservative Comedy Identity

To understand the place of humor in the construction of partisan identities, we analyzed a stand-up comedy act performed by Brad Stine at the 2012 Conservative Political Action Conference (CPAC), an annual political conference attended by conservative activists and elected officials from across the United States. The conference started as a small assembly in 1973 by the American Conservative Union and Young Americans for Freedom and has grown to include thousands of annual attendees. CPAC represents a critical recurring event in the formation of partisan based identity for political conservatives within the U.S. The annual CPAC Presidential straw poll has become a barometer of ideological purity for party loyalists and litmus test of a candidate's conservative bona fides. Recently, conservatives deemed too soft on Democrats were noticeably absent as CPAC featured speakers. Overall, CPAC is a moment whereby the meanings of association and membership within the context of conservative party politics become publicly performed and re-presented. The planning that goes into the orchestration of CPAC is highly strategic and geared toward maximizing intersubjective feelings of collective empowerment and effervescence among political conservatives. Like other political gatherings, CPAC is not devoid of entertainment offerings.

In 2011, at the Republican Leadership Convention in New Orleans, comedian and President Obama impersonator Reggie Brown performed in character, much to the delight of the Republican crowd. The audience rewarded Brown for his off-color jokes mocking the President, many of which bordered on racist. Once Brown turned his mockery on Republicans, satirizing their presidential candidates, he was showered with jeers only to have his microphone cut and the emcee usher him off-stage (Adams 2011). Questioning or ridiculing the ideological flag bearers of the party was not to be tolerated; hierarchy and difference in the social order had to be maintained. The decision to include comedian Brad Stine at the 2012 CPAC event marked a sharp contrast with previous performers. Stine is a somewhat unique figure in the realm of political humor as he is the rare breed of stand-up comic who explicitly identifies as a conservative comedian and inflects his humor with conservative political themes. The self-proclaimed "God's Comic" long toiled on the traditional, or secular, comedy circuit, never landing the coveted sitcom contract or filling large concert halls.

In an interview with *New Yorker*, Stine recounts the moment when he eschewed the search for mainstream success and followed a new calling as a Christian comedian, playing churches instead of comedy clubs and ministering to young men across the nation. Stine's career redirection has paid dividends (Green 2004). Stine now tours with conservative political groups, such as the Promise Keepers, and performs regularly on the television programs of Christian Right leaders, including Pat Robertson. In addition to his Christian books, comedy albums, and feature films, Stine is a regular on many FOX News programs. Stine's stage persona echoes that of Denis Leary. Beyond a physical similarity, Stine rapidly paces across the stage, spewing angry rants, sans cursing, against the liberal "wussification" of America. A selling point of Stine's image is that he repeatedly goes out of his way to announce his political identity and religious convictions to his audience. Stine's ideological allegiance has made him a celebrated figure with political conservatives, earning him a gig at the 2004 Republican National Convention as well as the 2012 CPAC.

The relative dearth of conservative comics coupled with Stine's high-profile appearances suggests that his performance offers unique insight into how conservative political actors strive to integrate humor into the construction of their political identities. Analysis of Brad Stine's 2012 CPAC performance not only offers a glimpse at how conservative political comedy works to enable a broader pursuit of electoral power among conservatives, but also why comedy has struggled to work its way into the tactical repertoire of conservative political actors.

Stine and the 2012 CPAC Routine

We located a full-length video of Brad Stine's 2012 performance on the video sharing website, YouTube.com. After viewing Stine's performance several times we transcribed and then coded his act using qualitative methods of open and axial coding (Corbin & Strauss 2008). The primary questions that served to guide our coding included: What are the salient themes and tropes present in Stine's act? How do the themes and tropes present in Stine's humorous discourse link up to struggles for power within the domains of electoral politics? How does Stine weave humor with a conservative ethos? And, most importantly, how does Stine's discourse contribute to the production of partisan based political identities through burlesque? The total length of Stine's performance was about 15 minutes and 30 seconds. We focus primarily on Stine's construction of conservative and liberal political identities. Stine renders these identities through the construction of an "Us" (the Protagonist Self) and "Them" (the Antagonist Self) dichotomy, defining the conservative political identity as rebelling against prevailing liberal forces. Stine's comedy act presents itself as a satirical corrective to liberal ideology, however his "Us" and "Them" dichotomy constructed within his performance is better understood as burlesque, symbolically foreclosing a chance to dialogue in favor of identity construction.

Stine presents a conservative identity as an amalgam of Christian piety and masculinity couched within particular understanding of American Constitutionalism. Stine begins his routine with an explicit framing of conservatism: "Let me tell you why I love conservatives: They're people who believe in the Judeo-Christian values that our founding fathers stood on to make this great nation." Stine parlays notions of Christianity into a narrative of self-sufficiency that uniquely ties America's *raison d'être* to the conservative identity. Such observations are reinforced through consistent critiques of government intervention, the byproduct of Americans losing their way. For example, "The Founding Fathers were about as conservative as you get: They didn't believe in tax breaks … Let me tell you something, if you didn't have a house back then, they didn't give you subsidies, they gave you an axe. 'Hey Jedediah, See them woods over there? That's your new duplex.'"

This conservative imaginary casts the Founding Fathers as anti-government libertarians who eschew the crutch of government support, echoing the tropes of the "American Dream." Conservatism becomes not an ideology of orderly tradition, but of defiant individualism. The humor does not play out as a satirical commentary on rugged individualism or as a send-up of governmental overreach, but as a bold statement on self-evident gumption. The tropes of individualism and safeguarding the legacy of America's founding fathers have become commonplace in conservative discourse; however, it is Stine's characterizations of traditionally more progressive ideologies that presents the unique force of his burlesque.

Stine gestures toward some progressive ideals (strong women are good), but appropriates them as valuable insofar as they support conservative articulations of masculinity. Stine reinforces manly individualism noting: "Conservatives make strong women, but they don't take their men down in the process. They allow men to be men." These observations are cast against the image of the liberal as soft and feminine. This characterization of the liberal identity is the foray to Stine's main target: political correctness. He positions political correctness as a byproduct of distancing ourselves from our masculine roots, framing it as the root cause of social decay. Stine quips: "It's the wussification of America that's killing us … Where does this wussification come from? From that cancerous ideology, or should I say idiotology, that has made us begin to crumble from within … Of course, I'm speaking about political correctness." Of course, while defining political correctness as an ideology stretches the meaning of the term, Stine's connection between political correctness and his neologisms for America's failings begin to cast conservatives as the victims of an oppressive discursive regime, one that seeks to avoid offending others in the body politic. In other words, conservatives are losing the privilege of unfettered expression, a freedom now only reserved to those once subject to discrimination. Stine doubles down on the feminine hue to political correctness: "They came to us and tried to take away our masculinity: 'Find your feminine side.'" Stine aligns the feminization of America with a liberal penchant for cultivating a blameless society that resents the successful. Stine continues: "It's the false world that liberal idiotology creates … we'll make everything nice and if you get hurt it's never your fault, it's always somebody else's fault, preferably someone with assets." To be sure, highlighting the irony is low-hanging fruit. However, Stine's comedic moves reflect an aspirational satire that does little to move beyond burlesque. The history or purpose for political correctness is rendered absent, glossing over a legacy of disenfranchisement that is both discursive and structural. Political correctness, whatever its shortcomings, seeks discursive inclusion, an effort to curtail exclusive language that performs linguistic violence. However, Stine passes on the satirical move to tease conservatives, his audience, for accepting a role of "victim" of political correctness and blaming it for the perceived downfall of society. Stine positions the conservatives, both himself and the audience, as cultural outsiders, victims who are the vanguards of the historical legacy of America. The outsider role is achieved only through the ridicule of others, and not by offering a corrective to the mistaken social order created by political correctness, as such a move would problematize the outsider identity. The anti-political correctness trope is common among conservatives, and for commentators such as Limbaugh, Lewis notes (2006), attacks on political correctness as quelling freedom of expression give him presumed license for offensive remarks in service of such attacks.

In their analysis of James Finn Garner's *Politically Correct Bedtime Stories*, Gring-Pemble and Watson (2003) argue that audience reception of ironic satire is often unpredictable, facilitating acceptance to the very thing being satirized. In Stine's rhetoric, the burlesque framing of political correctness in front of a conservative audience ensures that rejection of political correctness is inherently tied to the conservative identity. In essence, the arguably well-meaning intent of political correctness as a mode of inclusion and polite respect is not a practice in need of a comic corrective, but an oppressive and intolerable encroachment of liberty that requires complete rejection.

The closest Stine approaches satire is an extended rant on children growing up in "wussified" America. Using a stand-up comedy trope of calling out an audience member to serve as a foil for jokes, Stine identifies a 17-year-old kid in the audience who functions synecdochally – as a part representing the whole – as the shortcomings of contemporary America. Stine quips that the "seventeen-year-old" needs computers and Game Boys to pass time and lacks the toughness of yesterday's men (who wore neither bike helmets nor seat belts). Stine's nostalgia harkens to a Founding Fathers narrative that embraced difference, or the clear and celebrated distinctions between boys and girls, and the virtues of a melting pot discovered on the western frontier. This rendering of America has been sacrificed on the altar of political correctness, an ideology thrust upon America by nefarious liberals. The absence of the reflective, satirical move renders Stine's performance burlesque.

To be fair, Stine's other comedic acts offer more satirical moments. His other routines take shots at judgmental Christians and smug conservatives, discursive moves that invite the audience to laugh itself. The striking feature, however, is the noticeable absence of such satire in the CPAC performance. One would expect, given the reason for the convention, for the entertainment to "rally the base," and any criticism that faults Stine for fulfilling such a purpose would be staid and unproductive. However, the way Stine creates conservative and liberal identities through comedic tropes reveals larger dimensions of extant conservative political discourse. Moreover, that Stine relied on the burlesque during his performance at the 2012 CPAC, a high profile moment in the conservative limelight, is telling in that he sought resonance and appeal by editing out the satirical elements. This omission further suggests a policing of the identity construction process during his performance at the CPAC event in a way that largely eschews any humorous critical reflection on the complexities of the Self in favor of a much safer outwardly cynical derogation of the Other.

Articulating conservatives as victims, characterizing liberalism as the hegemonic force that subverts freedom and liberty in favor of secular government intrusion, works insofar as conservatives overlook the inherent irony of faulting others for one's failings over and against their own ideology. Stine's humorous rhetoric reaches for the satirical – challenging the assumed dominant order using a healthy dose of introspection – but is in practice best understood as burlesque – reducing opponents to a simplistic caricature. These caricatures are fundamental to the process of identity creation in that the Self is positively constituted through a negative definition of the Other.

Stine's discourse creates a particular identity for a conservative that operates on two levels: these are the qualities and commitments that mark "Us" as conservatives and "We" definitely do not possess those clearly liberal and socially destructive characteristics. However, Stine's comedy is not just marking identity as "Us" and "Not Us," but "Us" and "Not Them." All told, Stine creates the "Us" (the Protagonist Self) as fighting for: religious devotion, national pride and patriotism, constitutionalism, self-sufficiency, producerism, libertarianism, and masculinity. He also constructs the "Them" (Antagonist Others) as representing qualities the "Us" needs to fight *against*: atheism and secularism, socialism, moral and emotional weakness, emasculation, internationalism, political correctness, and historical revisionism.

Through this analysis, we attempt to understand this identity formation by overlaying the poetic categories of satire and burlesque onto Stine's humor to understand how his discourse constrains rhetorical action. With satire, there's typically an argument, a perspective that offers a point of departure for social criticism. Burlesque, on the other hand, does not care about such complexity. Burlesque does not suggest that there is a mistaken fool in need of comic correction, rather a clown that requires absolute ridicule and rejection, for the purity of the identity demands it. Stine, as evident in his other stand-up routines, fancies himself a satirist, believing he is engaging in the type of political work that comes with the territory. But for the CPAC audience, Stine elevates the liberal agenda to the level of the oppressive system in order to then reduce it, as if political correctness is this dominant force that is crushing freedom and liberty. The satirical element of mocking conservatives present in his other routines is noticeably absent for his CPAC routine, leaving the burlesque elements that construct irreconcilable identities untouched and hence intact. By suggesting that Stine is burlesque, we argue that his discourse forecloses any rational or legitimate critique of liberalism and thus limits the ability to invite productive political discourse. The boundaries between Self and Other are thus rendered impenetrable and exclusive rather than inviting and inclusive. The thickness of the boundary enclosing this partisan-based identity ultimately leaves little room for interaction and dialogue, a requisite of democratic politics in heterogeneous societies (Dahl 2000). Without the existence of spaces or modes of inter-partisan dialogue, politics becomes a zero-sum game leaving little to no room for collaboration and compromise.

Concluding Punchlines

Humor has often been a staple of biting political commentary, from the social critiques of Aristophanes to the liberal self-congratulatory mockery of Louis C.K.. Although humor enjoys a long history of performing rhetorical labor, rhetorical theorists and critics wonder if comedy promotes healthy deliberative practices or if it derails charitable discourses necessary for democratic dialogue. Even when humor is intended to offer critiques and commentaries that seek to open dialogue, the ideological leanings of the auditors ensures that the joke may not have its intended effect (LeMarre, Landreville, & Beam 2009). While satire invites the potential to expand discursive horizons and enrich democratic deliberations, burlesque often produces a chilling effect, foreclosing avenues for dialogue. The reflective and occasional self-mockery of satire offers opportunities for productive discourses, whereas outright unapologetic mockery of burlesque prevents the search for the commonplaces necessary for healthy democratic practices. The burlesque move evident in Stine's routine is not just mockery, but a mode of identity construction that feeds on the ridicule. To be sure, liberals, such as Bill Maher, use burlesque to mock conservatives. But liberal burlesque rarely moves beyond ridicule to offer an affirmative liberal identity that appropriates discourse of victimage. The burlesque dimension of Stine's comedy creates a conservative identity that does not allow for compromise; the casting of conservatives as a Protagonist Self pitted against the Antagonist Other undermines opportunities for discovering any commonplaces. Unlike the introspective move of satire that opens space for dialogue by challenging the "Us" and "Not Us" dichotomy, Stine's burlesque humor ignores any irony regarding the claim that the problem with society is that we are "wusses" who blame everyone else, and it's all the liberals' fault, recasting conservatives as the victim of liberal oppression. By elevating the liberal as oppressor, Stine looks to offer a more biting critique, where satirical humor is best expressed through the eyes of the oppressed.

Burke (1984) argues "methods of caricature [such as burlesque] do not equip us to understand the full complexities of sociality" (p. 93), but the frames of acceptance provide "the more or less organized system of meanings by which a thinking man gauges the historical situation and adopts a role in relation to it"

(p. 5). The mockery of burlesque alone does little to instruct Stine's audience on how to operate in the world; it is only through the identity construction of a conservative, articulated by the caricature of the liberal "Antagonist Other" that offers his audience a role in the world. This "frame of acceptance" is best understood as an epic "that enables the humble man [sic] to share the worth of the hero by the process of 'identification' … [that] becomes more accessible, and incidentally dignifies any sense of prosecution that may possess the individual, who may also feel himself [sic] marked for disaster" (pp. 36–37). Stine's burlesque constructs a heroic conservative figure who must stand up to the onslaughts of the imperialist liberals who silence expression in the name of political correctness. The existential struggle presents a conservative identity that is incommensurate with any putative liberal concepts, foreclosing the possibility of dialogue.

All told, the identity of the Protagonist Self in Stine's CPAC performance is rooted in notions of existential threat and persecution, endangering masculine strength, religious faith, personal autonomy, industriousness, patriotism and historical righteousness. The Antagonist Other, whose identity rests heavily upon notions of ideological duplicity, emotional weakness, moral idleness, pseudo-intellectualism, and statist paternalism, victimizes the values of the Protagonist Self. While Stine's act relies heavily on sardonic humor and is delivered to the CPAC audience in an aggressive-argumentative style, he periodically indexes religiosity and religious faith so as to temper what might otherwise come across as an angry tirade grounded upon hatred and resentment. One could thus view his act through the lens of the "superiority theory" of humor whereby humor works to build solidarity by tapping into the pleasure of finding the Self better than the Other and binds people through collective contempt for the disagreeable Other (Carroll 2014). Hence, in Burkean terms, Stine's act tends toward the tropes of the burlesque rather than the satirical.

The extant explanations for such moves are largely explained as resentment, or the more philosophically grounded *ressentiment*. However, an identity construction that combines burlesque with embracing the role of victim is further calcified by charges of resentment. To be sure, resentment functions as part of the identity construction, but explaining away such discursive techniques as primarily a product of the resentment does little to advance deliberative discourse. Stine did not enjoy success until he identified himself as a conservative, Christian comic. The *New Yorker* article on Stine possesses a cynical undertone, playing on the idea that Stine is a bit of a huckster searching for, but never experiencing, mainstream success. The article does not shy away from cheeky observations about his father's occupations and his penchant for swindling, noting that Stine long toiled as a magician with a clear desire for success (Green 2004). However, the overt move to label Stine's comedy as resentment works against the goal of finding commonplaces. Rather, Stine's conservative humor makes resentment part of the conservative identity. And yet, charges of resentment embolden conservatives and give further cover for burlesque humor. Characterizing Stine's conservative humor as resentment holds some rhetorical liabilities. First, it dismisses out of hand the legitimacy of their complaint. While many conservative complaints are informed by constructed boogeymen and prejudiced myopia, characterizing them as rooted in resentment plays into a narrative of victimization. This invites the second liability: conservatives wear the accusations of resentment and dismissals from the left as validation for their beliefs. Nothing helps create group cohesion like en masse belittling. In his CPAC routine, Stine blames the liberal media for preventing such success because he stood up for his beliefs, moral and political convictions that are risky ventures for conservatives in modern times. It is important to note that Stine ends his routine with a call for comedy, that conservatives must embrace comedy as a tool for group mobilization, as presumably coalition building. Stine cites Jon Stewart and Bill Maher as building an army of loyal liberals, and conservatives need to respond in kind. Despite the scarcity of conservative comedians, critics need to pay attention to the role of comedy in conservative identity construction.

Notes

1 While the crafting of broad-based coalitions of voters can prove to be a strategic path to electoral power, highly inclusive alliances can be prove fragile and difficult to maintain given the sheer diversity of interests that must be balanced (Dahl 2000).
2 To be sure, large swaths of Burkean scholarship place the identities of interlocutors at the center of its rhetorical analysis. Our argument is that scholarly treatments of burlesque typically focus on the characterization of the ridiculed.
3 Retrieved from www.gop.com/2012-republican-platform_Restoring/#Item3.

References

Adams, R. (2011). Republicans stop laughing after Obama impersonator turns jokes on them. *The Guardian*. Retrieved from www.theguardian.com/world/richard-adams-blog/2011/jun/20/republicans-barack-obama-impersonator
Appel, E.C. (1996). Burlesque drama as a rhetorical genre: The Hudibrastic ridicule of William F. Buckley, Jr. *Western Journal of Communication, 60*(3), 269–284.
Appel, E.C. (2003). Rush to judgment: Burlesque, tragedy, and hierarchal alchemy in the rhetoric of America's foremost political talkshow host. *Southern Communication Journal, 68*(3), 217–230.
Boskin, J. (1990). American political humor: Touchables and taboos. *International Political Science Review, 11*(4), 473–482.
Burke, K. (1969). *A rhetoric of motives*. Berkeley: University of California Press: Berkeley.
Burke, K. (1984). *Attitudes toward history*. Berkeley: University of California Press: Berkeley.
Carlson, C. (1988). Limitations of the comic frame: Some witty American Women of the Nineteenth Century. *Quarterly Journal of Speech, 74*, 310–322.
Carroll, N. (2014). *Humor: A very short introduction*. Oxford, UK: Oxford University Press.
Charland, M. (1987). Constitutive rhetoric: The case of the *Peuple Québécois*. *Quarterly Journal of Speech, 73*(2), 133–150.
Corbin, J., & Strauss, A. (2008). *Basics of qualitative research: Techniques and procedures for developing grounded theory*. Thousand Oaks, CA: Sage Publications.
Dagnes, A. (2012). *A conservative walks into a bar: The politics of political humor*. New York: Palgrave Macmillan.
Dahl, R.A. (2000). *On democracy*. New York: Yale University Press.

Faulks, K. (2000). *Political sociology: A critical introduction*. New York: New York University Press.
Fine, G.A., & de Soucey, M. (2005). Joking cultures: Humor themes as social regulation in group life. *Humor, 18*(1), 1–22.
Green, A. (2004, August 9–16). Standup for the Lord. *The New Yorker,* 46–52.
Gring-Pemble, L., & Watson, M.S. (2003). The rhetorical limits of satire: An analysis of James Finn Garner's *Politically Correct Bedtime Stories*. *Quarterly Journal of Speech, 89*(2), 132–153.
Hariman, R. (2008). Political parody and public culture. *Quarterly Journal of Speech 94*(3), 247–272.
Kline, K.N. (2010). Poking fun at midwifery on prime-time television: The rhetorical implications of burlesque frames in humorous shows. *Women & Language, 33*(1), 53–71.
LeMarre, H.L., Landreville, K.D., & Beam, M.A. (2009). The irony of satire: Political ideology and the motivation to see what you want to see in *The Colbert Report*. *The International Journal of Press/Politics, 14*(2), 212–231.
Lewis, P. (2006). *Cracking up*. Chicago: University of Chicago Press.
Meyer, J. (2000). Humor as a double-edged sword: Four functions of humor in communication. *Communication Theory, 10*(3), 310–331.
Stine, B. (2012). CPAC 2012 routine. *YouTube*. Retrieved from www.youtube.com/watch?v=MUdco-_bBeI

9
LIVE FROM DC, IT'S "NERD PROM"

Political Humor at the White House Correspondents' Association Dinner

Jonathan P. Rossing

At the 2012 White House Correspondents' Association dinner, late-night comedian Jimmy Kimmel quipped: "Members of the media, politicians, corporate executives, advertisers, lobbyists, and celebrities – everything that is wrong with America is here in this room tonight." So began another roasting of Washington insiders, political journalists, and our system of representative democracy. Such political humor rules contemporary popular culture. As such, scholars argue for the important relationship between humor and politics (e.g. Gray, Jones, & Thompson 2009). As political scientists Baumgartner and Morris (2008) remind us, "[A]lthough humor may take temporary hiatus from time to time, it has always been – and will continue to be – part of the political landscape" (p. xiv). The range of political humor is vast; it includes stand-up comedians (i.e., Hari Kondabolu; George Carlin), late-night talk show hosts (David Letterman; Conan O'Brien), sketch comedy (*Saturday Night Live*), news satires (*The Daily Show with Jon Stewart*; *The Nightly Show with Larry Wilmore*), Internet memes and videos (FunnyorDie.com; JibJab.com), television series (*South Park*; *The Simpsons*), and more. However, one genre remains largely under-examined: the roast.

A roast – a parody of a toast – is a stand-up performance where a celebrated guest becomes the target of good-natured jokes that ostensibly honor the individual through derisive jokes. Typically a host or "roastmaster" emcees the event while a series of roasters offer speeches that offer biting criticism of the "roastee." The comic abuse featured in the stand-up routines seeks to ridicule but not necessarily to harm both the guest of honor and the admirers in the audience. The roast could be considered a particular manifestation of insult comedy, a style of humor in which the comedian denigrates members of the audience or well-known public personas. Celebrity roasts arguably constitute the most common roast. The New York Friars Club roasts are, perhaps, the most famous, though Comedy Central has produced its own popular celebrity roasts since 2003.

Exploring the roast as a site for political humor, this chapter focuses on the stand-up performances at the annual White House Correspondents' Association (WHCA) dinners. Since 1983, the annual dinner has featured a headlining comedian who delivers a monologue for the President, the press, and celebrity guests who exemplify the blurring of entertainment and politics that political humor symbolizes. The stand-up routines at the dinner align with the genre of the roast. This chapter takes as its texts the 14 stand-up monologues from the WHCA dinners during the Bush and Obama Administrations from 2001–2015 (see Appendix A). These speeches are noteworthy because they emerge both in a heightened period of political humor and during a period of increased cultural attention to the WHCA dinner. These dinners feature roasts by stand-up comedians who also perform as late-night talk show hosts, *Saturday Night Live* performers, impersonators, and sitcom stars. Understanding these stand-up routines as roasts provides an opportunity to explore how the roast might operate as political humor. The roasts at these WHCA dinners target the press, politicians, and the public, thereby offering a tripartite roast of the true guest of honor: democracy.

I argue that this annual political roast or "demockery" – a mockery of democratic ideals and actors – represents a mode of stand-up comedy that can be used to take part in politics, to keep the governmental system on track. In the spirit of the roast, the comedians insult and ridicule democratic agents and processes not to harm democracy but to honor the system with all its flaws and, as Peterson (2008) argues of late-night comedy, to "nudg[e] it toward its ostensible goal of improving the common good" (p. 206).

I first offer context for these stand-up monologues with a brief history of the White House Correspondents' Association annual dinner. Then, drawing from 14 performances during the Bush and Obama administrations, I explore the three critical targets of these political roasts. In conclusion, I consider the critical limits of "demockery."

White House Correspondents' Association Dinner

Founded in 1914, the White House Correspondents' Association (WHCA) formed, in part, in response to President Woodrow Wilson's threat to cease presidential news conferences in 1913 and rumors that a congressional committee would invite only select journalists to presidential press conferences (Cohen 2012; Edwards 2011; "History of the WHCA" n.d.). Over its 100-year history, the organization has advocated for greater press contact with the President, demanded transparency from every administration, and encouraged vigorous reporting on the executive branch. In short, the WHCA was founded on ideals of free press, government accountability to the people, and the ethical responsibility of journalists to report public affairs accurately and fairly.

The White House Correspondents' Association dinner hosted its first annual dinner in 1921 with the purpose of inaugurating new officers. Today, the business of the WHCA also includes the awarding of several journalism scholarships. The dinner provides an opportunity for the press, the President, and other Washington insiders to mingle in a serious yet convivial affair away from briefing rooms and press conferences. Calvin Coolidge became the first president to attend the WHCA dinner in 1924; every President since Coolidge has attended at least one dinner.

Since the mid-1980s, however, a celebratory party atmosphere has increasingly overshadowed the dinner's business and called the organization's mission into question. Throughout its history, the WHCA dinner has featured popular entertainment to complement the business of the event. In early years, the dinner featured well-known singers, actors, and variety show performers. Now the dinner – also popularly known as "Nerd Prom" – has become a red carpet affair where news organizations invite A-List celebrities and outrageous guests to showcase in a parade of popular culture. A headlining comedian became the norm for the night's entertainment after comedian and political satirist Mark Russell performed at the 1983 dinner.

The dinner has long received criticism for encouraging too-close a relationship between Washington insiders and the journalists charged with reporting on the President. As the popularity of the event has increased, so has the criticism. In 2007, the *New York Times* withdrew its correspondents from the annual dinner because of the perception that such a close relationship between journalists and public figures jeopardizes the credibility of the news organization. *Times* columnist Frank Rich described the dinners as "propaganda events for a White House that has really staked almost its entire politics on creating propaganda events, whether it be uranium from Africa or mission accomplished" (Masters 2007). Former *Politico* reporter Patrick Gavin recently directed a documentary about the red carpet transformation of the dinner. Writing about his experience, Gavin (2015) called the dinner "a tacky and vainglorious self-celebration at a time when most Americans don't think Washingtonians have much to be commended for." Gavin continued, "[N]ow it's not just one night of clubby backslapping, carousing and drinking between the press and the powerful, it's four full days of signature cocktails and inside jokes that just underscore how out of step the Washington elite is with the rest of the country."

In sum, at the WHCA dinner the press, politicians, and the pinnacles of popular culture mingle in a spectacle that garners ample public attention. This three-ring circus environment makes the political roasts presented at the WHCA dinner wide-reaching and culturally important. The comic tone of the roast and the atmosphere of the dinner give the guest stand-up roastmasters license to speak directly to power. In this context of already blurred boundaries, the invited stand-up comedians take aim not only at the guests of honor – politicians and the press – but also at the public, thereby offering a three-pronged criticism through "demockery." The roasts illustrate the range of "serious comedy," a blend of aesthetics and politics, emotions and rationality, art and argument, that "is at once political and pleasurable" and "committed to the serious work of democracy" (Baym 2008, p. 35).

Roasting the Press, Politicians, and Public

Before detailing the "demockery" presented across this body of political roasts, I begin with a single performance that exemplifies the critical potentials of the political roast: Stephen Colbert's acclaimed (and lambasted) roast at the 2006 WHCA dinner.[1] With President George W. Bush sitting next to him on the dais and a ballroom full of prominent journalists and news organizations, Colbert launched a torrent of comic criticism against the President's miscues, the failure of the press to hold the Bush administration accountable, and the public's general disengagement from the political process. Of the WHCA dinner routines, Colbert's roast has received the most scholarly and popular attention for its artistic genius, its bold criticism, and its unrelenting barbs (e.g. Baym 2008; Bennett 2007; Colletta 2009; Rich 2006; Sternbergh 2006).

Colbert's model performance illustrates the three major targets of ridicule in these political roasts – the press, politicians, and the public – and offers an exemplar for the potential power of "demockery." The following excerpts from Colbert's roast at the White House Correspondents' Association dinner reveal "the power of satire and parody ... in enunciating critiques that were difficult to articulate (or be effective) in other ways" (Jones 2010, p. xi). Abiding by the conventions of the roast, Colbert couches ridicule in praise. For example, in a jab at the President, Colbert celebrates, "The greatest thing about [President Bush] is he's steady ... He believes the same thing Wednesday that he believed on Monday, no matter what happened Tuesday. Events can change; this man's beliefs never will." He extols the press for their limited reporting on important socio-political issues: "Over the last five years you people were so good over tax cuts, WMD intelligence, the effect of global warming. We Americans didn't want to know, and you had the courtesy not to try to find out. Those were good times, as far as we knew." The backhanded compliment lambasts the press for abrogating their responsibilities in democratic society to keep the public informed and to hold elected officials accountable. Colbert simultaneously implicates the public for their complicity in this failed system as well. One jab in particular skewers the dominant media's complicity in reporting the administration's agenda and the public's acceptance of this status quo:

> I stand by this man because he stands for things. Not only for things, he stands on things. Things like aircraft carriers and rubble and recently flooded city squares. And that sends a powerful message: that no matter what happens to America, she will always rebound – with the most powerfully staged photo ops in the world.

This triple attack hits the Bush Administration's restriction of information, the press' failure to challenge the Administration, and their willingness to report the Administration's desired agenda. Further, as the comic everyman who stands with the President and the media, Colbert implicitly attacks a complicit public who also fails to challenge these messages. Performances like this lead Waisenen (2009) to describe Colbert as more than a comedian, but as also a rhetorical critic who "creatively guide[s] audiences toward democratic possibilities" (p. 120). Indeed, by roasting key agents in the democratic system, Colbert's demockery challenges politicians, the press, and most importantly the public to rise to our respective civic responsibilities. Amid his roasting jabs, Colbert honors a flawed democratic system by accenting the shortcomings of its agents and calling us – shaming us – into continued work toward a more perfect union.

Arguably no other comic headliner during the Bush and Obama Administrations parallels the critical mastery of Colbert. However, with varying levels of critical savvy, the remaining roasts[2] illustrate the possibilities for the political roast as a site of socio-political critique. In addition, Colbert's performance marked a turning point in the WHCA roasts; while the majority of the roasts ridicule multiple aspects of our political system, the roasts following Colbert's have a sharper edge.[3] The next sections highlight the interconnected roasting of the press, politicians, and public at the WHCA dinners. First, these stand-up routines deride the press for privileging ratings over ethical reporting and for overt partisan bias. Next, they direct scorn at presidential administrations and politicians for their failure to serve the public they represent. Finally, the comedians roast the public for disengagement from civic life and complicity in the failures of the democratic system. This multifaceted attack suggests that our system of representative democracy is the true guest of honor at the roast. These WHCA dinner roasts serve up "demockery" that highlights the flaws of our system while also calling all parties to attend to their responsibilities within that system.

Pillorying the Press

As principal guests of the evening, the press figures as a primary target at the WHCA dinner roasts. The stand-up routines routinely skewer news organizations, journalists, and pundits. First, the roasts attack a press that often seems motivated by ratings rather than upholding journalistic ethics or ensuring political accountability. CNN figures as a frequent target for its ratings ploys. Late night talk show host and 2011 WHCA emcee Jimmy Kimmel (2012), for instance, mocked CNN's election coverage that featured holographic reporters asking, "Are the CNN tables real tables or virtual tables?" Just two weeks after CNN reporters notoriously reported misinformation in their rush to break the story about the Boston Marathon bombing, Conan O'Brien (2013) chastised, "Tonight's entrees were halibut and filet mignon or as CNN's John King reported it: lasagna and couscous." CNN's specious round-the-clock reporting about the mysterious disappearance of Malaysia Airlines flight 370 inspired Joel McHale's (2014) jab, "CNN is desperately searching for something they've been missing for months: their dignity." These barbs challenge CNN's journalistic integrity by highlighting the network's willingness to sensationalize stories, to report misinformation, and to report pure speculation as news.

Of course, CNN is not the only culprit in the press. Highlighting the histrionics with which Fox News reports political stories, McHale (2014) also asserted that pundits "Bill O'Reilly, Megan Kelly, and Sean Hannity are the Mount Rushmore of keeping old people angry." Extending the critique of ratings-driven news, Jay Leno (2004) questioned the urgency of live news coverage with a montage of reporters battling the elements as they attempt to file reports in the midst of impending hurricanes. Together these recurring digs stress an ongoing failure of the media to uphold its responsibility for accurate reporting amidst the pressure to maximize ratings and revenue.

Complimenting this ridicule of ratings-driven negligence, another recurring roast topic critiques biased, ideological reporting. Fox News and MSNBC receive the lion's share of these barbs. Leno (2004), for instance, in 2004, commented on the launch of Al Gore's left-leaning news station, Current TV, saying, "I guess [Gore] figures that if President Bush can have his own station [*Leno coughs under his breath*] – *Fox News* – then he should be able to have one as well." In 2010, Leno riffed on Obama's much maligned first pitch at a Washington Nationals baseball game. "It was not a good pitch," Leno told the President before he excused the athletic performance by explaining that Obama had just finished an interview with MSNBC so he was "used to softball." Seth Meyers (2011) also took shots at both news networks. Alluding to Fox News' frequent attention to President Obama's birth certificate, Meyers (2011) joked that "security is tough [at the Fox News after-party] so be sure to bring your driver's license and your long form driver's license." At the MSNBC party, however, "President Obama makes the Kool-Aid and everyone there drinks it." Meyers and Leno echo themes from most of the roasts that stress polarized media attitudes: on one hand, a media organization that appears set on celebrating Republican policy and discrediting the Democrats with little regard to the credibility of their claims; and, on the other hand, a media organization that seems eager to counter political bias with ideological purity of its own. In either case, the roastmasters ridicule how some journalists eschew their responsibility to hold politicians accountable through balanced reporting and instead represent an extension of partisan politics. To be sure, the roasts do not uncover hidden aspects of contemporary media; rather, they amplify these ideological prejudices in a way that keeps them present as problems to address rather than letting these flaws slide into a space of complacent familiarity.

Skewering ideological bias and ratings-driven reporting may not expose unknown flaws. However, the media roasting also attacks a less perceptible foible: the ease with which media storytellers distort political stories. Kimmel's (2012) opening bit exemplifies this criticism. The bit featured a montage titled "Unnecessary Censorship" in which strategically censored words invite crass interpretations for otherwise benign statements. For instance, the montage featured President Obama in a press briefing, saying, "I've told leaders of both parties that they must come up with a fair compromise in the next few days that can pass both houses of congress and a c— that I can s—." The President likely demanded a "copy" to "sign," but the censored words invited the audience to imagine a more untoward demand from Obama. The sequence also featured a reporter who explained, "Trying to find bi-partisan health care reform on Capitol Hill is sort of like children trying to f—— unicorns," and Texas Governor Rick Perry announcing, "I understand what pork-barrel politics is all about. I s—— your —ck and you s—— mine." The majority of the censored statements implied sexually explicit comments. Kimmel's bawdy gags critically demonstrate the ease with which editing distorts meaning. If cutting a single word radically transforms the public's understanding of a statement, then it is imperative to consider the effect of distilling socio-political issues into sound bites and 140-character tweets.

Leno's (2004; 2010) roasts offered similar insights about visual edits. For instance, Leno proved that Vice President Cheney's health was fine with a video showing Cheney leaving the hospital into which he spliced a body-double doing cartwheels down the street. Likewise, a video in which Michelle Obama advocates for the need to raise a healthier generation included a split screen of President Obama eating desserts, fried food, and hotdogs that discredited the First Lady's initiative. Leno's visual edits simultaneously demonstrate the powerful truth of the visual and invite careful scrutiny of the way the press uses the visual to create meaning. Together, Kimmel's verbal censorship and Leno's visual gags can be understood to indict the blend of ratings ploys, media bias, and manipulation typified by the media's scrutiny of a 2008 campaign photo in which President Obama appeared not to put his hand over his heart during the national anthem or the sensational speculation about Obama's "treasonous" bow before Japanese Emperor Akihito.

These examples showcase one dimension of demockery featured in political roasts: ridicule of the press's negligence to its ethical responsibilities. In the context of a dinner intended to honor the journalists who report on the political system, these stand-up routines must be understood as political roasts that identify the shortcomings of the press. As Jones, Baym, and Day (2012) assert:

> The moral voice of those who monitor and comment upon political life should not be limited by form – journalistic or comedic – and if it takes comedians to point out the moral and ethical lapses of those who dominate political processes and the discourses that structure public life, then so be it.

Amid their scorn, however, the stand-up comedians also display respect for the often unrealized power of the press in democratic society. Underlying this ridicule of ratings-driven hype and ideological bias rests the belief in the press' ability to inform the public of complex issues, to distinguish between fact and opinion, and to foster greater participation in public debates without sensationalizing or distorting stories. Of course, the press cannot shoulder the brunt of the ridicule; thus, politicians and political figures represent the second primary target of the WHCA dinner political roasts.

Pouncing on Presidents and Politicians

As the official guests of honor on the dais, Presidents Bush and Obama rival the press in their share of ridicule; the roasters, however, also spread the derision among elected officials and prominent political figures. Notably, the roastmasters jab the presidents lightly. During the Bush years, the headlining comedians target the president's verbal miscues, ample vacation time, and folksy mannerisms. Drew Carey (2002) jested that he loved watching President Bush speak "because every time he gets to a big word it's like watching a high wire act." Assuming the role of enthusiastic spectator, Carey continues: "Is he gonna do it? YES! He did it! Three syllables everybody! How about it?" Vice President Cheney's health and, specifically, his heart problems set up several punchlines about his seemingly cold, even ruthless demeanor. The roasts during President Obama's terms address benign topics such as the president's cool personality, his love of basketball, and moments that received public mockery such as his high-waisted "mom jeans" or his off-target first pitch at a professional baseball game. Comics target Vice President Biden as the boneheaded, gaffe-master to Obama's cool-headed straight man. Kimmel (2012), for instance, confessed at the top of his routine: "It's hard to be funny with the President of the United States sitting right next to you," then delivered the blow, "but somehow, day-in, day-out Joe Biden finds a way to do it." These roast topics appear less politically charged, but they serve an important function for the roast as a mode of political humor. The comic must carefully navigate the line between hostility and respectful criticism; these tempered barbs help the comedian establish goodwill and suggest that their critiques should be understood as productive rather than irrevocably damaging. Such gestures of deference create space for sharper rebukes throughout the routine that target both the Administration and the cast of politicians in Washington.

The roasts lampoon political partisanship and dysfunction, a theme that increased during the Obama administration. For instance, after President Obama addressed the audience with a comic monologue in 2013, O'Brien (2013) joked, "You got to do what I do, now for the next 15 minutes I get to do what you do – stand up here in a tense dysfunctional stand-off with Congress!" His quick take on partisan gridlock represents a problem the majority of the WHCA roastmasters seek to deride. Meyers (2011), for example, turned a riff on Representative Paul Ryan into an indictment of political dysfunction writ large. He explained that Ryan's budget proposal sharply cut social welfare programs "because he believes the American people have said loud and clear, 'Stop using my tax dollars to take care of me!'" The punchline contrasts Congress' duty to protect the common good for all citizens with the policies that gradually dismantle social safety nets. Meyers noted that Ryan's budget proposal garnered him praise as a "serious adult" before lamenting, "Nothing is more depressing about politics than the fact that 'adult' is now a compliment. Adult is only a compliment to a child." He then amplified the mockery, adding, "I'm so proud of you. You acted like an adult tonight. I'm glad I brought you to my boss's house for dinner. You even cut your own meat like a big boy." Meyers' recontextualized praise for adult-like behavior both maligns the petulance of partisan politicians and criticizes the press for its celebration of these behaviors. Exposing these norms, Meyers implies a need for higher expectations and standards of professionalism among our elected representatives. He also attacked members of Congress for stunts that fall within this frame of questionably "adult" behavior. "We are not impressed that you sat next to each other at the state of the Union," he argued. "You know what the rest of Americans call an evening spent sitting next to a person with wildly different political views? Thanksgiving." Turning to the Affordable Care Act, Meyers charged:

> We're not impressed when you complain about how bills are too long to read. The health care bill is almost 2,000 pages. Good. A bill that insures every person in America should be longer than *The Girl with the Dragon Tattoo*. I don't think you read bills anyways. I think you guys vote on bills the same way the rest of us agree to updated terms and conditions on iTunes.

Meyers roasts Congress members' failed responsibilities as public officials and implicitly chastises both the press and the public for enabling this lack of accountability. However, he also balances his ridicule with a moment of praise. He notes that from the partisanship and unprofessionalism emerged a health care bill, a sign that the democratic system with all its current flaws and warts can still be celebrated for such a significant accomplishment.

The roasts also take aim at political messaging. Some roasts attack political spin in general. Leno (2004), for example, named the head of the Home Shopping Network as the person "who first realized you could take a bunch of crap and sell it to the public" before amending his claim: "I'm sorry that's [Bush Senior Advisor] Karl Rove." He also targeted accusations that Senator John Kerry changed positions on key policy issues during the 2004 presidential campaign: "Kerry could be the first president in history to deliver the state of the union and the rebuttal." Rove and Kerry symbolize the ubiquity of political spin. Foregrounding this inescapable reality of framing, Leno invited his audience toward heightened consciousness about political meaning-making practices.

Other roasts model a critical stance toward political messaging strategies. Meyers (2011) tackled the title of Mitt Romney's book, *No Apologies*. "*No apologies*?" he asked, "When you have to claim 'no apologies,' isn't that a tacit admission you've made a lot of mistakes?" He recontextualizes the slogan to create a new framework for understanding: "If I come home from a trip to Vegas and the first thing I say to my girlfriend is 'No apologies!,' we're going to have a follow up conversation." Wanda Sykes (2009) addressed Cheney's defense of torture as an interrogation strategy, saying, "Defending torture is like robbing a bank and then saying 'Yes, your honor, but look at all these bills I paid.'" By repackaging these common-place slogans and political arguments, Meyers and Sykes scrutinize dominant meanings and show how they could be otherwise. Rather than roasting the fact of political spin, these comedians instead attack the certainty and dogmatism with which politicians often assert their truths. Acknowledging the reality that all politics are a matter of perspective and competing arguments, these roastmasters ridicule political messaging that treats political judgments as foregone conclusions.

Finally, these roasts critique elected representatives for failure to attend to the shifting demographics of a pluralistic country. Specifically, they critique political attitudes, policies, and practices that marginalize and disenfranchise members of the public. The roasts during President Obama's terms featured a number of attacks on racial attitudes, inspired perhaps by Obama's historic presidency. Meyers (2011), for instance, warned the President, "If your hair gets any whiter the Tea Party is going to endorse it." With a double-barbed joke that attacked both coded speech and racial attitudes, O'Brien (2013) noted that Representative Paul Ryan attributed Obama's re-election to the "high turnout of urban voters. Then, when he was asked how he liked his coffee, he said, 'No milk, no sugar, just urban.'" Each of these jokes brings to the foreground what critical race theorist Ian Haney López (2015) has called "strategic racism," the use of carefully coded racial appeals by politicians that speak almost subliminally to racial grievances and promote white solidarity. This type of political messaging constitutes a new racism, "inaudible and also easily defended insofar as it fails to whoop in the tones of the old racism, yet booming in its racial meaning and provoking predictable responses among those who immediately hear the racial undertones" (p. 4). Meyers alludes to the implied racial appeals that have constituted the Tea Party as a predominantly white organization – concerns over immigration, welfare, and homeland security, for example. Complementing these examples are ample jokes that roasted political leaders who consistently questioned Barack Obama's nationality.

Cecily Strong (2015) also attended to political marginalization in her roast. Commenting on racial profiling and police violence in communities of color she described the Secret Service as "the only law enforcement agency in the country that will get in trouble if a black man gets shot." Later in her roast, a joke about the aging President Obama attacked institutional racism and privilege again: "Your hair is so white now it can talk back to the police." Hypothetically placing the President in the role of victim, she creates alternative frames of reference on the viral 2014/2015 social campaign refrain, Black Lives Matter. *This* life matters, her joke suggests, but only because Obama ascended to the Presidency. Her follow-up jibe about Obama's hair exposes the disparity between black and white experiences with law enforcement. These quips, while not direct roasting any particular politician, indict a political system that fails to value a large swath of its citizenry.

The roasts also target institutional sexism and homophobia. McHale (2014) introduced himself as host of a show on the E! network before explaining, "To Republicans in the audience E! is the channel that your deeply closeted gay son likes to watch. Democrats, it's the same channel that your happy, openly gay son likes to watch." His comparison amplifies the psychological and emotional violence caused by political attacks and policies targeting gays and lesbians. Later, commenting on Hillary Clinton's probable presidential run, McHale argued that Clinton "has experience, she's a natural leader, and as our first female president we could pay her 30% less. That's a savings this nation could use!" Calling attention to the gender discrimination that disadvantages half the country, McHale's ironic quip about fiscal advantage punctuates how capitalist logics and political benefit trump the needs of marginalized populations. In another attack on sexism in politics Strong (2015) assured her audience, "Since I'm only a comedian I'm not going to tell you politicians how to do politics … That's not my job. That would be like you guys telling me what to do with my body, I mean, can you imagine?" Her satiric analogy, of course, both belies her critical intentions and underscores the patriarchal logic driving some legislation related to women's health.

These critiques of coded racism, political platforms that marginalize gays and lesbians, gender discrimination, and more assail a political context and political practices that decidedly devalue some lives. Peterson (2008) claims that comedy and politics are both "profoundly moral undertakings," which, at their best, "share a common goal of making human society freer, fairer, and more just" (p. 205). In these cases, the headlining comics use the roast to check a political system that fails, at times, to live up to its moral undertaking. These hits against institutional racism, sexism, and homophobia typify what Krefting (2014) calls "charged humor," which affirms marginalized communities, illuminates disparities in the political system, and creates possibilities for restructuring society for the better. The roastmasters incorporate charged humor to ridicule political processes that systematically fail to serve members of the populace. Yet, at their core, these roasts also honor the potential of the political system to address the very flaws it perpetuates.

Pressuring the Public

Traditionally, a roast attacks the guest/s of honor at the event – in this case, the President, politicians, and members of the press. However, the WHCA dinner features an honorary, absentee guest: the public. Both the press and the political leaders share the responsibility of serving the public. By virtue of these relationships, the dinner necessarily invokes the presence of the public and the stand-up comics target this imagined audience. The public, the third target of scorn, transforms the WHCA dinner into a "demockery" – jeering at the flaws of our democratic system and the primary agents of the system. The jibes at the public suggest that we, the people, share complicity for the socio-political shortcomings of the nation with the press and our elected officials. The comics highlight two symptoms of civic disengagement: disinvestment from the political process and over-investment in popular culture.[4]

C-SPAN, the cable network that broadcasts the dinner, typically figures as the butt of several jokes. The network's paltry viewing audience figures as the most common target; however, the jokes imply a harsher critique of the public's disinterest and disengagement from political processes. Meyers (2011) joked, for example, how honored he was to be performing for the audience at the dinner "as well as the handful of people watching at home on C-SPAN." O'Brien (2013) told his audience he needed to share something that would not leave the room adding, "I say that with absolute confidence because we're on C-SPAN." And Strong (2015) greeted her audience watching at home by saying, "Meow," implying that C-SPAN was broadcasting, at best, to rooms with only pets. Under the guise of roasting the network, these comedians turn up the heat on an indifferent public. With a dedicated channel providing transparent and unedited access to the "forums where public policy is discussed, debated, and decided" ("About C-SPAN" n.d.), the public simply does not tune in.

The type of ridicule directed at political figures also suggests an implicit critique of the public. The comics target politicians' physical characteristics, mannerisms, and idiosyncrasies, suggesting that the public is more familiar with politicians as entertaining caricatures than with the platforms and policies these figures endorse. For instance, the roasts ridicule the hue of Representative John Boehner's skin, Senator John Kerry's long face, and Donald Trump's toupee, New Jersey Governor Chris Christie's weight, Senator John McCain's age, and much more (e.g. Kimmel 2012; Leno 2010; McHale 2014; Meyers 2011; O'Brien 2013). On one hand, such physical jokes would be customary for any roast. On the other hand, a typical roast would also move to ridicule personal, insider information. The immediate audience of Washington insiders and journalists possess intimate knowledge of current public affairs, policies, and debates; thus, the absence of ridicule that speaks more specifically to public affairs is notable. I suggest that these roasts' focus on visible characteristics and personality quirks punctuates a paltry awareness of civic affairs among the imagined public audience, thereby implicitly roasting the public for its disinvestment from civic obligations.

The public receives criticism for a lack of concern about *civic* affairs followed by a roasting for its passionate involvement in *popular* affairs. Leno (2004), for instance, joked with the press that their readers would rather engage sports and entertainment than political news. He explained, "The News section [of a newspaper] protects the Entertainment and Sports section from the elements." Punctuating this disregard for public affairs, he noted that he had heard discussions about bringing back the draft. "We don't need the draft," he suggested, "Make it a reality show: *GI Average Joe*." During a heightened period of reality television programming, Leno maligns the public's fascination with this entertainment. His roast argues that a reality TV program would generate more engagement with the consequences and implications of the war in Iraq than the notion of a draft.

O'Brien (2013) also indirectly roasted the public's investment in entertainment over politics through a visual gag that extended the mockery of physical appearances. Hollywood's obsession with Washington, DC, has led to a new movie, O'Brien explained, before revealing the fictitious casting list with photos of politicians juxtaposed with their pop culture look-alikes: Secretary of State John Kerry played by an Easter Island head, Senator Harry Reid played by the "old man from the *American Gothic* painting," etc. O'Brien also compared politicians' appearances to those of figures like Grandpa Munster, Buzz Lightyear, and "the face-melt guy from *Raiders of the Lost Ark*." Like the physical jokes mentioned above, this bit offers customary fare for a roast. However, the roast humorously punches the politicians precisely because of the public's familiarity with the popular characters. O'Brien presumes the public's thorough knowledge of popular culture. In the context of the WHCA dinner celebration – an event grounded on principles of access and transparency in politics – such jokes offer a critical statement about the topics and personalities that dominate public attention.

McHale (2014) offered one of the most direct roasts of the public and its relationship to politicians and the press. "America has seen its share of challenges," he claimed, but then reassured the audience that the country is still great. His examples, however, call into question national priorities. He noted that Americans' biggest concern is TV spoilers adding, "In other countries a spoiler consists of 'Hey! I haven't been back to the village yet, so don't tell me who survived the drone strike. No spoilers!'" He compares the "threats" of gluten and peanuts to the threat of warlords creating child armies, and he commends the country for leading the way with the fourth installment of the *Transformers* franchise despite lagging in education, the economy, and the environment. Juxtaposing pop cultural obsessions against more ethically-laden issues such as the morality of drone strikes or educational opportunity, McHale roasts the public devotion to entertainment culture. Moreover, his routine implies a failed civic duty to hold leaders and the press accountable and, therefore, complicity in the ethical failures of the country. McHale concludes, America is the greatest country because a "guy like me can stand before the President, the press, and Patrick Duffy and tell jokes without severe repercussions. And instead of being shipped off to a gulag I'm going to the *Vanity Fair* after party. That's right. This is America where everyone can be a Pussy Riot." This *coup de grâce* simultaneously celebrates freedoms of speech and press while implying that the press neglects its responsibility in favor of glamour, celebrity, and popularity. It also suggests that the public's interest in popular culture and politics must not represent an either/or proposition. First, McHale offers himself as a model: he attends the celebrity-studded *Vanity Fair* party *and* he demonstrates fluency in and critical awareness of public affairs. More importantly, he calls on the public to do the same. McHale invokes the Russian, feminist, guerrilla performance protest group Pussy Riot, political activists who blend entertainment with sharp political critique even in the face of political repression and limited freedoms. Suggesting that our freedoms demand political engagement, McHale calls the public to a greater investment in public affairs without pitting this responsibility in a zero-sum game against popular entertainment.

In a bit about Hillary Clinton's candidacy for President, Strong (2015) invited journalists to raise their hands and take the following oath: "I solemnly swear not to talk about Hillary's appearance because that is not journalism." As the journalists in the audience follow her lead, they are tricked into roasting themselves. However, Strong offered an addendum that both complicates the oath and exemplifies the implicit roast of the public: "Also, Cecily Strong looks great tonight."

On one hand, she rejects the emphasis on female candidates' looks because it demeans these serious candidates and reflects journalistic bias. On the other hand, she urges the press to cover *her* appearance at the dinner. In effect, she marks herself as complicit in the press' sexism. This move symbolizes the subtle roast of the public throughout these routines. The comedians ridicule the press for infotainment and bias and politicians for partisanship and ethical lapses. And yet, a public with the power and responsibility to hold these agents and institutions accountable must also face scrutiny, particularly when a general disengagement from public affairs renders us complicit in the shortcomings of our democracy.

Conclusion and Implications

This chapter offers the political roast as an important and unexamined mode of political humor with the potential to provoke reflection on democratic failures and responsibilities as well as the capacity to nudge democratic culture toward its ideals. "True political satire," Jones (2009) argues, "always attacks power with cheekiness rather than tickling its cheeks powerlessly" (p. 60). Having the captive ear of the President, the press, and many of the most influential people and organizations in the country, the WHCA dinner headliners turn to the roast to attack not only the power of the press and politicians but also the public. Ridiculing three important pillars of our democratic system, these roasts present a "demockery" that highlights the flaws and shortcomings of democracy and the failed responsibilities of the agents of democracy. However, a roast – after all, an insult comedy version of a toast – is also a mode of speech intended to honor and celebrate. Thus, amid the critiques and barbs these political roasts celebrate the latent potential of the democratic system and the potential of all democratic agents to contribute to a more just, equitable, and functional system.

This argument is not meant to suggest that political humor nor the roasts at the WHCA dinners will ultimately transform democracy. Elsewhere I argue that humor is a *necessary but not sufficient* style for activism and social change (Rossing 2013). Stand-up comics roasting the agents of democracy might offer alternative interpretive frames, inspire new alliances, and shift terms of debate, but alone they will not correct the flaws of a democratic system. Their attacks might momentarily provide a sense of leveling, but they cannot create equity amidst imbalanced power relationships and structural inequalities. I do not argue that these political roasts will *fix* journalistic bias, political partisanship, and political disengagement. As entertainers, and more importantly, as fellow citizens, it is not these comics' responsibility single-handedly to define precise solutions. Rather, they enter the conversation as one participant among many, contributing critical insights that both celebrate our democratic potential and punctuate our shortcomings.

The political roast displays prominently the flaws and failed responsibilities of all those with a vested interest democracy and, in so doing, invites the interested parties to mend those flaws cooperatively. In the genre of the roast, this invitation takes the form of loving shame and ridicule. The roast is not a radical critique that seeks to dismantle a system, but a critical genre that warmly embraces the target it derides. Day (2011) documents how satire, irony, and parody serve as "methods of intruding into the public conversation" intended to disrupt the status quo, unite the disaffected, and engage in meaningful transformation (p. 193). This chapter offers the well-crafted political roast as another participant in that conversation. At best, the WHCA dinner comics intrude into the ongoing public conversation about political accountability, responsibilities of a free press, civic responsibility, and much more. Their "demockery" of the political system reveals shortcomings, flaws, and missteps so as to challenge all interested agents to better the system together.

Appendix A

White House Correspondents' Association Dinner comedy headliners, 2001–2015.

Bush Administration		Obama Administration	
Date	Headlining Comic	Date	Headlining Comic
2001, April 28	Darrell Hammond	2009, May 9	Wanda Sykes
2002, May 4	Drew Carey	2010, May 1	Jay Leno
2003, April 26	—*	2011, April 30	Seth Meyers
2004, May 1	Jay Leno	2012, April 28	Jimmy Kimmel
2005, April 30	Cedric the Entertainer	2013, April 27	Conan O'Brien
2006, April 29	Stephen Colbert	2014, May 4	Joel McHale
2007, April 21	Rich Little	2015, April 15	Cecily Strong
2008, April 26	Craig Ferguson	2016, April 30	Larry Willmore**

* Because of the war in Iraq, the organization skipped comedy in 2003 and musician Ray Charles performed throughout the dinner.
** Wilmore's roast exemplifies the themes discussed in the chapter; however, because of publication timelines, examples from his performance are not included in the chapter.

Notes

1 At the time of his performance, Colbert was a relative unknown – less than one year into his hit Comedy Central news satire *The Colbert Report* in which he famously parodied conservative news media.
2 The exception is Rich Little's strategically apolitical performance in 2007, the year following Colbert's roast. At the outset of the routine Little assured his audience, "I'm not a political satirist. I'm not going to make any political point. I'm an impressionist." Indeed, Little made no reference to current socio-political issues during his routine. Little's politically safe and defanged impersonations of the six presidents from Richard Nixon to George W. Bush offers a sharp contrast with Colbert's satirical roast the year before.
3 It is plausible that the WHCA dinner roasts in the early years of the Bush Administration lacked the punch of later performances due to the political atmosphere following the September 11, 2001 attacks and the early years of the wars in Iraq and Afghanistan.

The organization's decision to forgo comedy altogether in 2003 is indicative of an atmosphere that was less receptive to the tone of the political roast.
4   I do not mean to suggest that popular culture is apolitical or trivial and somehow less than "real" politics. Indeed the stand-up comics featured at the WHCA are evidence of the political importance and potential of popular culture. However, the investment in the popular I describe here reflects a particular type of uncritical, capitalist investment in the commodities of popular culture.

References

About C-SPAN: Mission (n.d.). *CSPAN*. (n.d.). Retrieved from www.c-span.org/about/mission/ (accessed June 15, 2015).
Baumgartner, J.C., & Morris, J.S. (Eds.). (2008). *Laughing matters: Humor and American politics in the media age.* New York, NY: Routledge.
Baym, G. (2008). Serious comedy: Expanding the boundaries of political discourse. In J. Baumgartner & J.S. Morris (Eds.), *Laughing matters: Humor and American politics in the media age* (pp. 21–36). New York: Routledge.
Bennett, W.L. (2007). Relief in hard times: A defense of Jon Stewart's comedy in an age of cynicism. *Critical Studies in Media Communication, 24*(3), 278–283.
Carey, D. (2002). White House Correspondents' Association Dinner. *CSPAN*. May 4. Retrieved from www.c-span.org/ (accessed May 26, 2015).
Cohen, J. (2012). History of the White House Correspondents' Dinner [Electronic resource]. *History in the Headlines.* April 27. Retrieved May 25, 2015, from www.history.com/ (accessed May 25, 2015).
Colbert, S. (2006). White House Correspondents' Association Dinner. *CSPAN*. April 29. Retrieved from www.c-span.org/ (accessed May 26, 2015).
Colletta, L. (2009). Political satire and postmodern irony in the age of Stephen Colbert and Jon Stewart. *Journal of Popular Culture, 42*(5), 856–874.
Day, A. (2011). *Satire and dissent: Interventions in contemporary political debate.* Bloomington: Indiana University Press.
Edwards, J. (2011). White House Correspondents' Dinner: 25 memorable moments. *National Journal.* April 27. Retrieved from www.nationaljournal.com/ (accessed May 25, 2015).
Ferguson, C. (2008). White House Correspondents' Association Dinner. *CSPAN*. April 26. Retrieved from www.c-span.org/ (accessed May 26, 2015).
Gavin, P. (2015). Nerd Prom is a mess: How to fix Washington's worst week. *Politico.* April 23. Retrieved from www.politico.com/ (accessed May 25, 2015).
Gray, J. Jones, J.P., & Thompson, E. (Eds.). (2009). *Satire TV: Politics and comedy in the post-network era.* New York, NY: New York University Press.
Hammond, D. (2001). White House Correspondents' Association Dinner. *CSPAN*. April 28. Retrieved from www.c-span.org/ (accessed May 26, 2015).
History of the WHCA. (n.d.). Retrieved from http://whca.net/history.htm (accessed May 25, 2015).
Jones, J.P. (2009). With all due respect: Satirizing presidents from *Saturday Night Live* to *Lil' Bush*. In J. Gray, J.P. Jones, & E. Thompson (Eds.), *Satire TV: Politics and comedy in the post-network era* (pp. 37–63). New York: New York University Press.
Jones, J.P. (2010). *Entertaining politics: Satiric television and political engagement,* 2nd ed. Lanham, MD: Rowman & Littlefield.

Jones, J.P., Baym, G., & Day, A. (2012). Mr. Stewart and Mr. Colbert go to Washington: Television satirists outside the box. *Social Research*, 79(1), 33–60.

Kimmel, J. (2012). White House Correspondents' Association Dinner. *CSPAN*. April 28. Retrieved from www.c-span.org/ (accessed May 26, 2015).

Krefting, R. (2014). *All joking aside: American humor and its discontents*. Baltimore, MD: Johns Hopkins University Press.

Kyles, C. (2005). White House Correspondents' Association Dinner. *CSPAN*. April 30. Retrieved from www.c-span.org/ (accessed May 26, 2015).

Leno, J. (2004). White House Correspondents' Association Dinner. *CSPAN*. May 1. Retrieved from www.c-span.org/ (accessed May 26, 2015).

Leno, J. (2010). White House Correspondents' Association Dinner. *CSPAN*. May 1. Retrieved from www.c-span.org/ (accessed May 26, 2015).

Little, R. (2007). White House Correspondents' Association Dinner. *CSPAN*. April 21. Retrieved from www.c-span.org/ (accessed May 26, 2015).

López, I.H. (2015). *Dog whistle politics: How coded racial appeals have reinvented racism and wrecked the middle class*. New York: Oxford University Press.

Masters, K. (2007). "Times" opts out of Correspondents' dinner. *Morning Edition*. May 2. Washington, DC: National Public Radio. Retrieved from www.npr.org/ (accessed May 25, 2015).

McHale, J. (2014). White House Correspondents' Association Dinner. *CSPAN*. May 3. Retrieved from www.c-span.org/ (accessed May 26, 2015).

Meyers, S. (2011). White House Correspondents' Association Dinner. CSPAN. April 30. Retrieved from www.c-span.org/ (accessed May 26, 2015).

O'Brien, C. (2013). White House Correspondents' Association Dinner. *CSPAN*. April 27. Retrieved from www.c-span.org/ (accessed May 26, 2015).

Peterson, R.L. (2008). *Strange bedfellows: How late-night comedy turns democracy into a joke*. New Brunswick, NJ: Rutgers University Press.

Rich, F. (2006). Throw the truthiness bums out. *New York Times*. Nov. 5.

Rossing, J.P. (2013). Dick Gregory and activist style: Identifying attributes of humor necessary for activist advocacy. *Argumentation & Advocacy*, 50, 59–71.

Sternbergh, A. (2006). Stephen Colbert has America by the ballots. *New York Magazine*. Oct. 16.

Strong, C. (2015). White House Correspondents' Association Dinner. *CSPAN*. April 25. Retrieved from www.c-span.org/ (accessed May 26, 2015).

Sykes, W. (2009). White House Correspondents' Association Dinner. *CSPAN*. May 9. Retrieved from www.c-span.org/ (accessed May 26, 2015).

Waisenen, D.J. (2009). A citizen's guide to democracy inaction: Jon Stewart and Stephen Colbert's comic rhetorical criticism. *Southern Communication Journal*, 74(2), 119–140.

RESPONSE: STAND-UP AND POLITICS

WISE FOOLS

The Politics of Comedic Audiences

Mary Stuckey

There is a tradition of wise fools dating back hundreds of years, jesters who unmask power and who get away with it because of their ability to pass unpalatable truths under the guise of humor. Probably used most famously in *King Lear*, the wise fool offers a corrective to concentrated power. In democratic contexts, the role of the wise fool is both important and, as these chapters illustrate, quite complex. In democracies, even representative ones like the U.S., there is a presumption that the people are already participating in, if not actually governing, the nation. Correction in the form of the wise fool comes from below, but in a democracy, the power is spread among the people, or, among the governed. Because of the nature and the extent of the public's presumed role in governance, the fool's position is not unambiguously powerless. But such fools speak for the people, and therefore speak in important ways. As these chapters demonstrate, the wise fool fulfills many important functions in our contemporary politics.

These chapters are a delightful combination precisely because they work so well together to illuminate the potential and complexity of wise fools in democratic politics. They allow us to focus on the relationship between an "audience" and a "people." Audiences are temporary collections of spectators. A "people," in the sense that I use the phrase here, is a more stable entity, comprised of individuals who consciously participate in a collectivity. Together, these chapters provide evidence that contemporary stand-up comedians can challenge the system and, in so doing, can unite an audience as a people. At the same time, their comedy can have the opposite effect, increasing national divisions and exploiting the partisan divide, making it hard to find reasonable ways to agree to disagree, and making it much harder for the nation to see itself as a unified people. Finally, these chapters show that stand-up comedy can push the boundaries between insider and outsider communication, and can encourage all the players in national politics –

politicians, the media, and the mass public – to reevaluate their actions and role in the national democracy. These chapters all make it quite clear that we depend upon, but must also be careful of, our wise fools. They also indicate the ways in which our comedy reveals something about ourselves as democratic audiences and as a democratically inclined people.

The Wise Fool as an Empowering Force

In "The Comedic Prince," Aaron Duncan and Jonathan Carter use both political and rhetorical theory to make the case that stand-up comedy, at least as it was practiced by Bill Hicks, has the potential to unite a fractured audience and influence the ways the mass public thinks about politics. Arguing that Hicks – and, by implication, conceivably other comedians – was as much a rhetorical critic as a comedian, these authors stress the ways that he pointed to both political practice and political speech (which is, of course, a specific kind of political practice) to point to the hypocrisies, inconsistencies, and absurdities of our national politics. These authors treat this as a unifying, empowering force, rendering an audience into a people, and enabling them to push back against the powerful.

As Roderick P. Hart and Johanna Hartelius (2007) argue, however, this kind of humor can separate people from politics, rendering them cynical and passive. They note that it can be profoundly disempowering to consider the manifold ways in which are national politics are corrupt, empty, or wrong-headed. It can be much worse to conceive of those politics as (mis)managed by elites to the exclusion of the common person. All of these conceptions can easily be imagined as leading to a populace that throws up their hands in disgust or buries their heads in their hands in despair. Either of these reactions, of course, contributes to either the fact or the appearance of quiescence, which is unhelpful to a participatory democracy.[1] Indeed, the authors quote Hicks as envisioning his work as being akin to that of Shiva the Destroyer, but do not seem to take that claim as seriously as they might, preferring to concentrate on the creative capacities of such destruction.

Duncan and Carter insist that Hicks' comedy encourages mass participation (or at least insofar as his audiences can be understood to represent "the mass"). He does this in two ways. First, they argue that Hicks interpolates the audience into a critique of the American class structure as well as its political structure by focusing on systemic, rather than individual elements. He does not, they claim, search for scapegoats. Second, they argue that he does this by referencing his lived experience rather than theoretical constructs, thus allowing him to appeal to a broader audience. His reliance on lived experience marks him as an "organic intellectual." And certainly, his regular appearances in forums like the *Letterman* show would support the argument that Hicks had a broad comedic reach. These two strategies, for Duncan and Carter, mean that Hicks' comedy was empowering rather than disempowering; that by sharing a laugh over the systemic elements that govern us, we can deconstruct the tactics that members of the ruling elite use to fracture and divide us and focus instead on deconstructing the system and the illusion of difference upon which it depends.

In this way, Duncan and Carter offer an overtly optimistic view of the potential of at least one comic, if not of stand-up itself. They understand Hicks' comedy to be both creative and destructive, and find in that an empowering force. They do not, in this chapter, consider the ways in which these arguments might tend the other way, and lead to apathy and anomie. In this, they display not a lack of intellectual acuity, but a certain faith in the democratic audience – for them, the potential of the comedy can be met by the reaction of the audience. And yet, it is worth considering whether audiences merit this faith. Mainstream Americans lack both interest in and acknowledgement of their own political system;[2] at least some of them support candidates with only rudimentary understandings of the U.S. Constitution;[3] and despite the rise of the Internet and the increased availability of political information, the norms and practices of civic democracy remain restricted among citizens.[4] Given the chance to analyze the system and the opportunity to see themselves as participants in a radical kind of restructuring of it, Duncan and Carter implicitly argue that the audience of American voters is up to this task. Other authors in this collection would appear to dispute that possibility.

The Wise Fool as a Divisive Force

The audience for Bill Hicks' comedy, at least to the extent that it was part of the *Letterman* show, can be presumed to be broadly national – although we cannot either speak to the size of those audiences or the reaction to his comedy, except, of course, for the fact that CBS executives appeared to think that at least some of that comedy was too dangerous for our delicate ears or democratic sensibilities. Ron Von Burg and Kai Heidemann, on the other hand, examine the political comedy of a very different sort, with a very different audience in mind. They unsurprisingly, then, arrive at different kinds of conclusions.

They take as their text Brad Stine's explicitly conservative and avowedly Christian comedy and find that while comedy in general can be unifying and can enable deliberation, there are explicitly undemocratic possibilities as well. Von Burg and Heidemann, appropriately relying on a Burkean frame, argue that satire can have very useful social and political functions, facilitating both critique and participation. Burlesque, on the other hand, offers no sense of identification. It is instead a search for scapegoats. Burlesque depends upon the exploitation of difference and requires an Other who, by definition, cannot be (re)incorporated into society, but must remain forever alien to it. Burlesque is thus an explicitly undemocratic (if not antidemocratic) form of humor. Comedic audiences are fragments of the overall polity, and, in responding to burlesque, may understand themselves as separate from others. But the polity itself is a unified collection of citizens; it survives on common ground, and burlesque undermines that common ground.

Von Burg and Heidemann imply that this divisive humor is not restricted to Stine, although it is clear in his work, but also fits more or less naturally into conservative ideology. This is so because conservatism is a structurally-conforming rather than structurally-challenging ideology, and prefers therefore to foreclose debate rather than to facilitate it. I'm not sure I agree with this interesting postulate, as it seems to me that this may perhaps ignore the more incendiary tendencies of many conservatives, who, like Donald Trump, thrive on conflict and confrontation. Stressing the structurally-conforming aspect of conservatism also seems to imply a lack of good faith politics on the part of those on the right who challenge the political order. By this I mean that many conservatives, such as the more vehement adherents of the Tea Party, are not necessarily order-affirming. And there are, of course, conservatives who are both willing to cross the partisan divide and eager to do so. It is also entirely possible that none of these people are in Stine's audiences. But it would seem important to be careful about how we understand audiences and how we associate those audiences with political ideologies.

But the main point here is worth considering. Political comedians do not organize their audiences in the same way that political parties organize coalitions. Parties strive to unite as many people as possible. Stine may well have less interest in themes that unify broadly, and more interest in appealing to a fairly narrow segment of the conservative audience. Such comedy is unlikely to challenge individual beliefs or require compromise in the name of a greater goal. It is very likely to offer affirmation and encourage resistance to compromise. And that may well have important consequences for our shared politics.

This means, of course, that this chapter is interesting and important not least because it offers a window into a kind of comedy that may suit specific kinds of political ends. If a given political actor, for instance, seeks to unite an audience, she might look to the kinds of humor wielded by Hicks. But if her goals are more easily attainable by division, then Stine may well be a more useful kind of model. We think of political humor as driven by content; this chapter makes it abundantly clear that it can be profitably understood as a matter of form as well.

Equally important, it seems to me, is how the burlesque humor exemplified by Stine is also a matter of content – and assaultive content at that. The ways in which he encourages his audiences toward a narrow view of political possibility and a restrictive understanding of the polity seem to be profoundly antidemocratic and even troubling. Some of these possibilities, especially the ways in which this comedy may offer affirmation and reassurance at the price of accepting the necessity of compromise, may also be profoundly undemocratic. Audiences aren't the same as political constituencies, but how comedians construct their audiences may have consequences for their practices as citizens. A politics rooted in anger has some kinds of democratic potential, according to Duncan and Carter. Von Burg and Heidemann aptly demonstrate that it has darker potentials as well.

The Wise Fool as a Corrective Force

The first two chapters in this part concentrated on stand-up comedy directed at either mass or narrowly conceived public audiences. Jonathan Rossing's chapter analyzes a much more elite audience, the one either attending or viewing the White House Correspondents' Dinner. Rossing is interested in the possibilities of what he calls "demockery," or humor that both pokes fun at and honors the political system, "with all its flaws." For Rossing, this humor, directed at elites, may help nudge the system and its participants toward better enactments of democracy. Rossing argues that there are three major targets of the gentle humor of the roast: the president, who is treated with at least some deference; the press, which is lampooned with less care; and the public, which is treated as complicit in the failures of the first two. For Rossing, the combination of praise and blame characterized by the humor on this occasion offers a corrective potential, in that it neither alienates the audience nor completely exculpates it. It offers a political view that privileges incremental change.

The WHCA Dinner's characteristic comedy relies on both amplification and hyperbole, and is thus able to make its corrective point without being unduly jarring. The comedians in question point to the manipulations and hyperpartisanship of political actors, journalists' untoward attention to ratings over informed coverage, and the inattention and shallowness of the mass public. They also point to institutionalized sexism, racism, and homophobia. Rossing explicitly argues that the comedians in question consider both politics and journalism as fundamentally moral undertakings, and implicitly claims that their humor both polices the boundaries of morality and helps guide political actors, journalists, and the mass public toward appropriately moral behaviors. He indicates that this kind of corrective is a necessary, but not a sufficient condition for improving our national politics.

There is another possibility here, of course, that Rossing does not explicitly acknowledge: the ways in which the Correspondents' Dinner serves to unite the elites who are present at it. These dinners are very much insider affairs, complete with insider humor and a kind of self-referential and thus highly self-congratulatory mood. Indeed, these occasions may work something like the early British inversions, where common folk reaffirmed the rulers' power by playing at governing for a day and mocking that power. It is quite possible that these dinners offer more of a pretense of challenge to power than an actual corrective. That is, the press appear to criticize political actors and critique the political system, but they do so from within; no one really takes either criticism or critique seriously, and no one expects change. The roast is, as Rossing himself notes, "gentle."

It is interesting though, that Rossing trusts the audience of these dinners to take the humor as a learning experience, and to profit from it. He has a certain faith that those in power – whether in politics or the media, as well as the mass public – are open to correction. Of all the humor studied here, that of the roast is clearly the most order-affirming, and seems to open the way for incremental rather than more radical change. It is corrective, not revolutionary and is thus best suited for its largely elite audience. Like the other chapters in this collection, this one indicates the connection between comedic audiences and democratic publics – each kind of comedy evokes both affective and reasoned responses to democracy, and cultivates a different kind of political sensibility.

Conclusion

Traditionally, wise fools had royal audiences. The audiences for stand-up comedy are more varied, and, as these fine studies indicate, include a broad expanse of possibilities, ranging from the elite audiences of the White House Correspondents' Dinner through nationally televised talk shows to the more narrow confines of a conservative convention. Comedic audiences are not the same as political constituencies; they do not combine to constitute the polity. But attention to the overlap between the concepts of "audiences" and "the people" can be instructive. Each of these chapters offers a different conception of the capacities of audiences. Duncan and Carter see the national audience as at least potentially engaged in social, political, and rhetorical criticism, wielding, along with Hicks, a kind of democratic practical reason in the service of a more democratic system. Von Burg and Heidemann, on the other hand, find in Stine's more narrow audience a response to a rhetoric that moves along, and thus enables, national politic divisions, hardening the identities in which those divisions are rooted. And finally, Rossing looks to an audience of elites, and finds in it a limited space for correction.

These chapters thus unite to make some interesting claims about our national politics. First and most obviously, we constitute ourselves as political audiences in manifold ways, not all of them being explicitly political. This of course means that addressing the pathologies of our politics without relating those pathologies to our culture more broadly is likely to prove unsuccessful. Second, these insightful chapters reveal the fact that the kinds of truth our wise fools offer us may not always be terribly wise. Different styles of humor carry different kinds of consequences for our national life, and we need to attend to form as well as content. Finally, these chapters indicate that like Lear's fool, ours can only educate us to the degree that we are able and willing to listen to them. Wise fools can critique, however carefully or explicitly, the system and those who act in it, but critique is not the same as social change. In a democracy, even in a representative one like the U.S., such change, it seems, is ultimately, up the fools' audiences, the people. In this, our comedy may well also be our politics.

Notes

1 Concerns about quiescence go back at least as far as the 1980s. See, most prominently, Edelman 1985 and Gaventa 1982.
2 See, for instance, Pew Research Center 2014.

3   Republican candidate Donald Trump has made arguments against birthright citizenship (Sakuma 2015). At the time of drafting this chapter, numerous Republican candidates object to the 14th Amendment (Stein & Terkel 2015).
4   See Smith et al. 2009.

References

Edelman, M. (1985). *The symbolic uses of politics*. Urbana: University of Illinois Press.

Gaventa, J. (1982). *Power and powerlessness: Quiescence and rebellion in an Appalachian valley*. Urbana: University of Illinois Press.

Hart, R.P., & Hartelius, J. (2007). The political sins of Jon Stewart. *Critical Studies in Media Communication, 26,* 263–272.

Pew Research Center. (2014). Beyond red vs. blue: The political typology – Section 10: Political participation, interest and knowledge. *Pew Research Center*. June 26. Retrieved from www.people-press.org/2014/06/26/section-10-political-participation-interest-and-knowledge/

Sakuma, A. (2015). GOP candidates rethinking constitution to end birthright citizenship. MSNBC. Retrieved from www.msnbc.com/msnbc/gop-candidates-rethinking-constitution-end-birthright-citizenship

Smith, A., Schlozman, K.L., Verba, S., & Brady, H. (2009). *The internet and civic engagement*. Washington, DC: Pew Internet and American Life Project.

Stein, S., & Terkel, A. (2015). A good chunk of the GOP field wants to repeal the 14th amendment. *Huffington Post*. August 17. Retrieved from www.huffingtonpost.com/entry/a-good-chunk-of-gop-field-wants-to-repeal-the-14th-amendment_55d24915e4b055a6dab12015

PART IV
Standing Up, Breaking Rules

> Isn't this the most fascinating country in the world? Where else would I have to ride on the back of the bus, have a choice of going to the worst schools, eating in the worst restaurants, living in the worst neighborhoods – and average $5,000 a week just talking about it!
>
> (Dick Gregory)

10

HOW CAN RAPE BE FUNNY?

Comic Persona, Irony, and the Limits of Rape Jokes

Christopher A. Medjesky

> I can prove to you that rape is funny. Picture Porky Pig raping Elmer Fudd.
> (George Carlin 1990)

In 1990 when comedian George Carlin used this Looney Tunes example to defend the idea that anything, including rape, can be funny, there was no recorded public outrage about his claims. A little over 20 years later, media and Internet critics immediately censured comedian Daniel Tosh for making what Tosh claims was a similar observation.[1] Carlin's point is that, given the circumstances, a joke – even one about rape – can make a contribution to public discourse. Tosh has since argued he was making a similar point, but I contend otherwise. I argue Tosh has used his comic persona and a deceptive form of irony, one that I call pseudo-satire, to make it *appear* as if the outrage attacks the same idea as Carlin's when, in fact, Tosh's comedy accomplishes something much different and potentially dangerous.

In July of 2010, Daniel Tosh – noted stand-up comic and host of Comedy Central's *Tosh.0* – was performing at the Laugh Factory in Long Beach. According to a Tumblr blog post, that night Tosh began a bit in which he "start[ed] making some very generalizing, declarative statements about rape jokes always being funny, how can a rape joke not be funny, rape is hilarious, etc." A female audience member "felt provoked" and "yelled out, 'Actually, rape jokes are never funny!'" Then, according to the author of the post, Tosh responded, "Wouldn't it be funny if that girl got raped by like, 5 guys right now? Like right now? What if a bunch of guys just raped her …"[2]

Soon a flood of commentary began. Some writers, like *BuzzFeed*'s Amy Odell (2012), were quick to point out that nobody should have been surprised, as Tosh has been making rape jokes for years. Lindy West (2012) of *Jezebel* critiqued

Tosh's overall approach to comedy as dangerous and pointed to several comedians such as Louis C.K. that have successfully, in her opinion, used rape humor to provide social commentary. C.K., however, was one of many comedians to come to Tosh's defense via Twitter (Comedians 2012). And the most pertinent tweet to my argument came from stand-up comedian Kumail Nanjiani (2012), who said, "Comedians have personas. Are you offended by [fellow comedian Anthony Jeselnik's] rape jokes? Probably not, and you shouldn't be. Tosh uses shock and always has."

Giving validity to the Tumblr blog post, Tosh soon apologized with a tweet: "The point I was making before I was heckled is there are awful things in the world but you can still make jokes about them" (Hibberd 2012). Tosh's tweet is a restatement of Carlin's 1990 commentary on rape humor presented through his joke about Porky Pig raping his cartoon foil, Elmer Fudd. Expanding on the idea, Carlin uses the setup to comment on how people would inevitably construct Porky Pig's masculinity as filled with natural, uncontrollable horniness while simultaneously slut-shaming Elmer. Carlin ends the bit noting, "Don't seem fair to me. Don't seem right. But you can joke about it. I believe you can joke about anything. It all depends on how you construct the joke." Through Carlin's construction, the Porky-Elmer rape becomes a satire of the social and mediated response to rape. By the end of the bit, it is clear Carlin is using rape as a humorous *topos* – or topic – to critique society.

Carlin dedicated his long career to using comedy for the purposes of social commentary. As he put it in an interview with Todd Leopold (2004) at *CNN*, "Part of what my impulse is with things I've said or done, I think it is an attempt to demystify these things, to take them out of the realm of the forbidden and the disgusting and the off-base, and to at least bring them into the discussion." On the other hand, Tosh has been making these types of jokes for years, and he relies on the "fetishization of not censoring yourself, of being an 'equal-opportunity offender,'" to produce his humor (Odell 2012; West 2012, paragraph 10).

These descriptions are key characteristics of each of the comedian's comic persona. As Ware and Linkugel put it, "Persona, in its strictest sense, is a Latin word referring to the masks worn in Greek and Roman theater … a 'mask' or 'false face' … 'worn by actors'" (1982, p. 50). Recall that Kumail Nanjiani used persona as an excuse to defend Tosh's action suggesting that the persona concurrently awards the comedian the power to joke about certain *topoi* and immunity from criticism about those jokes. Despite Nanjiani's claims, however, not all personae are created alike.

Each persona develops alongside what Elise Kramer (2011) calls humor ideologies, which suggests that humor builds on the history of similar jokes to establish a "shared set of beliefs in order to be socially meaningfully" (pp. 138–139). Thus, as jokes such as those about rape are told, a taxonomy of what is understood as a rape joke begins to be developed and shared between joke-tellers and the audiences. Similarly, as a comic develops a persona, the comic's ideological perspective shapes that persona. As a result, we can think of irony or satire, for example, as humor ideologies that create a taxonomy of the comic persona and these ideologies determine "the types of meanings the humor can take on" (p. 138).

Keeping their different comic personae in mind, we can return to the jokes by Tosh and Carlin to note that, despite saying similar things in their jokes, what makes Tosh's point different than Carlin's can be seen in the jab, "before I was heckled," at the beginning of his tweet. Carlin uses the moment in his bit to comment on the commonality of finding an excuse to shift the blame from the rapist to the raped. Tosh, on the other hand, explains in his response that heckling, not the joke, instigated the controversy. This action shifts the blame from Tosh to the woman, placing responsibility on the victim for the verbal attack. Just as the woman (or Elmer Fudd) should not wear a short skirt, had the audience member kept her mouth shut it would never have happened. In the tweet, Tosh becomes the type of man Carlin is critiquing.

Simply being a comedian, however, grants neither Carlin nor other comics immunity from criticism when joking about subjects such as rape. Often, jokes about the taboo are approached via an ironic comic persona, which some have suggested permits the comic to address taboo *topoi* with the audience (Lowrey, Renegar, & Goehring 2014, pp. 63–64). However, irony alone does not provide the comic with a shield from criticism when using rape as a *topos*. In this chapter, I argue that such ironic comedy must pull from a satiric humor ideology to grant the comedian immunity when joking about the taboo. Comedians with satiric personae such as David Cross, a stand-up comic and actor who regularly uses his stage time to perform social critique, have used jokes about rape to dare the audience to think about the subject in ways that challenge prevailing ideological perspectives. While these comics use stand-up to evolve our thinking about the taboo, others abuse the ironic persona and use jokes about rape as an opportunity to ridicule the victims and the oppressed. I contend that a satiric persona provides the comic and the audience a momentary shield from criticism in order to afford an opportunity to discuss and critique the taboo and possibly produce social change. However, I believe a pseudo-satiric persona, one that uses irony without satire merely to deride, must be critiqued as it can reproduce hegemonic ideologies and, as I will argue is the case of Daniel Tosh, endanger its victims.

In this chapter, I will discuss the rhetorical power of stand-up comedy and the role a comic persona plays in shaping a/the stand-up comic's rhetorical influence. Others have discussed that comic persona shapes not only the comic but also the message and the comic's audience. Extending this, I argue that we must consider the function of irony as an associated humor ideology in the comic persona before accepting the idea that a comedian can freely joke about the taboo and simultaneously be granted a shield from criticism.

Comedy and Rape

For this chapter, I will focus on the taboo subject of rape for several reasons. First, keeping rape a taboo *topos* is problematic, and I will argue that, when strategically used with a satiric comic persona, comedy can help society overcome discomfort with speaking to/about rape. Of course, a different strategy can result with troubling impacts on society, potentially reinforcing the subject as taboo or even normalizing rape culture. Such concerns have a long history connected to contemporary stand-up comedy. In fact, rape humor was typical of early Roman satirists who often performed like today's stand-up comics, before audiences in recital halls (Richlin 1992, p. 63, p. 66). Even from its earliest origins, rape humor has walked the line between potential critique or commentary and a detriment to society. As Amy Richlin, argues, "Cultures where rape is a joke are cultures that foster rape. We need to know our history and our present" (p. xxviii).

Contemporary empirical research supports Richlin's argument. Kathryn Ryan and Jeanne Kanjorski (1998) conclude, for men, enjoying sexist humor was linked with psychological aggression and "rape-supportive beliefs … behavioral intentions (i.e., the self-reported likelihood of forcing sex), and behavior (i.e., sexual and physical aggression)" (p. 752). Manuela Thomae and G. Tendayi Viki (2013) argue exposure to rape humor, particularly those that have a preexisting proclivity toward hostile sexism, "may create a situation which not only enhances tolerance of discrimination against women, but also appears to elevate to the propensity to commit rape" (p. 264).

These examples show the need to study the relationship between humor and rape, but the work of Elise Kramer (2011) suggests that it is not as simple as reducing all jokes about rape to "bad." In her study of online discussions about rape humor, Kramer found that supporters of rape humor often suggested that the jokes allowed the taboo to be discussed (p. 154). Furthermore, the ability of the joke to engage with the taboo subject as opposed to exploiting its victims was often tied to the moral dimension of the comedian (pp. 152–153). This focus on morals is what links rape humor to the comedian's comic persona and the ideology that shapes and guides that persona. Those ideologies construct not only what is funny, but what is rape and how we should respond to rape beliefs and behaviors.

The second reason for using rape as the focus of this study is its increasing impact on the stand-up landscape. Rape jokes may not be new, but they have fallen under public scrutiny in recent years. While some such as Sarah Silverman have been praised for their use of jokes to force engagement with the subject (Lowrey et al. 2014), others have been heavily scrutinized. Even old comedy bits have come under criticism – most notably those bits by Bill Cosby. An explosion of actual rape allegations against Cosby in 2014 led many to rethink his 1969 "Spanish Fly" bit from the comedy album *It's True! It's True!*. Initially viewed by many as a story about how boys will be (unabashedly horny) boys thanks in large part to Cosby's well-established fatherly comic persona, Cosby's alleged real life actions have cast a new light on the bit, leading some to reconsider the joke as normalizing date rape behavior (Fondy 2014).

When it comes to rape humor, however, Bill Cosby's straightforward, fatherly comic persona is quite rare. It only succeeded in its time because of the shared humor ideology that accepted such behavior as normal for men. Today, it would be hard to imagine the glorification of rape being discussed so brazenly even in a joke. Instead, many comics approach rape humor ironically. Using primarily the jokes about rape from comedians David Cross and Daniel Tosh, two comics who are viewed as particularly ironic, I argue that it is how irony functions as a humor ideology in the fostering of the comic persona that shapes the rhetoric of rape humor. It is this use of irony that drives the rhetoric of rape as a humorous *topos*, allowing, at times, for rape humor to viciously attack problematic ideologies and, at others, tragically reinforce ideologies that promote violence and oppression.

Humor Ideologies and the Comic Persona

More than merely for laughs, stand-up comedy provides an opportunity for a speaker and an audience to connect and discuss important societal issues. Andrea Greenbaum argues, "Stand-up comedy is an inherently rhetorical discourse; it strives not only to entertain, but to persuade, and stand-up comics can only be successful in their craft when they can convince an audience to look at the world through their comic vision" (1999, p. 33). The comic's persona presents the audience the comic vision. It is through that persona that a comic can position the audience to accept or challenge political stances or reconsider dominant discourse regarding current events or otherwise taboo *topoi* (Wuster 2006, p. 29; Waisanen 2011, p. 25).

The term comic persona is not used universally. Dan Waisanen (2011), for example, uses the term rhetorical persona. Tracy Wuster calls it comic character (2006, p. 25). Andrea Greenbaum refers to the concept as simply persona (1999, p. 35), while Lowrey et al. narrow the concept more to refer to the ironic persona (2014, p. 60). While the term may change, the function of the comic persona remains consistent, stemming back to the original understandings of the use of a rhetorical persona.

Ware and Linkugel (1982) describe the rhetorical persona as separate from the rhetor, a character created that is a reflection of expectations of the rhetor in the eyes of the audience. "Rhetorical *personae* reflect the aspirations and cultural visions of audiences from which stems the symbolic construction of archetypal figures. An archetype, of course, is the original model, a prototype; it is the pattern from which copies are made" (p. 50). As an archetype, the persona serves as not only a representation of the audience but an *ideal* representation. As comedians continue to use this persona at individual performances, the persona builds to become the overarching vision of how the comic desires to be viewed and, thus, how the comic views her or his audience.

Both the tone of the persona and the associated humor ideology shape the comic persona. Developing a clear and coherent tone is an essential mark of a successful comic (Greenbaum 1999; Pérez 2013). Many comics, including Larry the Cable Guy (né Dan Whitney), have famously changed their persona, particularly the tone of the character and jokes, to find a niche and an audience (Booth 2004).³ Tone remains only part of the persona, however. It is the ideologies that are imbued in all of the comic's works that further shape the persona. Extending beyond a single joke or even an entire routine, the comic persona is matched with ideologies that help define who that comic is to the audience. Jokes and routines build up one another to establish and promote particular ways of viewing the world via comic personae that can have legitimate influence over the public discourse by "[asking] their audiences to ingest certain structures of thinking and choices of interpretation" (Waisanen 2011, p. 25), as can be seen in bodies of work such as George Carlins or even, as Wuster (2006) argues, in individual albums such as Steve Martin's *A Wild and Crazy Guy* (p. 26).

Stand-up, thus, becomes a common form of ideological critique that permeates the popular culture (Lowrey et al. 2014, p. 74). But stand-up is not just a static text in the academic sense of popular culture. While often viewed in recorded form, live stand-up engages directly with an audience, making the audience an integral part of the speech process (Greenbaum 1999, p. 34). This relationship between performer and audience allows stand-up comics to serve as an intermediary between the often complex teachings of academics and the larger population (Bingham & Hernandez 2009, p. 349). The performance, when the audience uses it to discuss the topics, has been found to yield meaningful conversation about the issues (Bingham & Hernandez 2009, p. 345). These issues, removed from the serious and couched in comedy, now provide "the common people with an insulated means of argument to challenge the dominant view of the social order" (Greenbaum 1999. p. 33).

The ability for stand-up comedy to perform this rhetorical function relies heavily on an often unstated mutual understanding between performer, audience, and society whereby "stand-up comedians are often granted momentary immunity when discussing certain controversial social issues" (Lowrey et al. 2014, p. 74). The relationship between comic and audience transfers this immunity, allowing the audience to see themselves with the same protection to discuss controversial topics. It is this immunity that allows a topic like rape to be discussed with levity when, in common conversation, this would not be socially tolerated.

However, comedians often work diligently to craft strategies to engage with taboo *topoi* in front of an audience. Raúl Pérez (2013), whose work is featured in this collection, enrolled in a stand-up comedy course in order to better understand how comedians use comedy to discuss a topic that is often as controversial as rape: race. In his ethnographic study, Pérez found comedians often understood their comedy as rhetorical speech as well as the inherent immunity of their performance, but they used the view of themselves as social and cultural critics to justify the use of racial stereotypes in their humor (p. 479). In this process, comics develop numerous strategies to deflect any charges of racism against them. Pérez notes that such practices can be a false shield from criticism, and that "[c]ritical scholars contend race-based humor walks a fine line between challenging racial inequality and strengthening hegemonic notions of race" (p. 482).

Similar practices can be found in comedians' approaches to rape. Already, I have discussed George Carlin's use of rape not only to comment on how men respond to accusations of rape but also on the nature of rape humor itself. Here, Carlin is using his persona as social critic to address and challenge the ideology found in rape discourse. This ideological tie is essential to what Elise Kramer calls humor ideologies (2011, p. 138). Kramer argues that humor ideologies are a "corollary" to language ideologies, which "enable specific linguistic interactions to take on broader social meaning." Humor, Kramer states, "requires a shared set of beliefs in order to be socially meaningful, and the specific nature of those humor ideologies determines the types of social meaning that humor can take on" (p. 138). It is, thus, not just a single joke that shapes a rhetoric of humor, but a "structuring taxonomy of humor" constructed by humor ideologies shared between comedians and audiences that enable the reading of humor to be seen as producing social commentary or outwardly ridiculing (p. 139).

Kramer's (2011) argument ties the concept of humor ideologies to joke types, specifically rape jokes, but I believe the concept can be applied to persona types as well. As I described earlier, comics' material pulls from ideological perspectives that shape what jokes are told and the message of those jokes (Waisanen 2011, pp. 35–36). But comics also develop in their persona humor-related shared sets of beliefs that make their jokes socially meaningful. Take, for example, insult comics like Don Rickles or celebrity roast comedians like Jeffrey Ross. Outside of the shared humor ideology of what it means to be an insult comic or a roaster, the humor would extend beyond the border of cruelty. But developed and shared as a humor ideology, the cruelty becomes part of the humor and instrumental in the success of the joke. Not only does the cruelty suddenly become funny, but it also provides a means to jest about the shortcomings of the joke's victim that would otherwise often be ignored. We can think of Bill Cosby's fatherly persona in a similar way as it pulls from a humor ideology that assumes a degree of comforting wholesomeness. Forms of irony such as satire would also serve as humor ideologies that may guide the comic's persona. As I will argue, both David Cross and Daniel Tosh use forms of irony as the humor ideology influencing their respective personae, with Cross using irony as satire to embrace the persona of a social critic and Tosh using irony as pseudo-satire to develop the persona of an innocent, jokester "frat boy."

Like traditional views of ideology, which are never shaped by a single text, person, or event, humor ideologies are fashioned through continued experiences with particular forms and purposes of humor. Considering these humor ideologies, one can see how, at least to Tosh and his audience, Tosh's gang-rape joke/response makes sense. In the case of Daniel Tosh, the gang-rape response was treated as a response to a heckling. Greenbaum found comedians saw heckling as a difficult interaction, as it forces the comic to retain or maintain control of the room, often through ridicule of the heckler, without losing likeability with the rest of the audience. Furthermore, this requires the comic to make an impromptu response that may deviate from their material or their overall comic persona (1999, pp. 37–38) and sometimes employ conflicting sets of strategies to control the room (Pérez 2013, pp. 483–485). In the moment, the woman was a heckler and Tosh responded as best as he could to remain consistent with his current material and the humor ideology that weaves throughout his work. But not crafted and controlled, this spontaneous moment revealed the flaws of the performance and its dangerous influence. The audience may choose to reject Tosh's response; however, doing so means the audience must reject themselves as Tosh's response was based on their shared understanding and acceptance of the humor ideology. Accounts suggest that did not happen. It appears, based on the Tumblr blog post, the audience, steeped in the same humor ideology as Tosh, accepted his response to the heckling as appropriate and moved on, treating her challenge to Tosh as no different than a drunk's outburst.[4] Combined, Tosh's and the audience's responses reveal the power humor ideology has on comic material.

Thus, while at times comedy may serve to produce social commentary, at others times it may strengthen hegemonic and dangerous beliefs (Pérez 2013, p. 482). The direction the comedy takes is dependent on the humor ideologies tied to the comic persona. It is through the dialogic nature of stand-up comedy, a dialogue not only between comic and audience but between the performance and the culture from which it draws (Gilbert 1997, p. 317), that the comic establishes *ethos* (Greenbaum 1999, pp. 38–39). But it is the *ethos* of the comic persona that "invites the audience to respond to the conversation by laughing" and grants the comic and audience the shared moment of immunity to address controversial subject matter with humor (p. 35).

Ware and Linkugel (1982) further stress, "We draw a sharp distinction here between the rhetor's personal ethos and the ethos represented by the rhetorical *persona* the speaker assumes when he reminds the listeners of its archetypal hero – that prototype in their psyches whom they imagine will be their deliverer" (p. 51). This aspect of the comic persona may be the driving force behind the rhetorical power of the comedian, but it is not without potential consequences. There is no guarantee the comic has established a persona intended to produce commentary that improves public discourse. Pérez (2013) argues, for example, that to help defend the use of racist humor, comedians attempt to construct a "veil of *authentic inauthenticity*" that suggests, "I am not racist even as I say racist things" (p. 483). Certainly, this approach helps open up the conversation to discuss race, but the comic can use it as a shield from criticism. Rape humor can present the same authentic inauthenticity. It is this authentic inauthenticity that, I will demonstrate, permits Tosh to use his comic persona to defend his problematic rape humor while simultaneously denying its negative influence. But to understand the rhetorical function of Tosh's specific comic persona, it is important to understand the function of irony as it relates to the comic persona.

Rape Humor and Forms of the Ironic Persona

To establish a working definition of irony, I rely upon David Kaufer, who notes, "Rhetorical scholars … recognize irony as a figure of speech in which the words of a speaker express a meaning that is directly opposite to the intended meaning" (1977, p. 90).[5] There is some legitimate concern about the overuse of irony as a blanket term for any sort of double-meaning as it collapses a multitude of approaches into one too simplified concept (Kolb 1990, p. 133). This problem with defining irony is often made worse by its frequent use as a rhetorical strategy in satire and parody, resulting several different rhetorical devices treated by some as the same (Hutcheon 2000, p. 52). Hutcheon (1995) reminds us, though, that rhetoricians have traditionally viewed irony as an approach that "involves certain judgmental attitudes (beyond simple criticism) on the part of the ironist" (p. 38). Thus, despite some concern that the double-meaning nature of irony may cause confusion and distract an audience (Purdy 1999), many rhetoricians have argued for irony's *potential* as a powerful form of political engagement.[6]

Many comics take on an ironic persona, using the irony to produce social satire (Wuster 2006, p. 29; Lowrey et al. 2014, p. 60). The relationship between irony and stand-up makes sense. Not only does the irony, when used as satire, provide a vehicle for the comic to explore their humor ideologies, it also requires a similar relationship between rhetor and audience. Kaufer is correct when he asserts that simply because an audience recognizes the use of irony it does not mean the audience must agree with the rhetor (1977, p. 98). But when used specifically in the context of stand-up comedy, it is much more probable to assume the audience and rhetor are connected.

It is also true, as Kaufer (1977) points out, that irony itself "does not constitute intimacy," but the intimate relationship that often exists between comic and audience via the comic persona allows for irony to serve the function of encouraging and, at times, constituting agreement and strengthening that intimacy (p. 96). The developed relationship also may abate the rhetorical limitations brought on by the polyvalent nature of irony (Gring-Pemble & Watson 2003, p. 146). These caveats noted, the use of irony here works with Wayne C. Booth's (1975) construction in which irony requires the audience to engage with the material and rhetor in such a way that the audience understands the inherent dual meaning behind the ironic message, rejects the literal meaning, and embraces the perspective of the rhetor (pp. 10–11). The shared understanding of perspective is required for both irony and stand-up, allowing the approaches to merge often seamlessly.

An ironic comic persona stands to gain rhetorical power for several reasons. First, irony is the force, for example, that grants what Pérez called authentic inauthenticity (Pérez 2013, p. 483). Kaufer (1977) points out why: "[T]he ironist invariably dissociates himself from what he says, it follows that he will equally dissociate himself from audiences who agree with his literal statement" (p. 98). Irony also provides justification for the period of immunity granted to the comic and audience. Olson and Olson (2004) argue, "Like a rubber band stretched to its utmost, irony captures and can prolong that point in which incongruous meanings are points in mutually informing, yet unresolved symbolic tension" (p. 27). Just like that stretched rubber band, irony produces a moment full of energy, with the shared understanding that something powerful can and should happen. Permitted via irony to speak about controversial material, the comic can use an ironic persona to tackle issues humorously but effectively. Third, comic irony "allows the speaker to utilize communication that is not necessarily the opposite of its intended meaning, but rather simply different than its intended meaning" (Lowrey et al. 2014, p. 72). Creating a space for discussion rather than bifurcating the discourse allows a comic with an ironic persona to serve a democratic function. Finally, as Lowrey et al. (2014) argue, the audience has a responsibility to recognize the irony and react accordingly. Thus, unlike those who warn irony opens up meaning and leads to rhetorical slippage, these authors believe comic irony requires the audience "to interpret [the ironic message] and understand why this type of communication is ironic and rhetorically significant" (p. 63).

These characteristics assume the ironic persona is being employed with a purpose, and the commentary is positioned to be a critique. However, commentary is not an actual requirement of irony. Such an expectation would be found in a more accurately labeled satiric persona. I use the term satire here as an argument that employs irony for the purposes of specific inquiry and critique. As Linda Hutcheon (2000) puts it, satire "is both moral and social in its focus and ameliorative in its intention" (p. 16). Kenneth Burke (1973) saw satire as one form of equipment for living, a means by which people, either individually or collectively, use discourse to approach the complexities of life (p. 304). Scholars such as Amber Day (2011), Robert Hariman (2007), and Christine Harold (2007) have noted ways satire provides a space to dissent actively against dominant power structures and ideologies. As a result, satire can serve as a means toward social change.

Not all scholars, however, agree that such change is inevitable simply because the message is satiric. Dustin Griffin (1994), for example, believes the satirist is "quite certain in his [sic] own moral position; he [sic] also assumes such certainty in his [sic] readers" (p. 35). Such certainty may be unfounded. Others have noted that the double-codedness of satire encourages clarification by the satirist to state which interpretation is intended, thus, limiting its rhetorical effect (Tindale & Gough 1987, p. 6). These are potential limitations of satire. But, as I have argued, when satire functions as a humor ideology, it builds from a history and persona that helps assure the comic that the audience understands her or his position and will direct that audience to the appropriate layer of meaning without requiring the comic to state his or her position directly each time. Thus, satire retains a rhetorical advantage over irony alone when it functions as a humor ideology. Remembering that satire assumes the critique, while irony alone does not, gets to the point that it is *how* the irony functions in a comic persona that shapes the rhetorical message.

To understand why this is an important distinction to make regarding the comic persona, in general, and rape humor, specifically, I conclude this chapter by examining the rape humor of two comedians. First, I look at a bit by David Cross, who I believe successfully employs a satiric persona in his stand-up. Then I return to Daniel Tosh, who performs with an ironic persona but, instead of using it for criticism, uses it to reinforce problematic beliefs and shield himself and his audience from criticism.

Exploring David Cross's Satiric Persona

David Cross is an American comedian known for his work in film, television, and stand-up comedy. Although also known for his voice-over work in children's programming, Cross's stand-up as well as his work on television programs like *Mr. Show* and *Arrested Development* is often racy, profane, and challenging of dominant culture. Cross has worked as a comedian for two decades, developing a satiric persona that frequently critiques the prevailing ideological values of America (Nelson 2015).

David Cross's persona succeeds as satire because he offers stinging jokes in which neither the dual meaning nor the commentary can be easily misunderstood. Often appearing bitter and frustrated with the world's idiocy, Cross's humor exploits every bit of the immunity granted to him and the audience, forcing the hearer to address things society is often relieved to ignore. At times his critique is so harsh it may be only those constituted by the same humor ideology that drives Cross's satiric persona that find humor in his jokes. While Cross's comedy attacks a multitude of controversies, an example of his use of rape humor illustrates how a satiric persona can use the taboo as a humorous *topos* to challenge prevailing problematic discourse and ideological perspectives.

In the bit "My Daughter's First Date" from his 2002 album *Shut Up You Fucking Baby!*, Cross attacks the Catholic Church and its seeming acceptance of the rape of youths by priests. "In the last couple months, the Catholic Church has gotten a whole lot sexier," Cross begins. Immediately, the object of ridicule is established and, given the cultural context at the time and the shared humor ideology between Cross and his audience, it is likely everyone knows where he is going. He continues:

> Like, if you're caught or accused of molesting or raping children … then, like, you or I, obviously, because we're normal people, we're not anointed by God, we would go to jail … But the priests, they don't go to prison. They get a much, much worse punishment. They get taken out of their parish from whence they were there molesting people, where people know that they're molesting. And they're taken out of that parish, the safety and sanctity of that parish, and then they're moved to a completely new parish where it's "HELLO FRESH MEAT!"

Here Cross points to the freedom granted to the Catholic Church to not only regulate their problem but to do so in a way that hides the issue further and endangers new victims. Cross continues the bit, connecting the crime to the faith by suggesting that if the priests and Pope represent God and they fornicate with children, then God must do so as well. This conclusion is intended to be highly offensive, but it is presented in a way to point out that blind faith must be shaken, even to those that remain devoted Catholics. However, it is the next portion of the bit that challenges the hearer to go beyond humor to see the real horror of what the church ignores.

Cross continues, "Maybe, maybe that explains why, maybe that gives an answer to all those grieving women who are holding onto their child's casket going, 'Lord God why did you take him at such an early age? He was so innocent!' Yeah. They're all up in Heaven servicing the priests and God." The groan-worthy moment undoubtedly upset audience members, although not because they rejected the premise, but because they were forced to address just how far this line of thinking could be taken to justify turning a blind eye to the Church's actions. It is difficult to take this extreme exaggeration seriously. But it can force the audience to shake off any shackles faith may have over their reasoning and see the situation as Cross does, one in which religion and faith in Christianity blindly drive society and permit the Catholic Church to perpetuate the rape of children quietly throughout the world.

Cross drives home his criticism at the end of the bit, suggesting that blame for the rapes should actually be placed on the children. Cross points out, "The priests are sitting there and all these kids are sitting there going (in a kid's voice), 'I'm sorry father forgive me father for I have sinned.' How do you not fuck that?" In a satirical attempt to reinforce the distance between himself and the audience from the Church's practice while simultaneously criticizing the implicit condoning of the rapes, Cross continues, "You'd do the same thing if you were in a confessional booth and you weren't allowed to have sex for the rest of your life." The bit finishes by again suggesting this was all in accordance with the Church's teaching and that the rapes were God's will: "God made it. God made that fucking perfect ruby starfruit. Don't tell me. Do not tell me."

And that is where it finishes. There is no real end to the joke. Cross wanders off and we are left to contemplate why we, as a society, put up with these actions just because they are done in the name of religion. The audience is positioned to critique the idea that God would allow such horrors to exist, as if God was the one that created the children for the purposes of pedophilic rape. The extreme and ridiculous nature of the bit is often humorous, but undeniably discomforting. But it is not necessary to be perpetually funny as a comic. Cross's satiric persona posits serious critique. David Cross works as an example of a comic successfully using this form of the ironic persona, the satiric persona. But what happens when irony is deployed through a comic persona without commentary? To understand the rhetorical influence of this pseudo-satiric persona, I will return to Daniel Tosh and his attempts at rape humor.

The Problem of Daniel Tosh's Pseudo-Satiric Persona

The Laugh Factory incident described earlier is by no means Tosh's only encounter with controversial material. Tosh regularly uses *topoi* such as race, sex, and even rape on his show *Tosh.0* and in his stand-up. During the Comedy Central special, *Daniel Tosh: Happy Thoughts*, for example, Tosh begins a bit by talking about how "people have always told [him he] had a sick sense of humor." Tosh downplays the accusation, suggesting it is relative. He says, "To my circle of friends, I'm tame. My sister's off the chart." With his sister positioned as a person with a sicker mind than his, Tosh tells a story of switching out her pepper spray with silly string, leading to her rape. In the joke, Tosh's sister calls him the next day, ribbing him about how he "really got her that time." On the phone, his sister jests to Daniel that, in the moments before her rape, she quipped, "Daniel! This is really going to hurt!" The joke concludes in such a way that, in the end, everyone (Tosh, his sister, and the audience) found hilarious (McCarthy 2011).

This joke is more than an opportunity to laugh at rape, though. While the rape plays a major role in the punchline, the joke also serves to normalize Tosh's comic persona as the playful, jokester frat boy. By the end of the joke, we see that he simply has a dark sense of humor and, as long as everyone sees it as a joke, there is not real harm, even to his now raped sister. This joke is an instance in which the persona emphasizes the idea that as long as we recognize that whatever he is mocking is bad, he is free to joke about it and the audience is free to laugh about it, because any reasonable person would know already know it is bad. Tosh openly admits this is his approach. In a 2011 interview, Tosh was quoted as saying, "I'm not a misogynistic and racist person … But I do find those jokes funny, so I say them" (Hibberd 2012). Daniel Tosh presents his humor with the same perspective as someone starting a sentence, "I'm not racist, but …" when it is almost certain the next thing said will be undeniably racist. What makes Tosh different and more rhetorically troubling, however, is that his voice reaches far and wide and – most importantly for this argument – uses irony disguised as satire to defend his comedy and persona.

Note the significance of Tosh's use of irony. Clearly, his performance is filled with the dual-layered meaning expected of irony, and he proceeds as if it was not even worth hinting at the idea that someone would take the literal meaning (that he did indirectly cause his sister's rape or that she was actually raped at all) seriously. But the ironic layer provides no commentary on rape or even his persona. It exists simply as a layer of humor, in which we can laugh at the idea that someone would set someone up to be raped without encouraging any form of criticism of that type of behavior. Yes, we are positioned to consider such behavior is reprehensible, but his example reaches a level of hyperbole that any suggestion that he was serious could be itself easily mocked.

This use of irony presumes a standing critique of rape that Tosh feels no need to provide himself, ironically or otherwise. If the commentary were within the joke, it would turn his act into satire. But because it does not exist within his routines, Tosh uses irony to construct a pseudo-satiric persona. In performing the role of satirist without actually being satirical, Tosh's persona allows him and his audience to laugh at the ills of the world without really doing anything about it or, worse, perpetuating problematic notions of rape.

As a result, I argue, this pseudo-satiric persona gives Tosh and his audience a free pass to behave in ways that a satirist would be mocking, all the while using the satiric humor ideology to shield themselves from criticism. The impact of this characteristic of Tosh's comedic persona on attitudes toward aspects of culture and society flamed in July of 2012, when the Laugh Factory rape jokes propelled Tosh's bad behavior into the national spotlight. Like most controversies in contemporary media, though, the attention on Tosh's rape humor died out fairly quickly. One might hope that this would have influenced Tosh to reconsider his use of irony as a humor ideology and alter his comic persona. But such idealistic thinking does not gel with the needs of a comedian's persona or the audience. Much like all ideological thinking, challenges are reevaluated and incorporated into the humor ideologies and often serve to reinforce existing thought. A year after the rape joke controversy, I attended a live performance by Daniel Tosh in Toledo, Ohio that revealed Tosh's pseudo-satiric persona had not changed and, in fact, the controversy had been built into his routine to reaffirm his persona.

At the performance, Tosh proceeded through a large portion of his act before starting a routine about humor itself. During the bit, he emphasized that he was the type of guy that could find anything funny. He stressed that if a person could complete the line, "There's nothing funny about (blank)," there was no chance of them being friends. There was no particular performative difference about this bit, and every indication of his verbal and physical communication suggested he was about to move on to something else. It was here, though, where Tosh stopped. Standing perpendicular to the crowd, Tosh cocked his head toward the audience with a knowing smile and said, "That was the joke, by the way." Tosh's lack of additional energy or enthusiasm continued throughout the following moments as he explained that was the joke that caused the woman to interrupt his Laugh Factory performance (Tosh 2013).

There was no time given to the audience to be surprised by Tosh's decision to address the controversy. In fact, the rhetorical power of the staging left no doubt that the controversy was now fully integrated into his act. What was remarkable was Tosh's presentation of the joke and his unexcited delivery. By treating the joke as mundane, the woman's response was constructed as a clear overreaction by someone who was not part of the in-group. As quickly as it was brought up, Tosh moved on to another bit. The controversy, much like the joke itself, was insignificant. It was worthy to be addressed, but no more important than a cheap laugh in the middle of an hour-long set.

As there is no recording of the Laugh Factory performance and, as I have noted, descriptions of events have been inconsistent and sometimes contradictory, it is difficult to say if Tosh's Toledo delivery mirrored how the set and the related interruption occurred a year earlier in Long Beach. Then again, it is not what happened that matters. Tosh, given the power to tour and construct that evening as part of his act, has rhetorically shaped the controversy as trivial, sparked only by the reaction of a woman who clearly did not get it. Note that the reason for her true outrage and the outrage of the wider public, the call for her to be gang raped right there inside or outside of the Laugh Factory, was not stressed by Tosh in his retelling. With a rhetorical sleight-of-hand, that portion of the controversy in his act had been erased, leaving only the "anything can be funny" joke. Thus, while Cross uses his satiric persona to challenge dominant discourse about rape, Tosh uses his pseudo-satiric persona to perpetuate rape culture all the while using the authentic inauthenticity to shield himself from criticism.

Conclusion

Tosh's explanation of the joke and the resulting controversy reaffirmed his pseudo-satiric comic persona as kind of ironic frat boy that encouraged a form of philandering much like Cosby's comedy appears to endorse. Only this time, instead of hiding that the humor is about rape, as in Cosby's case, the irony is used to shield Tosh against criticisms that he was propagating rape culture. This shield allows both Tosh and his audience to downplay the controversy. Troublingly, throughout all of the controversy and even beyond, Tosh asserts the notion that rape can be funny without explanation, example, or – most importantly for an ironic comedic persona discussing rape – commentary.

One can take the structure of Tosh's joke to demonstrate the problem of the implementation of such irony without turning it into satire. Carlin suggests he (and, thus, his audience) should never be able to fill in the blank to "You can't joke about (blank)." Tosh's pseudo-satiric persona functions with the similarly constructed idea, "Look. I know (blank) is bad. Because I know it's bad, I get to joke about it." The same concept, be it rape or other forms of oppression or violence, can fill in that blank. But unlike Carlin, who urged his audience to fill in that blank in order to comment on the horrors of the world, Tosh strips away the commentary, implying that it exists already outside of his humor. That element of his persona presents himself and his audience with a blank check to ridicule without any responsibility to use comedy to improve the world. Someone else, like David Cross, did the hard work of critiquing society, and, as such, Tosh and his audience freely mock with an "all stereotypes are based in fact" mentality.

Such an approach highlights the privileged position of Tosh's pseudo-satiric persona. Tosh's comedy suggests that, because he acknowledges he has power as a straight, white male and he can nod to that privilege with a smirk, he is free to do whatever he desires with that privilege. His television program, *Tosh.0,* consistently reveals his persona's acceptance of power as he mocks sexuality, race, women, disability, class, and other taboo *topoi,* but the rape joke – regardless of whether we consider the joke to be Tosh's "anything can be funny" joke or the alleged "wouldn't it be funny if that woman got raped right now" joke – has shown how such a pseudo-satiric persona can cause immediate terror for one woman.

Furthermore, in the long run, this persona and the subsequent rape jokes play a role in normalizing the idea that women overreact to issues of rape, and sexual assault is a reasonable, even humorous, recourse for women who step out of line. The political and personal implications of such humor reveal that Tosh's pseudo-satiric persona and those that derive from the same humor ideology provide a layer of defense that is, at best, not warranted and, at worse, dangerous to the rights and safety of the marginalized and oppressed.

This chapter has argued that to study the rhetoric of stand-up comedy that engages with taboo topics requires an examination of the comic persona, the function of irony in that persona, and the humor ideologies that shape it and guide it. This argument is especially relevant to the rhetoric of rape humor. I have argued stand-up comics are right to defend the idea that rape can be *topoi* for jokes. Examples from George Carlin and David Cross demonstrate that, with attention to social commentary, rape humor can challenge the norms of rape culture. But not all rape humor is equal. Depending on the humor ideologies driving the comic persona, rape humor can produce drastically different results. While a satiric persona from Cross may use rape to force the audience to expand what is considered rape and encourage action against rapists, a fatherly persona like Bill Cosby's or a pseudo-satiric persona like Daniel Tosh's may normalize rape culture. The empirical evidence suggests rape humor, if delivered poorly, can solidify or exacerbate acceptance of and even proclivity to rape (Kramer 2011; Thomae & Viki 2013; Ryan and Kanjorski 1998). If, as Bingham and Hernandez claim, comedians are the teachers of ideology (2009, p. 349), then they have a deep moral responsibility. Comics who use rape humor and the audiences who laugh at/with them must be aware how their comic personae constitute audiences and shape discourse, because using irony to joke about subjects like rape without critiquing the associated politics and ideological influences will often normalize oppressive discourse. Those who do so should not be given a free pass, for comedy, even ironic comedy, is not alone a shield from criticism.

Notes

1 See, for just a few examples, Hibberd (2012), Odell (2012), and Read (2012).
2 It is unclear if the Tumblr blog is written by the woman in the audience that night, or if it is from someone writing on behalf of the woman. See So a girl walks into a comedy club … (2012).
3 Dan Whitney has not always used the Larry the Cable Guy persona. Earlier in his career, Whitney struggled to find a persona that resonated with the audience. His Larry the Cable Guy persona draws not from his own lived history, but his experiences with people such as his college roommates. See Booth (2004).
4 So a girl walks into a comedy club … (2012); West 2012.
5 Definitions and descriptions of irony could and do fill volumes. My choice of definition here is not to ignore the larger conversation about irony, but to keep the discussion focused on irony's role in the comic persona.
6 See Burke (1969); Booth (1975); Kaufer (1977); and McDaniel (2002; 2005).

References

Bingham, S.C., & Hernandez, A.A. (2009). "Laughing matters": The comedian as social observer, teacher, and conduit of the sociological perspective. *Teaching Sociology, 37,* 335–352.

Booth, W. (2004). Guffaw guys. *The Washington Post.* September 4. Retrieved from www.washingtonpost.com/wp-dyn/articles/A59508–2004Sep3.html

Booth, W.C. (1975). *The rhetoric of irony.* Chicago: University of Chicago Press.

Burke, K. (1969). *A grammar of motives.* Berkeley, CA: The University of California Press.

Burke, K. (1973). Literature as equipment for living. In *The philosophy of literary form,* 3rd ed (pp. 293–304). Berkeley, CA: The University of California Press.

Carlin, G. (1990). Rape can be funny. *Parental advisory: Explicit lyrics.* Atlantic.

Comedians defend Daniel Tosh rape joke on Twitter (NSFW). (2012). *Huffington Post.* July 12. Retrieved from www.huffingtonpost.com/2012/07/11/comedians-defend-daniel-tosh-rape-joke-twitter_n_1666072.html

Cosby, B. (1969). Spanish Fly. *It's true! It's true!* Warner Bros.

Cross, D. (2002). My daughter's first date. *Shut up you fucking baby!* Sub Pop.

Day, A. (2011). *Satire and dissent: Interventions in contemporary political debate.* Bloomington, IN: Indiana University Press.

Fondy, A. (2014). Bill Cosby and the 1960s. *Daily Kos.* November 22. Retrieved from www.dailykos.com/story/2014/11/22/1346782/-Bill-Cosby-and-the-1960s

Gilbert, J. (1997). Performing marginality: comedy, identity, and cultural critique. *Text and Performance Quarterly, 17,* 317–330.

Greenbaum, A. (1999). Stand-up comedy as rhetorical argument: An investigation of comic culture. *Humor, 12,* 33–46.

Griffin, D. (1994). *Satire: A critical reintroduction.* Lexington, KY: The University of Kentucky Press.

Gring-Pemble, L. & Watson, M.S. (2003). The rhetorical limits of satire: An analysis of James Finn Garner's *Politically correct bedtime stories. Quarterly Journal of Speech, 89,* 132–153.

Hariman, R. (2007). In defense of Jon Stewart. *Critical Studies in Media Communication, 24,* 273–277.

Harold, C. (2007). *OurSpace: Resisting the corporate control of culture.* Minneapolis, MN: The University of Minnesota Press.

Hibberd, J. (2012). Daniel Tosh apologizes for rape jokes at comedy club. *Entertainment Weekly.* July 10. Retrieved from www.ew.com/article/2012/07/10/daniel-tosh-rape-jokes

Hutcheon, L. (1995). *Irony's edge: The theory and politics of irony.* New York, NY: Routledge.

Hutcheon, L. (2000). *A theory of parody: The teachings of twentieth-century art forms,* 2nd ed. Urbana, IL: University of Illinois Press.

Kaufer, D. (1977). Irony and rhetorical strategy. *Philosophy and Rhetoric, 10,* 90–110.

Kramer, E. (2011). The playful is political: The metapragmatics of Internet rape-joke arguments. *Language in Society, 40,* 137–168.

Leopold, T. (2004). George Carlin confronts reality. *CNN.* October 29. Retrieved from www.cnn.com/2004/SHOWBIZ/books/10/28/george.carlin/

Lowrey, L., Renegar, V.R., & Goehring, C.E. (2014). "When God gives you AIDS … make lemon-AIDS": Ironic persona and perspective by incongruity in Sarah Silverman's *Jesus is Magic. Western Journal of Communication, 78,* 58–77.

McCarthy, B. (Director). (2011). *Daniel Tosh: Happy thoughts* [Television broadcast]. Comedy Central.

McDaniel, J.P. (2002). Liberal irony: A program for rhetoric. *Philosophy and Rhetoric, 35,* 297–327.
McDaniel, J.P. (2005). Speaking like a state: Listening to Benjamin Franklin in the times of terror. *Communication and Critical/Cultural Studies, 2,* 324–350.
Nanjiani, K. [@kumailn]. (2012, July 11). Comedians have personas. Are you offended by jeselnik's rape jokes? Probably not, and you shouldn't be. Tosh uses shock and always has. [Tweet]. Retrieved from https://twitter.com/kumailn/status/223163055981338625
Nelson, S. (2015). Sharp satire and uncomfortable laughs in *Hits*. *The Stranger.* February 11. Retrieved from www.thestranger.com/film/features/2015/02/11/21710523/sharp-satire-and-uncomfortable-laughs-in-hits
Odell, A. (2012). Daniel Tosh has been making rape jokes for years. *BuzzFeed.* July 10. Retrieved from www.buzzfeed.com/amyodell/daniel-tosh-has-been-making-rape-jokes-for-years#.nxz1v5zyY2
Olson, K.M., & Olson, C.D. (2004). Beyond strategy: A reader-centered analysis of irony's dual persuasive uses. *Quarterly Journal of Speech, 90,* 24–52.
Pérez, R. (2013). Learning to make racism funny in the "color-blind" era: Stand-up comedy students, performance strategies, and the (re)production of racist jokes in public. *Discourse & Society, 24,* 478–503.
Read, M. (2012). Comedy Central host Daniel Tosh should not tell people how funny it would be if they were raped. *Gawker.* July 10. Retrieved from http://gawker.com/5924948/comedy-central-host-daniel-tosh-should-not-tell-people-how-funny-it-would-be-if-they-were-raped
Richlin, A. (1992). *The garden of Priapus: Sexuality & aggression in Roman humor,* revised ed. New York: Oxford University Press.
Ryan, K.M., & Kanjorski, J. (1998). The enjoyment of sexist humor, rape attitudes, and relationship aggression in college students. *Sex Roles, 38,* 743–756.
So a girl walks into a comedy club … (2012). *Cookies for Breakfast Tumblr.* July 10. Retrieved from http://breakfastcookie.tumblr.com/post/26879625651/so-a-girl-walks-into-a-comedy-club
Thomae, M., & Viki, G.T. (2013). Why did the woman cross the road? The effect of sexist humor on men's rape proclivity. *Journal of Social, Evolutionary, and Cultural Psychology, 7,* 250–269.
Tindale, C. & Gough, J. (1987). The use of irony in argumentation. *Philosophy and Rhetoric, 20,* 1–17.
Tosh, D. (2013). *June gloom tour.* June 10. Stranahan Theatre, Toledo, OH.
Waisanen, D. (2011). Satirical visions with public consequences? Dennis Miller's ranting rhetorical persona. *American Communication Journal, 13,* 24–44.
Ware, B.L., & Linkugel, W.A. (1982). The rhetorical persona: Marcus Garvey as Black Moses. *Communication Monographs, 49,* 50–62.
West, L. (2012). How to make a rape joke. *Jezebel.* July 12. Retrieved from http://jezebel.com/5925186/how-to-make-a-rape-joke
Wuster, T. (2006). Comedy jokes: Steve Martin and the limits of stand-up comedy. *Studies in American Humor, 3,* 23–45.

11

LOUIE C.K.'S "WEIRD ETHIC"

Kairos and Rhetoric in the Network[1]

James J. Brown, Jr.

In December 2011, comedian Louie C.K. captured headlines with his self-produced and self-distributed comedy special, *Live at the Beacon Theatre*. A former writer for Chris Rock and Conan O'Brien, a film director, and a stand-up comedian known for his absurdist brand of humor, C.K. has become one of the most popular comedians in the U.S. His stand-up act is wide-ranging, dealing with his life as a father, white privilege, and everything in between. C.K. filmed, edited, and produced *Live at the Beacon Theatre* with his own money and then released it on his website as a $5 download. The project's success surprised everyone, including C.K., who was hoping that the experiment would break even financially. Instead, it grossed more than $1 million. The distribution model of *Live at the Beacon Theatre* takes advantage of a media environment in which authors and artists can distribute their work with fewer intermediaries, and C.K. has continued to use it for his own content and that of others. He also helped to distribute comic Tig Notaro's now famous 2012 set in which she discussed her diagnosis – received just three days earlier – of cancer in both of her breasts.[2] And while this model is relevant to digital rhetoricians since it demonstrates how digital networks allow for new ways of finding an audience, C.K.'s primary contribution to digital rhetoric resides not in how he has decided to distribute his comedy but rather in his method of invention. C.K.'s approach to *kairos* – the timing and crafting of rhetorical invention in response to situation – offers an alternative to some of the dominant modes of rhetorical action in networked life. As I'll argue in the postscript to this chapter, his approach is particularly useful in considering the snide, sarcastic tone, or "snark," that moves through contemporary networked spaces.

In this chapter, I'll focus more on C.K.'s creative processes than individual stand-up acts (though, I will address the latter as well) in order to argue that he offers a useful approach to rhetorical invention. That approach is not necessarily offered with digital spaces in mind, but it is useful to the digital rhetorician (indeed, to any rhetorician) nonetheless. C.K.'s creative process thrives on vulnerability by embracing constraints. Faced with the uncertainties of audience and of *kairos*, C.K. aims not to control a rhetorical situation but rather to practice succeeding in difficult situations. More than this, he constructs those situations himself in order to practice his escape acts in public. What we see in Louie C.K.'s stand-up (and in his self-produced television show, *Louie*) is a willingness to pull back the curtain on his method of invention. This is particularly useful to rhetoricians theorizing networked spaces, since the complexity and unpredictability of those spaces call for the ability to negotiate and respond to audiences and other rhetorical forces.

Comedy and Networked Rhetoric

Comedians are rich sources for understanding networked rhetoric because they address myriad audiences in myriad rhetorical situations. The stories of the "road comic" make this clear, as comedians drive or fly from city to city, delivering their routine to an audience that may or may not be receptive, that may or may not know who they are. The comedian must be ready for the heckler, since she or he might receive a warm welcome or be confronted with a group that has never been to a comedy club and has little understanding of what's expected of an audience. All of these variables emerge at once as the comic takes the stage, and this situation is a nice analogue for our networked lives. Yes, we may have some control over certain digital spaces – on social media, we can "friend" or "follow" certain people, "block" or "unfollow" others – but we can never truly predict the forces that will cut across our rhetorical action online. This is the clearest demonstration of *kairos* in the network, which reminds us, over and over again, that a rhetor is at the mercy of the network. The comedian lives this life every day, online and offline, and thus offers us a model for how to navigate the complexities of networks that welcome the troll and the friend, in equal measure.

Networked rhetorical situations mean that audiences and critics arrive from all angles, regardless of invitation. Networks, for all of their promise, raise difficult questions about audience and expose the rhetor's vulnerability. Jeff Rice (2006) points to these contradictory forces when he describes networks as "open places of rhetorical production" that make for fluid relations: "because of the influence of new content, other ideas, and alternate places of meaning, a connection that exists right now might not exist later" (p. 131). These connections that link up and then dissolve make for difficult rhetorical relations. Others arrive all the time, and these arrivals invite us to consider how the rhetor is called to respond. This problem is not created by networked life, but life in the network certainly exposes the predicaments of vulnerability to others. For Diane Davis (2010), these guests that arrive on our doorsteps (digital or otherwise) indicate a rhetorical imperative, "an originary (or preoriginary) rhetoricity – an affect*ability* or persuad*ability* – that is the condition for symbolic action" (p. 2). Before we act or argue or persuade, we are affected and called forth by various others.

Similarly, Richard Marback (2010) has argued that rhetorical theory might benefit from a different consideration of vulnerability, one that moves beyond understanding it in terms of weakness. Instead, he argues for a more sustained consideration of how vulnerability lays the groundwork for rhetorical action:

> What we gain in acknowledging and accepting our vulnerability to the appeals of others is an awareness of ourselves in our responsiveness to others. If we are aware of our responsiveness to others, we are aware of ourselves as being affected by them; we are aware at some level and in some sense of the irresistible power of their persuasiveness. Such awareness cannot but sensitize us to the subtleties and gradations of our vulnerabilities.
>
> *(pp. 10–11)*

Marback goes on to argue that recognizing vulnerability would mean "acknowledge[ing] our openness to the conditions of living" (p. 12). Both Davis and Marback show us that vulnerability is an unavoidable condition, one with which rhetoricians must continually engage. Vulnerability and affectability are unavoidable, and this is particularly clear in our networked encounters.

For this reason, a networked rhetoric needs to be attuned to *kairos*, a term that has received a great deal of attention in recent decades. The term has been used to describe the seizing of an opportune moment by the rhetor, a definition that presumes a fully present, willing, and controlling rhetor who commands the rhetorical situation. More recently, rhetorical theorists have moved to a more complex notion of *kairos*, one that does not presume a willing rhetor but rather understands how *kairos* itself, as a complex set of forces, acts upon a rhetor and his or her situation. This latter meaning is in line with the vulnerable, affectable rhetor described by Davis and Marback. The vulnerable rhetor may be called to respond at any moment by a wide variety of forces, interlocutors, and audiences. This predicament calls for something more than scripted responses.

In such situations, the rhetor is left in a strange predicament. How does one recognize that she or he is not controlling all aspects of a rhetorical ecology while also attempting to engage in rhetorical action? One way to prepare for such predicaments would be through practice. A rhetor can prepare for the unpredictability and mess of rhetorical situations through practice. The rhetorical tradition of the *progymnasmata* – a set of pedagogical exercises such as writing fables or paraphrasing poetry – was designed for just this type of practice. With these exercises, teachers in the rhetorical tradition have helped students attune themselves to the unpredictability of rhetorical situations. The practices themselves are not simple scripts that we run – if they were, they would be wholly inadequate for kairotic encounters. Instead, they offer us tools for tinkering with various rhetorical styles and strategies. Through experimentation, students can use the *progymnasmata* to craft a rhetorical sensibility.

Louie C.K. uses just this method, but he often acts as his own instructor. He attunes himself to the possibilities and predicaments of *kairos* not only by responding to unpredictable rhetorical situations but also by *constructing his own predicaments*. By creating (or, better, composing) difficult situations, C.K. forces himself to confront the vulnerability and shame of the kairotic moment. Placing himself in front of an audience and opening himself to the possibility of failure, C.K. must respond to the opportunities and pitfalls of *kairos*. Of course, every stand-up comedian does this (Greenbaum 1999). However, we can see C.K. taking this method to his other activities as well. In effect, he is allowing us to see his ever-evolving rhetorical education – he is continually performing his rhetorical experiments in public. This practicing in public stems from C.K.'s willingness to be exposed, to be placed in a vulnerable situation, to open himself up to risky situations in front of an audience. Again, nearly any stand-up comedian stands exposed in this way, but C.K. seems especially focused on forcing himself into situations that call for invention. As I will argue in this chapter, his methods for generating new stand-up material as well as his approach to his popular television show *Louie* insist upon vulnerability and unpredictability. It is this approach that offers those of us interested in rhetorical theory, and especially those who study networked spaces, a novel mode of engaging *kairos*.

C.K.'s method is a response to the vulnerability of life in a networked society. In a 2010 interview on Marc Maron's popular *WTF* podcast, C.K. described his processes of invention. Based on that interview, we can glean a great deal about C.K.'s method of invention, a "weird ethic" of practicing in public. If teachers of ancient rhetoric used tools like the *progymnasmata* for attuning students to the unpredictability of *kairos*, C.K. is showing us how such rhetorical practice need not always be performed behind closed doors or in the classroom. In the pages that follow, I will describe C.K.'s inventional method and its relationship to the *kairos* of networked life. I'll close the chapter with a brief postscript on "snark," a mode of rhetorical engagement that guards against and shields us from the vulnerability and exposedness that define C.K.'s method. What we find when we examine Louie C.K.'s weird ethic is an approach that avoids the safe space of snark and opens up toward new and complex notions of rhetorical invention.

On a High Wire

C.K's appearance on Maron's *WTF* podcast is particularly useful for understanding his methods and processes. Maron has known C.K. since his early days as a stand-up comedian, and his interview questions link C.K.'s recent success to his early days in stand-up comedy. During the interview, Maron offers an interesting encapsulation of C.K.'s guiding ethic: "You very consciously let things get so fucking bad for yourself in order to see if you can rise from it ... that's always been this weird ethic you had" (2010a). Maron provides various examples of this from early in C.K.'s career, including his decision to purchase a BMW on his American Express card (he subsequently defaulted). This early behavior was erratic and reckless, and his stand-up comedy at the time did not necessarily benefit from it. C.K. admits that his stand-up act, until recent years, was a scripted one that could be thrown off by a simple comment from an audience member. In other words, it was crafted in way that attempted to fend off the complexities of *kairos* and vulnerability. More recently, he has demonstrated a willingness to emerge from a kairotic moment by constructing predicaments and responding to them.

As Debra Hawhee (2002) argues, Gorgias offers the best known example of this approach to the kairotic encounter among ancient rhetoricians. The famous sophist would take the stage and ask the audience to recommend any topic, much the way that improv troupes do: "Gorgias would exploit the possibilities immanent in a particular rhetorical moment – a *kairos* – to create a discursive offshoot, and along with that a new *ethos* to go somewhere else. 'Invention-in-the-middle' occurs always on the spur of the moment, as a response to the forces at work in a particular encounter" (p. 18). Hawhee turns to this understanding of *kairos* to theorize invention not as a tool wielded by the rhetor but rather as a complex process that emerges in-the-middle. For Hawhee, this is more than understanding the forces, ideologies, and arguments at play in a rhetorical situation:

> It is important to distinguish "invention-in-the-middle" and its partner term *kairos* from what is often called exigence. While a commonly held notion of exigence requires the "rhetor" – a discrete, rational being – to decode a "rhetorical situation" from outside (step one), and then consciously to select "appropriate" arguments (step two) *kairos* provides a point of departure from reasoned, linear steps – even from consciousness.
>
> *(p. 24)*

This understanding of invention means that "rhetoric emerges from encounters" and that the rhetor is only one factor in complex, kairotic encounters.[3]

What C.K. shares with Gorgias is a willingness to embrace the mess of a kairotic encounter. He seems less interested in full control of that encounter than he is in becoming folded in to an ambient, complex environment. In the interview with Maron, C.K. expresses admiration for performers with this more risky sensibility, and he offers Jackie Gleason as an example:

> Gleason didn't come to rehearsals. Everybody rehearsed without him, and then he would just come in and go, "Alright what are we doing?" And he'd know half his lines, and he didn't know the blocking … Back then, everyone on the planet Earth watched *The Honeymooners* … It was like 50 million people. So, in front of all those people … you could see him in some scenes like "I'm not sure where I am or what's supposed to happen in this scene. I'm just going to do this: Bwaaa!" And he would just be hilarious.
>
> *(Maron 2010b)*

Gleason was forced to respond in front of a massive audience, and he did so by relying on an attunement to *kairos* rather than the memorization of a script. C.K.

expresses an admiration for this approach, saying that Gleason "put himself on a high wire." He knew he had to perform his way out of the situation.

This same approach is evident in C.K.'s own work as he insists that material he has performed be discarded as soon as it airs on television. While waiting for his HBO series *Lucky Louie* to air, C.K. created a one-hour stand-up special of brand new material. Knowing that the TV show would either be a success (meaning the end of his stand-up career) or a flop (meaning that he needed to make money to support his family), C.K. began developing material for this special, entitled *Shameless*. As he explains, every stand-up set that he did in preparation for *Shameless* was high stakes. Forced into this situation, C.K. filmed *Shameless* and then made a daring choice: "I threw away every minute of it … I'm never telling those jokes again. Never" (Maron 2010b). This approach is somewhat rare in the stand-up comedy community. While comedians are always developing new material, they rarely commit to throwing away all previous material. In fact, comedians are often much like musicians, relying on their "hits" during performances. What is the rhetorical value of painting oneself into a corner in this way, throwing away material that has proven successful? This method insists upon an opening up to *kairos* and vulnerability. The rhetor exposes herself to shame. S/he is placed in a vulnerable position, crafting material in ways not unlike Gleason during his work on *The Honeymooners*. She or he is not practicing behind the scenes to guard against unpredictability. Instead, the rhetor practices in front of the audience, creating a high stakes situation to which she or he must respond effectively.

One particular scene from the pilot episode of the hit television show *Louie* (this is not the same show as *Lucky Louie*, which was not renewed after its first season on HBO) is a perfect example of C.K.'s absurdist humor. At the end of a disastrous first date, C.K.'s ends up yelling at his companion (played by Chelsea Peretti). The date has been a mess, and Louie has attempted to smooth things over at every turn, but he finally hits a breaking point. At the end of his rant, his date is so uncomfortable that she jumps up from the bench they are sitting on and escapes via helicopter. The scene arrives, seemingly, out of nowhere. But for C.K., it is the most important part of the episode for a number of reasons: "Things like the helicopter exist for two reasons. One is just that I like it … [but] also I get off on squeezing a lot out of very little money. The budget for this show was tiny, and I wanted to show FX [the show's network] that I could do a lot with money" (Maron 2010b). When shooting for *Louie* started, C.K. asked his production manager, Blaire Breard, for the helicopter: "I said to her: 'Can you get me a helicopter?' That was like one of the first things I said to her" (Maron 2010b). This was not an easy task, and Breard continued to try to talk C.K. out of it, due to its expense. But the helicopter scene happened because C.K. committed to the absurd request and insisted that his crew do so as well:

> She would say to me "I'm not finding a helicopter yet. Start thinking of an alternate," and I'd say to her "There isn't an alternate. Get a helicopter." And

she'd keep working on it and working on it. And then she found this dude who, he's a new helicopter guy. He's the new guy in town.

(Maron 2010b)

Typically, the helicopter scene might be seen as an extravagance, a way to flaunt a large budget. For C.K., it's precisely the opposite. He committed to this scene knowing the risks involved. There was no plan B. Yes, this is a commitment to absurdist comedy, but it is also a commitment to a manufactured constraint, one that forces C.K. and those around him into a predicament and the possibility of failure.

C.K.'s willingness to embrace risk and failure dovetails with his stand-up material as well, which often deals with his own shame. He discusses his penchant for Cinnabon cinnamon rolls: "I'm buying a Cinnabon … at the airport that I arrived at. You understand why that's extra disgusting, right? … I'm 20 minutes from my house where I have bananas and apples, and I'm sitting on my luggage just eating a Cinnabon with a fork and knife." He also addresses his frequent masturbation: "You know, it's bad to, like, jerk off and run out the door. 'Cause you run into somebody … uh, she knows. You gotta take some time alone to process the shame." Both of these bits come in the aptly named special *Shameless*, which is actually anything but shameless. In the wake of *Live at the Beacon Theatre*, designer and writer Frank Chimero (2011) blogged about C.K.'s recent success and made specific reference to C.K.'s willingness to address his own shame. In his hit television show and in sold-out theatres, Chimero argues, C.K. has tapped into a collective discussion about shame and embarrassment:

> Louie CK has jokes because he is ashamed of his body, ashamed of his thoughts, his culture, his whiteness, whatever. Every joke seems to be about shame in some way. Ashamed of the things he doesn't do that he knows he should.

Another example of C.K.'s discussions of shame might help here. In *Live at the Beacon Theatre*, C.K. says that he's not a good person but that he enjoys "the idea of being a good guy." He describes flying in the First Class cabin and seeing people come on the plane, miserably walking to their seat in coach, and he focuses on the soldiers that he often sees getting on the plane, joining this procession to coach:

> Every time that I see a soldier on a plane I think, "You know what? I should give him my seat." It would be the right thing to do, it would be easy to do, and it would mean a lot to him. I could go up to him, hey son – I get to call him son – hey son, go ahead and take my seat. Because I'm in first class why? For being a professional asshole. I'm in first class because I talk about babies with big dicks. That's what got me my seat. This guy is giving his life for the country, he thinks. [pause for laughter]. But that's good enough! That's good enough. The fact that he thinks it. I'm serious. He's

fuckin' told by everybody in his life system that that's a great thing to do, and he's doing it. And it's scary, but he's doing it, and he's sitting in this shitty seat. And I should trade with him. I never have. Let me make that clear. I've never done it once. I've had so many opportunities. I never even really seriously came close. And here's the worst part: I still just enjoy the fantasy, for myself to enjoy. I was actually proud of myself for having thought of it. I was proud! "Uh, I am such a sweet man. That is so nice of me, to think of doing that and then totally never do it."

In this bit, C.K. shares with us his own shame, expressing something universal about how we fantasize about good deeds in order to provide ourselves with enjoyment. Chimero argues that "shame is diffused through its publication and distribution. Shame is reduced through its sharing." While I'm not sure that shame is reduced through sharing, it seems clear that the material is rhetorically effective. Chimero is right. The commonplace of shame runs through all of C.K.'s material, from his stand-up comedy to his television shows. And this commonplace is tied directly to the method of invention I've been tracing out here. Stripped of the support of a previous material or the scaffolding of old jokes, committed to absurd premises, open and affectable, C.K. is forced (and forces himself) to stand naked in front of his audience (see Marc 1992, p. 13). He insists upon designing difficult situations, leaving open the possibility of shame, and then responding.

This display of vulnerability makes C.K. a useful model for digital rhetoric, which must always take up the forces shape and constrain kairotic encounters. But there are other ways to link Louie C.K. to rhetoric and technology. During their interview, Maron reminisces about a computer that he and C.K. found on the street. C.K., whose mother was a computer programmer and who was a self-described junior high AV nerd, fixed it and ended up mining various files for stand-up material. He writes and edits his television show on a 13-inch MacBook Pro. He shoots the show on the RED digital camera and uses fixed focus lenses, meaning that lenses have to be changed out for every shot. In his own words, he does things in "the most complicated way possible." Like his choice to distribute his comedy special online, this use of technology is really just one more example of his "weird ethic," his willingness to put himself on a high wire. With his talent for creating tight spots, for constructing situations that he will have to write or perform his way out of, for remaining open to vulnerability, failure, and shame, C.K provides us with a useful model for rhetorical invention in the network. By cultivating an attunement to *kairos* and a recognition of the value of exposedness in the network, the rhetor can learn how to thrive in kairotic encounters.

Postscript: Shame, Snark, and Rhetoric in the Network

Given that contemporary rhetorical practice is largely defined by snark, C.K.'s willingness to place himself in tight spots and unpredictable situations provides a novel mode of invention. Snark – a portmanteau of "snide" and "remark" – defines contemporary rhetoric in the network. From the mocking tone of Gawker blogs to YouTube comment trolls to flame wars, digital spaces can be caustic places. Snark is one response to this set of problems. It offers jabs and opinions in a knowing tone, attacking the opposition coldly or preemptively insulating the author against attacks and trolling. In fact, it was the tone of such postings that led C.K. to quit Twitter, arguing that it didn't make him feel very good (Blistein 2015). It's difficult to deny that snark and sarcasm dominate rhetorical practice in digital spaces. Thrown into a kairotic situation where various audiences will view your video or listen to your podcast or respond to your blog post, the digital rhetor can use snark to make it clear that the various others with whom they collide are doing no damage. Snark attempts to protect against shame and vulnerability.

Snark emerges as a defense mechanism against the vulnerability of a networked world. But an attunement to *kairos* requires that the rhetor resist falling back on the callous, cynical, scripted defense mechanisms built in anticipation of the judgment of others. By recognizing an exposure to others, C.K. offers an answer to snark, which is allergic to failure and vulnerability. It's important to note that this is not about meeting snark with a saccharine form of sincerity. Anyone who has seen Louie C.K.'s act knows that this would be a radical mischaracterization. Instead, C.K.'s commitment to shame is a result of his willingness to emerge from *kairos* by forcing himself to, as Chimero notes, distribute his shame. This is the true significance of *Live at the Beacon Theatre*, an hour of material that continues C.K.'s penchant for shame and humiliation (his own and ours). He offers an alternative to the armor that snark attempts to create – a shell that guards against the shame of being exposed to/by others, an exposedness that is unavoidable in a networked society.

Notes

1 An early version of this chapter appeared in the journal *Present Tense*. See Brown (2013).
2 Since the original publication of this chapter, Tig Notaro has demonstrated an embrace of vulnerability and *kairos* in a particularly striking way. Laying her body bare and vulnerable to the audience, Notaro performs a portion of her most recent HBO special topless, showing her double mastectomy scars while performing material. This exposure to her audience is perhaps the most extreme example of a stand-up comedian forcing and then responding to a kairotic moment. But in addition to exposing her physical body to the audience, Notaro's performance can be seen as the manufacturing of a constraint. Notaro's aim is not to make her act about performing topless or about breast cancer. In fact, it is just the opposite. Performing in this exposed way, Notaro aims to make the audience forget entirely that she is not wearing a shirt, a seemingly impossible task. According to Jason Zinoman (2014) of the *New York Times*, Notaro succeeded in doing just this: "She showed the audience her scars and then, through the force of her showmanship, made you forget that they were there. It was a powerful, even inspiring, statement about survival and recovery, and yet, it had the larky feel of a dare."
3 Thomas Rickert (2004) extends Hawhee's conception of invention-in-the-middle even further, arguing that networked life requires a more extreme understanding of how the rhetor and her arguments emerge from complexity. In his theorization of ambience (a metaphor he finds more appropriate than "network") he wants to "pursue

as far as possible the implications that obtain from dismantling the interior/exterior opposition, which perhaps means that the concept of middle is itself transformed, or perhaps even effaced" (p. 913). As I have already begun to argue here, networked life means that cleanly separating "me" from "you" is nearly impossible. I am vulnerable to the various audiences and forces that will shape, constrain, and extend my rhetorical actions. For Rickert, this means that we are better served by a metaphor of ambience than by that of the network: "From this perspective, language and environment presuppose each other or become mutually entangled and constitutive. Further, becoming aware that there is no tidy separation of language and environment opens us up to forms of 'connection' that are not solely link driven" (pp. 903–904). Here Rickert's argument is persuasive. If the metaphor of a network evokes clearly defined nodes and edges, then it is perhaps not the best way of understanding rhetorical situations in which "no element can be singled out as decisive, for they are all integral to its singular emergence" (p. 904). Still, in this chapter, I will retain the language of the network and networked life more as a reference to the digital spaces I am most interested in theorizing. While the network may be too clean a metaphor for understanding networked culture, as a cultural reference is still carries useful weight when attempting to understand the rhetoric of (and rhetoric in) digital spaces.

References

Blistein, J. (2015). Louis C.K. on why he quit Twitter. *Rolling Stone*. April 30. Retrieved from www.rollingstone.com/tv/news/louis-c-k-on-why-he-quit-twitter-20150416

Brown, J.J. (2013). Louis C.K.'s "weird ethic": Kairos and rhetoric in the network. *Present Tense: A Journal of Rhetoric in Society*, *3*(1), www.presenttensejournal.org/volume-3/louie-c-k-s-weird-ethic-kairos-and-rhetoric-in-the-network/

Chimero, F. (2011). Louis C.K.'s shameful dirty comedy. *Frankchimero.com*. December 19. Retrieved from http://frankchimero.com/writing/louis-cks-shameful-dirty-comedy/

Davis, D. (2010). *Inessential solidarity: Rhetoric and foreigner relations,* 1st ed. Pittsburgh: University of Pittsburgh Press.

Greenbaum, Andrea. (1999). Stand-up comedy as rhetorical argument: An investigation of comic culture. *Humor, 12,* 33–46.

Hawhee, D. (2002). Kairotic encounters. In J. Atwill and J. Lauer (Eds.), *Perspectives on rhetorical invention*. (pp. 16–35). Knoxville: University of Tennessee Press.

Marback, R. (2010). A meditation on vulnerability in rhetoric. *Rhetoric Review, 29,* 1–13.

Marc, D. (1992). *Comic visions: Television comedy and American culture*. New York: Routledge.

Maron, M. (2010a). Episode 111 – Louis C.K. Part 1 [audio recording]. *WTF with Marc Maron*. Retrieved from http://wtfpod.libsyn.com/episode-111-louis-ck-part-1

Maron, M. (2010b). Episode 112 – Louis C.K. Part 2 [audio recording]. *WTF with Marc Maron*. Retrieved from http://wtfpod.libsyn.com/episode-112-louis-c-k-part-2

Rice, J. (2006). Networks and new media. *College English, 69,* 127–133.

Rickert, T. (2004). In the house of doing: Rhetoric and the *kairos* of ambience. *JAC, 24,* 901–927.

Sydell, L. (2012). Website editors strive to rein in nasty comments : NPR. *NPR.org*. June 1. Retrieved from www.npr.org/templates/story/story.php?storyId=126782677

Zinoman, J. 2014. Going topless, Tig Notaro takes over town hall. *New York Times*. November 7. Retrieved from www.nytimes.com/2014/11/08/arts/going-topless-tig-notaro-takes-over-town-hall.html

12

LATE NIGHT APOLOGIA

A Critical Analysis of David Letterman's On-Air Revelation

Casey R. Schmitt

Over the last several decades, following a string of cases involving high-ranking American politicians, the public disclosure of sexual indiscretions has become something of a rhetorical genre unto itself. The most infamous of such cases, perhaps, dates to 1998, when, via televised address to the nation, President Bill Clinton confessed to having had an inappropriate physical relationship with former White House intern, Monica Lewinsky. Since Clinton's confession, however, numerous other public figures have, amid allegations and accusations, publicly acknowledged and repented for extramarital affairs and similar improper liaisons. In 2008, for instance, New York Governor Eliot Spitzer admitted to his involvement as a client of an illegal prostitution ring in a public letter of resignation. Later that year, in response to scrutiny from the press, former North Carolina Senator and presidential candidate John Edwards released a statement affirming reports of a 2006 adulterous relationship between himself and a former campaign worker. In 2009, South Carolina Governor Mark Sanford, too, in a series of press conferences and Associated Press interviews, remorsefully disclosed details of his own extramarital relationship with an Argentine journalist.

In fact, both before and after Clinton, there has been no shortage of rhetoric prompted by public questions of private judgments. In an era of investigative journalism and increasingly invasive media coverage of political and celebrity figures, an accusation of sexual misconduct presents a rhetorical situation for the accused, by which he or she must address the moral implications of his or her actions.[1] Public figures speak to a constituency, or community of support; politicians speak to their electorate, clergy to their congregations, and celebrities to their audience and fan base. As the maintenance of power and renown in the American democratic system relies in a great part upon personal reputation in public opinion, the accused public figure must therefore address the concerns of this audience. The admission of and apology for sexual indiscretion tends to take on similar forms in its multiple incarnations. The fitting response allows the speaker to admit wrongdoing and express remorse, but also to refocus audience attention on public matters and reassert his or her moral dedication to a public charge, regardless of – and distinctly separate from – private matters (Bitzer 1968, pp. 9–12). The words of Clinton, Spitzer, Edwards, Sanford, and others resemble each other remarkably in their serious and somber tone (communicating earnest reflection upon transgressions), emphasis upon the unpleasant personal experience of laying bare such intimate details (when, in fact, providing very little explicit detail unless legally bound to do so), declaration to protect other involved parties, rededication and affirmation of continued public service, and gratitude to a gracious and understanding audience. Such similar arrangement of substantive and stylistic characteristics suggests that the "sexual misconduct apologia" is indeed a kind of sub-genre of public address.[2]

Yet on Thursday, October 1st, 2009, the American public witnessed a uniquely unorthodox admission of indecent conduct which stood apart from these other examples, not merely for its unusual stylistic qualities, but for its reception of a notably positive audience response. Popular late night television comedian and stand-up comic David Letterman used a portion of his nightly talk show to reveal not only that he too had engaged in inappropriate sexual relationships with workplace subordinates (similar to those so often mocked and satirized on the program), but that the affairs had, as of late, made him the target of a previously unreported $2 million extortion scheme. In many ways, Letterman's on-air revelation resembled the admissions of the several public and political figures before him – it included an open confession, an emphasis of unpleasant experience, and a declaration to protect those involved by refocusing further attention on the show and not the private life of the speaker – but the audience response to his ten-minute confession distinguished Letterman's address as markedly different. While other speakers may have fallen under immediate scrutiny or even vilification, Letterman's unsuspecting audience received his confession with cheers, laughter, and applause. Something in the comic's delivery and his confession's reception had radically altered the standard form of sexual misconduct disclosure rhetoric.

This chapter shall consider Letterman's on-air revelation as a means of exploring the unique rhetorical avenues available to the habitual comedian when speaking in situations of unusual gravity. Under circumstances that call for intensely somber or serious tones, the comedian becomes inherently out-of-place, and may respond in one of two ways: either by shifting out of comedic persona and, in effect, presenting a jarringly poignant tonal distinction for the audience, or by maintaining comedic persona paradoxically and, thus, imbuing weighty circumstances with a degree of levity wholly inappropriate for and inaccessible to the non-comic rhetor. A close textual analysis reveals Letterman to be engaging in both strategies, though relying more heavily upon the latter. Through both subtle and overt comedic language, as well as capitalization upon a well-established comic-to-audience relationship with his listeners, Letterman presents a confession that may also be read and alternately received as an apology, a pre-emptive power move, an informative account, a "little story," or simply (and, perhaps, ultimately) a mere variation upon his regular nightly comic monologue.

While other admissions of sexual misconduct have forced impeachment, indictment, and resignation amidst audience reproach and outrage, the comic host received applause, with no decrease in ratings or withdrawal of advertisers over the subsequent weeks (Elliott 2009). Analysis of Letterman's linguistic and structural choices, combined with a critical reading of the performative aspects and the special role of the studio audience in determining the ultimate reception of serious words in a regularly light-hearted and humorous atmosphere, helps to explain how the comedian in serious times might manipulate accepted forms of rhetoric and achieve such an otherwise improbable response.[3]

In the following pages, I present a close, point-by-point analysis of Letterman's now infamous address. This case study analysis of a single rhetorical performance helps demonstrate the unique rhetorical opportunities available to the stand-up comic, the ways in which audience reception influences stand-up oratory, and the means by which stand-up comedy and stand-up persona may diffuse otherwise serious or taboo *topoi*.

Setting the Stage

The first major distinction separating Letterman's confession from those of the politicians and public figures preceding him can be recognized in its contextual and structural framing. Letterman's confession itself was indeed rather brief – no more than three sentences, delivered over a matter of seconds – but the manner in which it was presented, following seven and half minutes of preamble, plays a crucial role in its ultimate efficacy.

Before dawn on September 9th, 2009, Letterman had received a small package from Robert Joel Halderman, a producer for the CBS news program *48 Hours Mystery*, indicating that Halderman had significant evidence of Letterman's workplace affairs and threatening to make those details public by way of a screenplay unless Letterman should meet certain demands. In a series of meetings with Letterman's personal lawyer over the next several weeks, Halderman – himself romantically linked to one of the women implicated in the affairs – requested $2 million in exchange for his silence. After consulting the New York District Attorney's office, Letterman and his lawyer drafted and delivered a bogus $2 million check to Halderman in order to evidence and strengthen the case that blackmail had actually occurred. On the morning of Thursday, October 1st, Halderman was arrested. While he posted bail later that afternoon, neither news of the blackmail attempt nor the affairs themselves had spread by the time Letterman prepared to tape his nightly show (Carter & Stelter 2009a).

However, aware that the story would soon reach the public, and that he would inevitably be required to address the situation, Letterman prepared his response. In a way, he enjoyed a degree of self-presentational liberty not always available to accused philanderers, knowing that, in the hours before reports of the incident would be widely circulated, he maintained some control of how the information might be initially presented. His decision to address the incident before his studio audience allowed him a unique rhetorical opportunity. Instead of the podium of a press conference, surrounded by flashing bulbs and news network microphones, he spoke from behind his hosting desk, at center stage, in Manhattan's Ed Sullivan Theater. After 16 years of nightly broadcasts, this location provided a comfortable atmosphere for Letterman as a speaker, while presenting a familiar image to the viewer, suggesting that, despite the confession, little of the moment was entirely out of the ordinary. In fact, Letterman's studio audience had no knowledge of the affairs or extortion plot before entering the theater or, indeed, during the entire first portion of the program. Letterman began with a customary topical comic monologue before breaking for commercial and taking his seat in what in-house and at-home audiences would both view as a natural, casual environment.

Upon returning from commercial and acknowledging the in-house band, however, Letterman launched into his remarkable, extended revelation by speaking to the studio audience directly. "I'm glad you folks are here tonight," he began, "and I'm glad you're in such a pleasant mood, because I have a little story that I would like to tell you and the home viewers as well. Do you feel like a story?" The audience responded with cheers and applause.

From that point onward, Letterman's revelation could be characterized by three distinguishing frames. First, it had been framed as a familiar exchange between intimate acquaintances. By addressing the in-house audience directly and distinguishing them from the viewers at home (who would watch the program later that evening, likely after news of the extortion incident had spread), Letterman implied a special confidence between himself and his listeners, encouraging their sympathy through the immediacy of direct contact. This relationship was further developed in his use of the colloquial "you folks" and a voiced concern for the audience's well-being, or "pleasant mood." Secondly, the revelation had been framed as comedic and light-hearted merely by virtue of its contextual atmosphere. From David Letterman, behind the desk, during a taping of *The Late Show*, the audience expected and anticipated humor. As Letterman had presented his opening monologue in typical fashion, they had no reason to expect anything else. Thirdly, Letterman had framed and identified the speech which followed as a "little story" – not an account, not a confession, and not an incident to report. As a "story," it could be seen as entertainment, likely presented for the audience's behalf, especially since Letterman had expressly asked whether or not they should like to hear one. Ignorant of the story's contents, the in-house audience agreed and, with the implication that the story was "little," they could hardly expect that it should have any grave or important consequences.

In the words that followed, Letterman relied heavily upon these three frames of presentation. The confession of sexual misconduct was thus *nested* within a cushioned blend of storytelling, comedy, and friendly exchange between familiar acquaintances. A closer reading of Letterman's speech – stylistically, structurally, and in direct response to immediate audience reactions – reveals how such a nest could have been constructed.

Analyzing Letterman's "Little Story": Omission, Levity, and "Terrible Things"

Upon re-watching and reanalyzing the ten-minute segment, one begins to notice specific stylistic elements at play. Ultimately, though, Letterman's overall narrative style is most notable for two key characteristics, which both work to distract from the gravity of the confession he eventually presents.

The first of these characteristics is a selective omission of specific or licentious details. During the entire telling of the "story," Letterman carefully withholds crucial pieces of information. For instance, upon gaining the audience's support for tell his tale and launching into a careful account of the Halderman incident (beginning with the arrival of the initial package three weeks earlier), he avoids identifying the extortion scheme explicitly from the start. Instead, he presents details to the audience as the story unfolds, carefully and notably revealing information in cryptic fragments so that the listener might experience the confusion and uncertainty that he himself had felt. The contents of the package, its origins, and Halderman's identity are never mentioned. Not knowing the particulars of the incident, the audience is left unsure of where the story will lead, and, in effect, Letterman thus builds a particularly strong sense of audience empathy with his own disorientation. Furthermore – and, perhaps, more importantly – he withholds the crucial detail of his affairs for the entire narrative portion of the speech. Referring, instead, merely to "terrible things," he avoids even hinting at what kind of information had been leveraged against him. An audience member is allowed, thus, to speculate about the nature of these "things," but they are ultimately overshadowed by the more vivid details of the blackmail plot, and the mysterious blackmailer (the unidentified Halderman) becomes a kind of nameless, faceless villain to Letterman's personable victim.

The second defining characteristic of Letterman's narrative style is more active than passive. In telling the tale, he heavily drenches his narrative in humorous commentary, and it is this stylistic strategy that most merits an extended close analysis. From beginning to end, the comic punctuates every few lines of the story with a small joke or humorous aside. There is a notable pattern by which he follows presentation of legitimate detail with droll or sarcastic remarks, waiting for laughter to subside before revealing graver details.[4] The laughter – especially from the perspective of the television viewer – contributes to the shape and tone of the discourse ultimately produced. Letterman is, after all, a comedian in a comedian's venue, reliant in some part upon his interaction with the immediate audience. In social and psychological studies of stand-up comedy as a communicative medium, Oliver Double, Pam Wells, and Peter Bull have all remarked upon this crucial interaction. Double (2005) compares comic delivery to a dialogue in which laughter constitutes one half, and by which discourse is created through an exchange of expressive energies (pp. 106–107). Wells and Bull (2007) explore applause and laughter as "affiliative" actions, which shape subsequent communication. A thorough analysis of Letterman's confession must, therefore, analyze the speaker's use of humor in relation to audience response. Whether these moments of levity and laughter arise as a calculated distraction, a means of cutting narrative tension, or merely out of Letterman's own nervous discomfort in the revelation matters not; they ultimately serve the same role in re-emphasizing the speech's overall frames of story, humor, and friendly banter.

The opening portions of Letterman's "story" are especially filled with lightened moods. After describing how he had found a mysterious package, Letterman notes that it was an odd occurrence, as he does not "usually receive packages [at] six in the morning in the back of [his] car," and this comment receives laughter from the audience.[5] He acknowledges the response by shrugging, "I guess you can. I guess some people do," which, in turn, relieves narrative tension by casually stepping outside of the immediate tale. At this point, the levity briefly is countered by a shift into serious confession, as Letterman reveals that a letter in the package read, "I know that you do some terrible, terrible things," but this statement, too, becomes a paradoxical combination of gravity and humor. Despite its serious implications, the audience receives the words with laughter.

It is quite possible that, unsure of the story's ultimate direction, Letterman's audience is still anticipating that the tale will eventually end in a punchline, and that the word "terrible" is not meant to be taken seriously. Yet the phrase also represents one of the key rhetorical strategies in Letterman's comic playbook: a kind of "repetition ad absurdum," by which the mere repetition of a word or phrase makes it humorous. In his comic monologues, Letterman is well known for using repetition of specific words for comic effect, and, in his revelation speech, the word "terrible" becomes a punchline, despite its implications. After repeating the word twice in his initial quotation of the letter, Letterman immediately employs a repetitive cadence, ending the next two phrases with the same exact words, followed each time by a slight pause, suggesting room for audience reaction. "I can prove that you do these terrible things," he says, quoting the letter, then adds, after a beat, "And sure enough, contained in the packet was stuff to prove that I do terrible things." Within the course of one minute of delivery, Letterman uses the word "terrible" seven times, without once clarifying what those "terrible things" might be. In effect, a grave accusation, stripped of its actual meaning, becomes humorous and, by extension, harmless.

Letterman continues his pattern of following serious revelation with casual, comedic commentary after describing the threatened screenplay, noting, sarcastically, "You know, that's good news for anyone, isn't it really?" The question once more presents an opportunity for audience involvement and the crowd laughs and applauds at the remark. Letterman presents Halderman as a menacing figure, but also as a mundane and unthreatening one, referring to him only as "a guy." When, after two minutes, Letterman finally reveals the "guy's" threat of extortion, several members of the audience react with audible sympathy, but a smiling Letterman counters the seriousness of the moment by describing it with a consciously comical qualifier – "a little hinky" – and the crowd returns to laughter once more.

At this point – once an extortion plot has been clearly identified, and when audience members might begin to question what Letterman had done that was so "terrible" as to legitimize such threats – the comic switches focus in order to create emotional empathy with his plight. He is in full narrative mode, concerned with maintaining the emotional tone of the situation he describes. "I just want to reiterate," he says, "how terrifying this moment is, because there's something very insidious about [it]," then poses a series of three short questions about the blackmailer's position in present tense, stressing a sense of paranoia. "Is he standing down there?" he asks, "Is he hiding under the car? Am I going to get a tap on the shoulder?" Then, he shifts yet again from serious to comic tones, adding to terror and paranoia the emotion of guilt. "I'm motivated by nothing but guilt," he says. "If you know anything about me, I am just a towering mass of Lutheran Midwestern guilt." This comment receives hearty laughter and cheers, for which Letterman actually pauses his narrative and thanks the audience.

From here, Letterman launches once more into his "little story," which, beneath a nest of comedy and casual banter, briefly resembles a legal report in its inclusion of Letterman's attorney and the Special Prosecution Bureau of the Manhattan D.A.'s Office. Still, Letterman maintains a friendly, relatable demeanor, stressing that he hates involving lawyers and referring to law enforcement agents in informal tones. He counters the legal elements with humor by repeating the word "hinky," by suggesting he could forgive Halderman's initial threat because "we all have bad days," and by channeling a law enforcement official with the comic recognition, "Whoa! Hello! This is blackmail!" In a narrative structured upon successively intensifying encounters, he recounts a series of three successive meetings with Halderman, who he begins to mock more and more frequently. After noting that Halderman ("the guy") threatened also to write a book about the "terrible things" (again repeated), Letterman poses a series of mocking questions which build in their absurdity. "So I thought, well, that's nice," he says, "you have a companion piece. You have the film, and you have the book. What do you [do], read the book first, then go to the film? Do you watch the film, then you read the book? Do you take the book and read along at the film?" The blackmailer becomes an absurd figure, while Letterman himself is further cast as the wronged party.

Yet when he remarks, to loud and buoyant laughter, "It's all coming up roses for me now," after speaking for nearly five minutes, he has still not revealed what it is *he* had done. If his audience's response is any indication, though, they no longer care. Amidst the engaging narrative and supportive environment, then, Letterman accomplishes a deft rhetorical maneuver. Anticipating the eventual revelation of his sexual misconduct, he gradually and subtly tweaks the term "terrible things" to hint slightly more explicitly at his actual actions. After repeating variations of the phrase eight times, he ceases to use it in its original form. "Terrible things" first become "embarrassing, terrible things." Then, by the time blackmail is established as both a real and ridiculous threat, Letterman replaces the term entirely with the phrase "creepy stuff." He cautions his audience to "remember, this guy knows creepy stuff about me," where before he had only known "terrible things." By substituting one term for the other, Letterman is able to transfer the jovial audience acceptance of the term "terrible," built upon comic repetition, to the slightly more vivid (and perhaps more accurate) term, "creepy" – a transference that foreshadows his later shift from "creepy stuff" to sex with workplace subordinates.

Midway through his speech, Letterman implicitly acknowledges the overall gravity of the situation by remarking that he is "not sure there really is" a "lighthearted moment in any of this," despite the jocular atmosphere his words have encouraged. As if to accompany this conscious recognition of narrative disconnect with the reality of the narrated situation, he then also openly admits that he has withheld information. "I don't think I've mentioned the amount up 'til now," he says, "but he was asking $2 million." Several members of the audience react with an audible gasp, at which the rest of the audience then laughs again. Letterman, in reaction to the gasp, scans the audience with his eyes, before smiling and asking, "Was that the foreigners?", a reference, in all likelihood, to a specific group in the audience, encountered during his customary pre-show in-studio meet-and-greet session. The staggering amount of money at play highlights a key difference between the multimillionaire Letterman and those individuals in his audience, but his personalized response to specific audience members' comments reemphasizes an intimate, friendly frame for their relationship. Letterman downplays his wealth by referring to himself as a "bonehead" and returning to humor in his narrative by describing how he had envisioned Halderman (still "the guy") walking about New York City with a giant-sized novelty check in place of an actual $2 million note. This image makes "the guy" even more absurd, while Letterman highlights his immorality by stressing that, despite the payoff, he still threatened to one day write the proposed screenplay.

Letterman then signals the climax of his story by shifting into a more immediate time frame, saying, "So this morning, I did something I've never done in my life." In comparison to the story's ridiculous and immoral extortionist, Letterman becomes an innocent and courageous foil. He ceases making comedic commentary and focuses his language with a serious tone. "It was a combination of just unusual and scary," he says, "this whole thing has been quite scary – I had to go downtown to testify before the grand jury. And I had to tell them how I was disturbed by this. I was worried for myself. I was worried for my family. I felt menaced by this." His language here, through stiff and earnest parallelism, reflects a sudden shift from the comedic persona he had maintained up to this point. The lack of comic counterbalance to matters of his own fear and his own sense of duty implies that these two are unique aspects of the ordeal that ought not be mocked or questioned. Through repetition of the words "scary" and "worried," and through an expressed concern for his family, he begins to conform to the regular characteristics of sexual misconduct apologia.[6] He seeks audience empathy and support, attempting, apparently, to perform what Robert P. Abelson, along with B.L. Ware and Wil Linkugel, have termed "bolstering" of his case (2000, p. 429).[7] For a moment, Letterman's speech almost adheres to the generic norm.

Yet, at that very instant, Letterman's confession's quintessential difference is made manifest. Describing his experience before the grand jury, he remarks, "And I had to tell them all of the creepy things that I have done." When he attempts to continue speaking in serious tones, he is interrupted by audience laughter. He pauses and asks, "Now why is that funny?" in an exasperated manner. The audience, again, applauds him for this effort. Such an exchange would be thoroughly unimaginable in a more formal setting, during the admissions of a politician or other, non-comedic public figure, yet, intentionally or not, Letterman gets away with it. In fact, the phrase is funny because the audience associates "creepy things" with the speech's earlier punchlines. They have no knowledge yet of what those "creepy things" might be, and therefore the words, for them, are a mere cue for laughter.[8] After seven minutes of story, humor, and casual banter, the speech has created a lighthearted environment incongruous with its ultimate subject matter.

Recovering from this incident, Letterman quickly draws his story to a conclusion, announcing that "a little bit after noon today, the guy was arrested." The audience cheers as the narrative ends. Victory has been achieved, and they have good reason to be jovial. A blundering villain has been defeated. With the arrest as the climax, any details to follow are implicitly secondary in nature. A full three quarters of the ten-minute speech is spent in the narrative, which has reached a satisfying conclusion and, here, Letterman finally presents his confession, almost as a footnote or minor afterthought to the larger story at hand. He pauses during the cheers to have a sip from his mug and clear his throat.

"Now, of course," he says, "we get to, what was it? What was all the creepy stuff that he was gonna put into the screenplay and the movie?" He poses the question that members of his audience may have in mind, implying he understands their immediate concerns. The confession itself is straightforward and succinct. He slows his pace, pausing between words, to admit, "The creepy stuff was that I have had sex with women who work for me on this show." The revelation is startling in comparison to the previous announcement of Halderman's arrest. The audience falls silent. And at this crucial moment, when other speakers might continue solemnly and apologetically, the comic demonstrates his remarkable rhetorical liberty by using humor yet again. Breaking the silence, he states, bluntly, "Now. My response to that is," and, after a slight pause, "yes I have." The laughter and applause return.

In part, no doubt, to contextual and structural framing, the audience perceives the confession as an appropriate place for laughter whereas, in other contexts, such a reaction would be extraordinarily inappropriate. But Letterman also cues his listeners onto the humor of the situation outside of mere context by continuing to utilize a strategy of comedic repetition. The confession begins with repetition of the phrase "creepy stuff," still marked as humorous from the "terrible things" of the speech's beginning. More importantly, though, Letterman manages to repeat the very core of his revelation as a kind of punchline. When first he says the words, "I have had sex with women who work for me on this show," they are part of an accusation and are met with silence. Breaking this silence with the blunt confession, "yes I have," which triggers a burst of audience laughter, he immediately repeats the phrase, almost word-for-word: "I have had sex with women who work on this show." This time, it is a confession – or perhaps, even, a declaration – building upon the humor of the blunt "yes I have," and is met with even louder laughter and stronger applause. Once the initial shock of its first mention is overcome, the word "sex," too, becomes something of a new cue word, to replace "terrible" and "creepy." Letterman repeats the word five times before finishing the speech, in increasingly joking contexts. He repeats the word "embarrassing" – earlier linked to "terrible" – with the question, "And would it be embarrassing if it were made public?", only to answer with another repeated phrase: "Perhaps it would. Perhaps it would." With his confession delivered, Letterman falls back on the pattern of countering legitimate detail with humorous remarks, adding the self-deprecating comment that publicity of the affairs would be "especially" embarrassing for the women involved, and once more mocking his extortionist – this time in a nasally, condescending vocal impersonation.

Returning to Halderman refocuses attention on the extended extortion narrative and not on the admission of affairs. The narrative and humor deflect concentration from Letterman's own misdoings while emphasizing those of "the guy" who had been arrested. Before cutting to commercial, though, Letterman does, once more, include a brief series of serious statements which mimic the more political, solemn form of sexual misconduct rhetoric. He thanks the officers of the Manhattan Special Prosecution Bureau. He emphasizes the difficulties he has experienced in the ordeal, as if they have provided sufficient punishment for his transgressions on their own. He highlights a self-appointed duty to take responsibility for the protection of individuals immediately affected by his choices, through repetition in the words, "I feel like I need to protect these people. I need to certainly protect my family. I need to protect myself – hope to protect my job – and the friends, everybody that has been very supportive through this." He vows not to "say much more about this on this particular topic," then thanks his audience for their patience.

Then, in one final movement, he stays true to form in countering this solemnity with colloquialisms and one-liners. To his audience, he says, "thank you for letting me bend your ears," before making a joke about their potential shock over the news that he had ever had sex at all. "I'll be darned," he exclaims, "Dave's had sex!" The audience laughs again, and Letterman adds, "That's what the grand jury said also."

At that point, the segment concluded. Letterman's house band played into the commercial break and, upon returning from the advertisements, the show went on as usual.

Conclusions and Implications

Ultimately, then, Letterman's confession is structured in four major parts – a narrative recounting the Halderman incident, an admission of sexual misconduct, an expression of gratitude to authorities and other involved parties, and a final joke to relieve the tension and signal an official return to the comic talk show format – though it is the narrative that dominates the piece. In presenting his story, Letterman maintains his comedic persona, only briefly refraining from humorous remarks, even when addressing his most morally questionable actions. The narrative and humor, in effect, overwhelm and overshadow the concise confession, deflecting attention from the speaker's vulnerability.

Letterman's revelation is a confession, but it is also many other things. It is a humorous story for those sitting in his studio audience. It is breaking news for those viewers watching him at home. It is a pre-emptive power play against media critics, by which he might defend himself as the victim of a greater evil before falling under public scrutiny. It is a unique variation of apologia, in which guilt is admitted but no true apology ever offered. And, nested as it is, nicely between opening monologue and celebrity guest interview, it is merely an unusual segment in an otherwise un-noteworthy episode of the typical nightly show.

The revelation was not without critics. Many did, and have since, lambasted Letterman for his seemingly cavalier attitude towards the allegations. Others have criticized his apparent manipulation of an unwitting studio audience, unprepared for anything but laughter, which ultimately legitimated his nonchalant, humorous tone with its applause. *New York Times* television critic Alessandra Stanley (2009), for instance, noted, "His confession … was less shocking than it was confusing. Mr. Letterman admitted 'creepy' affairs with CBS employees in a tone so glib and deadpan that the audience couldn't be blamed for assuming that this stand-up comedian … was still joking," and that the admission "looked a lot like calculation" as "Mr. Letterman made himself answerable to an audience that doesn't answer back." Such accusations are valid, as Letterman's unprepared studio audience set a tone and precedent for the reactions of television viewers at home, and such audience sympathy towards a speaker may, in fact, be infectious, but, by and large, Letterman still managed to escape the admonishment and scorn generally thrust upon philandering public figures.

Upon returning from commercial break during the Thursday, October 1st broadcast, Letterman noted that he had taken audience questions from the in-studio crowd off-camera. His remark that one gentleman had claimed he would have liked to have seen Halderman's movie inspired laughter and applause. When Letterman returned to the air on Monday evening (having taped Friday's show in advance, as usual), his studio audience was full and television ratings were up. While Letterman's affairs had not been lauded or necessarily excused, neither viewers nor guests nor advertisers seemed willing to condemn him or hold him immediately accountable for his actions (Carr 2009).[9] And while ratings may have enjoyed a boost simply from the scandalous gossip surrounding the case, several media critics agreed that Letterman's head-on, open, and honest approach would "position him in the best way he could be positioned," given the situation (Elliott 2009).

It is, of course, probable that we Americans do not necessarily hold celebrities and comedians to the same ethical standards as politicians and other elected or morally instated officials, but one might have expected at least a slightly stronger backlash against an individual so well known for mocking the likes of Clinton, Spitzer, Edwards, and Sanford. Instead, Letterman managed to build upon his comic-to-audience relationship to address sexual misconduct in a unique and casual way. Like other accused philanderers, he expressed remorse for his actions, admitted his guilt, stressed that he had already experienced sufficient internal turmoil, and vowed not to speak on the issue again, before thanking his audience and refocusing the conversation, but unlike them, he was able to nest such unpleasantries in an extended story to a warm and encouraging audience. What he presented may not have been exactly an apologia – especially as he felt the need to present a second, shorter speech during Monday's program, explicitly apologizing to his wife and coworkers – but his unorthodox October 1st address had been deemed fitting by the general populace.

The comedian, it seems, is given a sort of carte blanche in our society, to address solemn or tabooed topics in otherwise inappropriate ways.[10] Once a speaker has been identified as a comedian, the audience expects that speaker to conduct him or herself in a humorous or satirical manner. To do otherwise would breach expectations. David Letterman had engaged with his studio and television audience within the frame of comic monologues and goofball routines on a nightly basis for over 30 years. Viewers expected the familiarity, the storytelling, and the humor with which he presented and nested his revelation, regardless of the revelation's content. Perhaps simply by recognizing him as David Letterman, speaking in his usual manner and exhibiting his usual comic persona, viewers were inclined to excuse the accused speaker.

A further study of this special place of the comic in addressing non-comic topics would present a useful perspective for the continued criticism of rhetoric in comedy. Like the Fool in Shakespeare's *King Lear,* the comedian retains a seeming immunity from restrictions placed upon other speakers, with an ability to speak bluntly and without reproach where those others may not. The comic may provide commentary on society and upon him or herself in a way unique to the special give-and-take relationship he or she shares with a receptive and participatory audience.

In the case of David Letterman's late night revelation, we need not worry whether the speaker's unusual style was preplanned as a means of constructing a more stalwart defense, whether it bubbled up naturally as a result of his inherent discomfort, or if, after a quarter decade of televised discourse, he truly knew of no other way in which to clearly express himself. Instead, we must merely recognize that when he confessed, we laughed. Few other rhetors could have done such a thing.

Notes

1 "Rhetorical situation may be defined as a complex of persons, events, objects, and relations presenting an actual or potential exigence which can be completely or partially removed if discourse, introduced into the situation, can so constrain human decision or action as to bring about the significant modification of the exigence" (Bitzer 1968, p. 6).
2 Campbell and Jamieson 2000: "A genre is a group of acts unified by a constellation of forms that recurs in each of its members" (p. 417) and "A 'genre' is a classification based on the fusion and interrelation of elements in such a way that a unique kind of rhetorical act is created" (p. 421).
3 This chapter also includes studio audience response as an aspect of Letterman's rhetoric itself. In-house audience applause and laughter alter the way the in which the speech was ultimately perceived by at-home viewers during its television broadcast.
4 Letterman and his audience, here, appear to demonstrate what Wells and Bull (2007) identify as "synchrony" in stand-up comedy, marked "when members of an audience respond at, or immediately before, the intended completion of the speaker's utterance" in the form of "invited applause." Wells and Bull expand on both the "invitationality" and "rhetoricality" of a comic's delivery, by which he or she encourages active audience response through vocal and nonvocal cues and by rhetorical devices, respectively. Letterman's delivery is notable for its several invitational and rhetorical cues encouraging the applause, especially in the early portions of his speech. By the latter section of his revelation, when garnering laughter and applause is no longer appropriate, the audience demonstrates what Wells and Bull call "uninvited applause," initiated, they say, by the audience, yet I would argue that, in Letterman's case, the comic has set an earlier precedent for applause which the audience merely continues to adhere to once the speaker moves on to more serious confessional tones.
5 This comment also works to enhance Letterman's familiarity and relatability with his audience, as it neglects to mention that the "car" was in fact a chauffeured limousine. By merely calling it a "car" and not mentioning the presence of a driver, Letterman again exhibits an omission of detail and presents himself as more of an everyman.
6 Clinton, for instance, in his 1998 address, stressed that testifying before a grand jury involved answering "questions no American citizen would ever want to answer," and stressed that protection of himself and his family remained the primary motivating factors through the ordeal.
7 Ware and Linkugel explain, "When he bolsters, a speaker attempts to identify himself with something viewed as favorable by the audience" (p. 429).
8 Wells and Bull (2007) note that stand-up comedy garners higher amounts of interruptive applause than political speech, and that less formal, comedic speech generally accepts such outbursts. "Interruptive applause," they note, "can be an indicator of speaker popularity." However, they also claim that "uninvited applause" does not "relate to rhetorical devices and is initiated by the audience." The laughter at Letterman's mention of "creepy things" presents a kind of paradox for the Wells and Bull system then, as it does seem to stem from the rhetorical repetition of words, but also to start among the audience members. Letterman's comic repetition was perhaps unintentional, but, either way, his modesty in questioning the laughter – whether genuine or feigned – may have further encouraged audience sympathy, as, according to Wells, Bull, and J.M. Atkinson, the refusal of applause is generally attributed to "a highly charismatic orator" (pp. 323–324, 339).
9 Nearly two weeks after Letterman's revelation, the *New York Times*' David Carr (2009) noted that "the court of public opinion has been kind, with many lauding his forthright disclosure of the unpleasant business at hand."
10 For further reading, see Achter 2008.

References

Achter, P. (2008). Comedy in unfunny times: News parody and carnival after 9/11. *Critical Studies in Media Communication, 25*(3), 274–303.

Bitzer, L.F. (1968). The rhetorical situation. *Philosophy and Rhetoric, 1,* 1–14.

Campbell, K.K., & Jamieson, K.H. (2000). Form and genre in rhetorical criticism: An introduction. In C.R. Burgchardt (Ed.), *Readings in rhetorical criticism*, 2nd ed. (pp. 408–425). State College, PA: Strata Press.

Carr, D. (2009). The big tests for Letterman are still ahead. *New York Times.* Oct. 12.

Carter, B. (2009). David Letterman reveals extortion attempt. *New York Times.* Oct. 2.

Carter, B., & Stelter, B. (2009a). Extortion case raises questions for Letterman and his network. *New York Times.* Oct. 3.

Carter, B., & Stelter, B. (2009b). Letterman apologizes on the air to his wife. *New York Times.* Oct. 6.

Clinton, W.J. (1998). Clinton addresses the nation – August 17, 1998. *Online NewsHour.* Retrieved from www.pbs.org/newshour/lewinsky_address/address.html (accessed November 20, 2009).

Dagostino, M., & McNeil, E.F. (2009). Inside his affair. *People,* Oct. 26.

Double, O. (2005). *Getting the joke: The inner workings of stand-up comedy*. London: Methuen Publishing Ltd.

Edwards, J. (2008). Edwards statement on affair. *CNN.com.* Retrieved from www.cnn.com/2008/POLITICS/08/08/edwards.statement/index.html (accessed November 20, 2009).

Elliott, S. (2009). Letterman's sponsors appear to be unperturbed. *New York Times.* Oct. 8.

Leff, M. (1986). Textual criticism: The legacy of G.P. Mohrmann. *Quarterly Journal of Speech, 72,* 377–389.

Lennon, R. (1994). *David Letterman: On stage and off.* New York: Pinnacle Books.

Letterman, D. (2009). Full transcript: David Letterman's on-air statement about his affairs and the $2 million attempt to blackmail him. *The Comic's Comic.* Retrieved from http://thecomicscomic.typepad.com/thecomicscomic/2009/10/full-transcript-david-lettermans-onair-statement-about-his-affairs-and-the-2-million-attempt-to-blac.html

Rice, L. (2009). David Letterman: Surviving a scandal. *Entertainment Weekly,* Oct. 16. Retrieved from www.ew.com/article/2009/10/09/david-letterman-surviving-scandal

Stanley, A. (2009). A serious admission, with comic delivery. *New York Times.* Oct. 3.

Stelter, B. (2009). CBS removes David Letterman's mea culpa from YouTube. *New York Times.* Oct. 5.

Ware, B.L., & Linkugel, W.A. (2000). They spoke in defense of themselves: On the generic criticism of apologia. In C.R. Burgchardt (Ed.), *Readings in Rhetorical Criticism*, 2nd ed (pp. 426–436). State College, PA: Strata Press.

Wells, P., & Bull, P. (2007). From politics to comedy: A comparative analysis of affiliative audience responses. *Journal of Language and Social Psychology, 26,* 321–342.

Zoglin, R. (2008). *Comedy at the edge: How stand-up in the 1970s changed America.* New York: Bloomsbury.

RESPONSE: STANDING UP, BREAKING RULES

RETURNING THE FAVOR

Ludic Space, Comedians, and the Rhetorical Constitution of Society

Stephen Olbrys Gencarella

First, let's deal with the obvious. In this part and in America at large, there are a significant number of straight white men – including myself – talking about the comedic performances of other straight white men, often at the expense or neglect of comedians who are not straight white men. There is something telling, I think, when I look back to another collection of essays that hit the scene when I first began to cultivate an interest in humor studies as an undergraduate. The collection was *New Perspectives on Women and Comedy,* edited by Regina Barecca (1992). Many of the collection's articles struck me, but one by Laura Kightlinger, "Return the Favor," was particularly illuminating and disturbing in a helpful way. Kightlinger reflected upon her personal experiences as a woman in stand-up, including the rough treatment and open hostility she received not only from men but from female agents and managers who refused to assist women to break into comedy. These observations shook my own ignorance and comedic dogmatism at the time. They made me acutely aware of the problematic industry I admired as a spectator, but more importantly, they contributed to an awareness that warranted a rethinking of my own allegiances to masculine (and white) domination in the arts and in society as a whole.

Things have changed since 1992, of course, including the advent of the Internet, the flourishing of alt comedy, and the dethroning of the mainstream networks as arbiters of comedic success. But I consider it lamentable how readily Kightlinger's observations – and the greater spirit of her commentary – stand today. As I write these lines in the early autumn of 2015, no woman hosts a late-night television show (*Full Frontal with Samantha Bee* is months away and its success is not guaranteed). *The Wanda Sykes Show, Lopez Tonight, Totally Biased with W. Kamau Bell*, and *Chelsea Lately* have been off the air for years with no successors. *Saturday Night Live* took six years to hire a woman of color after the departure of Maya Rudolph, and only after widespread critical discourse lambasted its lack of diversity. Improv remains dominated by both men and masculinist attitudes, as well as entrenched whiteness. Similarly, *Sirens*, a situation comedy with a protagonist embodying the aggrieved masculine aggression of Denis Leary (who adapted the show from its British version), was renewed immediately following its inaugural season despite lackluster narrative innovation, whereas *Playing House*, a series about two female friends that frequently passed the Bechdel test, required a massive online campaign to secure a second season on the same channel.

As we consider the celebrity, notoriety, and complexity of responses to the comedians under investigation in this part – Daniel Tosh (and David Cross), Louis C.K., and David Letterman – let us not pretend, then, that their success or failure is only an issue of rhetorical prowess. (Let us also not dismiss the issue of command of rhetorical resources, either.) Let us admit that in mainstream U.S. American society, the privilege of humor performances – formal comedy especially – has historically been a grant to men. The shock of a performance such as Amy Schumer's headline-making turn on the *Comedy Central Roast of Charlie Sheen* (Gallen 2011), for instance, has as much to do with the confrontation of masculine domination as with the humorous abuse of the specific target of the event. While Schumer may be culpable for past comedic indiscretions about race, one cannot easily reject the premise that her appearance on that roast and her subsequent television series (on a channel that failed to support Amy Sedaris and Sarah Silverman) is remarkable for taking up the function of comedy as taboo-breaker while turning it on comedy itself to demonstrate how such activity has been traditionally relegated to men.

In other words, ludic space and ludic performance – space and performance that playfully, even subversively, upend rules of form and propriety – cannot escape critical considerations of gender (to mention only one example) simply because comics have been marked – and frequently condemned by moralists – as free to experiment, to break taboos, to say what cannot be said in polite society, and to push the line. Such resistance to the suffocating forces of pious expectations is useless if the only bodies allowed on its stage are the same bodies and same experiences representing the dominance or political correctness against which they rebel. Those of us who are invested in the study of humor and comedy proper cannot forget this point: the establishment of a play frame, while creating an arena for the interrogation of values through the imaginary, allows for license that so-called "serious" or "normal" experience would reject; while we may praise the beneficial applications of this liminality, we cannot do so with a blind eye towards its potential disadvantages, especially if it protects freedoms of speech, gesture, and thought for only a select few.

To strengthen the ludic as a rhetorical resource for the investigation (and plausible transformation) of society, I do not think we can simply accept the idea that the "anything goes" ethic of much contemporary stand-up in the mainstream United States is justifiable on the grounds that such comedy is merely entertainment. That critical vantage point is not novel; every contributor to this collection recognizes it. But as humor and comedy studies are maturing in scholarship, old theories of how their content "works" are giving way to a more richly provocative engagement with notions of play itself. Johan Huizinga's (1955) *Homo Ludens* was not originally read for contributions to humor studies, for example, nor was Roger Caillois' (1961) distinction in *Man, Play, and Games* between *ludus* and *paidia*. It may be time for reconsideration of these works – and, indeed, one now finds references to play theories in copious studies of humor and comedy – but in doing so one will find a mixture of ideas that require sophisticated rather than facile appreciation.

Caillois notes, for example, that the ludic is play that is structured and rule-bound, whereas paidia is more closely associated with entertainment and the creative free play of children. While both may result in the experience of fun that Huizinga identifies with play or with the mirth that countless scholars recognize as the core constituent of the humorous, I would further note that the ludic space occupied by stand-up comedians not only attends to and regulates the specific rules of stand-up performance but also the rules of the society and cultural context in which they are performed. Historically and frequently, these rules line up – for example, the mistaken belief that women are not funny and therefore not deserving of the performance stage (Gilbert 2004) – even as a given performer may specialize in mocking social rules. (Tosh, C.K., and Letterman are all examples of such performers, although their acts and shtick vary widely.) Cracks in the unspoken and overt rules of comedy may have positive social consequences, then, but only if they do not replicate an alliance with dominant norms regarding the regulation of bodies and experiences to be seen and heard.

The idea of the ludic further implicates the rhetorical constitution of society in other ways. The term *ludus* in Latin (akin to the term *paideia* in Greek) suggests education as well as play and training as well as games. In an age of unrelenting testing and the deprivation of recreation in schools (and the ideological perception of adulthood as the general absence of play except in commodified and controlled experiences), the growth of cognition, emotions, the body, and social roles implicated in the term may seem woefully antiquated. Stand-up comedy, as a site for ludic display, is important, therefore, because it bears the potential to rehabilitate those interrelations: hence, in the "simple" act of laughing at a comedian's performance, we may indulge the risk of enjoying new thoughts, emotional eruptions, awareness of our bodies, and reconsiderations of our social roles. But if we wish to suggest – and I do – that stand-up comedians are contemporary *ludi magistri et magistrae* (that is, teachers), then it is imperative we take the educative contours of such performances very seriously.

This places more than a moderate onus of responsibility on the audiences or consumers of comedy to be aware of the history (including the recent history) of neglect in stand-up comedy, and on scholars of humor and comedy to spread the word that a far greater commitment to diversity is necessary than what currently exists. Perhaps all commercialized arts suffer the same fate of prohibition against diversity. I cannot attend to that issue here, but as a scholar and critic of the humorous and the comedic I am able to recognize the stage to which I am tasked to respond. If the educative elements of stand-up comedy are as significant as the playful ones – that is, if the art of stand-up comedy deserves appreciation as a ludic constituent of our social world – then the growing scholarship around these issues has more weight than those who would dismiss the non-serious might recognize. It would suggest that the rhetorical force of the humorous and the comedic is far more potent than, say, the observations of the utility of jokes and mockery that Aristotle and Cicero mentioned. It would mean that the rhetorical foundations of society are grounded in the division between the serious and the non-serious and that "society" is often shorthand for the exclusion of the playful, the humorous, and the comedic. But this would also mean students of this rising field had best be on their game and ready to return the favor to the excluded by doing more than praising humor and comedy that one finds pleasing or copasetic with one's own politics.

I mention this concern as I move towards a response to the three chapters in this part in order to ask the reader to see them as scholarship that must remain the first word, not the last. I hope that the success of this volume will spur other collections and conversations on the same topic, widening the examples increasingly beyond straight white male comedic experience. I recognize such a change requires the promotion (and a stance against the demotion) of the experiences of comedians who are not straight white men in mainstream culture in the United States as well as in scholarship. I would like to imagine that the undergraduate who reads this collection the year it is published will look back as a professor a quarter of a century later and remark that so much has changed for the better in comedy – and with it, in U.S. American society. In following the advice of Allison Fraiberg (1996), who herself sought to observe Kightlinger's (1992) call, I will draw upon the comedic performances of women and non-whites in my responses; my intention is not to submit a transparent compensation but to foster the depth of the conversation initiated by this part's three chapters.

I think Christopher Medjesky's distinction between a satiric persona and an ironic (or pseudo-satiric) persona is helpful. Indeed, if I may venture to say so playfully, it may be *too* helpful. Its elegant simplicity lends itself to be applied almost universally, when like all heuristic devices, it best serves specific (rhetorical) situations. His comparison between the personae of David Cross and Daniel Tosh, for example, is quite convincing. But I would be worried that an enthusiastic reader, especially one new to humor and comedy studies, might be tempted to apply this distinction too readily. Conservative comedians such as Steven Crowder, Greg Gutfield, Michael Loftus, and Brad Stine regularly employ satire, and do so in a manner that is as consistently constructed into a persona of social critic as is Cross. In other words, the comparison that Medjesky establishes resonates, but its further applicability requires a similar deftness as his in setting up a thoughtful comparison between personae and performances.

I would also caution fellow progressives about their recent investment in satire as a means to enact social change (and, in doing so, agree with arguments made by Ron Von Burg and Kai Heidemann in Chapter 8 of this collection). While it may be true that satire functions as equipment for living, it is equally true that Kenneth Burke understood satire as a species of the negative, originally noting that a satirist "attacks *in others* the weaknesses and temptations that are really *within himself*" (1984, p. 49) and hence operates from a more ambiguous rhetorical position than substantial social change necessitates. Furthermore, satire is not always a weapon of the weak. It has not been so historically, and may not be so in the future. While the distinction Medjesky offers illuminates the problem – perhaps even cowardice – of pseudo-satiric performers such as Tosh who create elaborate reasons for failures in performance, it would be risky to extrapolate from this example the assurance that satire could not be employed to assist the dominant.

This is one reason why I disagree with Medjesky regarding George Carlin. I am grateful to Carlin as an untiring defender of free speech, whose use of ludic space made a case for facing issues that polite society would ignore. But as a rhetorical critic, I cannot agree with Carlin's claim in the same album in which he joked about rape that "they're only words." That is, while I can allow for virtually anything to be performed in spaces marked for such activity, I am not willing to accept the idea that words only matter in context (as Carlin suggests) and without history. There was, for example, a poignant video posted online a few years ago (The word n.d.) with a mashup of Carlin's ruminations about the word "nigger" (including the declaration that we do not care when Richard Pryor uses it because he is one) and Pryor's routine in which he explains why he will no longer use the word. Similarly, the very next routine that Carlin performs after his rape joke is entitled "Feminist Blowjob" (1990) in which he depicts feminists only as women, and as uptight controllers of language. These are hardly the jokes of a social critic who wishes to resist white masculine domination.

Carlin's general rhetorical strategy is to deny the very power of rhetoric itself as a socially-constituting force that directs and normalizes action over long historical periods. My point is that the comparison between Carlin and Tosh regarding the specific rape jokes that Medjesky analyzed convinces me, but I do not think that any persona – even a well-crafted satiric persona – should ever be allowed a shield from criticism. I am quite willing to allow the comedic stage to be a place for freedoms we aspire to in liberal democratic society, and I am furthermore a believer that we must staunchly defend the stage as a locus for the performance of taboos, but that does not mean any comedian – or any of us – should be automatically off the hook. And if I am reading Medjesky correctly, I think he would agree; hence my respectful admonition to the reader not to mistake a useful heuristic for a universal solvent.

I am also grateful that Medjesky has made evident that the redress of our rape culture requires the participation of men in the discussion. I think David Cross has much to offer this conversation, especially a willingness to model a masculinity that examines rather than exiles uncomfortable subjects that constitute it. But again, I would petition the reader not to rest on this point. Rape jokes are a common stock in the humor of female and gay comedians, many of whom are not as well-known as David Cross (or Wanda Sykes or Sarah Silverman or Amy Schumer, who have garnered positive and negative critical attention for theirs). I am thinking especially of Ever Mainard's (2012) "Here's Your Rape" routine and Adrienne Truscott's (2013) "Asking For It," but there are countless others who deserve attention and who would foster the conversation in nuanced ways. But they are not likely to be welcome in the mainstream, and certainly not as likely as straight, white men playing the jokester frat boy persona. This is one of the reasons that I encourage readers to seek out underground or fringe venues.

Before I respond to James Brown's compelling chapter, let me admit something: I don't like Louie C.K. I used to champion his work, and I might again someday if he changes his tune. But after five seasons of his show (each one more misogynistic without consequences than the next) and seemingly endless praise for his honesty (which strikes me as little more than the anxiety of influence over Woody Allen), I cannot help but think that all of his comedic inquiry into white male privilege is, well, an act. I get it: He's brave enough to be sullen and angry and occasionally ashamed of himself. But to borrow the structure of an old joke, I liked it better the first time when it was called "Achilles" and "Archilochus." At least then those heroic emotions made sense in a patriarchal, violent, war-soaked culture. Today, they seem to animate the politics of political candidates who wish to push back women's rights and send brown bodies out of the country as much as they fit widely-praised comedic observers of society and auteurs such as C.K.

That admission made, I would like to praise Brown's overall contribution as another rewarding heuristic for understanding the rhetorical impact that comedians may actualize in contemporary society. Although I myself prefer Rickert's notion of ambience to the idea of networks – we are always already in-the-middle of a conversation, as Burke once noted – I appreciate Brown's exploration of how our networked society and the snark it inspires creates conditions in which people are unwilling to face up to shame and vulnerabilities. (This also makes me think the time has come to reconsider the work on shame and guilt cultures with respect to comedic performance.) I also find his case for reconfiguring *kairos* extremely helpful. Scholars of rhetoric may sigh at yet another appearance of the term; it has become one of the buzzwords of recent scholarship. But as Brown notes, it remains important for rethinking the notion of a rhetorical situation. This idea – the rhetorical situation – has evolved since Lloyd Bitzer introduced it in 1968. Telling of the evolution of rhetorical studies itself, rhetorical situations were first conceived as things to which rhetors responded; over the decades they became conceptualized as things created by rhetors. The concept of *kairos* negotiates the event and the invention.

The ways comedians risk themselves (beyond the general possibility of failure in any performance) and "practice" escaping from predicaments is a fascinating topic certain to inspire further scholarship in humor and comedy studies. As a respectful adaptation of Brown's contribution, I would like to suggest that we should also examine moments in which a comedian is decidedly and deliberately *not* kairotic. As a formidable example, I have in mind Thea Vidale's (2002) appearance on the *Tavis Smiley Show* during which she joked:

> Osama Bin Laden – He ain't mad at us. He mad at y'all [white people] … America was shocked 'cause it's not so much that we got bombed – it's *where* they bombed us. They bombed us at the World Trade Center … You know, 'cause if it had been … Compton … or Harlem, they would've been saying, "Osama Bin Laden has bombed Compton, California and Harlem, New York. Next, Jim with Sports … "

Vidale's appearance occurred in August 2002, nearly a year after the attacks. She (along with show host Tavis Smiley) was pummeled for these comments, especially as they echoed sentiments expressed by KRS-One and other African Americans who wanted to draw attention from 9/11 to the long history of racial injustice in the United States and its global reach.

The *untimeliness* of Vidale's joke made her vulnerable, but her humor then and in her acts now (which tend towards unapologetic sensual and sexual indulgences, tensions inherent in family life – including domestic abuse – and critique of white dominance) hardly advocated shame. In mentioning her comedy, I am attempting to extend Brown's observations but to free them from upholding C.K. as the ideal and to encourage readers who follow this lead not to associate shame with authenticity. I think it is necessary to mention that Louis C.K. is a comedian who has the privilege of being shamed – and the privilege of putting himself in difficult situations to see if he can escape. It is difficult for me to compare him with Gorgias, therefore, because I can imagine no circumstance in which he would face exile or execution for interrogating the values of the dominant. I can imagine something along those sorts befalling Vidale and other African-American comedians or to the members of the Axis of Evil Comedy Tour, and I think it would be helpful to consider a recent genealogy of vulnerability in comedy that traced a line without white men – say, from Kate Clinton to Emily Heller, Carmen Esposito, and Maria Bamford. In reflecting on Brown's chapter, it is my hope that readers extend its insights quickly and well beyond anyone *Rolling Stone* nominates as "the funniest comedian in America," aware that the occupant of such a position may simply be rehearsing the anxieties of the dominant rather than offering countercultural resistance to them.

Casey R. Schmitt's chapter is different from the other two in that the subject is a comedian whose oeuvre is late-night television rather than strictly stand-up (and a comedian whose career is now winding down), but the continued themes of a satiric persona, vulnerability, and even guilt illuminate this study of David Letterman's non-apologetic apologia. I will cut to the predictable quick. It is my opinion that, in addition to all the reasons Schmitt details in his meticulous study of the apology, we must also consider Letterman's status as a powerful straight white male in the entertainment industry as a contributing reason that his admission of creepy and salacious exploitation of subordinates was regarded as a peccadillo rather than an indictment of his ethos capable of rendering the end to his career. Although Clinton, Spitzer, Edwards, and Sanford are apt examples of politicians caught in similar circumstances, I also think it pays to mention that all of them survived their falls to some extent (Clinton and Sanford continued on as politicians, for example, and Spitzer and even Edwards have done fine financially since their scandals).

This is not to suggest that I disagree with Schmitt's premise that Letterman survived his scandal in a manner uniquely accountable to his status as a comedian – and I would point to Rush Limbaugh as a similar figure whose importance to the entertainment industry coupled with the cultural allowances for white men to behave badly allowed him to rebound from moral hypocrisy. I am just not certain that it is solely Letterman's comedic authority rather than his additional personal capital and the importance of the *Late Show* to the mainstream entertainment and political industries in the United States that allowed for his escape in the first place. There is a reason, I think, that Jerry Seinfeld appeared on the *Late Show* in 2006 to introduce Michael Richards' apology for his n-word laced tirade at the Laugh Factory, and these two apologies resonate with the 1995 appearance of actor Hugh Grant on *The Tonight Show* following his arrest in a prostitution sting. That is, national late-night talk shows are perhaps not such an uncommon stage for white men to confess their faults to compliant viewers, especially since (as Schmitt keenly notes) the audiences to these performances attend with the expectations of a light-hearted play frame and are therefore much more amenable to acceptance of things that unfold within that frame.

A reader may quibble with my assignment of masculinity as the reactant initiating the force of public forgiveness in the case of these comedians, and might note that comedian Chelsea Handler survived a potential sex tape scandal in 2010 by dismissing it as a joke on her own late-night talk show (Handler 2010). This is a fair retort, but I would also note that Handler's own confessional style as a comedian and humorist, her continued assault on both puritanism and pornographic attitudes, and her critique of masculine domination (such as her topless parody of Vladimir Putin's horseback photo) influence audience interpretation of her sexuality. Letterman's comedic persona was the epitome of snark, but his sexual identity was generally off the table throughout his career. Handler, to the contrary, continually risks vulnerabilities in placing her sexuality and penchant for conventionally defined vices at the forefront of her comedy. Chelsea Handler without scandal would not be Chelsea Handler, whereas Letterman long assumed a role of moral moderation even as his act indulged in the absurd and weird.

So I do not think that late-night talk show hosts are granted special rhetorical status simply by virtue of being late-night talk show hosts. In this way, I find Schmitt's analysis of Letterman's rhetorical ploy spot on, and only wish to complement his observations with a reminder that whiteness and masculinity had a role to play in the public acceptance of the apology as well. Further application of Schmitt's contribution would ask scholars in humor and comedy studies to examine the relative success and failure of other comedians who apologize for matters outside of the realm of the comedic (such as Steve Rannazzisi's [Kovaleski 2015] recent admission that he lied about escaping the 9/11 attacks) or their reputed attempts at humor (for which there are many examples, with Don Imus [Chiere 2007], Katt Williams [Hughes 2011], and Nicole Arbour [Olya 2015] leaping to mind) or their refusal to apologize for jokes (as Natasha Leggero unabashedly demonstrated in 2013, following a comedic jab at aging veterans [Luippold 2014]). As the public culture of the United States continues to debate the meanings of trauma with respect to words that people use, rhetorical analysis of the kind Schmitt offers will become ever more pressing and necessary. I also think this issue of the traumatic is heading for a collision and confrontation not only with comedians whose livelihood depends upon uttering the unspeakable, but for our general conversation about the constitution of our society, including the role of humor and comedy in that process.

The gift of ludic space is a complicated exchange. Like the *pharmakon*, that substance at once poison and medicine, capable of harming or healing depending on its usage, ludic space brings the possibility of both aid and disaster. Those who enter it – and here I mean comedians and their audiences – are at once removed from and deeply invested in the so-called "real world." Ludic space, although playful, is a ground of consequences; only the truly naïve would argue otherwise. But it does not quite play by the rules of the normative or polite society; this allows its participants to exploit the inconsistencies of the dominant or to cement those cracks and stabilize them. As scholars and consumers of humor and comedy, we cannot simply pretend that "anything goes" in ludic space, but we also must not demand that it function merely as an extension of the pieties and moralities we insist upon to influence the rhetorical constitution of society. Ludic space, then, is demanding space. The three chapters in this part – and, indeed, all of the chapters in this collection – remind us of its demanding and complicated nature, and ask us to do our part by extending their insights to other venues, performances, and comedians. I appreciate this call and in the spirit of reciprocity, I would only insist that we consider extensions inclusive of bodies and experiences frequently exiled or prohibited or ignored in ludic space, and in so doing return the favor of its promise.

References

Burke, K. (1984). *Attitudes toward history*. Berkeley: University of California Press.
Caillois, R. (1961). *Man, play, and games*. New York: Simon and Schuster.
Carlin, G. (1990). Feminist blowjob. *Parental advisory: Explicit lyrics* [CD]. Atlantic.
Chiere, R. (2007). Imus called women's basketball team "nappy-headed hos." MediaMatters.com. April 4. Retrieved from http://mediamatters.org/research/2007/04/04/imus-called-womens-basketball-team-nappy-headed/138497 (accessed October 26, 2015).
Fraiberg, A. (1996). Between the laughter: Bridging feminist studies through women's stand-up comedy. In G. Finney (Ed.), *Look who's laughing: Gender and comedy* (pp. 315–334). Philadelphia: Gordon and Breach.

Gallen, J. (Director). (2011). *Comedy Central roast of Charlie Sheen* [Television broadcast]. Comedy Central.

Gilbert, J. (2004). *Performing marginality: Humor, gender, and cultural critique.* Detroit: Wayne State University Press.

Handler, C. (2010, April 28). *Chelsea lately* [Television broadcast]. E! Entertainment Television.

Hughes, S. (2011). Katt Williams apologies for rant against Mexico. *The Washington Post.* September 1. Retrieved from www.washingtonpost.com/blogs/celebritology/post/katt-williams-apologizes-for-racist-rant-against-mexico/2011/09/01/gIQAUXZquJ_blog.html (accessed October 26, 2015).

Huizinga, J. (1955). *Homo ludens: A study of the play element in culture.* Boston: Beacon Press.

Kightlinger, L. (1992). Return the favor. In R. Barreca (Ed.), *New perspectives on women and comedy* (pp. 85–88). Philadelphia: Gordon and Breach.

Kovaleski, S. (2015). Steve Rannazzisi, comedian who told of 9/11 escape, admits he lied. *The New York Times.* September 16. Retrieved from www.nytimes.com/2015/09/17/arts/television/steve-rannazzisi-comedian-who-told-of-9-11-escape-admits-he-lied.html?_r=0 (accessed October 26, 2015).

Luippold, R. (2014). Natasha Leggero's stunning "not sorry" response over the controversial Pearl Harbor joke. *Huffington Post.* January 23. Retrieved from www.huffingtonpost.com/2014/01/04/natasha-leggero-not-sorry-for-pearl-harbor-joke_n_4541354.html (accessed October 26, 2015).

Mainard, E. (2012). "Here's your rape" at Chicago Underground Comedy. *YouTube.* Retrieved from www.youtube.com/watch?v=29ArdxWYBGQ (accessed October 26, 2015).

Olya, G. (2015). Nicole Arbour refuses to apologize for "dear fat people" YouTube video on *The View. People.* September 16. Retrieved from www.people.com/article/nicole-arbour-refuses-apologize-dear-fat-people-the-view (accessed October 26, 2015).

The word "nigger" – Richard Pryor & George Carlin mash up. (n.d.). Retrieved from www.dailymotion.com/us/relevance/universal/search/richard+pryor+george+carlin+n+word/1 (accessed October 26, 2015).

Truscott, A. (2013). Asking for it. Retrieved from www.adriennetruscott.com/asking-for-it/ (accessed October 26, 2015).

Vidale, T. (2002, August 2). *The Tavis Smiley show* [Radio broadcast]. National Public Radio.

I've never told a joke in my life.

(Andy Kaufman)

INDEX

9/11 xi, 129–30, 243, 245

absurdity: for reduction 145, 155; of conventions 21, 26, 28, 32–3, 104; of stereotypes 6, 16, 101, 117
African American tradition xxii-iii, 41–6, 54, 60–61
All American Girl 3–4, 7–8
ambiguity 74, 76, 83, 85, 126
American Indian tradition *see* Native American tradition
Amos 'n' Andy 71
Anglo-American tradition xii-iv
Apollo Theater xii, 40, 48
apologia 224–5, 231, 233–4, 243–4
applause 81, 224–5, 228
"Are There Any Niggers Here Tonight?" 97
Aristotle xiii, 240
Asian American tradition 4–6, 8–9, 13–17
audience: 185–190, 223–7, 227–32; and complicit role in meaning 75–7, 165, 173, 196–7, 233–4, 239; and engagement 63, 78–86, 140–1; and identification 11–12, 14–17, 139, 199–210; and perspectives 29, 33, 176, 244; and persuasion 57, 60–61, 142, 146; and power 93, 155–6; and race 42, 44–50, 97–101, 112–123, 126–130; and reception 35, 159, 162, 214, 216–18, 220; as key to stand-up xi-ii, xv, xix-xxii, 65; creation 158, 178–9
Axis of Evil Comedy Tour 129–30, 243

Bakhtin, Mikhail xii, 76, 98
Barr, Roseanne xxii, 3, 59
Berman, Shelley xvii-iii, 127
bisexuality 4, 59
Brown, Reggie 159
Bruce, Lenny xvii-iii, 92–107, 125, 127–8, 135
Burke, Kenneth 149, 153–5, 164, 187; and identification 136–7, 158; and identity 30; and perspective by incongruity 144; and power 140; and rhetoric 26–7, 34, 59; and satire 204, 241–2
burlesque 34, 153–7, 160–5, 187–8
Bush, George W. xxvi, 146, 169, 171–3, 175–6, **182**
Butler, Brett 3, 59, 135

C.K., Louis 153, 164, 196, 213–22, 242–3
Carey, Drew 175, **182**
Carlin, George xvii-iii, 74, 195–7, 200–1, 209–10, 241
carnivalesque xii, 76
catachresis 25, 28–9, 32
catharsis xxiv, 75, 82, 85, 88, 142
Cedric the Entertainer **182**
censorship 146–7, 149, 173–4, 196
Cho, Margaret xi, xx, 3–17, 58–60, 65
Civil Rights movement xii, 50, 61, 93, 125; and race humor 71–81, 85–88, 97, 101, 127–128

class *see* middle class, working class
Clinton, Bill 24, 223–4, 234, 244
Colbert, Stephen xiv, 97, 171–2, **182**
Comedy Central 97, 129, 168, 195, 207, 238
Conservative Political Action Committee (CPAC) 153, 159–60, 163–6
community 15, 121; among audience members 59, 65, 81–2; between stand-up and audience 6, 12, 16, 154–5, 157, 159
Cosby, Bill 40, 198, 201, 209–10
court jester *see* fool
Cross, David 197, 199, 201, 205–6, 209–10, 240–42

Daily Show with Jon Stewart, The 92, 136, 145, 153, 168
Dana, Bill 72, 74, 76, 79
Danson, Ted 74, 76, 126
de Ceretau, Michel 94, 96–8, 102
democracy xiv, 152–4, 164, 185–90, 241; and critique of leaders xii; and "demockery" 168–72, 174, 176, 178, 181; and race 85–6
dialect xii, 41, 72, 80, 83
Dickinson, Emily xi
Diller, Phyllis xix, 59
Dressed to Kill 21–36
Dunham, Jeff 87

eiron xii
epithet 98–100, 126
equal opportunity offender 72, 76, 79, 82, 85–8, 196
ethos 149, 160, 217; of speaker xix, 35, 107, 202, 244
ethnic humor 71–6, 78–88

female *see* women
fool: fooled individual 24; jester 65, 76, 129, 153, 157, 163; King Lear 234; "wise fool" 34, 48, 185–190
Franklin, Benjamin xii–iv
free speech xvii–iii, 74, 87, 161–3, 238, 241; and obscenity 92; and politics 180
freedom of speech *see* free speech

gay 4, 24, 30–1, 48, 64, 177–8
gender 238; and race 40–54, 79; discrimination 178; non-binary xii, 21–36; roles 58–60

genre xiii, 22, 65, 154; see apologia, ethnic humor, roast
Goffman, Erving 77–8, 80–3, 85
Goldberg, Whoopi 48, 126
Gramsci, Antonio 136–40, 145–7, 149
Greenbaum, Andrea xix, 199–202
Gregory, Dick xvii, xxii, 193

Hammond, Darrell **182**
Handler, Chelsea 244
HBO 48, 54, 63, 135, 218
heckling 57, 122, 126, 196–7, 201–2, 214
hegemony 42, 136–7, 139, 141–9, 157, 197; and patriarchy 52, 60; and race 95, 201–2
Hello Dummy! 72, 77
heteronormativity 21, 24, 59–60, 64
Hicks, Bill 135–50, 186–8, 190
Hill, Charlie 111–12, 114, 122–3
Homo Ludens xi, 239
homosexuality *see* gay, lesbian
Hope, Bob 126
"How to Relax Your Colored Friends at Parties" xxiv, 93, 100, 128

identity 24–7, 57–65, 95; black female 40–4, 48–53; class 126; civic 21–23, 28–33; cultural and ethnic 3–17, 73, 99, 101–4, 117, 122–3; management 76–9, 85, 152–66
I'm the One That I Want 4–7, 10–11, 15
imitation xiii, 5, 35, 141
impersonation xii, 31, 159, 169, 232
incongruity xiv, xix, 50, 76; for effect 62, 96, 157, 204; in delivery 22, 28, 60, 231; perspective by incongruity 144, 157
ironic essentialism 5–6, 9–12, 15–16, 58–9
irony 25; pseudo-satirical 195–9, 201–4, 206–10; rhetorical 144; satirical 155, 162–4, 182
Izzard, Eddie xi-ii, 20–36, 59–60, 64–5

jester *see* fool
Jewish American tradition 74–5, 78–80, 87–8, 99, 102, 127
Jim Crow xii, 41, 54, 61, 127–8

kairos xiii, xix, 213–222, 242
Kimmel, Jimmy 168, 172–5, **182**
Ku Klux Klan 51, 104–5

Lampanelli, Lisa 87, 91
Larry the Cable Guy 199

Index

Late Show with David Letterman, The 135, 224–234, 244
Latino American tradition 74, 79
Laugh Factory, The 74, 195, 207–9, 244
laughter: as communal act xxvii, 65, 72, 81–5, 115–16, 121–3; as release 75; as rhetorical xi, xix, 77, 96, 112, 227–33; as situational xii, 224; subversive 27
Leno, Jay 136, 173–4, 176, 179, **182**
lesbian 29, 40, 59, 63–4, 99, 177–8
Letterman, David 135, 146–8, 186–7, 223–35, 238–9, 243–4
Limbaugh, Rush 24–5, 157, 162, 244
Limon, John 116–17
Little, Rich **182**
Live at the Beacon Theatre 213, 219, 221
ludic xxiii, xxvii, 238–45

Mabley, Jackie "Moms" xi–ii, 40–54, 59–61, 63, 65
Maher, Bill 154, 164, 166
marginality xxvii, 24, 57–65, 128, 147, 177–8; of class 126; of race and culture xix, 95–6, 99, 102–7, 130; of sex and gender xix, 21
Mason, Jackie 87
McGee, Michael Calvin xvii
McHale, Joel 172–3, 177–8, 180, **182**
metalepsis 23, 32, 34, 36, 60, 62
Meyers, Seth 173, 175–9, **182**
middle class xiii, 75
minstrel shows xii, 42, 44–5, 61, 71–4, 79
Modern Prince 136–7, 139–40, 148–50
Monty Python xii, 20–1, 34, 36
Murphy, Eddie 40, 43, 53, 54
music halls xii

Nanjiani, Kumail 196
National Association for the Advancement of Colored People (NAACP) 72
Native American tradition 111–24
networked rhetoric 213–16, 221, 242
New Deal xiv
New York City xii–iii, xvii, 65; in jokes 31, 47, 141–2, 230, 243
New York Friars Club 74, 168
Newhart, Bob xvii
Notaro, Tig 213

O'Brien, Conan 172, 175, 177, 179–80, **182**, 213
Obama, Barack xxvi, 159, 169, 172–3, 174–5, 177

obscenity xvii–iii, 48, 74, 92, 146
offense xi, 114, 125–6, 162; offensive acts 27, 36; offensive language or content 16, 74–9, 84–6, 98–102, 106, 206
offensive *see* offense
organic intellectual 136–40, 143–4, 147, 149, 186

parrhesia xx
persona 58–63, 240–4; adopted persona 126; comic persona xii, xix, xxiii, 81, 195–210, 224–5, 230–4; stage persona 41–3, 45, 48–9, 51, 54, 119, 160; television persona 13; textual persona xiv
piety 144
political correctness 24, 86, 120, 156–7, 161–5, 238
Politically Incorrect 87, 136
poros 22, 26, 34
Powwow Comedy Jam 111–124, 125, 128–9
prolepsis 84
prosopopoeia 31
protest xviii, 72, 74, 81, 85–6, 180
Pryor, Richard xi, xvii, xix–xx, 40, 69, 135, 241

queer 20–3, 26–7, 31–6, 59, 71, 80

racism 49, 52, 61, 126–30, 177–8, 189; critiquing racism xii, xvii; racist humor 71–88, 92–107, 159, 200, 202, 207; reducing racism 115, 124; *see* stereotype
radio xiv, xviii, 71
rape humor 63, 195–210, 241–2
relief theory of humor 75, 88
religion 25, 74, 128, 138, 146, 206
rhetorical situation xxiii, 213–21, 223, 242
Richards, Michael 74, 76, 126, 244
Rickles, Don 25, 71–88, 125–8, 201
Rivers, Joan 3, 59
roast 126, 168–82, 189, 201, 238
Rock, Chris xxii, 213
Rogers, Will xiv, 84
Ruel, Jim 112, 115–21, 123, 129–30

Sahl, Mort xi, xviii, 127, 133
satire 92–4, 96–107, 162–4, 171, 187, 240–1; and reflexivity 127; political 145, 154–7, 181–2; pseudo-satire 195–7, 201–10
Saturday Night Live 61, 146, 168, 169, 237
Schumer, Amy xxii, 238, 242

self-deprecation 6, 12–17, 42, 58–9, 118; as rhetorical tactic xix, 123, 126, 232; negative self-presentation 78–80, 85
September 11 attacks *see* 9/11
"Seven Words You Can Never Say on Television" xvii-iii
sexual misconduct 223–6, 229, 231–4
sexuality xvii, 3, 33–4, 41–2, 209, 244; black 103; female 52–4, 146, 244; in specific routines 28, 79; *see* bisexuality, gay, lesbian
Shakespeare, William xii, 234
shock xix, 77, 97–9, 196, 232–3, 243
Silverman, Sarah 130, 153, 198, 242
slur *see* epithet
snark 213, 216, 220–1, 242, 244
social change xi–xv, xvii–xxii, 88, 93, 106, 155, 240–1; activism 181; politics 189–90; race 75–7, 112, 129–30; satire 197, 204; sex and gender 34–6, 54
speaking truth to power xii, xx, 96, 155, 185, 190
spectacle xix, 136–7, 139–50, 170
stereotype 8, 36, 58–62, 127, 130, 209; age 54; Asian 4–6, 10–17; mammy 41–2, 44; Native American 111–17, 121–3, 129; sex and gender 25, 27, 34; *see* racism
Stern, Howard 24–5
Stewart, Jon 92, 166, 168
Stine, Brad 152–66, 187–8, 190, 240
Strong, Cecily 177–80, **182**

subversive comedy xxvii, 60–1, 65, 111–12, 238; as tool for social critique xix, 6, 10–11, 16, 86
superiority theory of humor 73, 76, 165
Sykes, Wanda 61–5, 176, **182**, 237, 242

taboo 75, 80, 85, 197–200, 205–10, 234; breaking xxii, 77, 111, 238, 241; linguistic 98; questioning 58; racial xvii, 46, 126; sexual xvii, 53
Tonight Show, The 116, 136, 244
topoi see topos
topos 36, 196–200, 205, 207, 209–10, 225
Tosh, Daniel 195–210, 238–41
trickster 44–6, 111–24, 128–9
Twain, Mark xiv

vaudeville xii, xiv, 41–2, 44–5, 59
vernacular xiii, 99, 129

White House Correspondents Association (WHCA) 168–82, 189–90
whiteness 92–107, 125, 127–30, 219, 238, 244
Williams, Robin 25
women xiv, 58–63, 155, 178, 237–42; female comics xix, 3–4, 40–54, 178, 237–42; jokes about women 78–9, 84, 198
working class 24, 73, 126, 138
Wright, Steven 25

Milton Keynes UK
Ingram Content Group UK Ltd.
UKHW031502071224
451979UK00019B/197